STUDIES IN CHRISTIAN HISTORY AND THOUGHT

Prisoner of Conscience

John Bunyan on Self, Community,
and Christian Faith

STUDIES IN CHRISTIAN HISTORY AND THOUGHT

A full listing of all titles in this series
will be found at the close of this book

STUDIES IN CHRISTIAN HISTORY AND THOUGHT

Prisoner of Conscience

John Bunyan on Self, Community,
and Christian Faith

Galen K. Johnson

Wipf & Stock
PUBLISHERS
Eugene, Oregon

Wipf and Stock Publishers
199 W 8th Ave, Suite 3
Eugene, OR 97401

Prisoner of Conscience
John Bunyan on Self, Community, and Christian Faith
By Johnson, Galen K.
Copyright©2003 Johnson, Galen K.
ISBN: 1-59752-094-2
Publication date 2/15/2005
Previously published by Paternoster, 2003

Paternoster
9 Holdom Avenue
Bletchley
Milton Keyes, MK1 1QR
Great Britain

STUDIES IN CHRISTIAN HISTORY AND THOUGHT

Series Preface

This series complements the specialist series of *Studies in Evangelical History and Thought* and *Studies in Baptist History and Thought* for which Paternoster is becoming increasingly well known by offering works that cover the wider field of Christian history and thought. It encompasses accounts of Christian witness at various periods, studies of individual Christians and movements, and works which concern the relations of church and society through history, and the history of Christian thought.

The series includes monographs, revised dissertations and theses, and collections of papers by individuals and groups. As well as 'free standing' volumes, works on particular running themes are being commissioned; authors will be engaged for these from around the world and from a variety of Christian traditions.

A high academic standard combined with lively writing will commend the volumes in this series both to scholars and to a wider readership.

Series Editors

Alan P.F. Sell, Visiting Professor at Acadia University Divinity College, Nova Scotia, Canada

David Bebbington, Professor of History, University of Stirling, Stirling, Scotland, UK

Clyde Binfield, Professor Associate in History, University of Sheffield, UK

Gerald Bray, Anglican Professor of Divinity, Beeson Divinity School, Samford University, Birmingham, Alabama, USA

Grayson Carter, Associate Professor of Church History, Fuller Theological Seminary SW, Phoenix, Arizona, USA

To my wife Lori, with love and gratitude

Contents

Acknowledgements	xiii
List of Abbreviations	xv

Chapter 1
Introduction — 1

Chapter 2
Conscience and Individualism in Bunyan's Anti-Quaker Writings — 9
- Scripture and Conscience — 10
  - *Bunyan's View of Scriptural Authority* — 11
  - *The Quakers' Views of Scriptural Authority* — 16
- Christ and Individualism — 19
  - *Bunyan on the "Christ Without"* — 20
  - *The Quakers on the "Christ Within"* — 30
- The Road to Modern Individualism — 34
  - *The Enlightenment* — 36
  - *Romanticism* — 38
  - *Protestant Liberalism* — 41
- Conclusion — 44

Chapter 3
***Grace Abounding to the Chief of Sinners*: Bunyan Between Luther and Modernity** — 47
- Bunyan's Attraction to Luther's *Galatians* — 53
- Luther's Understanding of Conscience — 55
- Luther's *Galatians* and *Grace Abounding*: Parallels — 58
  - *The Law* — 59
  - *Death* — 64
  - *The Devil* — 66
  - *Hell* — 73
- The Emerging Picture of the Self in *Grace Abounding* — 76

Individualism and Subjectivism in Bunyan and Luther	82
Conclusion	86

Chapter 4
Conflicts of Conscience in Bunyan's Political Writings — 89

Liberty of Conscience in William Perkins and William Ames	90
The Debate Over Liberty of Conscience Between John Cotton and Roger Williams	96
Individualism and Traditionalism in Bunyan's Political Theory	101
Religious Liberty	103
"Fear God, and Honour the King"	106
Bunyan's Political Conservatism in Comparison to Milton	112
Religious Liberty vs. Orthodoxy in Milton's Political Writings	113
Milton's Antimonarchicalism	120
A New View of Freedom	122
Conclusion	124

Chapter 5
Christian Selfhood in *The Pilgrim's Progress*, Parts I and II — 127

The Role of Conscience in *The Pilgrim's Progress*, Parts I and II	132
The Emerging View of "Self" in *The Pilgrim's Progress*, Parts I and II	139
Individualism and Subjectivism in *The Pilgrim's Progress*, Parts I and II	141
The Desire for Company	143
The Church	145
Church Ordinances	153
The Pilgrim's Progress and Modernity	161
Conclusion	164

Chapter 6
Conscience and Citizenship in *The Life and Death of*
   Mr. Badman **and** *The Holy War*   167
    The Life and Death of Mr. Badman   168
       "Good Conscience" and Christian Economic
       Ethics   172
    The Holy War   178
       The Role of Conscience in The Holy War   181
       Citizenship in The Holy War   187
    The Perseverance of the Saints through
    Gospel-Informed Conscience   189
    Conclusion   192

Chapter 7
A Test Case for Bunyan's Subjectivism: Bunyan and
    Richard Baxter   195
    Bunyan's Opinion of "Church Fathers"   197
    Bunyan and Baxter on Justification by Faith   203
    Conclusion   210

Bibliography   211
Index   229

Acknowledgements

Many persons have contributed immeasurably to the improvement of this work, and so my praise is inadequate to express my appreciation for them. I thank especially Dr. Ralph Wood, University Professor of Theology and Literature at Baylor University, who both suggested this project and directed to completion its earlier incarnation as my doctoral thesis. As Bunyan's Christian said, "Above all, I found it hard work to get up this hill, and truly if it had not been for the good man, the Porter that stands at the gate, I do not know, but that after all, I might have gone back again: but now I thank God I am here, and I thank you for receiving of me."

The community of scholars at Baylor nurtured my work and helped bring its conclusions to maturity, particularly Professors Barry Hankins, Bob Patterson, Rosalie Beck, Barry Harvey, Bill Pitts, Glenn Hilburn, David Jeffrey, Gordon Grant, Paula Woods, Roger Olson, William Brackney, and Jeff Hensley. Drs. Ann McGlashan and Francoise Ghillebaert have checked my translation of articles in German and French, respectively. I have also benefitted from the comments of several members of the International John Bunyan Society, particularly Vera Camden, Greg Randall, and Robert Collmer. A faculty development grant from John Brown University facilitated the preparation of my research for publication by Paternoster Press, whose editorial staff has been of invaluable assistance. Thank you all very much.

The interest shown in Bunyan and the themes of this book by family, friends, colleagues, and students has been immensely gratifying. But if I have misrepresented such matters to my readers in any way, the flaw lies with none of the consultants listed above but solely with myself.

The love and support of my wife Lori have provided the fuel on which my commitment to this book operated, and it is my honor and pleasure now to dedicate it to her.

List of Abbreviations

Badman	John Bunyan, *The Life and Death of Mr. Badman*, ed. James F. Forrest and Roger Sharrock (Oxford: Clarendon Press, 1988).
CG	Martin Luther, *A Commentary on St. Paul's Epistle to the Galatians*, ed. Philip S. Watson (Westwood, NJ: Fleming H. Revell Company, 1953).
GA	John Bunyan, *Grace Abounding to the Chief of Sinners*, ed. Roger Sharrock (Oxford: Clarendon Press, 1962).
GAOSA	John Bunyan, *Grace Abounding with Other Spiritual Autobiographies*, ed. John Stachniewski with Anita Pacheco (Oxford: Oxford University Press, 1998).
HW	John Bunyan, *The Holy War*, ed. Roger Sharrock and James F. Forrest (Oxford: Clarendon Press, 1980).
MW	John Bunyan, *The Miscellaneous Works of John Bunyan*, 13 volumes, gen. ed. Roger Sharrock (Oxford: Clarendon Press, 1976-1994). Full editorial information for each individual volume is provided in the bibliography.
PP	John Bunyan, *The Pilgrim's Progress*, ed. James Blanton Wharey and Roger Sharrock (Oxford: Clarendon Press, 1960).

CHAPTER ONE

Introduction

In December 2001, the Graduate Center of the City University of New York released the findings of its second American Religious Identification Survey. The survey revealed that a significant trend of religious identification in contemporary America is the bifurcation of individuals' religious beliefs from their participation in a religious community. It also suggests that "this mix-and-match, come-and-go attitude may be the logical outcome of America's sanctification of individualism and personal autonomy."[1] In the same month in which this survey appeared, a book entitled *Self Matters: Creating Your Life from the Inside Out* became a *New York Times* top-five bestseller soon after its release. This book encourages readers to reclaim an "authentic self" by not bowing to what others think they should be.[2] Such rugged individualism is one of the most defining features of contemporary Western culture, including the Christian church. Stanley Hauerwas observes, in fact, how Christians in America often appear more American than Christian: they interpret the Bible on the basis of their own experience or "common sense" and not from within the authority of a truth-seeking community.[3] Sociologist Robert N. Bellah, invoking the forecast of the Frenchman Alexis de Tocqueville's *Democracy in America* a century and a half ago, frankly wondered in 1985 if American individualism had not already become "cancerous."[4]

Roger Pooley summarizes a scholarly commonplace when he claims that the real turn toward individualism in the West came in the sixteenth century, when the Renaissance and the Reformation each encouraged human individuals to think of themselves *as* indi-

---

1 Cathy Lynn Grossman and Anthony DeBarros, "Still One Nation Under God, But Survey Finds Shifting Beliefs," *USA Today*, 24 December 2001, sec. D, p. 1.
2 Phillip C. McGraw, *Self Matters: Creating Your Life from the Inside Out* (New York: Simon and Schuster, 2001), inside back sleeve.
3 Stanley Hauerwas, *Unleashing the Scripture: Freeing the Bible from Captivity to America* (Nashville: Abingdon Press, 1993), 15.
4 Robert N. Bellah, *et al.*, *Habits of the Heart: Individualism and Commitment in American Life* (New York: Harper and Row, 1985), vii.

viduals rather than as members of a people, nationality, or family.⁵ Charles Taylor identifies the further growth of individualism in the seventeenth century as the new "independence of the subject, [and] his determining of his own purposes without interference from external authority." Taylor locates the importance of the seventeenth century for development of self-perception in the internalization of moral authority, particularly in the thought of René Descartes and John Locke: "relative to Plato and relative to Augustine, it brings about in each case a transposition by which we no longer see ourselves as related to moral sources outside of us, or at least not at all in the same way."⁶ Friedrich Schweitzer maintains that the largest buoys in the stream of modernity between the seventeenth century and our own were Immanuel Kant and Sigmund Freud, the latter of whom particularly summoned men and women to become truly adult by exercising autonomous judgment.⁷ But the headwaters of *early* modern individualism, observe Michael Mascuch and Cecile M. Jagodzinski, flowed not from Kant's and Freud's Germany but from John Bunyan's England.⁸

Much of the recent critical study of individualism has focused on the peculiar mix of religious, social, and political unrest in mid-seventeenth century England that fostered the social mobility and heightened introspection which eventually left human lives as ends in and of themselves, without obligation to the communal whole. Keith Thomas, for instance, calls seventeenth century England "the Age of Conscience" because of the intense scrupulousness with which its citizens responded to religious and political conflicts.⁹ Yet no one has fully reconstructed Bunyan's conceptions of conscience

---

5   Roger Pooley, "*Grace Abounding* and the New Sense of Self," in *John Bunyan and His England, 1628-88*, ed. Anne Laurence, W. R. Owens, and Stuart Sim (London: The Hambledon Press, 1990), 105.
6   Charles Taylor, *Sources of the Self: The Making of the Modern Identity* (Cambridge, MA: Harvard University Press, 1989), 143.
7   Friedrich Schweitzer, "Church, Individual Religion, Public Responsibility: Images of Faith Between Modern and Postmodern Adulthood," *The Princeton Seminary Bulletin* 21:3 (November 2000): 289-290.
8   See the overviews by Michael Mascuch, *Origins of the Individualist Self: Autobiography and Self-Identity in England, 1591-1791* (Stanford: Stanford University Press), 1996, 14, 23-24, and Cecile M. Jagodzinski, *Privacy and Print: Reading and Writing in Seventeenth-Century England* (Charlottesville: University Press of Virginia, 1999), 1, 169.
9   Keith Thomas, "Cases of Conscience in Seventeenth-Century England," in *Public Duty and Private Conscience in Seventeenth-Century England: Essays Presented to G. E. Aylmer*, ed. John Morrill, Paul Slack, and Daniel Woolf (Oxford: Clarendon Press, 1993), 29.

and selfhood, leaving Bunyan scholars unable to judge to what degree Bunyan both anticipated and rejected the self-defining, self-directing conscience that typifies modern individualism. In subsequent chapters, I shall deal with Bunyan's relationships to the political and ecclesiastical turmoil that characterized England after the civil wars, and how this complex dynamic also influenced his autobiographical and fictional works. But first I must identify the significance of Bunyan's theological writings, especially his anti-Quaker treatises, for the whole question of modernity and the rise of individualism.

The issue at stake is not *whether* Bunyan participated in the evolution of individualism, which I understand according to Bellah's definition as "a belief that the individual has a primary reality whereas society is a second-order, derived or artificial construct."[10] Bunyan certainly nurtured the individualist ethos in his refusal to comply with state worship and in his wayfaring protagonist Christian in *The Pilgrim's Progress*. Bunyan scholars have long recognized this. For example, Christopher Hill argues that for Bunyan and other seventeenth century dissenters, individual consciences were "the vehicles of change" in the shifting of social norms toward greater religious toleration.[11] M. Esther Harding and Monica Furlong describe Bunyan's religious maturation as a Jungian quest for individuation.[12] Vincent Newey says that Bunyan's Christian reveals "the individual's ability to live by his own devices."[13] Roger Sharrock finds that Bunyan "individualizes Biblical meaning,"[14] and other writers note that Bunyan advocated "liberty of conscience" or

---

10 Bellah, 334.
11 Christopher Hill, *A Tinker and a Poor Man: John Bunyan and His Church, 1628-1688* (New York: W. W. Norton and Company, 1990), 84.
12 M. Esther Harding, *Journey Into Self* (Boston: Sigo Press, 1993), 18; Monica Furlong, *Puritan's Progress* (New York: Coward, McCann and Geoghegan, Inc., 1975), 179.
13 Vincent Newey, "Bunyan and the Confines of the Mind," in *The Pilgrim's Progress: Critical and Historical Views*, ed. Vincent Newey (Totowa, NJ: Barnes and Noble Books, 1980), 24.
14 Roger Sharrock, "Bunyan Studies Today: An Evaluation," in *Bunyan in England and Abroad: Papers Delivered at the John Bunyan Tercentenary Symposium, Vrije Universiteit, Amsterdam 1988*, ed. M. van Os and G. J. Schutte (Amsterdam: Vrije Universiteit Press, 1990), 55.

suffered imprisonment "for conscience' sake."[15] Bunyan's appearance as the ultimate lonely individual wrestling with his private conscience would also appear to account for his great appeal to non-ecclesial, non-confessional modern artists such as the painter Vincent Van Gogh, the writers Samuel Taylor Coleridge and George Bernard Shaw, and the composer Ralph Vaughan Williams.

Ironically, however, these moderns are in fact not fascinated by the tormented soul of Bunyan's early autobiographical narratives but instead with his use of allegory, to which he resorted precisely to obviate his own subjectivist tendencies. The genius of Bunyan's work is not to be found in his allegedly modern assumptions about individualism. Furthermore, in his theological and political writings, Bunyan strongly *resisted* aspects of various spiritual and intellectual movements in his own century, such as "the inner light" of Quakerism and the libertarianism of John Milton, which were more direct precursors (if not progenitors) of the pronounced subjectivism of later centuries. Bunyan certainly resisted the deification of collective authority, but in these works, he did not view collective authority as the necessary antithesis of authentic Christian selfhood.[16]

My method combines literary critical, theological, and historical approaches. My literary study of Bunyan arises out of the form critical school, which advocates a "close reading" of the meaning of words on the page. Thus is the use of selective quotations important to establish precisely how Bunyan used the words "conscience" and "self." Yet these quotations are no mere proof texts, for I seek always to locate them within the theological and historical contexts in which Bunyan wrote, and I use supplementary citations from Bunyan's whole corpus to bolster conclusions drawn from the works under principal consideration: Bunyan's anti-Quaker and political writings, *Grace Abounding to the Chief of Sinners*, *The Pilgrim's Progress*, *The Life and Death of Mr. Badman*, and *The Holy War*. Theologically, I wish to demonstrate how Bunyan's understanding of scriptural authority and Christological orthodoxy, rather than rendering him the prototypically introspective modern man, kept him

---

15 For Bunyan's "liberty of conscience," see e.g., Stuart Sim and David Walker, *Bunyan and Authority: The Rhetoric of Dissent and the Legitimation Crisis in Seventeenth-Century England* (Bern: Peter Lang, 2000), 45, 131. For Bunyan's imprisonment "for conscience' sake," see e.g., Harry Emerson Fosdick, *On Being a Real Person* (New York: Harper and Row, 1943), 205.

16 I credit Eric C. Rust, *Towards a Theological Understanding of History* (New York: Oxford University Press, 1963), 128-129, for helping me think through this distinction.

Introduction

on the alert against subjectivist trends in his century. Historically, I want to show how Bunyan related to important seventeenth century movements that contributed so mightily to the evolution of the modern self, such as Puritan conversionism, religious radicalism, and Enlightenment individualism.

To these ends, Chapter Two treats Bunyan's first published writings, which were against the Quakers, because the early Quakers appear to be closer relatives to the modern autonomous self than does Bunyan, and his resistance to them is evidence of his further resistance to their affinity for the modern self. The Quakers believed that by the inner light of the Holy Spirit, individuals could communicate with God as closely and directly as did the twelve apostles with Jesus, and they held, moreover, that this light dwells within every person, whether a believer or not. Bunyan, representing the wider Baptist community on this issue, responded that the Quakers – in emphasizing a personal, mystical encounter with the divine – too easily bypassed the authority of Scripture on doctrinal matters, such as the Incarnation and resurrection of Jesus Christ. In Chapter Two, I cite the contention of Sacvan Bercovitch and L. John Van Til that the Quaker notion of the inner light was a forerunner of the romantic notion of the individual that flowered in the work of Ralph Waldo Emerson and that influenced the Western secularization of conscience. Yet Bunyan vehemently opposed it. Though I grant certain points of commonality between Bunyan and the Quakers, in the end, these only serve to emphasize their great differences in regard to conscience.

Chapter Three addresses Bunyan's autobiography, *Grace Abounding to the Chief of Sinners*, the chief test case for what appears to be a radical subjectivism and individualism: a solitary soul who seems to descend into a vortex of his own stricken conscience. I contend that to understand the conception of conscience that Bunyan there displays, one must appreciate Bunyan's fondness for and reliance upon Martin Luther's *Commentary on Galatians*. Since Bunyan acknowledged his great theological indebtedness to Luther, it will be appropriate to rehearse Luther's understanding of conscience. Randall C. Zachman's excellent study, *The Assurance of Faith: Conscience in the Theology of Martin Luther and John Calvin* (1993), argues that Luther was not really a champion of liberty of conscience in the modern connotation but rather of conscience freed to serve Christ alone. I will read Bunyan's treatment of conscience in *Grace Abounding* through this Lutheran lens, paying special attention to the context in which Bunyan speaks of "conscience" and "self." A thorough investigation of Bunyan's twenty-nine references to conscience in *Grace Abounding* reveals that they correspond closely to what Luther taught in his *Galatians*. Since Bunyan inherited his view of conscience from Luther – and I demonstrate this through numerous parallel passages – it is fitting to ask whether he joined Luther in denying liberty of conscience understood in the autonomous sense.

Then, in Chapter Four, I locate Bunyan along the Puritan spectrum of political ideas on conscience and its liberty.[17] Van Til points to the important difference between toleration and liberty of conscience: a tolerationist holds that the state has the authority to dictate a range of religious practices that nurture the commonweal, while an advocate of liberty of conscience holds that a person has a natural or God-given "right" to worship as he or she believes without any intrusion from the state. Both emphases were present in the political writings of such Puritan theologians as William Perkins and William Ames. One of the perplexities of Bunyan is that he appeared to applaud each school. Martin Schmidt states that the historical line to the modern Western notion of the self ran from Perkins through Bunyan, since their tendency to rely on the conscience for decision-making was easily separated later from their theological concerns. But, in fact, many of Bunyan's late political works were hardly modern in any sense; instead, they were tolerationist at best and astonishingly traditionalist. I will demonstrate this by comparing Bunyan's political writings to those of his contemporary John Milton. Attempts to see in Bunyan's talk of conscience something akin to modern concepts of liberty and freedom thus comprise an anachronistic reading by a later, more individualistic age.

In Chapter Five, I show that *The Pilgrim's Progress* is a masterpiece that has many individualist qualities but that also envisions the Christian struggle for authenticity before God as a communal and public reality rather than a merely private and personal one. I argue that *The Pilgrim's Progress*, Part II, has been wrongly maligned because it has not been interpreted via the themes of assurance of conscience and the gradually sanctified self. Indeed, there is evidence to suggest that Bunyan himself believed the communal pilgrimage of Part II to be superior to Part I, though even in Part I Christian constantly seeks the companionship of fellow believers. Part II reveals a Bunyan who had a stronger notion of Christian confidence than before, which allowed him to depict Christian selfhood in less individualistic terms. I treat numerous sacramental and

---

17 Portions of Chapter Four are based on an article by me entitled "The Conflicted Puritan Inheritance of John Bunyan's Political Writings", published in *Baptist History and Heritage* 38:2 (Spring 2003): 103-115.

ecclesial images in Part II, whose full implications for Bunyan's ecclesiology have remained often unnoticed in secondary criticism.

I treat *The Life and Death of Mr. Badman* and *The Holy War* together in Chapter Six. After rehearsing the many negative evaluations of these two fictional works, I explain why they are in fact crucial for reading Bunyan's rejection of subjectivism. When diagnosing Mr. Badman's "bad" conscience, the characters Wiseman and Attentive offer a program for Christian citizenship and involvement in the economic life of the nation that could hardly be less sectarian or modernist. My treatment of *The Holy War* is largely a critique of Stuart Sim and David Walker's *Bunyan and Authority: The Rhetoric of Dissent and the Legitimation Crisis in Seventeenth-Century England* (2000). Sim and Walker argue that Diabolus' and Emmanuel's alternate possession of the city of Mansoul reveals Bunyan's awareness not only of the modern but of the postmodern self. Emanuel's final admonition to "Hold fast" thus serves as an encouragement toward individual "self-authorisation." Sim and Walker miss the fact that "Hold fast" comes from Revelation 2:25 and is spoken not in resignation that Mansoul will forever endure alternating leadership, but that the Christian soul, though it may indeed waver between Christ and the devil in this life, belongs to Christ alone and thus stands assured of ultimate triumph. The authors' failure to grasp Bunyan's eschatological beliefs thus prevents them from appreciating the comprehensive religio-cultural vision of *The Holy War*.

Finally, in Chapter Seven, I show how my accumulated research corrects accusations of subjectivism made against Bunyan by David Lyle Jeffrey in *People of the Book: Christian Identity and Literary Culture* (1994). Indeed, I demonstrate how the Puritan preacher Richard Baxter, Jeffrey's foil to Bunyan, can be called "early modern" or even "subjectivist" with much more validity than Bunyan because he mitigated the theological orthodoxy that tied Bunyan much more firmly to ancient Christian tradition. In 1845, church historian Philip Schaff called ecclesiastical subjectivism the "grand disease which has fastened itself upon the heart of Protestantism,"[18] and over a century later, theologian Wolfhart Pannenberg described it as an "irrational fanaticism" that debilitates all discourse about God

---

18 Philip Schaff, *The Principle of Protestantism as Related to the Present State of the Church*, trans. John W. Nevin (Chambersburg, PA: Publication Office of the German Reformed Church, 1845), 107.

and ecclesial life.[19] And although he does not necessarily find it a complete detriment, Philip E. Thompson has recently identified an anthropocentric individualism to be as nearly creedal as anything in Bunyan's own Baptist tradition since the early nineteenth century.[20] But Bunyan himself remained ever a churchman who offered his life and writings in protest against any interior authority that could become an individually *generated* and thus *subjective* authority.

French philosopher Alain Renaut stresses in his historical survey of the sweep of modern individualism that *"subjectivity and individuality must not be confused."*[21] Through discerning in Bunyan's writings, even those with individualist tendencies, what he thought individual conscience and selfhood should and should not involve, and comparing these ideas to Bunyan's more forward-looking contemporaries, one uncovers in Bunyan a consistent resistance to fully modern notions of autonomous, subjective conscience and forming one's self "from the inside out." Hence, much like Bunyan's Christian beneath his heavy load, Bunyan himself cannot always bear the burden of modernity that any number of observers have laid upon him.

---

19   Cf. Stephen K. Moroney, *The Noetic Effects of Sin: A Historical and Contemporary Exploration of How Sin Affects Our Thinking* (Lanham, MD: Lexington Books, 2000), 51. Though critical of Pannenberg for underestimating the effect of sin on human reason, Maroney provides a very useful review of the critique of religious subjectivism in Pannenberg's *Systematic Theology*.
20   Philip E. Thompson, "Re-envisioning Baptist Identity: Historical, Theological, and Liturgical Analysis," *Perspectives in Religious Studies* 27:3 (Fall 2000): 289-290, 293.
21   Alain Renaut, *The Era of the Individual: A Contribution to a History of Subjectivism*, trans. M. B. DeBevoise and Franklin Philip (Princeton: Princeton University Press, 1997), 128.

Chapter Two

Conscience and Individualism in Bunyan's Anti-Quaker Writings

While walking through Bunhill Fields Dissenters' Cemetery in London in 1999, Dr. Mary Trim from the University of Loughborough strolled not merely among the grave markers, but backward through time. Standing before the monument to John Bunyan, she recalled that it was there, "at Bunhill Fields, on the third of September, 1688, that Bunyan was laid in the tomb of another, like his Saviour. One can dimly imagine the sadness of the mourners, as well as the prayers, praise and testimonies of Christian faith that were bravely offered that day." Continuing through the grays, whites, and occasional mossy greens of this past world, Trim looked upon the graves of other religious nonconformists such as John Owen, Oliver Cromwell's great-great-grandson Henry, Isaac Watts, and William Blake. Some of the headstones were no longer legible, their inscriptions having been effaced by the eroding factors of rain and wind. Trim imagined the voices of all these dead dissenters telling in chorus "a story of individualism and fidelity to conviction of conscience, while communally offering testimony to the resoluteness of human spirit that should not be forgotten."[1]

Within three hundred yards of Bunyan's grave, in the Quaker burial ground, George Fox lies interred.[2] In death as they were in life, Bunyan and Fox remain near each other and yet separated by significant barriers. Both were preachers of enormous persuasive power who spent a good portion of their adult lives in prison for their nonconformity, yet the two men never met, even though Fox visited Bedfordshire several times during Bunyan's ministry there. In fact, they competed for converts among the same townspeople, and Fox countered Bunyan's theological offensive against the Quaker Edward Burrough with his own published reply. Their most vehement disagreement was precisely at the point of their closest

---

1   Mary Trim, "Bunyan's Burial Place," *The Recorder* 6 (Spring 2000): 2-3.
2   T. L. Underwood, *Primitivism, Radicalism, and the Lamb's War: The Baptist-Quaker Conflict in Seventeenth-Century England* (New York: Oxford University Press, 1997), 52.

affinity: both were willing to forfeit their civil liberty for the spiritual liberty to engage Christ directly, without any mediation from priest or Prayer Book. Yet their respective quests yielded significantly different perspectives on the authority of individual conscience in religious matters relative to "objective" scripture and Christology. Bunyan strongly resisted those aspects of Quakerism whose displacement of theological orthodoxy with one's own "inner light" was a precursor (if not progenitor) of the extremely individualistic subjectivism of later centuries.

Bunyan's negative reactions to those emphases where the Quakers most closely prefigured modern individualism bring into relief to what degree he thought conscience merited fidelity, and whether he saw himself, as Trim suggests, as "offering testimony to the resoluteness of human spirit." The task of this chapter is to demonstrate that in the major points of dispute between Bunyan and the Quakers – particularly those which pertained to conscience, the self, and individualism – the Quakers often jumped the demarcating stream of modernity that Bunyan stood astride. The two most significant sources for understanding Bunyan's position are his first two published works, *Some Gospel-Truths Opened* (1656) and his reply to the Quaker Edward Burrough's *The True Faith of the Gospel of Peace Contended For*, called *A Vindication of Some Gospel-Truths Opened* (1657). Bunyan also alluded to the Quakers in *A Few Sighs from Hell* (1658), *The Doctrine of the Law and Grace Unfolded* (1659), *The Heavenly Foot-man* (written ca. 1671; published 1698), *A Defence of the Doctrine of Justification, By Faith* (1672), *The Strait Gate* (1676), *The Pilgrim's Progress*, Part I (1678), the fifth edition of *Grace Abounding to the Chief of Sinners* (1680), *A Discourse Upon the Pharisee and the Publicane* (1685), *Questions About the Nature and Perpetuity of the Seventh-Day Sabbath* (1685), and *Israel's Hope Encouraged* (posthumous, 1692). My evaluations of the Quakers' own perspectives come predominantly from George Fox's *Journal* and *The Great Mystery of the Great Whore Unfolded*, as well as apologetic writings by the early Quakers Burrough, William Penn, and Robert Barclay, along with Quaker historians.

Scripture and Conscience

Henri Talon dismisses any lasting importance of the theological arguments in Bunyan's polemical works and instead looks there only for intellectual developments in Bunyan's ideas of selfhood.[3]

---

3   Henri Talon, *John Bunyan: The Man and His Works*, trans. Barbara Wall (Cambridge, MA: Harvard University Press, 1951), 94.

But as I have suggested elsewhere, readings of Bunyan's corpus which tend to minimize the living personal force of his theology often reveal only the ideological agenda of the evaluator, including Talon's apparent assumption that Bunyan's understanding of "the genesis of self through self" developed independently of, and was only illustrated by, his theology.[4] In Bunyan's anti-Quaker writings especially, the most effective way to understand how Bunyan perceived the relationship between conscience and self is to learn how they were inextricably interwoven together with his dogmatic claims for the authority of scripture and the historic Christological confessions of the church.

Bunyan's View of Scriptural Authority

In the opening letter to the reader in *Some Gospel-Truths Opened*, Bunyan was fearful of how the devil "laboureth by all meanes possible to keepe thy Conscience asleep in Securitie and self conceitednesse, keeping thee from all things that might be a meanes to awaken and rowse up thine heart."[5] What are these "things" that rouse the heart and conscience and thereby vanquish the soporific fiend? They are the ordinances of Christ, Bunyan said: not baptism and the Lord's Supper in this case, but hearing (that is, through preaching), reading, and meditating on the word of God. How does the word invigorate the conscience? It does so by making one feel the smart of personal sin. Faced with scripture as the antidote to his stupefying potion, Satan "cannot so blind, and benumb thy conscience, but that it doth see and feele sin to be a burden, intolerable and exceeding sinful."[6] The burdened conscience then tries to purge its guilt in a manner that anticipates Christian's attempt to rid his burden in *The Pilgrim's Progress*: at first it is despondent, and then it tries to absolve itself through works of law. Failing at that, in the process of time, it drives the soul to the gospel of Christ and salvation by grace. But a conscience not first "seared as with an hot iron" by scripture does not do "thee the least good."[7]

---

4 Ibid.; Galen K. Johnson, "'Be Not Extream:' The Limits of Theory in Reading John Bunyan," *Christianity and Literature* 49:4 (Summer 2000): 447-464.
5 John Bunyan, *Some Gospel-Truths Opened*, in *The Miscellaneous Works of John Bunyan*, vol. 1, ed. T. L. Underwood and Roger Sharrock (Oxford: Clarendon Press, 1980), 13. Throughout my study, I follow the original italicization and the original spelling of all Bunyan's works.
6 Ibid., 14.
7 Ibid., 15.

Yet some *"deluded"* persons were teaching the *"pernicious"* doctrine that a person's search for Christ did not need to follow the progression that Bunyan described.[8] They advocated a direct spiritual encounter with Christ that allegedly superseded the intercession and authority of the Bible. For Bunyan, however, there was no other way but the scriptural way; the person whose conscience was untaught by the objective word of God could never know nor be saved by the objective Christ.[9] This was the foundation for his argument against the Quakers.

> Therefore what a sad doctrine is that which saith, follow the light that Christ hath enlightened every man withall which commeth into the world, which light is the Conscience that convinceth of Sinnes against the Law; and that you may see clearly if you mind that Scripture, Jo. 8.9. which saith, that the Pharises which had neither the love of God, nor yet his word abiding in them, Jo. 5.38.43 when they heard Christ speaking thus to them, He that is without sin among you, &c. being convicted by their own Consciences, went out one by one, beginning at the eldest, even to the least.[10]

Here lies the difference that Bunyan saw between his own theology of conscience and that of the Quakers. For the Quakers, the conscience was the inner light of Christ which all persons naturally possess and is sufficient for communing with Christ. For Bunyan, conscience was not autonomous, for only when it learns from the preached scriptures to feel the terrible burden of personal sin does it begin its progression toward Christ.[11] A quiet conscience for Bunyan was subject to divine wrath; only a "pricked" conscience was a healthy one.

Even in defending the word of God as objective, Bunyan could nonetheless interpret it individualistically. As *Grace Abounding* reveals, Bunyan's own arrival at salvation came after tortuous years

---

8 Ibid., 15-16.
9 Cf. Richard L. Greaves, *Glimpses of Glory: John Bunyan and English Dissent* (Stanford: Stanford University Press, 2002), 78.
10 Bunyan, *MW*, 1:22-23.
11 Note Bunyan's emphasis on the preached word: "Again, Man at his coming into the world hath this conscience given him, which doth convince of sinne, *John* 1.9. *John* 8.9 yet man as he commeth into the world, hath not the spirit of Christ in him, for that must be received afterward, by the preaching of the word, which is preached by the Ministers and servants of Jesus Christ" (Ibid., 57). The title page of *Some Gospel-Truths Opened*, in fact, describes the author as *"John Bunyan*, of Bedford, By the grace of God, Preacher of the Gospel of his dear Son" (Ibid., 5).

of alternately aligning himself with biblical texts that either assured him or damned him. Yet against the Quakers, he believed "he was defending the Bible to which he owed his conversion,"[12] for they appeared to bypass the Bible's regulative authority, and so, like Formalist and Hypocrisy in *The Pilgrim's Progress*, they were bound to destruction for not coming in through the narrow door.[13] Bunyan did not deny that the particular pangs of each chastened conscience are different, but he certainly thought that some form of anguish should be a universal experience of all true followers of Christ. For instance, although the character Faithful in *The Pilgrim's Progress* is not long detained, as is Christian, by the Slow of Dispond, "whither the scum and filth that attends conviction for sin doth continually run," Faithful nonetheless must resist the seductress Wanton, who, Christian says, *"did not promise you the content of a good conscience."*[14] Talon's assessment of Bunyan's reaction to the Quakers is thus quite appropriate: "He had weighed up his own unworthiness and nothingness, and now they wanted him to believe that man could find redemptive force with his own self. Against the pretensions of this Quaker teaching he had the irrefutable evidence of his own experience, his own interior certainty."[15] But how could Bunyan claim that his conscience was submissive to scripture if his conscience was his only guide in interpreting scripture? Did Bunyan's evidence for the objectivity of scripture – at least in these early writings against the Quakers – lie ironically in his own individual perceptions?

In *A Vindication of Some Gospel-Truths Opened*, Bunyan again emphasized that the conscience must be submissive to scripture, for otherwise, it, like the Mosaic law, cannot actualize the salvation to which it points (cf. Romans 7:10). Indeed, Bunyan's equation of the law with conscience and also with nature is the substratum upon which *A Vindication* stands. He understood conscience as "Nature it selfe, because it can controule, and chide them for sin," "the law of

---

12 Hill, *Tinker*, 79.
13 Bunyan, *The Pilgrim's Progress*, ed. James Blanton Wharey and Roger Sharrock (Oxford: Clarendon Press, 1960), 40.
14 Ibid., 15, 68.
15 Talon, *John Bunyan: The Man and His Works*, 96. Cf. Bunyan's response in *The Doctrine of the Law and Grace Unfolded* to Paul's statement in Romans 7:9-11 that sin lured him precisely through its prohibition by the Mosaic law: "And indeed to speak to my own experience, together with the experience of all the Saints, they can seal with me to this, more or lesse" (John Bunyan, *The Miscellaneous Works of John Bunyan*, vol. 2, ed. Richard L. Greaves [Oxford: Clarendon Press, 1976], 138).

nature," and "the [Mosaic] law;" conscience is furthermore "but a creature, a faculty of the soul of man."[16] It did not matter to Bunyan which of "these Scripture terms" one employed: conscience, the law, and nature all denote the same agent by which the Holy Spirit impresses upon the reader/hearer of scripture his or her sinfulness. Therefore, of themselves and unregenerated, consciences are "poor low, empty, beggerly things," and "if thou or any one else, shall leave the Scriptures, to follow the convictions of their own conscience, ye are not like to know Christ Jesus the Lord, for they may be defiled."[17] Moreover, "Our consciences naturally are evil, having (saith the Scripture) our hearts sprinkled from an evil conscience, *Heb.* 10.22."[18]

Therefore, when Harry Emerson Fosdick suggests that Bunyan became "a prisoner in Bedford jail for conscience' sake," this holds true only with the realization that Bunyan's conscience, in turn, was

---

16 Bunyan, *MW*, 1:147, 148, 168-169; cf. 163, 165, 200-201, 206, 210-211, 214-215; see also Bunyan's *Christian Behaviour*, where he chastises "such who count the dictates and impulses of a meer natural conscience, as good, as high, and divine, as the leadings and movings of the Spirit of Christ" (*The Miscellaneous Works of John Bunyan*, vol. 3, ed. J. Sears McGee [Oxford: Clarendon Press, 1987], 20). Note further Bunyan's claim: "There is no Man by *Nature*, that hath any soundness in him, no, neither in Soul or Body; his understanding *is* darkened, his Mind and Conscience *is* defiled, his Wills perverted and obstinate: *There is no judgment in his goings*" (*A Defence of the Doctrine of Justification, By Faith*, in *The Miscellaneous Works of John Bunyan*, vol. 4, ed. T. L. Underwood [Oxford: Clarendon Press, 1989], 13). Bunyan's equation of the law of Moses with the law of nature followed the same by Martin Luther, for whose influence on Bunyan, see the following chapter. Also see Jaroslav Pelikan on Luther's position: "Although both the law and the gospel had come by the revelation of God, there was this difference between them: the gospel could be known only through such revelation, while the law of Moses was, at least in principle, coextensive with the law of nature and was valid only insofar as it was the same as the law of nature" (Pelikan, *The Christian Tradition: A History of the Development of Doctrine*, vol. 4, *Reformation of Church and Dogma (1300-1700)* [Chicago: The University of Chicago Press, 1984], 170).
17 Bunyan, *MW*, 1:152, 168. Cf. Bunyan's *Questions About the Nature and Perpetuity of the Seventh-Day Sabbath*: "For if the Law of Nature, as such, can predict, or foretel Gods Secrets, and that before he reveals them, and this Law of Nature is universal in every individual man in the world, what need is there of particular Prophets, or of their holy writings? (and indeed here the Quakers and others split themselves)" (*MW*, 4:338).
18 Bunyan, *MW*, 1:175.

captive to scripture.[19] It is very interesting that when Bunyan confessed in *A Vindication*, "For I am ruled, and would be ruled by them [the scriptures] through the Spirit," he anticipated the very language that would be turned against him three years later by Paul Cobb, Clerk of the Peace, when Bunyan was on trial: "Pray be ruled."[20] Bunyan's response to Cobb, that he actively obeyed only laws to which his conscience bound him, should be understood in terms of his expanded treatment of conscience in his early anti-Quaker works: conscience was a binding force only when it in turn was bound to scripture. Conscience was *not*, in Bunyan's perspec-

---

19 Fosdick, 204-205; cf. a similar description of Bunyan as "prisoner of conscience" by Graham Midgley (in John Bunyan, *The Miscellaneous Works of John Bunyan*, vol. 6, ed. Graham Midgley [Oxford: Clarendon Press, 1980], xxxiii) and W. R. Owens, "Reading the Bibliographical Codes: Bunyan's Publication in Folio," in *John Bunyan: Reading Dissenting Writing*, ed. N. H. Keeble [Bern: Peter Lang, 2002], 62). Compare Martin Luther's famous declaration before the Diet of Worms in 1521: "Unless I am convicted by Scripture and plain reason – I do not accept the authority of popes and [papal] councils, for they have contradicted each other – my conscience is captive to the Word of God. I cannot and I will not recant anything, for to go against conscience is neither right nor safe. God help me. Amen" (Roland H. Bainton, *Here I Stand: A Life of Martin Luther* [New York: Abingdon-Cokesbury Books, 1950], 185).

20 Bunyan, *MW*, 1:160; *A Relation of the Imprisonment of Mr. John Bunyan*, in *Grace Abounding to the Chief of Sinners*, ed. Roger Sharrock (Oxford: Clarendon Press, 1962), 124. The concern with "being ruled" is a recurrent one in *The Pilgrim's Progress*. For instance, in Part I, Bunyan says in his Apology, "This Book will make a Travailer of thee, / If by its Counsel thou wilt ruled be;" Obstinate chides Pliable, "What! more Fools still? be ruled by me and go back; who knows whither such a brain-sick fellow will lead you?" Worldly-Wiseman informs Christian of Evangelist, "I beshrow him for his counsel; there is not a more dangerous and troublesome way in the world, than is that unto which he hath directed thee; and that thou shalt find, if thou wilt be ruled by his counsel;" and Christian informs Formalist and Hypocrisy, "I walk by the Rule of my Master, you walk by the rude working of your fancies." In Part II of *The Pilgrim's Progress*, Steadfast says of Madam Bubble, "Then she made Offers again, and said, If I would be ruled by her, she would make me great and happy" (Bunyan, *PP*, 6, 12, 18, 40, 301). Also in Bunyan's *The Holy War*, Captain Conviction calls upon the city of Mansoul to "be ruled then" by the laws of King Shaddai (*The Holy War*, ed. Roger Sharrock and James F. Forrest [Oxford: Clarendon Press, 1980], 44). John Foxe's *Acts and Monuments*, which Bunyan read while in prison, also records Robert Barnes and John Philpot being asked by Queen Mary's inquisitors, "Will you then be ruled by us ...?" (John Foxe, *Foxe's Book of Martyrs* [Springdale, PA: Whitaker House, 1981], 325, 341).

tive, an autonomous authority. Likewise, "Judge not thereof by feeling, nor by the reports of thy Conscience," Bunyan advised in *The Jerusalem Sinner Saved; or, Good News for the Vilest of Men*, for "Conscience is oft-times befooled and made to go quite besides the Word."[21] And, in *Questions About the Nature and Perpetuity of the Seventh-Day Sabbath*, Bunyan hailed Martin Luther for yielding to the Bible "to get his Conscience clear from all those *roots* and *strings* of inbred errour."[22] Similarly, in *A Discourse Upon the Pharisee and the Publicane*, Bunyan further applauded the penitent publican of Luke 18:13 because "he went against the voice of Conscience, against Sense and Feeling, against the Curse and condemning Verdict of the Law," and toward the word of God.[23] And when, in the fifth edition of *Grace Abounding*, Bunyan added a list of eight theological errors made by the Quakers, the first was their alleged belief "that the Holy Scriptures were not the Word of God."[24] Thus, Bunyan believed that Quakers did not submit conscience to scripture.

The Quakers' Views of Scriptural Authority

Bunyan forged his understanding of conscience on the iron of the Quakers' apparently low view of scripture. Were the Quakers in fact guilty as charged? Hugh McGregor Ross, an eighth generation stepson of George Fox, admits that Fox's teachings did not include the authority of the written Bible, although "nevertheless he [Fox] implies that the passages he quotes carry authority – even though he used the bible very selectively."[25] Certainly, Fox used selections from scripture to support his teachings, even as Bunyan did, often citing passages that emphasized the direct personal encounter of the believer with God or Christ. William Penn's preface to Fox's *Journal* (1694) also praised Fox for having "an extraordinary gift in

---

21 John Bunyan, *The Miscellaneous Works of John Bunyan*, vol. 11, ed. Richard L. Greaves (Oxford: Clarendon Press, 1985)
22 Bunyan, *MW*, 4:380. Recall that when Luther was asked to recant his writings before the imperial Diet of Worms in 1521, he responded that "to go against conscience is neither right nor safe," but only because "my conscience is captive to the Word of God" (Bainton, 185).
23 Bunyan, *The Miscellaneous Works of John Bunyan*, vol. 10, ed. Owen C. Watkins (Oxford: Clarendon Press, 1988), 201.
24 Bunyan, *GA*, §123-124, pp. 38-39.
25 Hugh McGregor Ross, ed., *George Fox Speaks for Himself: Texts That Reveal His Personality – Many Hitherto Unpublished* (York, England: William Sessions Limited, 1991), 86.

opening the Scriptures."[26] In *The True Christians Distinguished* (1689), Fox called the Bible "the truest history that is upon the earth," encompassing God's actions both without mediation and intermediately through the prophets, Christ, and the apostles.[27] But the Bible for Fox remained only a *relative* authority: it gave examples of the divine encounters of others but was no substitute for having such an encounter oneself:

> And now, my friend, the holy men of God wrote the scriptures as they were moved by the holy ghost. All christendom are on heaps about those scriptures because they are not led by the same holy ghost as those were who gave forth the scriptures. Which holy ghost they must come to in themselves, and be led by, if they are to come into all the truth of the scriptures, and to have the comfort of God, of Christ, and of them.[28]

Theoretically, any emphasis on the direct encounter with Christ need not minimize the authority of written scripture.[29] Bunyan himself certainly affirmed the importance of inward communion with Christ, though not to the exclusion of Christ's outward work or scripture's objective authority. Geoffrey F. Nuttall even contends that if the Quakers relativized the authority of scripture, they did so "partly because of their very devotion to Scripture."[30] Whereas Protestants had always emphasized the essential role of the Holy Spirit in interpreting scripture, the Friends were incited by what they found in scripture to go a step further and claim that an authoritative Spirit need not speak only through the words of others in the Bible but could speak directly and no less authoritatively to each individual.[31] Yet there is no question that the Quaker bifurcation of Spirit and scripture tended to minimize the importance of scripture. By grounding authority more in the Holy Spirit rather than the Spirit-inspired scripture, as did Protestantism, or in church hierarchy, as did Roman Catholicism, Fox cultivated an "intensely

---

26 William Penn, in George Fox, *The Journal*, ed. Nigel Smith (London: Penguin Books, 1998), 500.
27 George Fox, in Hugh McGregor Ross, 41.
28 Ibid., 41.
29 Cf. Sidney E. Ahlstrom: "The distinctive Quaker testimony is to the direct revelation of Christ to the soul, although this is not understood to be contradictory to or even apart from the revelation in Scripture" (*A Religious History of the American People* [New Haven: Yale University Press, 1972], 177).
30 Geoffrey F. Nuttall, *The Holy Spirit in Puritan Faith and Experience* (Oxford: Basil Blackwell, 1946), 26.
31 Ibid., 28.

individualistic faith."[32] Scripture in Quaker perspective, according to D. Elton Trueblood, is something one uses to reach the same Spirit which originally inspired it.[33] And a corollary of this, says Horton Davies, is that "the experience of direct communication with God even meant bypassing the Scriptures."[34] Thus did William Penn's close friend Isaac Pennington say that the Bible is not an absolute authority for Quakers but that its rightful use is to prize the Spirit to which it points above what it contains.[35] And though the Quaker James Nayler received Fox's censure for reenacting Christ's triumphal entry into Jerusalem in Bristol in 1657, Nayler nonetheless spoke the logical conclusion of Quaker belief when he said flatly that one can know Christ *apart* from scripture.[36] Robert Barclay's

---

32   H. Larry Ingle, *First Among Friends: George Fox and the Creation of Quakerism* (New York: Oxford University Press, 1994), 42. It is only fair to point out that despite the individualistic tendencies of Fox's theology, the early Quakers nonetheless developed a strong sense of community. Perhaps this was partially a result of their persecution.

33   D. Elton Trueblood, *The People Called Quakers* (New York: Harper and Row, Publishers, 1966), 79. Cf. T. L. Underwood and Roger Sharrock, eds., in Bunyan, *MW*, 1:xviii: "It was the same testimony, they [the Quakers] asserted, which holy men of God had had before the Scriptures were written."

34   Horton Davies, *Worship and Theology in England: From Cranmer to Baxter and Fox, 1534-1690* (Grand Rapids: William B. Eerdmans Publishing Company, 1996), II.512. (Shirley Miller Bartell suggests that it was precisely Fox's failure to see the Bible as a regulative authority for Christian living that spared him the agonies which Bunyan recounted in *Grace Abounding*, when he debated whether verses of hope or condemnation best described his spiritual state. Shirley Miller Bartell, "Uncertainty in Bunyan versus Assurance in Fox," *Quaker History* 58 [Autumn 1969]: 100).

35   Isaac Pennington, letter, in Geoffrey Hubbard, *A Quaker by Convincement* (Middlesex, England: Penguin Books, 1974), 92.

36   Underwood, 113. Nayler's ride into Bristol on a donkey and his acceptance of the title of "Christ" from his admirers led to his imprisonment, in which condition he was when Bunyan wrote his two books concerning "gospel-truths." Bunyan probably had Nayler in mind when he wrote in *Some Gospel-Truths Opened*, "He is like to be deceived that will believe everything that calls it selfe a Christ" (*MW*, 1:47), though Leo Damrosch believes that *Some Gospel-Truths Opened* is "far less interesting than Nayer's writings of the same period" (Leo Damrosch, *The Sorrows of the Quaker Jesus: James Nayler and the Puritan Crackdown on the Free Spirit* [Cambridge, MA: Harvard University Press, 1996], 12). This reference lends credence to Dayton Haskin's contention that in light of Nayler's reception of "Hosanna to the Son of David!" Bunyan over the course of his career "sustained a concern to chasten the self-centered activities of those who presented themselves as

widely circulated "Confession of the Society of Friends," issued in the same year as Nayler's pseudo-Christic procession, also said that knowledge of Christ's death as proclaimed by scripture is "very profitable and comfortable, but not absolutely needful."[37]

Christ and Individualism

Some might contend that the Quakers would not have been aware of their conceptions of Christian selfhood being in any way "modern" and thus deviating from ancient Christian norms. Others may wonder whether Bunyan's own Baptist denomination was that much less individualistic than the Quakers, since the Baptist experience of scripture obviated the need for a regulative church hierarchy and tradition. Such was the accusation of Horace Bushnell in his 1861 book, *Christian Nurture*, which claimed that all Baptist theories of religion are based upon the error of extreme individualism.[38] However, in the seventeenth century, Baptist disputants against the Quakers perceived that exaggerated individualism was at the core of their disagreement. The Baptists saw the Quaker emphasis on "scripture within" and "Christ within" as a very dangerous displacement of objective, dogmatic authority. The ex-Quaker turned Baptist John Toldervy described his former religion as "'*Self for the justifying of Self*' where all was 'Resolved into Self.'"[39] Thomas Grantham, primary author of the Baptists' Ortho-

---

superior to the scriptural writers" (Haskin, "Bunyan's Scriptural Acts," in *Bunyan in Our Time*, ed. Robert G. Collmer [Kent, OH: The Kent State University Press, 1989], 65; cf. 73). Thomas H. Luxon describes the behavior of Nayler and some other seventeenth century radicals as taking figurative expressions about union with Christ too literally, "announcing the end of that dispensation under which such a dualistic ontology was required" (Luxon, *Literal Figures: Puritan Allegory and the Reformation Crisis in Representation* [Chicago: The University of Chicago Press, 1995], 13; cf. 2, 174, 198). Hugh Barbour and Arthur O. Roberts suggest that Edward Burrough's need to respond to Bunyan was also born somewhat of the disgrace which Nayler brought on the whole Quaker movement (Barbour and Roberts, eds., *Early Quaker Writings 1650-1700* [Grand Rapids: William B. Eerdmans Publishing Company, 1973], 298).

37 Philip Schaff, ed., *The Creeds of Christendom with a History and Critical Notes*, 6th ed. rev. David S. Schaff (Grand Rapids: Baker Books, 1998), 3:793.
38 Horace Bushnell, *Christian Nurture* (Grand Rapids: Baker Book House, 1979), 29.
39 John Toldervy, quoted in Nigel Smith, *Perfection Proclaimed: Language and Literature in English Radical Religion 1640-1660* (Oxford: Clarendon Press, 1989), 68.

dox Creed (1679), observed in *Christianismus Primitivus*, "If every Man have this Judg of all Debates in himself, and he aver, that what he saith and doth is according to the Voice of this Judg, (or that of God in him) no Man can take in hand to judg contrary thereunto, without becoming the Judge's Judg, and so violate the Rule proposed." Thomas Hicks, who wrote four anti-Quaker tracts in the 1670s, remarked that the Quakers' verification of truth could be nothing more than what William Penn decided. And John Tombes, who had a public disputation with George Fox, sarcastically volunteered that if every person was to follow the light within, his light revealed to him that the Quakers were wrong.[40] Despite professions of self-*denial* by both Fox and Penn,[41] the critical issue still came down to whether the Quakers' reliance on the "inner Christ" conflated Christ with human conscience to such a degree that the self eventually became an autonomous authority.[42] That is precisely what John Bunyan believed about the Quakers. James Nayler's self-identification as Christ, indicative of an extremely subjectivist inability to recognize any authority except that within, only confirmed Bunyan's suspicion.

Bunyan on the "Christ Without"

Bunyan suggested that his "correct" understanding of the Bible developed alongside his need to *separate* himself from the Quakers. Only two years after the publication of *A Vindication*, Bunyan expressed gratitude in *The Doctrine of the Law and Grace Unfolded* that "just before the men called Quakers came into the Countrey," he saw the importance of affirming Christ's virgin birth, crucifixion, resurrection, ascension, and second coming.[43] Bunyan related that he had reached his Christological convictions before he took up his pen against the Quakers – which he confirmed in the 1680 addition to *Grace Abounding* – but the Quaker errors reiterated to him his

---

40 Underwood, 115.
41 Christopher Hill, *The World Turned Upside Down: Radical Ideas During the English Revolution* (London: Penguin Books, 1991), 252; John R. Knott, *Discourses on Martyrdom in English Literature, 1563-1694* (Cambridge: Cambridge University Press, 1993), 245; William Penn, preface to George Fox, *Journal*, 502.
42 Nigel Smith seems to accept early Quaker claims of self-denial when he says, "The most extreme form of self-denial comes with the Quakers, who generally subordinate the sense of self entirely to the light within" (66).
43 Bunyan, *MW*, 2:157-158.

own position. So "besides these teachings of God in his Word, the Lord made use of two things to confirm me in these things, the one was the error of the *Quakers*, and the other was the guilt of sin; for as the *Quakers* did oppose his Truth, so God did the more confirm me in it, by leading me into the Scriptures that did wonderfully maintain it."[44] After Bunyan's affirmation of scripture as the Word of God in *Grace Abounding*, he listed in the addition seven doctrinal errors of the Quakers along the same lines as those in *A Vindication*, concerning the life, death, and resurrection of the incarnate Christ.

Several Bunyan scholars have lamented the exchange of verbal warfare between Bunyan and his first published Quaker respondent, Edward Burrough. Burrough was certainly an energetic young man: before the age of twenty years, he became an itinerant preacher who addressed hundreds of people, and though he often slept under hedges, and he still found time and place to write dozens of tracts in defense of Quakerism. He even pled before King Charles II on behalf of persecuted Quakers in Massachusetts. Like Bunyan and Fox, he was also imprisoned for nonconformist preaching soon after the Restoration, and he died in Newgate prison in 1662 at the age of twenty-eight.[45] Perhaps because Burrough's valor is reminiscent of Bunyan's own, even the champion of late nineteenth and early twentieth century Bunyan appreciation, John Brown, wishes "that these two good men could have had a little free and friendly talk face to face. There would probably have been better understanding and fewer hard words, for they were really not so far apart as they thought."[46] Roger Sharrock also describes their exchange as "unfortunate acrimoniousness," and more strongly, F. R. Leavis calls Bunyan's contributions to the debate "brutally bigoted polemic."[47] Henri Talon says that Bunyan misunderstood Burrough's conception of divine love but perhaps could do no differently because of his theological biases against Quaker presuppositions.[48] But in view of the thesis of this essay, that Bunyan conscien-

---

44 Bunyan, *GA*, 38-39 (§123).
45 T. L. Underwood and Roger Sharrock, in Bunyan, *MW*, 1:xxxiii; William York Tindall, *John Bunyan: Mechanick Preacher* (New York: Russell and Russell, Inc., 1964), 8.
46 John Brown, *John Bunyan (1628-1688): His Life, Times, and Work*, rev. Frank Mott Harrison (London: The Hulbert Publishing Company Limited, 1928), 108.
47 Roger Sharrock, *John Bunyan* (London: Macmillan, 1968), 36; F. R. Leavis, Afterword, in John Bunyan, *The Pilgrim's Progress* (New York: Signet Classics, 1981), 291.
48 Talon, *John Bunyan: The Man and His Works*, 98.

tiously resisted the most extremely individualistic tendencies of Quakerism because they subverted historic Christian faith, one must not reduce Bunyan's polemic to a simple misunderstanding. The issue for Bunyan was simple but momentous: "there is a difference between conscience and Christ."[49]

What prompted this assertion? "The new and false Christ," Bunyan had heard, "is a Christ crucified within, dead within, risen againe within, and ascended within in opposition to the Son of Mary, who was crucified without, dead without, risen againe without, and ascended in a cloud away from his Disciples into heaven without them."[50] Only the "Christ without" could offer the sacrifice to God which can atone for sin and mollify the law-inflamed conscience. Without invoking by name the fourth century Cappadocians (Basil of Caesarea, Gregory of Nyssa, Gregory of Nazianzus), whose legacy is the Niceno-Constantinopolitan Creed, or Anselm of Canterbury, the eleventh century arch-expositor of the satisfaction theory of atonement, Bunyan nonetheless took up their cause and so implicitly acknowledged their authority. Even as the Cappadocians insisted that Christ was fully human since a nature not assumed is not redeemed, so did Bunyan reason that Christ's death accrued no benefit for fallen angels since Christ did not take on angelic nature but the seed of Abraham.[51] Bunyan also affirmed Nicea's declaration of Christ's divinity, naming Christ "very God, Co-eternal, and also Co-equal with his Father."[52]

---

49 Bunyan, *A Vindication of Some Gospel-Truths Opened*, in *MW*, 1:175.
50 Bunyan, *Some Gospel-Truths*, in ibid., 19-20. Bunyan's use of "without" means "outside of " the human subject in the realm of history.
51 Ibid., 37.
52 Ibid., 47. Cf. Bunyan's *The Doctrine of the Law and Grace Unfolded* (1659): "For the Saviour, thou must look upon him to be very God and very man; not man onely, nor God onely, but God and man in one person, both natures joyned together, for the putting of him in a capacity to be a suitable Saviour: suitable I say to answer both sides and parties with whom he hath to do in the office of his Mediatorship, and being as Saviour"(*MW*, 2:189). This was surely a more sophisticated Christology than Bunyan's defense of the full divinity and full humanity of Christ through a reading of Revelation 5:6 in *Grace Abounding* (*GA*, 38 [§122]). In *A Book for Boys and Girls* (1686), Bunyan included a poem called "Upon the Creed" that summarized all the articles of the Nicene Creed, on the persons of the Trinity, the Church, the forgiveness of sins, and the resurrection of the dead (Bunyan, *MW*, 6:208). Sim and Walker make an unsubstantiated claim that Bunyan's equation of God the Father and God the Son somehow had subversive political implications (63).

Yet, this orthodox affirmation of the person of Christ was a preamble to Bunyan's larger concern for the work of Christ. At several places in *Some Gospel-Truths Opened* and its *Vindication*, Bunyan agreed with Anselm that the offence of human sin against God's justice required a satisfaction which only the Savior who was both God and human could pay.[53] Twenty years after these two early works, Bunyan in *The Strait Gate* again linked the satisfaction made to God by Christ and the two-natures Christology as self-evident condemnation of Quakers, "free-willers" and Socinians, who apparently denied this essential connection.[54] And in the posthumous *Israel's Hope Encouraged*, Bunyan accepted the accusation by "the quaking [William] *Pen*" of being a *"Satisfactionist."*[55] In *A Vindication*, Bunyan's favorite word to describe Christ's work was "justification," which he used forty-eight times.[56] He employed the term in

---

53 Bunyan, *MW*, 1:36, 52, 103, 140, 154. Cf. Bunyan's statement in *The Doctrine of the Law and Grace Unfolded*: "For if thou look upon any of these asunder, that is to say, the God-head without the man-hood, or the man-hood without the God-head, thou wilt conclude that what was done by the God-head, was not done for man, being done without the man-hood; or else, that that which was done with the man-hood could not answer Divine Justice, in not doing what it did, by vertue and in union with the God-head; for it was the God-head that gave vertue and value to the suffering of the man-hood, and the man-hood being joyned therewith, that giveth us an interest into the heavenly glory and comforts of the God-head" (Bunyan, *MW*, 2:189). Richard L. Greaves and Michael A. Mullett also comment on Bunyan's Anselmian atonement theory (Greaves, *John Bunyan* [Grand Rapids: William B. Eerdmans Publishing Company, 1969], 36-41; Mullett, *John Bunyan in Context* [Keele: Keele University Press, 1996], 131).
54 John Bunyan, *The Miscellaneous Works of John Bunyan*, vol. 5, ed. Graham Midgley (Oxford: Clarendon Press, 1986), 127. Bunyan punned in *Some Gospel-Truths Opened* that the Quakers "made light of " the outward work of Christ (*MW*, 1:73).
55 Bunyan, *The Miscellaneous Works of John Bunyan*, vol. 13, ed. W. R. Owens (Oxford: Clarendon Press, 1994), 81. As Owens points out in an endnote on p. 510, Penn decried in *The Sandy Foundation Shaken* (1668) the belief that Christ's death was necessary for God to forgive sins. Bunyan elaborated his theory of satisfaction in *Light for Them That Sit in Darkness*, in *The Miscellaneous Works*, vol. 8, ed. Richard L. Greaves (Oxford: Clarendon Press, 1979), 108-109. Cf. Richard L. Greaves, in ibid., 395, and *John Bunyan*, 36-41.
56 Bunyan, *A Vindication of Some Gospel-Truths Opened*, in *MW*, 1:140, 142, 145, 147-148, 150, 153, 155-157, 159, 167, 169-170, 172, 181, 197, 200-201, 203, 209-210, 212. Cf. Martin Luther's comment that the doctrine of justification "consoles our consciences before God" (Paul Althaus, *The Theology of Martin Luther*, trans. Robert C. Schultz [Philadelphia: Fortress Press, 1966], 224).

an economic sense, describing justification as a ransoming from bondage to the law.

Recall that for Bunyan, the "law" equally described the Mosaic proscriptions of the Old Testament and the human conscience. Bunyan had plenty to say about the conscience in his anti-Quaker works – usually in contradistinction to Christ, and thus usually in contradistinction to the Quakers' alleged confusion of the two. Bunyan hoped to refute what he thought to be the Quaker teaching on John 1:9, i.e., that each individual human conscience is the indwelling spirit of Christ. Bunyan agreed that every person has a conscience, but it did not follow for him that this conscience was the spirit that Christ actually gives only to the elect. The light of conscience which every person has is sufficient to give proof that there is an eternal God, Bunyan thought, but unredeemed by Christ, it plays no role in salvation. So, it is the devil's trick to say that this "inner light," as the Quakers called it, is sufficient to that end.[57] By contrast, the inner self can only become clean through the outer work of Christ's atoning blood. Michael A. Mullett captures Bunyan's thought well when he observes that Bunyan's "rejection of inner good conscience or of any inherent human capacity for righteousness was reflected in his constantly repeated phrase about 'that blood that was shed without the gate,' 'without' being his shorthand for the vicarious nature of redemption."[58]

Bunyan stepped up his attack in *A Vindication* in response to Burrough's denial in *The True Faith of the Gospel of Peace Contended For* (1656) that the Quakers depreciated Christ's Incarnation. Again, Bunyan declared that salvation comes only through the outward actions of the outward Christ. He was even more convinced, however, that the Quakers equated Christ with the conscience, thus obviating the need for Christ's literal work and making possible salvation by fiat. So he warned, "Friend, thou mayest call thy conscience, the man Christ Jesus, or the light (as thou callest it) in thy Conscience the man Christ Jesus; which if thou do, This is a delusion, and a dangerous doctrine."[59] Bunyan again compared conscience to the law of nature, which discerns between the good and the bad – but, since conscience is a material creation and not spiritually constituted, it has no spiritual power and cannot save from

---

57 Bunyan, *Some Gospel-Truths Opened*, in MW, 1:55-59. Cf. Bunyan's *Saved by Grace*, where Bunyan repudiated the idea that there is a light in every person that is the special grace of God and compared such an idea to relying upon the law for salvation (MW, 8:219).
58 Mullett, 132.
59 Bunyan, *A Vindication of Some Gospel-Truths Opened*, in MW, 1:145-146.

sin. Many come to feel sin by their sensitive consciences who still do not have the spirit of Christ, Bunyan argued, and it is ignorance to call the natural law "Christ" simply because it convinces of sin. Thus Bunyan believed that the Quakers identified the conscience with the spirit of Christ, while he strove to keep them distinct.

There could be no arbitration on this issue for Bunyan. "Surely," he said, "if salvation coms [sic] by our conscience, or by the conviction or commands thereof, *Christ Jesus died for nothing, Gal.* 2 last *ver.*"[60] Bunyan conceded the Quaker retort that scripture calls the church Christ's body, but this should not exclude "Christ without."[61] He concluded *A Vindication* by emphasizing the Reformation notion of Christ's imputed righteousness.[62] The Quakers, he said, valued their own obedience to the natural law more than Christ's obedience imputed to them, and their satisfaction came from their own consciences, not from Christ's blood.[63] Indeed, Robert Barclay criticized the notion of imputed righteousness as a deception in *An Apology for the True Christian Divinity* (1678).[64] Bunyan would liken this inward reliance in salvific matters to crypto-Catholicism in *A Defence of Justification, By Faith*, based on his perception that both Quakers and Roman Catholics exalted human works over Christ and the Bible. In a section showing alleged similarities between Penn and the latitudinarian Edward Fowler, Bunyan admonished Papist and Quaker alike for rejecting "these wholsome, and Fundamental [Thirty-Nine] Articles" (of the Anglican Church) in favor of "Papistical Quakerism," which is "quite denyed by the Lord Jesus, and by his blessed Testament."[65] In *A Discourse Upon the Pharisee and the Publicane*, Bunyan compared Quakers, Ranters, and Socinians to

---

60 Ibid., 173.
61 In *A Few Sighs from Hell*, Bunyan said, "If thou wouldest know that the Quakers hold an errour, that say the body of Christ is within them," to consider Acts 1:9-11 and Luke 24 (Ibid., 327).
62 Cf. Vera J. Camden, "'Most Fit for a Wounded Conscience': The Place of Luther's 'Commentary on Galatians' in *Grace Abounding*," *Renaissance Quarterly* 50:3 (Autumn 1997), 828.
63 Bunyan, *MW* 1:182, 212, 217.
64 Robert Barclay, *An Apology for the True Christian Divinity*, 14th ed. (Glasgow: R. Barclay Murdoch, 1886), 150-151, 180.
65 Bunyan, *MW*, 4:124, 121. In *Some Gospel-Truths Opened*, Bunyan reckoned the act of "quaking" as one of "legall holiness" and admitted, "I reckon Pharisees and Quakers together" (*MW*, 1:85, 178). Though himself a Baptist, Henry Denne defended the Quakers against Bunyan's accusations in *The Quaker No Papist* (1659).

the Pharisee of Luke 18:11, whose thanksgiving to God was hypocritical.[66]

But Bunyan's most famous analogy for Quakerism may have slipped the notice of many who have read it in *The Pilgrim's Progress* and been startled by what Nathaniel Hawthorne called "the most awful truth in Bunyan's book."[67] I refer to the fate of the character of Ignorance at the end of Part I. Talon, Hill, and William York Tindall believe that the skeletons of those who denied the bodily resurrection, which lie unburied at the foot of the Hill of Error, belong allegorically to Quakers.[68] Yet only three other articles argue that the stunning fate of Ignorance, who is carried "to Hell, even from the Gates of Heaven," is Bunyan's ultimate condemnation of the Quakers.[69] Richard Stauffer argues my case:

> Ignorant serait-il, pour notre auteur, l'archétype du papiste attaché à la fois à la religion des œuvres et à la notion de tradition? Je ne le pense pas. Il est plutôt, me semble-t-il, la figure du Quaker qui croit à l'existence d'une "lumière intérieure," une "lumière intérieure," qui implique, un même temps que la possibilité d'une révélation immédiate de Dieu, une certaine confiance en l'homme. En effet, aux questions que lui posent Chrétien et Espèrendiu. Ignorant ne répond pas en se fondant sur le térmoignage de l'Écriture, mais en

---

66 Bunyan, *MW*, 10:135.

67 Nathaniel Hawthorne, *The Blithedale Romance*, ed. William E. Cain (Boston: Bedford Books of St. Martin's Press, 1996), 215.

68 Talon, *John Bunyan: The Man and His Works*, 153; Tindall, 63; Hill, *Tinker*, 86. In *Some Gospel-Truths*, Bunyan ridiculed the Quaker notion that the resurrection is not of physical bodies from the dead but is only being raised into a state of grace (*MW*, 1:124). Cf. Haskin, "Bunyan's Scriptural Acts:" "With this radical [Quaker] theology there was no need to feel separated in space from the risen body of the Savior, nor in time from the era of Christ and the apostles. Such views are quite contrary to the imaginative conception that informs *The Pilgrim's Progress*, where the 'manner of … setting out' is the bearing of a guilty burden, and where paradise may be regained only with a 'safe arrival at the desired Country' that lies on the other side of death" (70-71). Also compare *HW*, where Captain Torment leads the battalion of Resurrection-doubters in Diabolus's army (187).

69 Two authors who identify Ignorance as a Quaker are Richard Hardin, "Bunyan, Mr. Ignorance, and the Quakers," *Studies in Philology* 69 (1972): 500, and Dayton Haskin, "*The Pilgrim's Progress* in the Context of Bunyan's Dialogue with the Radicals," *Harvard Theological Review* 77:1 (1984): 75. T. L. Underwood, in his introduction to Bunyan, *MW*, 4:xxiv, suggests that Ignorance betokens the Latitudinarian Edward Fowler, who accused Bunyan of antinomianism in *The Design of Christianity*. Hardin agrees with me that Bunyan "was not above having the last laugh" (500).

s'appuyant sur celui de son cœur. "Mon cœur me le dit," rétorque-t-il à plusieurs reprises à ses interlocuteurs qui l'invitent à déclarer d'où il tire ses arguments. Et quand Chrétien et Espèrendiu lui objectent le passage du livre des Proverbes où il est écrit que "celui qui a confiance dans son propre cœur est un insensé" (28, 26), Ignorant réplique que son cœur à lui est "innocent."[70]

Could Ignorance be, for our author, the archetype of papism attaching works and the notion of tradition to the faith of religion? I do not think so. He is rather, it seems to me, the figure of the Quaker who believes in the existence of an "inner light," which implies, at the same time, the possibility of an immediate revelation of God, a certain confidence in humanity. In effect, to the questions that Christian and Hopeful pose to him, Ignorance does not respond with the terminology of Scripture, but by placing on top of this what is in his own heart. "My heart tells me so," he retorts on several occasions when his questioners invite him to declare objectively to them where he finds [support for] his arguments. And then Christian and Hopeful put forward to him the passage from the book of Proverbs where it is written that "the one who has confidence in his own heart is a fool" (28:26), Ignorance replies that his heart is 'innocent' to him.

What is the evidence embedded in the text of *The Pilgrim's Progress* that establishes Ignorance as a Quaker? First, one must note that Stauffer overstates his denial of any "papist" dimensions of Ignorance's character. For in *A Defence of the Doctrine of Justification, By Faith*, the crypto-Catholic, "works righteous" dimension of Quakerism led Bunyan to find common opposition to enemies both to his ideological right and left. Thus, when Ignorance informs Christian that "Christ makes my Duties that are Religious, acceptable to his Father by vertue of his Merits; and so shall I be justified,"[71] what sounds to be a conventional Protestant description of late medieval Catholicism can be at the same time a Puritan's depic-

---

70 Richard Stauffer, "Le voyage du pèlerin," *Bulletin de la Societé de l'Histoire du Protestantisme Français* 134 (October-December 1988): 720. The translation is my own. Parenthetically, I doubt that Bunyan would have found any humor in Mark Twain's setting of *The Innocents Abroad, or the New Pilgrims Progress* onboard the ship *Quaker City*!
71 Bunyan, *PP*, 147. Cf. Sharrock on Ignorance: "This is the cool, sceptical language of a man of the new age, a man of latitude, anxious to ground his faith in conscience and conduct, not in twice-born experience. Bunyan had emerged from a bitter controversy with the Latitudinarian Edward Fowler; memories of that feud may have contributed to the harsh treatment bestowed on the 'brisk lad'" (*John Bunyan*, 93).

tion of Quakerism. Ignorance's response to Christian's insistence on Christ's imputed righteousness – "What! would you have us trust to what Christ in his own person has done without us?"[72] – surrenders both election and substitutionary atonement. When one further considers the frequency with which Bunyan describes the Quakers as "ignorant" in *Some Gospel-Truths Opened* and *A Vindication*,[73] it becomes highly plausible that Bunyan intended the character Ignorance in *The Pilgrim's Progress* as a Quaker.

One can see here once again the similarities and dissimilarities between Bunyan and the Quakers. One could understand Ignorance's confession, "I take my pleasure in walking alone, even more a great deal then in Company, unless I like it the better," as a revealing statement about Quaker individualism, but Bunyan's *doppelgänger* Christian also keeps a community of no more than one other person for most of the novel. He, too, rejects others' company when he first sets out from the City of Destruction. Thus, it would seem that the real force of Bunyan's apprehension of Quakers could be less that they sometimes kept no company than that Quakers did not keep company with *him*. Perhaps Bunyan even reserved such harsh judgment for Ignorance to purge the painful realization that his theological language could sometimes sound quite close to that of the Quakers. For instance, in *A Confession of My Faith*, he wrote, "I walk according to my Light with God."[74] Brian Nellist points out the further irony that Bunyan so sharply condemns Ignorance of theological naivety when Bunyan himself often paraded his own

---

72 Bunyan, *PP*, 148. George Bernard Shaw remarked on Ignorance's fate: "It is the Athanasian that damns him, not any fault of his own" (Scott McMillin, "G. B. S. and Bunyan's *Badman*," *The Shaw Review* 9:3 [September 1966]: 99).

73 Bunyan decried Quaker ignorance in *MW*, vol. 1: *Some Gospel-Truths*, 23, 90-91, 99, and *A Vindication*, 127, 166-167, 193-194, 214. Cf. Hardin, 502. Bunyan also ended *Instruction for the Ignorant* on a similar note as *The Pilgrim's Progress*, Part I: "Consider how sweet the thought of Salvation will be to thee when thou seest thy self in Heaven, whilst others are roaring in Hell" (*MW*, 8:44). Some of the ignorant who needed instruction were those who did not perceive that inward light was also the law of God that brought "convictions of Conscience" but could not save (16).

74 Bunyan, in Greaves, *John Bunyan*, 140-141; cf. Greaves, "Introduction: Bunyan, the Shadow of Persecution, and the Power of Awakening Words," in *Awakening Words: John Bunyan and the Language of Community*, ed. David Gay, James G. Randall, and Arlette Zinck (Newark: University of Delaware Press, 2000), 10. For a further explanation of Bunyan's sacramental theology, see Chapter Five, below.

lack of formal education as evidence that his oratorical skills and biblical knowledge came directly from God.⁷⁵

Moreover, Bunyan's very process of argumentation in the two early anti-Quaker tracts and *Grace Abounding* reveals his own individualist tendencies. Scripture essentially took the place of conscience as Bunyan's lens through which to see Christ, and its conclusions were right because they were right for *him*: "Many more vile and abominable things were in those days fomented by them, by which I was driven to a more narrow search of the Scripture, and was through their light and testimony not only enlightened but greatly confirmed and comforted in the truth."⁷⁶ If the triumph of rationalistic argumentation over the accepted dogma of the community made modernity a more individualistic phenomenon than whatever came before it, as Jürgen Habermas argues, then Bunyan tripped over the border of modernity despite his efforts to stay balanced on the other side.⁷⁷ At the same time, Bunyan still damns Ignorance because, unlike Christian, he comes to the Celestial City "alone; neither did any man meet him with the least incouragement."⁷⁸ In *The Heavenly Foot-man*, Bunyan valued the company of "the soundest Christians," but he did not expect that the beliefs and experiences he shared with them encompassed his more individualistic rivals: "Be sure thou have a care of *Quakers, Ranters, Free-Willers*: Also do not have too much Company with some *Anabaptists*, though I go under that name my self."⁷⁹

---

75 Brian Nellist, "*The Pilgrim's Progress* and Allegory," in *The Pilgrim's Progress: Critical and Historical Views*, ed. Vincent Newey (Totowa, NJ: Barnes and Noble Books, 1980), 150. In his preface to *Some Gospel-Truths Opened*, John Burton said that Bunyan "*hath through grace, taken these three heavenly degrees, to wit, union with Christ, the anointing of the spirit, and experience of the temptations of Satan, which doe more fit a man for that weighty work of preaching the Gospell, then all University Learning and degrees that can be had*" (John Burton, in Bunyan, *MW*, 1:11).
76 Bunyan, *GA*, §125, p. 39.
77 Julie Rivkin and Michael Ryan, "The Class of 1968 – Post-Structuralism *par lui-même*," in *Literary Theory: An Introduction* (Malden, MA: Blackwell, 1999), 353. In the words of Sim and Walker, "Recourse to Scripture fragmented rather than consolidated authority" (60). This was an argument which the Quakers did in fact level at Bunyan, as he reported in *A Vindication*: "Thy religion stands in Disputes and Controversies, and Quaeries, and many words. But our Religion stands in the exercise of a pure conscience towards God, and toward man; whether we speak, or be silent: These are thy words" (Bunyan, *MW*, 1:194).
78 Bunyan, *PP*, 162.
79 Bunyan, *MW*, 5:153.

The Quakers on the "Christ Within"

How did the Quakers answer Bunyan's Christological affirmations? Bunyan cited several of Burrough's objections from *True Faith* that seemed to confuse the necessity for inward appropriation of Christ's work with the actual conduct of that work in history. Burrough wondered why inward illumination was not sufficient for salvation, seemingly without a real referent exterior to the soul, such as in these comments cited by Bunyan:

> If Christ hath lightened all men as he is God (as thou confessest) then hath hee not lightened all men as he is the Son of God? and is not the light of God sufficient in itself, to lead to God all that follow it, yea or nay?
>
> Whether is it possible, that any can be saved without Christ manifested within. If no; then whether is not the doctrine of salvation, which is only necessary, to preach Christ within; and is it not the whole mystery of salvation, God manifest in the flesh.
>
> Whether is it not possible, that many professe as much of Christ without, as thou hast sayd of him, and yet be damned; and if this be the faith to professe him born, dead, risen and ascended without; then is there any unbeleever in England? seeing all in the outward sound beleevs, and professeth as much as thou hast said. Yea, or nay?[80]

Like Burrough, Fox also contended in *The Great Mystery* that "to witness Christ within is not to deny him come in the flesh."[81]

William Penn offered the strongest defense of Quaker orthodoxy when he adopted the language of the Nicene Creed in *Primitive Christianity Revived*:

> We bless God, religiously believe and confess, to the glory of God the Father, and the honour of His dear and beloved Son, that, Jesus Christ took our nature upon him, and was like unto us in all things, sin excepted: that he was born of the Virgin Mary, suffered under Pontius Pilate, the Roman governor, was crucified, dead, and buried in the sepulchre of Joseph of Arimathea; rose again the third day, and ascended into heaven, and sits on the right hand of God, in the power and majesty of his Father; who will one day judge the world by Him, even that blessed man, Christ Jesus, according to their works.[82]

---

80 Bunyan, *MW*, 1:199, 202-203. Cf. Edmund Arbuthnott Knox, *John Bunyan in Relation to His Times* (London: Longmans, Green and Company, 1928), 85-95.
81 George Fox, *The Works of George Fox*, vol. 3, *The Great Mystery of the Great Whore Unfolded* (New York: AMS Press, Inc., 1975), 337. Penn and Burrough stated the same: cf. Underwood, 39.
82 Penn, 254.

Although Penn's Christological confession appears quite in order, perhaps there is nonetheless significance in the phrase "took our nature upon him." The Quakers did not believe that Christ's human nature was his own or essential to his person; i.e., Quakers understood the Incarnation to mean that "Christ had assumed a human body but not that it was part of him."[83] With such an unmistakably docetic overtone, Quaker subscriptions to the Incarnation of Christ served to reveal the incipient "modernism" at the core of the entire debate: if many Quakers did not absolutely require Christ's living, material sacrifice on the cross, then their whole vision of the Christian life looked to depend on a subjective experience that could be verified by no one but themselves. This may explain why Bunyan often linked Quakers with the radically antinomian Ranters throughout his doctrinal works: both groups, Bunyan thought, operated on no authority outside their own autonomy. Christopher Hill confirms that "the whole early Quaker movement was far closer to the Ranters in spirit than its leaders later liked to recall, after they had spent many weary hours differentiating themselves from Ranters and ex-Ranters."[84]

Even should Leo Damrosch be correct that most Quakers did not doubt the importance of the historical Jesus, neither Burrough nor Fox expended the effort for which Bunyan was looking to claim the soteriological *necessity* of the Incarnation and Christ's actual death on the cross.[85] In Barclay's "Confession," which became the standard Quaker apology in the late seventeenth century, there is in fact no article on the person of Christ. Bunyan believed that human salvation depends on a real historical event by the historical Christ, and he did not discover that same concern in the Quaker writers. The bifurcation of the inner realm of subjectivity and external reality, says Stanley Fish, is most indicative of modernity.[86] And it was that very distinction which Bunyan believed to be at stake in his writings against the Quakers.

---

83 Underwood, 49.
84 Hill, *World*, 232. John Stachniewski notes, "Bunyan habitually bracketed Ranters and Quakers…. Perceptions depended on how far down the subjectivist track of spiritual liberty one had travelled" (John Stachniewski, in John Bunyan, *Grace Abounding with Other Spiritual Autobiographies*, ed. John Stachniewski with Anita Pacheco [Oxford: Oxford University Press, 1998], xxxv).
85 Damrosch, 92-93.
86 Stanley E. Fish, *How Milton Works* (Cambridge, MA: The Belknap Press of Harvard University Press, 2001), 42.

Fox retorted against Bunyan's Galatian charge that the Quakers preached an entirely different gospel by saying,

> If Christ that is crucified be not within, and Christ that is risen be not within, I say that you all are reprobates; and if the scripture be not within, which was spoken forth from within, you all want the spirit that gave it forth, and Christ the substance of it, and you have not eaten his flesh, neither are you of his bone; and this is not opposite to Jesus Christ without, that died at Jerusalem, but the same; for they who eat his flesh have it within him, and this is not a new gospel.[87]

It is not clear on what basis Fox claimed that the Christ whom believers eat "within" is "the same" Christ who died on the cross, for if the "eating" of Christ is only a metaphor for a spiritual activity, then Fox did not make a convincing case that speaking of Christ incarnate is anything other than a metaphor either. Fox's concern was to emphasize a mystical union with Christ that he found lacking not only in the Church of England but also in most other dissenters. But though Fox maintained that he followed the apostles in preaching "Christ that is crucified within," he accentuated Christ's manifestation in the illumined saints rather than in a physical body, saying, again somewhat docetically, that "to affirm Christ is human, is to say thy knowledge is not from Christ."[88] T. L. Underwood and Roger Sharrock note that the early Quaker writers were silent about Christ's objective work – even when trying to refute charges of heresy by Bunyan and others – owing to their emphasis on Christ's spiritual indwelling of individual Christians.[89] For Bunyan, objective atonement and spiritual indwelling were not exclusive, but Fox thought that Christ's body *was itself* a "spiritual indwelling" in the believer that did not demand the actual physicality of the incarnate Son of God.[90] One can see this difference between Fox's statement that

---

87 George Fox, *Works*, 3:338-339. Cf. Galatians 1:6-9.
88 Ibid., 339, 341.
89 T. L. Underwood and Roger Sharrock, in Bunyan, *MW*, 1:xix; Underwood, 4-5, 54. Roger Williams made very similar points in his *George Fox Digg'd Out of His Burrowes* (1676), in which he affirmed the authority of the Bible and the "Christ without" against Quakers who, by following an erroneous conscience (precisely the charge that John Cotton had once leveled against Williams for advocating religious liberty), "preached not Christ Jesus but Themselves" (Ahlstrom, 180; Edwin S. Gaustad, *Liberty of Conscience: Roger Williams in America* [Grand Rapids: William B. Eerdmans Publishing Company, 1991], 183; Edmund S. Morgan, *Roger Williams: The Church and the State* [New York: Harcourt, Brace and World, Inc., 1967], 134).
90 Richard Bailey, *New Light on George Fox and Early Quakerism* (San Francisco: Mellen Research University Press, 1992), 92.

Christ's priestly office is "in the midst of you," and Bunyan's conviction that Christ, after his sacrifice on the cross, now carries out his priestly intercession "in the heaven without [you] above the Stars."[91]

While Bunyan correctly diagnosed the Quakers' universally present "inner light" as Christ himself, he did not accurately distinguish this inner light from conscience. For as Fox replied to him, "Man at his coming into the world hath a light from Christ, him by whom the world was made, which is more than conscience; but he that hates the light abides in darkness, and so is not like to receive the spirit, but is reproved with it."[92] For Bunyan's purposes, conscience and the light/law of nature were equivalent, but he failed to see that they served different roles for the Quakers. The Quakers indeed asserted that every person has both a conscience and the inner light, but they did not equate conscience and the inner light. The Quakers agreed with the Baptists that the conscience was a part of the creaturely body, located somewhere in the human mind. But the Quakers further insisted that the conscience was essentially the "candle wick" of the human body, which God sets aflame by the inner light.[93] Every person receives this inner light from God, although not all persons live by it.

Thus did the Quakers not actually confuse the inner light – which they did often call "Christ" or "the Spirit of Christ" – with any "natural" human property, as Bunyan alleged. "Thy confusion is seen at large," Burrough wrote, saying that the light of Christ comes to the conscience and even unites with it, but is not originally the same as it.[94] Ironically, the Quakers' exclusion of anything human in salvation went even further than Bunyan's, for whereas Bunyan denied any human role in meriting the satisfaction of Christ, he still maintained, as the Quakers did not, that at least what *Christ* did in his human body was of utmost importance. For the Quakers, God's

---

91 George Fox, in Hugh McGregor Ross, 69; Bunyan, *Some Gospel-Truths Opened*, in *MW*, 1:82.
92 George Fox, *Works*, 3:342.
93 Underwood, 104-106. Cf. Susan Juster: "Carla Pestana locates the appeal of Quakerism to women in its elevation of the mystical experience of the inner light over the bible-centered ecclesiology of the Congregationalists and the Baptists in seventeenth-century New England" (Juster, "The Spirit and the Flesh: Gender, Language, and Sexuality in American Protestantism," in *New Directions in American Religious History*, ed. Harry S. Stout and D. G. Hart [New York: Oxford University Press, 1997], 343).
94 Edward Burrough, in William C. Braithwaite, *The Beginnings of Quakerism*, 2nd ed., rev. Frank Mott Harrison (London: The Hubert Publishing Company Limited, 1928), 287.

refusal of any human contribution to salvation potentially excluded even the need for Christ's body to hang on the cross.[95] Barclay wrote that saving light and grace come not exclusively from the *death* of Christ but also through the inner light in the individual, even "though ignorant of the history." Inward grace, he added, is sufficient alone for salvation without outward reference.[96] And so, despite whatever misunderstandings he certainly had about the relationship between conscience and Christ in Quaker thought, Bunyan's criticism remains valid that Quakerism made faith in the objective work of Christ a peripheral issue and not the center of faith. As Nayler was among the first to affirm explicitly, Jews, Muslims, and pagans could all conceivably know Christ only through inward illumination, without overt profession.[97] And that idea radically individualized faith, and even truth itself, as a subjective personal matter, as Geoffrey Hubbard confesses for Friends past and present: "What we mean by 'Christ the Light' is indeed a more subjective matter, and we cannot as a Society subscribe to any exclusive doctrines in relation to Christ."[98] Such a reliance on inward authority certainly stands closer than Bunyan to the modern self, whose identity is forged by how things have significance singularly, often relatively, for that person.[99]

The Road to Modern Individualism

Both Bunyan and the Quakers held notions of conscience that could call ecclesiastical and civil authorities into question. For instance,

---

95 Ibid., 43. For Burrough, Christ died because he was falsely judged a blasphemer for speaking the truth, but his death had no atoning significance (Greaves, *John Bunyan*, 38). The dissertation of Lawrence S. Kuenning explores the misconceptions that Bunyan and Burrough had of each other. Scholars of the Bunyan/Burrough debates can appreciate Kuenning's work in arranging the seventeenth-century writings in parallel columns according to accusations and responses. (Kenning, "The Bunyan-Burrough Debate of 1656-1657 Analyzed Using a Computer Hypertext" [Ph. D. diss., Westminster Theological Seminary, 2000]; available online at http://www.qhpress.org/texts/bvb/).

96 Barclay, "The Confession of the Society of Friends, Commonly Called Quakers," in Schaff, ed., 3:793.

97 Trueblood, 78, and Hubbard, 111-112, confirm this as the Quaker view.

98 Hubbard, 84; cf. 75-76. Cf. Pink Dandelion, *A Sociological Analysis of the Theology of Quakers: The Silent Revolution*, Studies in Religion and Society 34 (Lewiston, NY: Edwin Mellen Press, 1996), 312.

99 Taylor, 34.

when asked by such authorities after the Restoration why they would not cease their nonconformist preaching, Bunyan said it would "wound my conscience," and Fox refused on the basis of his "tender conscience."[100] Bunyan much more closely linked conscience to scripture than did the Quakers, but appeals to either conscience or scripture could have the same effect of elevating personal authority over that of the state and its church.[101] It is therefore reasonable for T. L. Underwood to say that "Fox, Bunyan, and others in the two groups [which they represented, the Quakers and the Baptists] had much in common with each other."[102] Yet Bunyan's unwillingness to discard scripture as a regulative authority shows how he resisted the cultural evolution toward modern individualism in which Quakerism participated.

In *The Great Mystery of the Great Whore Unfolded* (1659), Fox answered accusations against the Society of Friends leveled by writers such as Bunyan and John Burton, Bunyan's pastor who wrote an introductory letter to the reader in *Some Gospel-Truths Opened*. Fox responded:

P[rinciple]. They say, "It is a rendering of the scriptures odious ... to tell of the scripture within, which Christ never taught, nor his disciples: but God hath given them up to a reprobate mind."

A[nswer]. Were not all the scriptures from the spirit within? and were they not there before they came out? And must not all upon the earth have the spirit within that gave it forth, before they can understand the scripture without, given forth from the spirit of God within others? And was not the apostles' and Christ's preaching of the scripture within, the law in the heart, and the world in the heart? and the kingdom within, and the spirit within, leading into all truth, the spirit of the Father speaking in you, and

---

100 Bunyan, *A Relation of the Imprisonment of Mr. Bunyan*, in *GA*, 109; George Fox, *Journal*, 496-498.
101 Cf. Christopher Hill, *The Century of Revolution, 1603-1714* (New York: W. W. Norton and Company, 1980), 149. Yet, Hugh Ormsby-Lennon notes that when the Quakers, unlike Bunyan, "challenged custom as grand master of language and behaviour, they revealed an innate kinship with contemporaries ostensibly as different as Thomas Hobbes and Fellows of the Royal Society. For all of them strove to re-articulate the links binding *res et verba*, whether these were construed in terms of *usus loquendi* or of *ars significandi*" (Ormsby-Lennon, "From Shibboleth to Apocalypse: Quaker Speechways During the Puritan Revolution," in *Language, Self, and Society: A Social History of Language*, ed. Peter Burke and Roy Porter [Cambridge: Polity Press, 1991], 101).
102 Underwood, 4.

Christ within? and is not this extolling scripture of truth? and are not all they reprobates that have scripture without, and not within?[103]

Fox's restatement of Bunyan's and Burton's argument about scripture, along with his response, illustrates why Bunyan opposed the Quakers' reading of scripture. Bunyan's internalization of scripture always had an external referent, but once the Quakers internalized scripture, they transubstantiated it into a personal property that minimized the written word and the history it records – including the atoning work of Christ – making it for some even ultimately superfluous.

To illustrate Bunyan's comparative conservatism to the incipient modernism of early Quakerism, I will now identify the continuities and discontinuities of each with recognizable features of later "modern" cultural movements – the Enlightenment, Romanticism, and Protestant liberalism.

The Enlightenment

J. P. Kenyon believes that René Descartes (who, though a Catholic, wrote in Protestant Holland) simply carried out to its conclusion the Protestant preoccupation with the individual who must give a solitary account before God: the focus on the self became an end in itself, and so the personal God of Puritanism gave way to the detached God of deism, leaving human beings to fend for themselves without expectation of divine aid.[104] Roger Sharrock suggests that Bunyan was certainly a part of this transition of world views, saying that "the extreme self-consciousness of his [Bunyan's] method is modern and post-Cartesian."[105] But did Bunyan's explicit desire to subject self to the outward authority of scripture constitute at least some small resistance to the modern autonomy more clearly forecast by Fox? Consider how each compared to fellow Englishman John Locke.

Locke (coincidentally, a close friend of William Penn) died in 1704, sixteen years after Bunyan and thirteen years after Fox. In *An Essay Concerning Human Understanding* (1690), Locke denied the Pla-

---

103 George Fox, *Works*, 3:340 (emphases added). In this quotation, and in several by Bunyan to follow, the use of "without" does not mean "apart from" but "outside of." In this case, Fox's argument is that a person must be illuminated from within before being able to understand the written scripture.
104 J. P. Kenyon, *Stuart England* (London: Penguin Books, 1990), 202.
105 Sharrock, *John Bunyan*, 57.

tonic conception of "innate ideas" and held that all human knowledge comes either from experience or reflection upon experience (reason). He even understood knowledge thus acquired to be the comprehension of "natural revelation."[106] Although Locke's criticism in *An Essay* of those "enthusiasts" who relied on a non-empirical "internal light" may refer to the Quakers, his de-emphasis of the need for special revelation left him with a view of scripture very similar to theirs. In *The Reasonableness of Christianity* (1695), Locke used scripture to support his arguments, but he separated "the testimony of a good conscience" from creeds or other scripturally drawn articles of faith, of "which a good Christian may be wholly ignorant." Like a number of Quakers, he conceded that it was possible to know the Christian God apart from the Bible, saying, "He that made use of this candle of the Lord, so far as to find what was his duty, could not miss to find also the way to reconciliation and forgiveness."[107] According to Taylor, the pivotal contribution of Locke and Descartes to modern individualism was that knowledge must be self-constructed to be genuine.[108] This understanding of human selfhood is in more direct continuity with the Quakers than with Bunyan. Bunyan constituted his Christian self in conjunction with his increasing knowledge of scripture. He said plainly in *Some Gospel-Truths Opened*, "I deny that Paul biddeth listen within," and even more pointedly in *A Treatise of the Fear of God*, "Let the Word be true, whatever thy experience is. Dost thou not understand me[?]"[109] By contrast, for the Quakers, "the words on the biblical page become no more than the literary account of individual experience."[110]

A corollary of the diminution of scripture in the Enlightenment was the shift of focus on Christ from a propitiatory redeemer to an enlightened teacher. Although Locke affirmed with Bunyan the bod-

---

106 "Reason is natural revelation, whereby the eternal father of light, and fountain of all knowledge, communicates to mankind that portion of truth which he has laid within the reach of their natural faculties" (John Locke, *An Essay Concerning Human Understanding*, in *The English Philosophers from Bacon to Mill*, ed. Edwin A. Burtt [New York: The Modern Library, 1967], XIX.4, p. 397).
107 John Locke, *The Reasonableness of Christianity*, ed. George W. Ewing (Washington, D.C.: Regnery Publishing, Inc., Gateway Editions, 1965), §232, 245, 248, 243, 19; pp. 131, 146, 150, 141-145, 9.
108 Taylor, 167. Cf. Sim and Walker, 32.
109 Bunyan, *MW*, 1:172; Bunyan, *The Miscellaneous Works of John Bunyan*, vol. 9, ed. Richard L. Greaves (Oxford: Clarendon Press, 1981), 35.
110 Sim and Walker, 56.

ily resurrection of Jesus, his belief that the God/light of nature is sufficient for salvation for non-Christians sounds closer to the view of the Quakers,[111] and Talon perceives that "the 'Christ within' of Fox could well have been the natural morality of the deists," the natural religionists of the Enlightenment.[112] Indeed, while Bunyan equated "nature" with fallen conscience, Barclay's "Confession" defined Quaker beliefs as nothing other than "evident and clear ... natural truths."[113] In Bunyan's view, Quakerism was a new upstart phenomenon when compared to the heritage of orthodox soteriology in which he saw himself; correctly, then, Michael A. Mullett describes Bunyan's approach in his two books of *Gospel-Truths* as one of "a critic of current modernity."[114] And insofar as the Quakers foreshadowed "modernity" in the sense of an increased importance of the individual defined apart from a transcendent authority outside oneself, then Bunyan was indeed a critic of this kind of early modernity.

Romanticism

By describing Quakerism as "mere transcendentalism," John Brown, perhaps unwittingly, points to important similarities between the Quakers and later American Romantics, such as Ralph Waldo Emerson.[115] Emerson, whom John Michael and Richard Brantley believe was strongly indebted to Lockean philosophy, shared in common with the Quakers an emphasis on "the inspired perceiver" – except that for him, the heralds of self-awareness were to be philosopher-poets, not preachers.[116] Whereas sociologist Robert N. Bellah labels Locke's individualism as "utilitarian," a belief that human beings enter into contractual agreements to advance self-interest, he describes Romantic individualism as

---

111 Locke, *The Reasonableness*, §175, 232; pp. 105, 131.
112 Talon, *John Bunyan: The Man and His Works*, 96, ft. 9.
113 Schaff, ed., 3:790.
114 Mullett, 127.
115 John Brown, 107-108. Cf. Taylor, 39. Richard E. Brantley also likens William Wordsworth to the Quakers in *Wordsworth's "Natural Methodism"* (New Haven: Yale University Press, 1975), 113.
116 Richard E. Brantley, *Coordinates of Anglo-American Romanticism: Wesley, Edwards, Carlyle and Emerson* (Gainesville, FL: University Press of Florida, 1993), 79-81; Bunyan, *Anglo-American Antiphony: The Late Romanticism of Tennyson and Emerson* (Gainesville, FL: University Press of Florida, 1994), 194; Sacvan Bercovitch, *The Puritan Origins of the American Self* (New Haven: Yale University Press, 1975), 164.

"expressive," the idea that each person "has a unique core of feeling and intuition that should unfold or be expressed if individuality is to be realized."[117] Emerson's contrast of soul and church encouraged his readers, "first of all, to go alone," and he believed that Quaker and Swedenborgian enthusiasts, by doing precisely this, had "attained ... to the perception of God."[118] Taylor believes that Emerson and Walt Whitman were the most influential writers on "human potential" in America,[119] and so it is furthermore notable that Whitman wrote an essay explaining the personal influence made upon him by Elias Hicks (1748-1830), a Quaker whose declaration that the blood of Christ "was no more effectual than the blood of bulls and goats" split the Society of Friends in America into "Orthodox" and "Hicksite" factions in the late 1820s. Quaker historians John Sykes and D. Elton Trueblood observe that it was the Orthodox who had moved farthest from the vision of George Fox by rejecting the universality of the inner light and by hiring clergy.[120] Whitman was very interested in Fox's contribution to Western thought. "'I come,' wrote Whitman of Fox, 'to direct people to the spirit that gave forth the scriptures.' The range of his thought, even then, cover'd almost every important subject of after times."[121] Whitman thus believed that Fox's turn away from "scripture without" to "scripture within" showed the genius of a man who stood next to Shakespeare ("think of them! compare them!" Whitman says) as both an intellectual giant of his own age and a forerunner of more illuminated ages to come.[122]

Whitman saluted Fox for equating God and personal identity, and he knew Hicks' words, "Nor have I found a Saviour anywhere else / But in the light, spirit, and grace of God in my soul."[123] The subjectivism of *Leaves of Grass* (1891) is the Quaker heir:

---

117 Bellah, 333-334, 336.
118 Ralph Waldo Emerson, "An Address [to Harvard Divinity School]," in *Selected Writings of Emerson*, ed. Brooks Atkinson (New York: The Modern Library, 1940), 81; Brantley, *Coordinates*, 96; cf. Brantley, *Anglo-American Antiphony*, 196.
119 Taylor, 497. Bercovitch, 151, 162-163, 168, also compares Emerson to the Quakers and Emerson with Whitman.
120 Jessamyn West, ed., *The Quaker Reader* (New York: The Viking Press, 1962), 324, 332.
121 Walt Whitman, "George Fox (and Shakespeare)," in *Complete Poetry and Collected Prose*, ed. Justin Kaplan (New York: The Library of America, 1982), 1245.
122 Ibid., 1248.
123 West, 334.

> Divine am I inside and out, and I make holy whatever I touch or
> am touch'd from,
> The scent of these arm-pits aroma finer than prayer,
> This head more than churches, bibles, and all the creeds.
> We consider bibles and religions divine – I do not say they are not
> divine,
> I say they have all grown out of you, and may grow out of you
> still,
> It is not they who give the life, it is you who give the life,
> Leaves are not more shed from the trees, or trees from the earth,
> than they are shed out of you.[124]

Even though Richard L. Greaves reminds us that both Emerson and Whitman had read Bunyan, it is impossible to conceive these lines developing out of Bunyan's thought, it is easy to see their roots in Quaker thought.[125] Trueblood believes, in fact, that Quaker influence on Whitman was immense, and of Whitman's relationship to Hicks, he asks, "Was it an accident that one Long Islander [Hicks] loved to say that the fullness of the godhead dwelt in every blade of grass, and another Long Islander called his poems *Leaves of Grass*?"[126] The Quakers' antecedence to, and even influence on, Romantic Transcendentalism situated them closer than Bunyan to the modern autonomous self.

The Quakers' comparative lack of emphasis on the historical person and work of Christ also characterizes two philosophers who were children of both the Enlightenment and Romanticism, Immanuel Kant and Friedrich Schleiermacher. Kant believed that Christ's example of following the greatest good has force as a "model already in our reason,"[127] thus going even further than the Quakers in removing the need for a "Christ without" (although Kant also rejected the kinds of mystical experiences for which the Quakers were known). Schleiermacher's definition of Jesus' divinity was less the Incarnation of the Word than "the uniqueness of his [Jesus'] religiousness."[128] Despite Schleiermacher's apparent dis-

---

124 Whitman, ("Song of Myself ") §24, p. 211; ("A Song for Occupations") §3, p. 359.
125 Greaves, *Glimpses of Glory*, 631.
126 West, 333.
127 Immanuel Kant, *Religion Within the Boundaries of Mere Reason*, ed. Allen Wood and George di Giovanni (Cambridge: Cambridge University Press, 1998), 81 (6.62).
128 Friedrich Schleiermacher, *On Religion: Speeches to Its Cultured Despisers*, trans. Richard Crouter (Cambridge: Cambridge University Press, 1990), 219.

avowal of radical individualism in Speech 4 of *On Religion*, with his emphasis there on the social dimension of religion, his explication of the "feeling" of dependence upon God – with his residual minimization of Christ's incarnation and the satisfaction theory of atonement – fostered the subjectivist faith of Romanticism and picked up a theme characteristic of Quakerism.[129]

Tamsin Spargo notes that Bunyan's saying in *The Pilgrim's Progress* that he fell "suddenly into an Allegory" corresponded to the Romantic notion of literary inspiration, but she appreciatively adds that "it is also important to acknowledge the historical and textual differences between his model and the Romantics."[130] Specifically, she finds the Quaker stress on unmediated revelation – and, I might add, the favoring of individual sentiment over Bunyan's theological orthodoxy – much closer to the anthropocentric Romantics than was Bunyan.

Protestant Liberalism

The early Quakers' view of scripture had notable similarities with that of Protestant liberals in the nineteenth and twentieth centuries. The ex-Baptist Quaker Samuel Fisher, for example, argued in 1660 that the Bible could not be the Word of God since it contains too many inconsistencies. Fisher assumed that the Bible was a book subject to criticism, no less than any other book.[131] Although Fisher's own generation still had many people like Bunyan who insisted on the Bible's inspired character and unique authority, Fisher's approach to scripture was similar to the historical critical method which biblical scholars came to hold as axiomatic generations later.

For instance, in the nineteenth century, the left-wing Hegelian Ludwig Feuerbach said in *The Essence of Christianity* (1841) that it is ludicrous to honor both Nature and the Bible. Bunyan could have agreed, *except* that it was the latter and not the former that Feuerbach, who thought that God is a projection of humanity's highest hopes for itself, wanted to eliminate.[132] Adolf von Harnack, the most eminent ecclesiastical historian of his century, joined the quest for

---

129 Roger Olson, *The Story of Christian Theology: Twenty Centuries of Tradition and Reform* (Downers Grove, IL: InterVarsity Press, 1999), 546-547.
130 Tamsin Spargo, *The Writing of John Bunyan* (Aldershot, England: Ashgate Publishing Limited, 1997), 32-33.
131 Hill, *Tinker*, 83, 81.
132 Ludwig Feuerbach, *The Essence of Christianity*, trans. George Eliot (Amherst, NY: Prometheus Books, 1989), 104, 284.

the historical Jesus by claiming, almost Quaker-like, that the way to know Jesus in the present was not through treating the Bible as a source of doctrine but in recognizing that the inward-turned "individual religious life was what he [Jesus] wanted to kindle."[133]

Harnack described the work of Jesus in an unmistakably individualistic way: "Individual religious life was what he wanted to kindle and what he did kindle; it is ... his peculiar greatness to have led men to God, so that they may henceforth live their own life with Him."[134] For Harnack, the individual encounter with Christ is the kernel of Christianity's message, after one removes the husk of all dogmatic statements about Jesus' person both within scripture and after it (such as the two-natures Christology). Bunyan would have chafed at the suggestion that Christological confessions are unimportant, but William Penn sounded a great deal like Harnack when he described Fox's teaching as "the setting up [of] the kingdom of God in the hearts of men," which was the very core of Jesus' message according to Harnack as well.[135] Did Harnack's overt acceptance of the label "modern" for his approach to Christ and scripture not also speak for the very similar approach of the early Quakers?

---

133 Adolf von Harnack, *What is Christianity?* trans. Thomas Bailey Saunders (Philadelphia: Fortress Press, 1957), 11. Compare William Penn: "By liberty of conscience, we understand not only a mere liberty of the mind, in believing or disbelieving this or that principle or doctrine, but the exercise of our selves in a visible way of worship" (Penn, *The Great Case of Liberty of Conscience*, in *The Peace of Europe, The Fruits of Solitude, and Other Writings*, ed. Edwin B. Bronner [London: J. M. Dent/Everyman, 1993], 159). Cf. Richard S. Dunn's explication of Penn's pursuit of liberty of conscience, which includes primary and secondary citations, in "William Penn's Odyssey: From Child of Light to Absentee Landlord," in *Public Duty and Private Conscience in Seventeenth-Century England: Essays Presented to G. E. Aylmer*, ed. John Morrill, Paul Slack, and Daniel Woolf (Oxford: Clarendon Press, 1993), 308.
134 Harnack, 11. Notice the similarity to Hubbard's summation of the Quaker view: "As you go towards God, you will be led to the beliefs which answer to your personal need" (Hubbard, 77).
135 William Penn, in George Fox, *Journal*, 499; Harnack, 52-56. Cf. Richard Wightman Fox: "At least since the publication of Adolf Harnack's *Das Wesen des Christentums* in 1900 ..., liberal Christians had combined a critical-historical analysis of Gospel narratives with a veneration of Jesus as prototype of the modern man" (Richard Wightman Fox, "Experience and Explanation in Twentieth-Century American Religious History," in *New Directions in American Religious History*, ed. Harry S. Stout and D. G. Hart [New York: Oxford University Press, 1997], 409).

In the twentieth century, one finds overtones of the Quaker view in figures such as Rudolf Bultmann, who saw biblical interpretation as an exercise in demythologization and existential appropriation as opposed to doctrinal construction.[136] Bultmann wrote an introduction to Harnack's *What is Christianity?* in which he maintained that the best way to honor Harnack's liberalism was not to canonize it but to follow its lead and go even further in removing doctrinal accretions from the original *kerygma* of Jesus. For Bultmann, this proclamation was the kingdom of God in an eschatological sense. But since this kingdom did not imminently materialize on earth as Jesus and the early Christians expected it would, the only way to maintain any sense of the Bible's authority is to "demythologize" its fundamental message by reinterpreting its pre-scientific language. For example, the "mythological conceptions of heaven and hell are no longer acceptable for modern men since for scientific thinking to speak of 'above' and 'below' in the universe has lost all meaning."[137] Bultmann did not relinquish the God outside the human as did Feuerbach, but neither did the Quakers, although the practical effect of their thought was certainly to concentrate on God within. And for both Bultmann and the Quakers, Bunyan's emphasis on the historical event of the resurrection is displaced, not complemented or appropriated by, an individual encounter with Christ.

Hubbard even describes the Quaker view of Christ's crucifixion in quasi-Bultmannian language: "To say, 'I see the crucifixion as a symbolic myth' or 'I see it as a literal event, and the crowning intervention of God in the life of man' is to make different statements about ourselves, not about the crucifixion."[138] From Bunyan's perspective, the Quakers and Bultmann would obviously be docetic (that is, they minimized the importance of Jesus Christ's corporeality).[139] Of course, Bunyan, too, insisted on a personal encounter with the divine, which *Grace Abounding* makes abundantly evident. But for him, this was not an encounter that could conceivably bypass

---

136 Rudolf Bultmann, *Jesus Christ and Mythology* (New York: Charles Scribner's Sons, 1958), 57.
137 Bultmann, 20. Cf. Hubbard: "Quakers today would not ever offer the next life as either reward or punishment or consolation for the life on earth. And in my observation, they find this subject of little interest, preserving by-and-large either a robust conviction or a cheerful agnosticism" (104).
138 Hubbard, 83. Paul Tillich also thought of the two-natures Christology as a religious symbol which needs to be replaced in the modern era. It is not surprising, then, that Hubbard approves of Tillich's "shaking of the foundations" (108).
139 Cf. Bunyan, *MW*, 1:xx, 192.

the incarnate person and objective work of Christ, as expounded in Christianity's historic creeds.

I do not desire to push the comparison between liberal Protestants and early Quakers beyond the formal similarities in their treatment of the Bible. "Liberal Protestantism" and "Quakerism" are very broad terms which no single person embodies, and perhaps Bultmann, *et al.*, never even read the English Quakers, much less embraced their theological emphases. Yet, there is enough evidence to suggest that liberalism's rejection of scripturally-based doctrine, and its general treatment of the Bible through historical critical methodology and existentialist philosophy, is consistent with how the early Quakers also used the Bible. This does not entail an organic, historical connection between Quakerism and later Protestant liberalism in Germany, though the noted historian Sidney E. Ahlstrom does point out that Quakerism, which one anonymous seventeenth century observer called the "fag-end of the Reformation," did become "overwhelmingly the most important and enduring manifestation of Puritan radicalism in either England or America."[140] Certainly, the Quakers anticipated an individualist approach to both the Bible and the Christian faith with far more enthusiasm than did the still bibliocentric, dogmatic John Bunyan. Primal individualist though he sometimes was, Bunyan was still very much a medieval man when judged by his differences with the more progressive, and occasionally subjectivist, Quakers.

Conclusion

The purpose of this chapter has not been to disavow Bunyan's individualism nor his reliance on an introspective conscience. It has been, instead, to provide a much sharper conception of these ideas in Bunyan's writing in comparison with their more developed

---

140 T. L. Underwood, in Bunyan, *MW*, 4:xxxviii; Ahlstrom, 176; cf. 112, where Ahlstrom sees Quaker-led colonial Pennsylvania as the paradigm of American democracy. Barry Alan Shain believes that the individualism of early American Quakers so excluded "commitment to a local community (or a nation) and its corporate values, concerns, and restraints" that they "eventually proved to be effective solvents of American local communalism" (Shain, *The Myth of American Individualism: The Protestant Origins of American Political Thought* [Princeton: Princeton University Press, 1994], 73). Michael J. Sandel can thus lament how American individualism often forfeits any sense of conscious membership in the communal whole (Sandel, *Democracy's Discontent: America in Search of a Public Philosophy* [Cambridge, MA: The Belknap Press of Harvard University Press, 1996], 207).

usage by his Quaker contemporaries, whom Bercovitch calls "those most individualistic of Puritans" and Philip Schaff bluntly labels "subjective."[141] This does not mean that we cannot appreciate the Quakers' concern for dry institutionalism and sacerdotalism, nor recognize that there have probably always been Quakers who have been more or less committed to historic Christian orthodoxy. Fox was surely closer to the evangelical mainstream than Nayler, for example. But there were also undeniably significant differences between Bunyan and the Quakers. To reinvoke the opening image of this chapter – that Bunyan and Fox are buried so close together yet are separated by a deeply symbolic wall – Bunyan's simultaneous nearness to and distance from the Quakers on matters of outward religious authority and doctrinal standards were in many ways his same degrees of nearness to and farness from modernity. The result of this endeavor, therefore, is the establishment of a "Perspective Glass"[142] for future Bunyan studies which reveals that his theological traditionalism often tended to tug Bunyan back toward a medieval-Reformation milieu, even when he began to appear most recognizably individualistic and modern.

Notice, for example, how Bunyan and Fox were described by the people who knew them well. Penn said of Fox, "His authority was inward and not outward,"[143] whereas John Burton said that God had chosen "foolish" Bunyan to study in "the heavenly University, the Church of Christ," which teaches "a righteousness wrought by that God-man Jesus Christ without thee."[144] Already in the seventeenth century, Bunyan and some other fellow Baptists attempted to delimit the extent of their individualism by distinguishing themselves from the Quakers, and future scholarly treatments of Bunyan's own individualism should take this into account. Bunyan struggled to appropriate the inward leading of Christ in such a way that did not minimize the outward and objective work of redemption. And so Bunyan wrote in *Some Gospel-Truths Opened*:

> Here is my life, namely the birth of this man, the righteousnesse of this man, and blood of this man, the death and resurrection of this man; the ascension and intercession of this man for me, and the second comming of this man to judge the world in righteousnesse, *Acts* 17.31. I say here is my life, if I see this by faith

---

141 Bercovitch, 29; Schaff, ed., 1:869.
142 Cf. Christian's gift from the shepherds of the Delectable Mountains in Bunyan, *PP*, 122.
143 William Penn, in George Fox, *Journal*, 504.
144 John Burton, in Bunyan, *MW*, 1:9, 8.

without me; through the operation of the spirit within me; I am safe, I am at peace, I am comforted, I am encouraged, and I know that my comfort, peace, and encouragement is true.[145]

So what does one make of David Lyle Jeffrey's belief that "the doctrine of the indwelling spirit or 'light within' was considered by many to have been taken to extremes not only among Quakers, Levellers, Ranters, and Muggletonians, but [even] among more conservative Puritans [like Bunyan] it combined with the obligation for self-examination to bring about a preoccupation with self at least as troubled"?[146] Despite Bunyan's emphasis on the objective work of Christ "without," did the necessity of individual appropriation of that work become so great for him that its objectivity was in the end swallowed up by his subjective response? This is the critical issue of Bunyan's autobiography, *Grace Abounding to the Chief of Sinners*, to which I now turn.

---

145 Bunyan, *Some Gospel-Truths Opened*, in ibid., 112. Cf. Bunyan's *The Pharisee and the Publicane*: "So then Justification before God, is one thing; and Justification in mine own eyes, is another: Not that these are two Justifications, but the same Righteousness by which I stand before God, may be seen of God, when I am ignorant of it; yea, for the sake of it I may be received, pardoned, and accounted righteous of him, and yet I may not understand it" (*MW*, 10:182).

146 David Lyle Jeffrey, *People of the Book: Christian Identity and Literary Culture* (Grand Rapids: William B. Eerdmans Publishing Company, 1996), 276.

CHAPTER THREE

Grace Abounding to the Chief of Sinners: Bunyan Between Luther and Modernity

If Bunyan's anti-Quaker writings comprised the first defining stage of his theological understanding, then, as G. B. Harrison says, "the next stage was the accidental discovery of an old copy of Martin Luther's *Commentary on the Galatians.*"[1] Despite the fact that Harrison made this observation upon the tricentennial of Bunyan's birth in 1928, Henri Talon could still point out in 1951 that the influence of Luther upon Bunyan was "usually touched on and not given its due prominence by Bunyan's critics, with the exception of the always perceptive Coleridge."[2] In the half-century since Talon's remark, Bunyan scholars have given closer attention to Bunyan's reliance upon Luther. After Richard L. Greaves's theological biography, *John Bunyan*, made a convincing case that Bunyan's Calvinism was but the superstructure upon a Lutheran theological foundation,[3] subsequent researchers realized that Luther's influence on Bunyan's thought went far beyond the few lines in which Bunyan mentioned Luther by name in *Grace Abounding to the Chief of Sinners*. Vera J. Camden, Dayton Haskin, and Michael A. Mullett, for instance, are among those who have built upon Greaves's own foundation by exploring *why* Bunyan professed that he found his *own* story in what Luther revealed of himself in the Galatians commentary.[4] Yet, there is still surprisingly little *explicit* comparison, aside from Camden's article, of how Bunyan's word choices when describing "conscience" and "self" so imitated Luther's that to speak of one's understanding of conscience is to speak almost identically about the other. It is very important not simply to settle for the fruits of Bunyan's indebtedness to Luther but to dig to the the-

---

1 G. B. Harrison, *John Bunyan: A Study in Personality* (Garden City, NY: Doubleday, Doran & Company, Inc., 1928), 39.
2 Talon, *John Bunyan: The Man and His Works*, 272.
3 Greaves, *John Bunyan*, 156.
4 Camden, "Most Fit," 819-849; Dayton Haskin, "Bunyan, Luther, and the Struggle with Belatedness in *Grace Abounding*," *University of Toronto Quarterly* 50:3 (Spring 1981): 300-313; Mullett, *passim*.

ological roots – because only when one fully excavates the Lutheran ground from which Bunyan's speech about conscience grew can one finally determine whether his introspection in *Grace Abounding* reveals a subjectivist turn as some have charged, or whether Bunyan's seeming modernism does not run deep.

Luther and Bunyan were not the first Christians whose introspective religion served as a harbinger of the modern concept of individualism. L. John Van Til shows how St. Paul's view of conscience differed from that of his Hellenistic environment by making God and not conscience the final judge of human decisions.[5] Yet the Greek idea of conscience in Paul's Bible, the Septuagint, denoted a prosecutor and judge in ethical matters, and Paul retained this stress.[6] Paul used the Greek term for "conscience" (*suneidēsis*) fifteen times in his Corinthian and Roman correspondences to denote a human faculty that accuses of sins (Rom 2:15, 13:5), expresses sorrow over unbelief (Rom 9:1-2), and can be either "weak" or "strong" depending on a Christian's scruples over indifferent matters such as eating meat (1 Cor 8:7-12, 10:25-29). The conscience also has a cognitive ability to verify Christian truth claims (2 Cor 4:2, 5:11). Luther similarly spoke of the conscience as something naturally sensitive to sin that can be "educated" by the Christian gospel.

Yet Krister Stendahl argues that Augustine set the example for Luther's recasting of Paul by suggesting that Paul arrived at his view of conscience through a failed struggle for justification under the law.[7] Robert Jewett's word study of *suneidēsis* in Paul's writings indeed suggests a different context than legalism in 1 Corinthians, which produced an "original and remarkably modern view."[8] Paul did not make conscience the direct voice of God, Jewett says, because he defended Christian consciences that were "weak" (e.g., in regard to eating meat), and such forbearance is a condition of modern liberty of conscience. Moreover, Paul did not want to educate the conscience forcibly but allowed those with "weak" con-

---

5   L. John Van Til, "The Appeal to Conscience," *Christianity Today* 13:17 (23 May 1969): 6-7.
6   Hans-Christoph Hahn, "Conscience," *The New International Dictionary of New Testament Theology*, ed. Colin Brown (Grand Rapids: Zondervan Publishing House, 1986), 1:349-350.
7   Krister Stendahl, "The Apostle Paul and the Introspective Conscience of the West," *Paul Among Jews and Gentiles, and Other Essays* (Philadelphia: Fortress Press, 1976), 82-84. Cf. Haskin, "Bunyan, Luther, and the Struggle," 309.
8   Robert Jewett, *Christian Tolerance: Paul's Message to the Modern Church* (Philadelphia: The Westminster Press, 1982), 45.

sciences to remain weak rather than to experience pain through coerced belief. Thus, in Stendahl's opinion, Augustine's efforts to correct the soteriological value of human effort in Pelagianism, and Luther's efforts to correct the soteriological significance of legalism in late medieval Catholicism, colored their reading of Paul's language of "conscience."[9] For example, Luther spoke at length about conscience in his *Commentary on Galatians*, but Paul did not even use *suneidēsis* in that letter. So Stendahl's claim appears to have some merit. Jewett also suggests that medieval (= Augustinian/Lutheran?) preconceptions about conscience have clouded Western misunderstanding of Paul even to our own day.[10]

Surely there is some kinship in Paul's notion of Christian tolerance in 1 Corinthians to the modern notions of religious liberty espoused in Bunyan's century by the likes of Roger Williams and John Milton. Yet it is too far a stretch to claim Paul's view of conscience as completely modern since his only explicit discussion of weak consciences and their toleration occurred entirely within a confessional context. In other words, whether or not Paul thought non-Christians had "liberty of conscience," he never expressed any concern for conscience except when speaking about and to Christians. Thus, while Augustine and Luther focused on Paul's teachings on conscience in Romans to the relative neglect of 1 Corinthians, they were not at all contradicting Paul's approach when they dealt with legalism as a problem for *Christian* thought – indeed, a problem with which Paul also dealt extensively in Galatians.[11] Moreover, Augustine and Paul correctly understood Paul's explanation in Romans that the conscience registers awareness of misdeeds, and they also distinguished the conscience from God which, as we have seen, was an emphasis of John Bunyan against subjectivist tendencies within Quakerism. Such ancient ideas can still

---

9 E. P. Sanders and James D. G. Dunn have accepted Stendahl's "non-Lutheran" reading of Romans while moving beyond Stendahl to explain the role of the law in first century Judaism as that of "covenantal nomism," the idea that divine grace initiates the God/human relationship, while observance of the law, perhaps even divinely enabled, has something to do with that relationship's maintenance (cf. James D. G. Dunn, "The New Perspective on Paul: Paul and the Law," in *The Romans Debate: Revised and Expanded Edition*, ed. Karl P. Donfried [Peabody, MA: Hendrickson Publishers, 1991], 299-308).

10 Jewett, 45.

11 C. A. Pierce observes that Paul's problem with legalism in Galatians 3:26 ff. is indeed a problem of conscience itself (Pierce, *Conscience in the New Testament* [London: SCM Press Limited, 1955], 126, ft. 3).

seem individualistic and modern because, in Jewett's phrasing, discussions of the "weak" conscience are "intimately connected with the mechanisms of self-respect, moral autonomy, and psychic health."[12] So Stendahl contends further that Augustine's *Confessions*, in many ways the pattern for Luther's *Galatians* and Bunyan's autobiography, was "the first great document in the history of the introspective conscience."[13] I caution, however, that the apprehension of conscience by Luther and Bunyan, precisely because grounded in Paul, did not become an *autonomous* authority in the fully modern sense.

Mystical writers, such as Luther's fellow German Meister Eckhart and Bunyan's fellow Briton Julian of Norwich, were among those writers between Augustine and Luther whose works seem most individualistic,[14] and so perhaps it is not coincidental that

---

12 Jewett, 45; cf. 61.
13 Stendahl, 85. Cf. John Stachniewski's edition of *Grace Abounding*, which finds *Confessions* the most significant literary precedent for an introspective work of the scope and influence of *Grace Abounding* (Stachniewski, ed., in *GAOSA*, xxxviii). Although Sandra Lee Dixon does not compare Augustine and Bunyan, her psychological approach does raise several incidents in *Confessions* that have interesting parallels in Bunyan's writings: Augustine's pride in leading his youthful mates in debauchery and his later trust that God would catch him if he "jumped" into faith foreshadowed similar language in *Grace Abounding*, and his temptations by the tri-fold lust of the flesh, the eyes, and ambition are reminiscent of the three daughters of Adam-the-first who seduce Faithful in *The Pilgrim's Progress* (Dixon, *Augustine: The Scattered and Gathered Self* [St. Louis: Chalice Press, 1999], 63, 134).
14 R. W. Southern cites a sermon from the Dominican Eckhart which he believes is "a preview of the quiet evangelical purity of domestic life which is the most lasting contribution of Protestant puritanism to the Christian life" (Southern, *Western Society and the Church in the Middle Ages*, The Penguin History of the Church 6 [London: Penguin Books, 1990], 301-302). Much like Luther and Bunyan, Julian of Norwich believed that seeing "our self to be so foul" is the first step to "find rest of soul, and an easy conscience" (Julian of Norwich, *Revelations of Divine Love*, trans. Clifton Wolters [London: Penguin, 1966], 121-122). Cf. Galen Johnson, "Church and Conscience in William Langland and Julian of Norwich," *Fides et Historia* 32:2 (Summer/Fall 2000): 51-66, for a summary of Julian's view of conscience. Anna Maria Reynolds says that for Julian, "there is no distinction between the right knowledge of God and the knowledge of self" (Reynolds, "Julian of Norwich," in *Pre-Reformation Spirituality*, ed. James Walsh [New York: Fordham University Press, 1965], 200-201). This is also, of course, Calvin's starting point in the *Institutes of the Christian Religion*. Michael Davies warns, however, not to forget that despite Calvin's "exhortation to self-knowledge" at the beginning of the *Institutes*, he *discouraged*

Luther's beloved teacher Johannes Staupitz was a mystic, and even Bunyan, says Richard Stauffer, "*a la suite de Luther et avant Kierkegaard*," was a mystic in that his personal and allegorical pilgrimages moved along *"le chemin de l'angoisse."*[15] Then the Renaissance, first in Italy and later in western Europe, spurred the consideration of human particularity; alongside it, the Reformation emphasized that each individual must prepare to stand alone before God.[16] In England, economic woes forced many to reconsider their place in their world, while Puritanism, with its focus on private Bible reading and personal "calling," cast doubt on the idea of a common religion for all when it spun off into Independency and Separatism.[17] Christopher Hill concludes of the seventeenth century that "all roads in our period have led to individualism," and he identifies Luther's speech at Worms as the most significant milestone along the way.[18] Beyond Puritanism, says J. P. Kenyon, the emphasis on the individual became secularized, particularly with the independence of the subject in Descartes and Locke; Charles Taylor adds that "by the turn of the eighteenth century, something recognizably like the modern self is in process of constitution."[19]

Roger Sharrock believes that "nagging anxiety and the uneasy

---

    introspection over one's soteriological status (Michael Davies, "Bunyan's Exceeding Maze: *Grace Abounding* and the Labyrinth of Predestination," in *Awakening Words: John Bunyan and the Language of Community*, ed. David Gay, James G. Randall, and Arlette Zinck [Newark: University of Delaware Press, 2000], 101). Perhaps, says A. G. Dickens, Calvin sought "to bring order into a world where Luther's message seemed in process of degenerating into subjectivism, individualism and license" (Dickens, *The English Reformation* [University Park, PA: The Pennsylvania State University Press, 1993], 224).

15 Bainton, 56; Stauffer, 721.
16 Alister E. McGrath, *A Life of John Calvin: A Study in the Shaping of Western Culture* (Oxford: Blackwell, 1993), 6.
17 John Stachniewski, *The Persecutory Imagination: English Puritanism and the Literature of Religious Despair* (Oxford: Clarendon Press, 1991), 78.
18 Hill, *Century*, 217, 78.
19 Kenyon, 202; Taylor, 185. On Locke, cf. Taylor 82, 177, 307. On Descartes, cf. the contrast with Augustine on conceptions of interiority made by Jaroslav Pelikan, *The Christian Tradition: A History of the Development of Doctrine*, vol. 3, *The Growth of Medieval Theology (600-1300)* (Chicago: The University of Chicago Press, 1978), 306-307. Luxon says that the idea of a self separable from the body predates Descartes in Calvin's removal of the real presence of Christ from the elements of the Eucharist (6). Apparently Luxon alludes to Calvin's belief that communicants feast on the real body and blood of Christ even though Christ is not physically present in the elements.

conscience recommend Bunyan for consideration as a cousin of the modern mind" because Bunyan's self-conscious neuroses over his true identity as elect or reprobate reflect post-Cartesian doubt.[20] Taylor and John N. Morris further hail *Grace Abounding* as the prototype for modern subjectivist doubt, now cut off from the God whom Bunyan hoped to appease.[21] Indeed, the individualism of *Grace Abounding* is so pronounced, argue Michael Davies and Alick West, that the book discloses something quite different from what Bunyan probably intended: a new sense of self that is subjective in the extreme.[22] While there must surely be *some* sound explanation for why so many scholars find in *Grace Abounding* the same subjectivist turn, can their arguments be fully persuasive if they do not adequately consider the Lutheran "mechanics" according to which Bunyan's view of conscience operated, nor whether Bunyan's references to "self" were truly "inward" or simply synonyms for his person?

For instance, although Richard A. Muller states that "the entirety of Bunyan's life was a succession of cases of conscience,"[23] the Oxford English Dictionary lists no entries under "self" as "a permanent subject or successive and varying states of consciousness" before Thomas Traherne (1674), Sir Thomas Browne (1682) and John Locke (1690).[24] Was it *Grace Abounding* (1666) that actually first trod the path which they followed? Taylor also contends that Locke and Descartes were innovators in promoting awareness of the self *as* a self.[25] Though a contemporary of theirs, could Bunyan the biblically primitivist Puritan have thought of self-awareness in the same sense as these giants of the Enlightenment? I will investigate whether a close and theologically informed reading of Bunyan's use of the terms "conscience" and "self" actually warrants the charge of subjectivism that myriad commentators have made against *Grace Abounding*.

---

20 Sharrock, *John Bunyan* 57.
21 Taylor, 184; John N. Morris, *Versions of the Self: Studies in English Autobiography from John Bunyan to John Stuart Mill* (New York: Basic Books, Inc., 1966), 90.
22 Michael Davies, "Bunyan's Exceeding Maze," 100; cf. David Herreshoff, "Marxist Perspectives on Bunyan," in *Bunyan in Our Time*, ed. Robert G. Collmer (Kent, OH: The Kent State University Press, 1989), 168; Stauffer, 712.
23 Richard A. Muller, "Covenant and Conscience in English Reformed Theology: Three Variations on a 17th Century Theme," *The Westminster Theological Journal* 42:2 (Spring 1980): 321.
24 J. A. Simpson and E. S. C. Weiner, eds., *The Oxford English Dictionary*, 2nd ed., vol. 14 (Oxford: Clarendon Press, 1989), 907.
25 Taylor, 176.

Bunyan's Attraction to Luther's *Galatians*

Bunyan's notable commendation of Luther comes two-fifths of the way through *Grace Abounding*. Yet what escapes the concern of virtually all the commentators on this passage is Bunyan's explanation earlier in the same paragraph of exactly *what* in Luther's commentary so soothed him. Though Bunyan did not recall specific *citations* from Luther ("of Particulars here I intend nothing"), he did declare those *themes* of Luther that most impressed him:

> Besides, he doth most gravely also, in that book debate of the rise of these temptations, namely, Blasphemy, Desperation, and the like, shewing that the law of *Moses*, as well as the Devil, Death, and Hell, hath a very great hand therein; the which at first was very strange to me, but considering and watching, I found it so indeed. But of Particulars here I intend nothing, only this methinks I must let fall before all men, I do prefer this book of Mr. *Luther* upon the *Galathians* [sic], (excepting the Holy Bible) before all the books that ever I have seen, as most fit for a wounded Conscience. (§130)[26]

Did Luther enrapture Bunyan because he emphasized the *freedom* of human conscience, its ability to squelch anxiety and justify itself, or even to establish its inherent goodness? No: Bunyan's conscience did not find relief through an inward resource but rather ironically through the realization that it was leased to the law, the Devil, death, and Hell. Since Bunyan veritably equated these four horsemen of perdition with the natural conscience in his anti-Quaker writings, one can easily perceive why Bunyan felt such attraction toward Luther: each man spoke of the conscience primarily with the terminology not of liberation but of bondage. Indeed, because it is impossible to determine exactly how many years prior to the publication of *Grace Abounding* in 1666 that Bunyan first read Luther, it is surely credible that Luther's *Galatians* even influenced the anti-Quaker works of the mid-1650s. Bunyan did indicate, after all, that he would have thought it strange to link conscience with law, devil, death, and hell before he pondered the words of Luther, but he made those very same connections in *Some Gospel-Truths Opened* and its *Vindication*.

Bunyan's change in his understanding of conscience, which came because "I found my condition in [Luther's] experience, so largely and profoundly handled, as if his Book had been written out of my heart" (§129), did tend to locate personal authority within himself.[27]

---

26 Bunyan, *GA*, 41.
27 Ibid.

Bunyan believed that Luther's words had to be true words because they described *his* own experience; if the autobiographical elements of Luther's *Commentary on Galatians* had not resonated with "the state of Christians now" (§129) in which Bunyan lived and moved and had his being, would Bunyan's conceptions of conscience have grown to synchronize so completely with Luther's own?[28] One certainly sees the individualistic manner by which Bunyan derived his theological convictions. But did he also make the fully *subjectivist* turn of modernity, in which the inward search for authority yields self-*direction*? Bunyan certainly did not think that the incorporation of Luther's *Galatians* into his theological self-assessment was an autonomous act, for it was "the God in whose hands are all our days and ways" who "did cast into my hand, one day, a book of *Martin Luther*, his comment on the *Galathians*" [sic] (§129).[29] So, while Bunyan indeed assumed in *Grace Abounding* that he had the authority *within* himself to judge religious doctrine, that authority did not derive *from* himself but from divine providence.

Luther's *Commentary on Galatians*, which he developed with the help of student notes from classroom lectures delivered in 1531, first appeared in 1535. Its first English translation was published by Thomas Vautrollier in 1575 and included a preface from Vautrollier addressed to "all afflicted consciences." This edition went through eight reprintings by 1640.[30] Because Bunyan described his copy as being "so old that it was ready to fall piece from piece" (§129),[31] Mullett wonders if it was possibly an original 1575 issue that Bunyan owned.[32] "What is certain," says Greaves, "is that Bunyan recognised an immediate spiritual kinship with the German

---

28 Ibid.
29 Ibid., 40.
30 Roger Sharrock, in ibid., 144. For quotations from Luther's *Commentary on Galatians* in this essay, it is more profitable to use the translation with which Bunyan would have been familiar than the editions of *Galatians* in *Luther's Works* or *Weimarer Ausgabe*. Therefore, my source for citations from this work is Martin Luther, *A Commentary on St. Paul's Epistle to the Galatians*, ed. Philip S. Watson (Westwood, NJ: Fleming H. Revell Company, 1953). According to Jaroslav Pelikan, who translated *Commentary on Galatians* for the *Luther's Works* series, Watson's modernization is "the most satisfying" recent edition based upon Vautrollier's 1575 text (Jaroslav Pelikan, in Martin Luther, *Lectures on Galatians, 1535: Chapters 1-4*, ed. Jaroslav Pelikan, *Luther's Works*, vol. 26 [Saint Louis: Concordia Publishing House, 1963], x).
31 Bunyan, *GA*, 40.
32 Mullett, 36.

reformer."[33] Randall C. Zachman has conducted an extensive analysis of the meaning of conscience according to Luther and John Calvin, in which he establishes their respective positions on the concept of conscience in their writings, as well as their use of it in their theology. Zachman is particularly concerned to show how Luther's claims about conscience in fact undergirded his entire theological system.[34] In my attempt to demonstrate something comparable for Bunyan, I shall first rehearse Zachman's general findings about Luther before comparing particular passages between Luther's *Galatians* and *Grace Abounding*.

Luther's Understanding of Conscience

Even as Luther never wrote a systematic theology, neither did he write a single formal treatise that explained his understanding of conscience in a methodical way. However, Luther did mention the conscience frequently enough for the reader to deduce with some assurance of accuracy what he believed to be its most important characteristics. In an early work, the *Judgment of Martin Luther on Monastic Vows* (1521), Luther provided a working definition for conscience that foreshadowed his more extensive treatment of it in *Galatians*:

> For conscience is not the power to do works, but to judge them. The proper work of conscience (as Paul says in Romans 2[:15]), is to accuse or excuse, to make one guilty or guiltless, uncertain or certain. Its purpose is not to do, but to pass judgment on what has been done, and this judgment makes us stand accused or saved in God's sight. Christ has freed this conscience from works through the gospel and teaches this conscience not to trust in works, but to rely only on his mercy.[35]

Since the conscience according to Luther judges human works, it has, in Zachman's words, "a strongly empirical orientation."[36] Thus, all that is under its purview are acts of the flesh, for it can assess only physical deeds and not spiritual motives. This means that the

---

33 Greaves, *John Bunyan*, 18.
34 Randall C. Zachman, *The Assurance of Faith: Conscience in the Theology of Martin Luther and John Calvin* (Minneapolis: Fortress Press, 1993), 5.
35 Martin Luther, *Judgment of Martin Luther on Monastic Vows*, in *Luther's Works*, vol. 44: *The Christian in Society* I, ed. James Atkinson (Philadelphia: Fortress Press, 1966), 298.
36 Zachman, 21. Cf. Pelikan: "Zwingli viewed the law differently from Luther. For him, law was not opposed to gospel but was in fact renewed by Christ as the pattern for Christian living" (*The Christian Tradition*, 4:213).

conscience, at least in its pre-regenerate state, is incapable of gleaning any comfort from justification by *faith*. Since the conscience can only evaluate itself on the basis of works, it will try to justify its "owner" by obedience to the (Mosaic) law. But it is unable to do so, for by works of the law, no one will be saved (Gal 2:16).

On what basis, then, could Luther say before the Diet of Worms – in the same year in which he wrote his *Judgment on Monastic Vows* – that "to go against conscience is neither right nor safe"?[37] In other words, how could the testimony of the conscience become "good" for Luther? The conscience must receive the testimony of Jesus Christ by faith alone. When individuals receive the Christian gospel, their consciences lead them to deny themselves and confess the empirical evidence of sin that merits God's judgment. The conscience must yield its authority over the human person to God's objective and revealed will to save sinners.[38] It must forego its futile, even idolatrous, efforts to direct the human will to liberation and submit to the gospel truth that God alone justifies.[39] "The self-revelation of God thus directly contradicts the testimony of the conscience to itself about God…. God does not justify those who acquit themselves in their conscience, but justifies those who condemn themselves in their conscience."[40]

So why could Luther neither rightly nor safely go against his conscience and recant his books at Worms? By means of holy war, the word of God (Luther's double *entendre* on "word" as both Christ and scripture was probably intentional) had taken captive his conscience, Luther said, and through that act of mystical ravishment, the two had become one.[41] With Christ having displaced the suitor Moses as the true spouse of conscience, to dishonor conscience would now be nothing other than to violate ("to go against") the marriage bed of Christ and the disciple.[42] This union is not entirely

---

37 Bunyan likely knew of Luther's defense at Worms since it is recorded in John Foxe's *Acts and Monuments*, which Bunyan had with him in the Bedford jail. Cf. Foxe, 173.
38 Zachman, 6.
39 Ibid., 39.
40 Ibid., 41; cf. 57-58.
41 Cf. Heiko A. Oberman, *Luther: Man Between God and the Devil*, trans. Eileen Walliser-Schwarzbart (New York: Image Books, 1989), 204. Compare the words of Mr. Conscience in Bunyan's *HW*, 89: "*For he* [Prince Emanuel] *now, as you see, doth not only lye in close siege about us, but hath forced his entrance in at our Gates; moreover* Diabolus *flees before him*."
42 Zachman, 56; Camden, "Most Fit," 839-841. Luther said in his *CG*, 126: "Let the conscience have her bride-chamber, not in the low valley, but in the

"interior," however, as I shall show. Sometimes the sanctified conscience still feels the terrible threat of the law, but the preached word and the sacraments can reassure it that God's mercy endures forever.[43] In moments of crisis (*Anfechtungen*) – such as Luther experienced at Worms – one must turn a deaf ear to conscience itself in order not to sear ("go against") conscience and corrupt its sanctity. Therefore, even the redeemed conscience never became an autonomous (literally, "self-law") authority for Luther.[44]

Luther summarized the change from law to liberty that Christ effects in fallen human conscience in his preface to his lectures on Romans (1515-1516):

> Our conscience is bound to the law in its former state of the old sinful self. But when this self is put to death by the spirit, our conscience is set at liberty, and each is released from the other. This does not mean that our conscience has become inactive, but that now, for the first time, it can really cling to Christ as a second husband, and bring forth the fruit of life.[45]

The instruction of the conscience by Christ brings death to the "old" self. The new self, despite its occasional struggles in faith, escapes the never-ending cycle of doubt and matures into Christian sanctification ("the fruit of life"). Does this describe modern subjectivity? Bernhard Lohse observes that "the claim that Luther brought about the end of the Middle Ages and the beginning of the Modern Age has frequently been made [e.g., by Karl Holl, Emanuel Hirsch,

---

    high mountain: in the which let Christ lie and there rule and reign, who doth not terrify and afflict sinners, but comforteth them, pardoneth their sins, and saveth them" (2:14). In *Of the Law and a Christian*, Bunyan also believed "that the Christian Soul ... is Married to him that is raised from the Dead," and not the law (Bunyan, *The Miscellaneous Works of John Bunyan*, vol. 12, ed. W. R. Owens [Oxford: Clarendon Press, 1994], 412).

43 Zachman, 59, 63, 84-85. Bunyan also moved in this direction in his later works.

44 Ibid., 85-87. For an exploration of the concept of *Anfechtung* in Lutheran and Puritan thought, cf. Zachman, 64-66; Stauffer, 718; Martin Schmidt, "Biblizismus und natürliche Theologie in der Gewissenslehre des englischen Puritanismus," Zweiter Teil, *Archiv für Reformationsgeschichte* 43:1 (1952): 72.

45 Martin Luther, *Lectures on Romans*, in John Dillenberger, ed., *Martin Luther: Selections From His Writings* (New York: Anchor Press/Doubleday, 1961), 30. Compare Luther's comment on Galatians 2:19: "Therefore when I feel the remorse and sting of conscience for sin, I behold that brazen serpent Christ hanging upon the Cross" (Luther, *CG*, 161). Cf. Pelikan, *The Christian Tradition*, 4:133.

Theodor Siegfried, and others] by referring to his new conception of conscience."[46] Luther's defense at Worms is something so powerfully defiant that it is absurd to think that Luther did *not* hail a sea-change in Western appeals to conscience. But were it not for that one familiar speech, ineradicably engraved in our memories by the title of Roland Bainton's classic biography, *Here I Stand*, would a close reading of Luther's statements about conscience, imbedded in his commentaries and tracts, still bear, Atlas-like, the full weight of modern inwardness? What did Bunyan discover in Luther when *he* "had but a little way perused" the *Commentary on Galatians* (§129)?[47]

Luther's *Galatians* and *Grace Abounding*: Parallels

Luther believed that Paul's epistle to the Galatians contained the Christian gospel in miniature; his fondness for the letter was so great that he even jested that he had married it![48] If the index in John Dillenberger's serviceable and widely used compilation of Luther's major writings is an accurate indication, then Luther spoke disproportionately about conscience in the *Commentary on Galatians*. Of the twenty-seven page-number entries under "conscience" in that index, seventeen allude to the selections from *Galatians*, which in turn comprise only about one-seventh of the pages in the anthology. Of course, there are many more than seventeen references to conscience in *Galatians*, but this unscientific survey nonetheless offers a clue to the special concern which Luther had for conscience when he treated the Pauline letter that, more than any other, speaks critically of the law.

How did Luther's special concerns in Galatians influence Bunyan's purpose in *Grace Abounding*? In his preface, Bunyan said that "it is profitable for Christians to be often calling to mind the very beginnings of Grace with their Souls," even as God commanded Moses to institute the Passover as an occasion of eternal remembrance.[49] Bunyan did not write *Grace Abounding*, therefore, to describe a perpetual condition of doubt in which he still continued to dwell, but rather to look back upon his trials, much as Christian

---

46   Bernhard Lohse, "Conscience and Authority in Luther," in *Luther and the Dawn of the Modern Era*, Studies in the History of Christian Thought 8, ed. Heiko A. Oberman (Leiden: E. J. Brill, 1974), 158.
47   Bunyan, *GA*, 40-41.
48   B. A. Gerrish, *Grace and Reason: A Study in the Theology of Luther* (Oxford: Clarendon Press, 1962), 62.
49   Bunyan, *GA*, 2. I continue to follow Bunyan's own italicization.

does on the other side of the Valley of the Shadow of Death, and to credit his deliverance to "the Grace of God towards me."[50] His purpose in *Grace Abounding* was to present the same kind of spiritual balm to others that Luther's Commentary on Galatians gave to him. This is deducible from Bunyan's encouragement to his audience in the preface to "call to mind the former days, the years of ancient times," when one also recalls Bunyan's utter astonishment that Luther could speak so accurately of his condition though Luther "must needs write and speak of the Experience of former days" (§129).[51] Thus, Bunyan invited his readers to follow the way he had trodden: the way of former days, the way of Luther. Although it may appear that Bunyan's crises of faith continued without abatement, he could have said much more – "I could have enlarged much in this my discourse of my temptations and troubles for sin" – but he chose instead, at least comparatively, to "be plain and simple" because "God did not play in convincing of me."[52] Bunyan did not recount his struggles of faith simply for public documentation; *Grace Abounding* is apparently far from complete in that regard. It is abbreviated only because the worst of Bunyan's spiritual struggles had come to an end, and Luther had helped him in the process.

Bunyan explained that Luther's commentary made the strongest impression on him in its discussion of the Mosaic law, death, the devil, and hell. And with what things, according to Bunyan, did Luther adjoin the law in his *Commentary on Galatians*? "Even of sin, death, God's wrath, the devil, &c. Wherefore there is no greater or harder bondage, that [sic] the bondage of the law" (5:1).[53] It is possible to identify parallel passages between Luther and Bunyan in their descriptions of conscience relative to each of the four areas that Bunyan mentioned.

The Law

In his epistle to the Galatians, Paul strongly rebuked those who believed that their salvation depended to any degree on their maintenance of the Mosaic law. The law had the purpose of restraining human lusts until the advent of Christ, Paul said, but now that Christ has come to perform his atoning work, God has fully revealed that justification is found by faith alone. For Luther, it was

---

50 Ibid., 3.
51 Ibid., 3, 41.
52 Ibid., 3.
53 Luther, *CG*, 445.

the conscience which has the function of informing us that their obedience to the law has not only been inadequate but actually incapable of satisfying God. Therefore, Luther could say in the preface to his *Commentary on Galatians*: "Man's weakness and misery is so great, that in the terrors of conscience and danger of death, we behold nothing else but our works, our worthiness and the law: which when it sheweth unto us our sin, by and by our evil life past cometh to remembrance."[54] Similarly, Bunyan not only recollected his "evil life past" in *Grace Abounding* ("I was, notwithstanding my Religion, one that took much delight in all manner of vice;" §20), but he believed that in such remembrance he also found humility before God: "*Remember, I say, the Word that first laid hold upon you; remember your terrours of conscience, and fear of death and hell.*"[55]

Though *Grace Abounding* obviously did not adopt Luther's commentary style, Bunyan followed Luther in remembering that his earliest encounters with God's word produced only "terrors of conscience." At first, said Luther, "the conscience feeleth that it hath not satisfied the law," and so all alike does the human race cry, "We shall die, we shall die" (2:17).[56] Human reason then makes the false assumption, added Luther, that it can absolve itself through obedience to the moral law it had broken. Luther did not believe that reason of itself was unimportant; the Christian gospel is not a-rational or irrational. But reason has been corrupted through original sin: in seeking to understand more about God than lay in his natural capacity, Adam stretched human reason beyond its limits and left it limp, like an elastic band that has lost its tension. Luther was no innovator in this regard; he stood with Augustine and Thomas Aquinas before him, and John Calvin and the Reformed theological tradition shortly after him, in acknowledging the noetic effects of sin.[57] In its weakened state, Luther wrote, human reason relies upon the law to fortify itself; it sees no other way by which it may be saved than by good works. This is human reason's great misconception, however. For while the law itself is good, and indeed may

---

54 Ibid., 22. Cf. Luther's *The Bondage of the Will*: "If I lived and worked to all eternity, my conscience would never reach comfortable certainty as to how much it must do to satisfy God" (Dillenberger, 199).
55 Bunyan, *GA*, 9, 3.
56 Luther, *CG*, 153. Cf. Bunyan's *HW* where the first response of the Mansoulians to Emanuel's declaration that he will consider their request for clemency is, "*We must all be killed*" (97).
57 Cf. Moroney, 125-129. Contemporary explorations of the effect of sin upon human reason have been conducted largely by theologians in the Reformed tradition, such as Nicholas Wolterstorff and Alvin Plantinga.

be the highest good on earth, it cannot attain to the kingdom or righteousness of Christ. Justification by *faith* overturns what reason expects. And so, neither law nor reason, because illuminated by nature and not by Christ, can assuage a conscience that has been terrorized by the awareness of its sinfulness.[58]

Bunyan, too, originally thought that he could slake the terrors in his conscience through perfect obedience to the law: "I fell to some outward Reformation, both in my words and life, and did set the Commandments before me for my way to Heaven: which Commandments I also did strive to keep; and, as I thought, did keep them pretty well sometimes, and then I should have comfort; yet now and then should break one, and so afflict my conscience" (§30).[59] Again he said, "All this while, when I thought I kept this or that Commandment, or did by word or deed any thing that I thought were good, I had great peace in my Conscience, and should think with my self, God cannot chuse but be now pleased with me, yea, to relate it in mine own way, I thought no man in *England* could please God better than I" (§35).[60] Though Bunyan could thus be quite pleased with himself for a short while, the uncompromising expectation of the law would then become too much for him to bear: "I found that, unless guilt of conscience was taken off the right way, that is, by the Blood of Christ, a man grew worse for the loss of his trouble of minde, than better" (§86).[61]

Where did Bunyan find this conviction? He learned it from Luther's *Galatians*, where the Reformer had explained the law's sway over the conscience:

---

58 Gerrish, *Faith and Reason*, 30, 84-88, 98, 118.
59 Bunyan, *GA*, 12.
60 Ibid., 14.
61 Ibid., 28. This is precisely Christian's dilemma in *The Pilgrim's Progress*, Part I. Compare Bunyan's *The Doctrine of the Law and Grace Unfolded*: "First, if thou do get off thy convictions, and not the right way (which is by seeing thy sins washed away by the Blood of Jesus Christ), it is a question whether ever God will knock at thy heart again or no; but rather say, such a one, *is joyned to Idols; let him alone* [Hosea 4:17]. Though he be in a natural state, *let him alone*. Though he be in, or under the Curse of the Law, *Let him alone*. Though he be in the very hand of the Devil, *Let him alone*. Though he be a going poste haste to Hell, *Let him alone*" (*MW*, 2:17). And also from the same work: "The soul being under trouble of Conscience, and grieved for sin, the Spirit doth seal up the soul by its comfortable testimony; perswading of the soul, that God for Christs sake hath forgiven all those sins, that lie so heavy on the conscience, and that do so much perplex the soul, by shewing it that Law which doth utter such horrible curses against it, is by Christs blood satisfied, and fulfilled, *Eph.* 1.13,14" (*MW*, 2:215).

It is necessary that men's consciences be diligently instructed, that they may understand the difference between the righteousness of the law and of grace. The righteousness of grace, or the liberty of conscience, doth in no wise pertain to the flesh. For the flesh may not be at liberty, but must remain in the grave, the prison, the couch: it must be in subjection to the law, and exercised by the Egyptians. But the Christian conscience must be dead to the law, that is to say, free from the law, and must have nothing at all to do with it. It is good to know this; for it helpeth very much to the comforting of poor afflicted consciences. Wherefore, when you see a man terrified and cast down with the sense and feeling of his sin, say unto him: Brother, thou dost not rightly distinguish; thou placest the law in thy conscience, which should be placed in the flesh. Awake, arise up, and remember that thou must believe in Christ the conqueror of law and sin. With this faith thou shalt mount up above and beyond the law, into that heaven of grace where is no law or sin. And albeit the law and sins do still remain, yet they pertain nothing to thee; for thou art dead to the law and sins (2:19).[62]

This sequence is precisely the one that Bunyan believed not only he himself but also all other true Christians followed. "It is as though," says Camden, "each believer must experience in small the flow of Christian typology."[63] When Bunyan would feel particularly guilty from recollection of his sin, Christ would "so sprinkle my Conscience with his Blood, that I should find, and that before I was aware, that in that Conscience where but just now did reign and rage the Law, even there would rest and abide the Peace and Love of *God* thorow Christ" (§127).[64] For Bunyan as for Luther, the law, like the conscience, was not created evil, but because the law contained no salvific potentiality and was only given to restrain wickedness until the advent of Christ, it can only fan the fire of the burning conscience (Rom 7:7-13; Gal 3:19-26). Thus did Bunyan warn in *A Book for Boys and Girls*:

The Law is very Holy, Just and good,
And to it is espous'd all Flesh and Blood:
But this its Goodness it cannot bestow,
On any that are wedded thereunto.[65]

When the terrors of the law "lay heavy on my Conscience," Bunyan remembered, "I preached what I felt, what I smartingly did feel,

---

62 Luther, *CG*, 160.
63 Camden, "Most Fit," 827.
64 Bunyan, *GA*, 40.
65 Bunyan, *MW*, 6:236.

even that under which my poor Soul did groan and tremble to astonishment" (§276).⁶⁶ There is indeed a real turn in Christian parlance, which Bunyan could not avoid, toward subjective feeling. Yet Bunyan's primary concern was to prove people's "miserable state by the Law," and so he sought in his sermons "to demonstrate it, and to fasten it upon the Conscience of others" (§282-283).⁶⁷ In this, he was following Luther's instruction to those who "shall become instructors and guiders of consciences" to remain in constant prayer and study so "that in time of temptation ye may be able to instruct and comfort both your own consciences and others."⁶⁸

In *The Doctrine of the Law and Grace Unfolded* (1659), written before *Grace Abounding* but with a maturity that came after the events the autobiography describes, Bunyan could analyze what he "felt" more thoroughly:

> Christian, thou art not in this thing to follow thy sense and feeling; but the very Word of God. The thing that doth do the people of God the greatest injury, it is their too little hearkening to what the Gospel saith, and their too much giving credit to what the Law, Sin, the Devil, and Conscience saith: and upon this very ground to conclude, that because there is the certainty of guilt upon the soul, therefore there is also for certain by sin, damnation to be brought upon the soul. This is now to set the Word of God aside, and to give credit to what is formed by the contrary: but thou must give more credit to one syllable of the written Word of the Gospel, then thou must give to all the Saints and Angels in Heaven and Earth; much more then [sic] to the devil and thy own guilty conscience.⁶⁹

Bunyan's indebtedness to Luther for his understanding of the natural conscience – not as liberated but enslaved to the law – was thus not exclusive to *Grace Abounding*. Bunyan added in *The Doctrine of the Law and Grace Unfolded* that unregenerate human beings are as "prisoners at the bar, having offended the Law."⁷⁰ And in *Of the Law and a Christian* (posthumous), Bunyan encouraged his readers to silence the accusations of the law by directly addressing the conscience: "When this Law with its Thundering threatnings doth attempt to lay hold on thy conscience, shut it out with a promise of

---

66 Bunyan, *GA*, 85.
67 Ibid., 87. Elsewhere, Bunyan expresses gratitude to God for giving to him "some measure of bowels and pity for their Souls, ... if God would bless it, lay hold of and awaken the Conscience" of others (§272) (Ibid., 84).
68 Luther, *CG*, 27.
69 Bunyan, *MW*, 2:191.
70 Ibid., 37.

grace; cry, the Inn is took up already, the Lord Jesus is here entertained, and here is no room for the Law."[71] Bunyan's marginalia there even cited Galatians 5:1-5 as the authority for confronting the conscience in this way. When commenting on Galatians 5:2, Luther urged believers to rebuke the conscience directly for bringing to mind that one's deeds have deserved damnation, and in the commentary's preface, he addressed the law directly: "Trouble me not in these matters, for I will not suffer thee, so intolerable a tyrant and cruel tormentor, to reign in my conscience, for it is the seat and temple of Christ the Son of God, who is the king of righteousness and peace, and my most sweet saviour and mediator."[72] In *The Pilgrim's Progress*, Messrs. Worldly-Wiseman and Mr. Legality obviously advocate the very allegiance to the law from which Luther believed one must be freed, and Christian's harrowing experience at Mt. Sinai echoes Luther's description from *Galatians* that "the terrors which [the law] raiseth up in the conscience, are no less than was that horrible shew in the mount Sinai" (1:11).[73] Even as Luther feared allowing Moses "to have dominion over our conscience" (5:3), so did Bunyan also warn via Christian in *The Pilgrim's Progress* not to yield to the mastery of Moses, who has no ability *"to shew mercy to those that transgress his Law."*[74]

Death

In *The Doctrine of the Law and Grace Unfolded,* Bunyan assumed that the accusing voice of the law that had plagued him so violently

---

71 Bunyan, *MW*, 12:412. Luther observed in *CG*: "This place, touching the difference between the law and the Gospel, is very necessary to be known, for it containeth the sum of all Christian doctrine.... For as touching the words, the distinction is easy: but in time of temptation thou shalt find the Gospel but a stranger and a rare guest in thy conscience; but the law, contrariwise, thou shalt find a familiar and a continual dweller within thee" (123; 2:14).
72 Luther, *CG*, 449, 28. Cf. Pelikan: "Calvin likewise developed the distinction between the law and the gospel in a manner quite reminiscent of Luther: the law commanded, threatened, and urged, but did not promise the kindness of God; the gospel did not impel or press, but taught the supreme kindness of God" (*The Christian Tradition*, 4:214).
73 Luther, *CG*, 76. Cf. Bunyan, *Of the Law and a Christian*: "The Christian hath now nothing to do with the Law, as it thundereth and burneth on *Sinai,* or as it bindeth the conscience to wrath and the displeasure of God for Sin" (*MW*, 1:12, 413).
74 Luther, *CG*, 53; Bunyan, *PP*, 71.

could only plunge him into death. Explaining Romans 7:9-14, Bunyan said that *"when the commandment came* (that is, to do and exercise its right office on me, which was to kill me, then) *sin revived, and I died* (and I was killed), *and the commandment* (or the Law) *which was ordained to be unto life, I found to be unto death."*[75] But it was in being "killed" by the law, as he described the law's effect on him, that Bunyan discovered its spiritual purpose to push him toward the mercy of Christ. He was already seasoned enough in the understanding of his faith to believe that his experience could be the pattern for others to follow, even as he, through Luther, had followed the pattern of Paul: "And indeed to speak of my own experience, together with the experience of all the Saints, they can seal with me to this, more or lesse."[76] Since Bunyan could articulate the stark Lutheran distinction between law and grace at least by 1659, this is further evidence that Bunyan did not write *Grace Abounding* in 1666 for self-diagnosis but rather to share the assurance he had won over a long period of time as an encouragement to others.[77] Again, Bunyan did hold an individualistic understanding of what might have been normative about his personal conversion – note, for instance, his observation when he recounted his call to ministry "that I could not be contented with saying, I believe, and am sure; methought I was more then sure, if it be lawfull so to express my self, that those things which then I asserted, were true."[78] Even Bunyan's most convinced moment of theological certitude was grounded in his own personal thought. But at the same time, it was precisely in this personal pattern that he looked for the objective signs that could break him out of subjective uncertainty; individualism for Bunyan here should not be taken as equivalent with solipsism, the idea that the self is the only reality. Luther, too, specifically rejected "this liberty [that] the people seek and embrace at this day," which was but "liberty in their opinions and in all their doings, to the end they may teach and do whatsoever they dream to be right, without reprehen-

---

75 Bunyan, *The Doctrine of the Law and Grace Unfolded*, in *MW*, 2:138.
76 Ibid. Bunyan even calls himself "your Father" in the preface to the reader of GA (5). In *Christian Behaviour* (1663), Bunyan also suggested to biological fathers that toward their children they should "be often indeavouring to fasten on their consciences ... their Death and Judgment to come" (Mullett, 106).
77 Cf. Martin Luther, *The Bondage of the Will*: "Take the Apostle Paul – how often does he call for that 'full assurance' which is, simply, an assertion of conscience, of the highest degree of certainty and conviction[?]" (Dillenberger, 168).
78 Bunyan, *GA*, 87 (§282).

sion. These stand in that liberty wherein the devil hath made them free" (5:1).[79]

In his preface to *Galatians*, Luther explained that "the afflicted and troubled conscience hath no remedy against desperation and eternal death, unless it take hold of the promise of grace freely offered in Christ."[80] He also wrote there, "Wherefore like as we have borne (as St. Paul saith) the image of the earthly Adam, so let us bear the image of the heavenly (I Cor. xv.49), which is the new man in a new world, where is no law, no sin, no sting of conscience, no death, but perfect joy, righteousness, grace, peace, life, salvation and glory."[81] And of Galatians 2:19, Luther added that when the gospel lodges firmly in a person's heart, "it will make him able to stand against all dangers of death, and all terrors of conscience and sin."[82] Bunyan's spiritual torments, likewise, were so keen that "indeed I have been as one sent to them from the dead; I went my self in chains to preach to them in chains, and carried that fire in my own conscience that I perswaded [sic] them to be aware of " (§277).[83] The effect of the gospel for both men was to make them realize that Christ had triumphed over, and thus killed, death. So said Luther: "Trouble not me, not Conscience, I say, ...: for I am dead to thee, and now I live to Christ" (2:19).[84] In *Come, and Welcome, to Jesus Christ*, Bunyan also cited the master himself: "*Luther* saith, *When Christ speaketh, he hath a mouth as wide as Heaven and Earth*: That is, to speak fully to the incouragement of every sinfull *him*, that is coming to Jesus Christ."[85] Greaves has good grounds to believe, therefore, that the reassuring "voice of a man" that Bunyan's Christian hears while traveling through the Valley of the Shadow of Death is probably the voice of Luther.[86]

The Devil

Both Luther and Bunyan recounted many personal encounters with the devil. Certainly, they were far from being the only two individuals of their own or any other age to make such claims, but again,

---

79 Luther, *CG*, 442.
80 Ibid., 23.
81 Ibid., 25.
82 Ibid., 163.
83 Bunyan, *GA*, 85.
84 Luther, *CG*, 160-161.
85 Bunyan, *MW*, 8:296.
86 Bunyan, *PP*, 64; Richard L. Greaves, in Bunyan, *MW*, 2:xviii.

their particular images are strikingly similar. For instance, Luther in *Galatians* described feeling the "fiery darts of the devil" pierce his flesh as well as hearing the devil's blood-curdling cries, while Bunyan's Christian barely escapes the arrows of Beelzebub at the Wicket-gate and also hears "a continual howling and yelling" from the demonic pit that runs alongside the Valley of the Shadow of Death.[87]

According to Luther's preface to *Galatians*, the devil tries to take advantage of the weak conscience by reminding it that it does not deserve salvation: "Satan abusing the infirmity of our nature, doth increase and aggravate these cogitations in us. Then can it not be but that the poor conscience must be more grievously troubled, terrified and confounded."[88] In other words, the devil tries to reinvigorate the force of the law over the conscience which has received the gospel, and he does so through the double-edged capability of memory. "For the devil is wont, in affliction and in the conflict of conscience, by the law to make us afraid, and to lay against us the guilt of sin, our wicked life past, the wrath and judgment of God, hell and eternal death, that by this means he may … pluck us from Christ."[89] Luther found personal strength against the devil, "that master of subjectivity" as Heiko Oberman calls him, in what he called the "alien righteousness" of Christ.[90] Because of the elective decision of Christ to absolve human sins by imputing his righteousness to their "account" with God, Luther believed that he was objectively saved – even though Christ's righteousness never actually became his by personal possession. Luther even said that the one who does not fully comprehend the "passive righteousness" of Christ will *lose* his conscience to the devil and the judgment of God.[91] Thus, Luther's cure for the "sick soul" – William James's label for both Luther and Bunyan[92] – was not a saccharine fillip but the meaty sustenance of soteriological doctrine, made "of high and weighty matters, as how we may overcome the flesh, sin, death, and the devil" (5:19).[93] Similarly, Bunyan wrote in *Saved by Grace*,

---

87 Camden, "Most Fit," 832; Bunyan, *PP*, 25, 62. Cf. Camden, "Most Fit," on the place of the devil in the spiritual formation of Luther and Bunyan (829-833).
88 Luther, *CG*, 22. This is the sign of a still-medieval world, whereas guilt has been replaced by anxiety in the modern world.
89 Ibid., 27; cf. Althaus, 259.
90 Oberman, 227.
91 Luther, *CG*, 22-23.
92 William James, *The Varieties of Religious Experience* (New York: Vintage Books, 1990), 122-123, 147, 150.
93 Luther, *CG*, 517; cf. Althaus, 224.

STUDY therefore this Doctrine of the grace of God, Suppose thou hast a Disease upon thee, which is not to be cured by such or such Medicine, the first step to thy Cure, is to know the Medicines: I am sure this is true, as to the Case in hand; the first step to the Cure of a wounded Conscience, is for thee to know the grace of *God*, especially the grace of *God* as to justification, from the Curse, in his sight.[94]

Constance A. Douglas is incorrect to conclude, therefore, that it was *only* the similarities in personal experience to Luther, but not the German Reformer's theology, that comforted Bunyan.[95]

With Luther, Bunyan was aware that the devil constantly seeks to desensitize the conscience to the sin-fighting powers of Christ's blood. "I am very confident," he said, "that this temptation of the Devil is more than usual amongst poor creatures than many are aware of, even to over-run their spirits with a scurvie and seared frame of heart, and benumming of conscience" (§25).[96] During his early struggles of faith, Bunyan would receive mental messages from Satan informing him of his hopeless condition (§48) and pressuring him "to *sell and part with Christ*" (§139). Even after Bunyan had become a preacher, sometimes the devil would suggest to him right before he began to preach that he should forego his intended sermon since, rather than awaken others, it would only condemn himself (§295).[97] But Bunyan gave thanks to God for preventing him from yielding to "these so horrid suggestions," even though his sermon might indeed "bring guilt upon my own Conscience" (§295).[98] Then Bunyan declared that when actually preaching, he would call upon God to "make the Word effectual to the salvation of the Soul; still being grieved lest the Enemy should take the Word away from the Conscience, and so it should become unfruitful" (§280).[99]

---

94 Bunyan, *MW*, 8:218-219. In one of Luther's sermons on his Catechism, he preached that "one must pray God to give us a conscience unafraid, which is assured that its sins are forgiven" (Dillenberger, 224).

95 Constance A. Douglas, "Rebirth Through Narrative: John Bunyan's Autobiographies" (Ph. D. diss., Louisiana State University and Agricultural and Mechanical College, 1987), 15.

96 Bunyan, *GA*, 11. Compare Bunyan's evaluation of those who reject the convicting words of a preacher in *The Acceptable Sacrifice*: "Hence they endeavour to *stifle* Conscience, to *choak* Convictions, to *forget* God, to *make* themselves Atheists" (*MW*, 12:51).

97 Bunyan, *GA*, 18, 43, 90. Contrast Bunyan's early temptation to sell Christ with the justification images of his theological works, where he in turn was *bought* by Christ.

98 Ibid., 90.

99 Ibid., 86.

What did Bunyan learn from these temptations? "It is far better that thou do judge thy self, even by preaching plainly to others, then that thou, to save thyself, imprison the truth in unrighteousness: Blessed be God for his help also in this" (§295).[100] For Bunyan, conscience without the word of God is damnable, but by God's help, it draws near to the righteousness of Christ. There is no *ontological* change in the nature of the conscience itself, however. It only undergoes a *relational* change from self-directedness to God-directedness. Hence, again *contra* Douglas, Bunyan did not make the subjective turn in which the inward reliance upon God became inward reliance *apart* from God.[101] It is far better to *judge* oneself by the light of conscience than to attempt to save oneself, Bunyan taught, in opposition to the devil's seemingly sound logic to the contrary.

According to Luther, to defeat the devil one must "play the cunning logician" oneself by giving to the law no more than belongs to it, for the law excludes the joy which comes through faith. Because the sacrament of baptism symbolized for Luther the unmerited grace of God in the new covenant, it was a particularly vivid reminder for him that although he was *peccator*, he was *simul iustus*. When Luther considered that he had been baptized, he found that "my conscience is at rest, where no law is, but altogether forgiveness of sins, peace, quietness, joy, health and everlasting peace."[102] Bunyan's comparatively "lower" sacramentology when he composed *Grace Abounding* did not allow him to see in baptism the outward sign of consolation that Luther found when he warded off the devil by writing, "*Baptizatus sum*."[103] For Bunyan in *Grace Abounding*, God portrays his good will toward men and women most vividly not in baptism, which he did not accept with Luther as an initiation into the church, but in the other chief sacrament, or ordinance, the Lord's Supper. In Christ's instruction, "This do in remembrance of me," Bunyan found the corrective to the devil's invocation of all his past sins. Therefore, Christ's formula of institution "was made a very precious word unto me; for by it the Lord did come down upon my conscience with the discovery of his death

---

100 Ibid., 90.
101 Douglas, 18.
102 Luther, *CG*, 28. In *The Babylonian Captivity of the Church* (1520), Luther also defended his retention of the practice of confession as a half-sacrament because it can serve "as a singular medicine for afflicted consciences" (Dillenberger, 319).
103 Oberman, 105. Cf. ibid., 226-231, for an excellent treatment of how Luther understood baptism as sign and seal of Christ's triumph over the devil.

for my sins, and as I then felt, did as if he plunged me in the vertue of the same" (§253).[104] It was an objective status before God which Bunyan desired – though it is unclear from what he wrote whether he sought it in the actual Supper itself or Christ's verbal command – one by which he could be assured of his standing despite the devil's accurate reminders of his unworthiness.

The objective condition of salvation that Bunyan desired would have been impossible to attain if he were judged by God on the basis of his own righteousness, even a righteousness that had been entrusted to him by Christ. But when the phrase, *"Thy righteousness is in heaven,"* entered his conscience, he thought he could see, as did Stephen (Acts 7:55), Jesus himself at the right hand of God (§229-230).[105] While there is no such exact quotation in scripture as the one which "dashed" upon Bunyan's conscience, Bunyan knew from Luther's *Galatians* that "heavenly righteousness is given us of God without our works or deservings."[106] Bunyan repeated this emphasis in *The Pharisee and the Publicane*: "I am then made righteous first, by the righteousness of another; and because I am thus righteous, God accepteth of my person as such, and bestoweth upon me his Grace .... I am convinced that the means of peace is not to be found any where but in Jesus Christ. Now, by my thus adhering to him, I find stay for my Soul, and peace to my Conscience."[107]

Another term for the process by which the alien righteousness of Christ acquits believers of sin is "imputation." Only the imputed righteousness of Christ can silence the devil's voice, for it provides the objective reality that stills subjective doubt. As Paul Althaus explains, the twin effects of Christian faith for Luther were the

---

104 Bunyan, GA, 79. George Herbert, the English divine who died when Bunyan was five years old, expressed a similar sentiment in his poem entitled "Conscience:" "If thou persistest, I will tell thee, / That I have physic to expel thee. / And the receipt shall be / My Saviour's blood: whenever at his board / I do but taste it, straight it cleanseth me, / And leaves thee not a word; / No, not a tooth or nail to scratch, / And at my actions carp, or catch" (George Herbert, *George Herbert: The Complete English Poems*, ed. John Tobin [London: Penguin Books, 1991], 97-98).
105 Bunyan, *GA*, 72. Cf. Bunyan, *The Doctrine of the Law and Grace Unfolded*: "He [Jesus Christ] is also thy righteousness now at Gods right hand alwayes shining before the eyes of his glory: So that there it is unmoveable, though thou art in never such a sad condition, yet thy righteousness, which is the Son of God, God-man, shines as bright as ever, and is as much accepted of God as ever" (*MW*, 2:222).
106 Luther, *CG*, 23.
107 Bunyan, *MW*, 10:183.

imputation of Christ's righteousness for forgiveness of sins and the establishment of a new self which lives increasingly in righteousness.[108] However, the former effect never depends on the latter effect but in fact, said Luther in *Two Kinds of Righteousness* (1519), always precedes and produces it.[109] Christ imputes his righteousness to the sinner and then induces a desire for lived righteousness in that sinner, but it is always on the basis of Christ's righteousness alone that the sinner is saved. So, Christ's righteousness is imputed to the sinner, but it is not *imparted* to the sinner so as to become the person's personal possession. While some of the later Puritans came to believe that the faith and righteousness by which they were saved became their own "property," Luther and Bunyan always believed that saving righteousness remained the possession of Christ alone.[110] Human faith cannot be adequate for obtaining saving righteousness because it is tainted by original sin; "faith is indeed a formal righteousness, and yet this righteousness is not enough" (3:6).[111] Therefore, human faith may make an effort toward righteousness, "but imputation maketh it perfect unto the day of Christ" (3:6).[112] As Luther further explained in his *Sermons on the Catechism* (1528), "justification by faith" means more precisely justification *through* faith, with the distinction as sharp as possible between any human contribution to salvation (even so much as returning to Christ that which he gives) and Christ's alien, imputed righteousness: "He who believes that he will be saved by his own works and not through Christ [does not believe that Christ is his Lord]."[113]

It is not surprising that Bunyan adopted Luther's use of "imputation" in the *Commentary on Galatians*, since Luther said in the preface that there is no saving righteousness for sinners "unless God himself by mere imputation and by his unspeakable gift do bestow it upon us."[114] "And this acceptation, or imputation, is very necessary," Luther said of Galatians 2:16, so "it is not without good cause, therefore, that we do so often repeat and beat into your minds the forgiveness of sins, and imputation of righteousness for Christ's sake," thereby "pacifying and quieting the conscience."[115] Could it

---

108 Althaus, 235.
109 Luther, *Two Kinds of Righteousness*, in Dillenberger, 86-89.
110 Bunyan, *MW*, 4:47; 10:183.
111 Luther, *CG*, 223.
112 Ibid., 224.
113 Martin Luther, *Sermons on the Catechism*, in Dillenberger, ed., 211.
114 Luther, *CG*, 23.
115 Ibid., 137-139.

be, as with Christian in the Valley of the Shadow of Death, that Bunyan again heard the "voice" of Luther expounding to him the comforts of imputation?

> Now was I as one awakened out of some troublesome sleep and dream, and listening to this heavenly sentence, I was as if I had heard it thus expounded to me; Sinner, thou thinkest that because of thy sins and infirmities I cannot save thy Soul; but behold my Son is by me, and upon him I look, and not on thee, and will deal with thee according as I am pleased with him: at this I was greatly lightened in my mind, and made to understand that God could justifie a sinner at any time; it was but looking upon Christ, and imputing of his benefits to us, and the work was forthwith done. (§258)[116]

Nor should one forget that Bunyan asked his Quaker opponents in *A Vindication of Some Gospel-Truths Opened* if "you did ever see your selvs undone and lost, unlesse the righteousness, blood, death, resurrection, and intercession of that man Christ Jesus (in his own person) was imputed to you? and until you could by faith owne it as done for you, and counted yours by imputation, yea, or no?"[117] Bunyan tried to explain to the Quakers how only the objective work of Christ could prevent "this mercilesse butcherer of men, the Devil," from commandeering the conscience.[118] And in *The Advocateship of Jesus Christ*, he exhorted:

> I know I put thee upon a hard and difficult task, for believing, and expecting Good, when my guilty Conscience doth nothing but clog, burden, and terrifie me with the Justice of God, the Greatness of my Sins, and the burning Torments is hard and Sweating work. But it must be, the Text calls for it, thy case calls for it, and thou must do it, if thou wouldst glorifie Christ. And this is the way to hasten the issue of thy Cause in Hand, for believing Daunts the Devil, pleaseth Christ, and will help thee before-hand, to sing that Song of the Church, saying, *O Lord, thou hast pleaded the Causes of my Soul, thou hast redeemed my Life*, Lam. 3.[119]

According to his own advice in *Grace Abounding*, Bunyan was able to respond to the temptations and rumors that the devil devised against

---

116 Bunyan, *GA*, 80.
117 Bunyan, *A Vindication of Some Gospel-Truths Opened*, in *MW*, 1:182. Bunyan continued to defend the imputed righteousness of Christ soon after *A Vindication* in *The Doctrine of the Law and Grace Unfolded* (1659).
118 Bunyan, *Some Gospel-Truths Opened*, in *MW*, 1:58.
119 Bunyan, *MW*, 11:116.

him with "a good Conscience" – that is, a conscience engaged by imputation in "good conversation in Christ" (§306-310).[120]

Hell

Luther's doctrine of imputed righteousness also influenced Bunyan's perception of hell. All Christians are indeed declared righteous before God through the imputed righteousness of Christ, Luther said. But because they will not be made wholly righteous before the eschaton, then they still will encounter *Anfechtungen* from time to time. Luther often identified these moments of doubtful conscience with hell, which meant that, for him, hell was primarily the condition of feeling terrified under the wrath of God and only secondarily, but no less truly, an actual place.[121] "The real torture of hell, as it already begins to be felt in this life, comes when a man feels in his conscience that God is against him and he cannot endure to be close to God."[122] Such agony of soul was a frequent concern of Luther, "for the devil is wont, in affliction and in the conflict of conscience, by the law to make us afraid, and to lay against us the guilt of sin, our wicked life past, the wrath and judgment of God, hell and eternal death, that by this means he may drive us to desperation, make us bond-slaves to himself, and pluck us from Christ."[123] Because Luther frequently joined together as co-agitators of conscience the law, sin, wrath, death, the devil, and hell, it is easy to see why Bunyan siphoned off from these themes the comforts of Christ's atonement which he said that Luther gave him.

Bunyan recalled trembling "both night and day" over "the fearful torments of Hell-fire" before he was even ten years old (§6), understandably wishing at that point that there was no hell at all (§7). His preoccupation with hell obviously did not begin when he read Luther.[124] Nor did his dread of hell end there. Even after he had gained considerable maturity in Christian faith, a particularly fierce assault from the devil made him think "as if I had my self already descending into the Pit; methought, I said, there was no way but to

---

120 Bunyan, *Some Gospel-Truths Opened*, in *MW* 1:58; *GA*, 93. "Conversation" in this quotations refers to Christian behavior, not simply chatting.
121 Althaus, 208; cf. Richard Marius, *Martin Luther: The Christian Between God and Death* (Cambridge, MA: The Belknap Press of Harvard University Press, 1999), 60-63.
122 Althaus, 177.
123 Luther, *CG*, 27.
124 Bunyan, *GA*, 6.

Hell I must [go]" (§260).¹²⁵ And he knew that he was far from the only person who possessed this dread, for he recalled later in *The Acceptable Sacrifice* (posthumous) that he had "known some that have been made to *Roar* like bears, to *Yell* like Dragons, and to *Howl* like Dogs, by reason of the weight of Guilt, and the lashes of Hell upon their Conscience, for their evil deeds."¹²⁶ Indeed, some of Bunyan's own writings, particularly *A Few Sighs from Hell*, were meant to show his readers the horrors of hell. Recalling his description of the devil as a merciless butcher in *Some Gospel-Truths Opened*, Bunyan further elaborated on the dissected conscience in a section of *One Thing is Needful* (1665) entitled, "*Of Hell, and the estate of those that perish*:"

> Oh Conscience is the slaughter-shop,
> There hangs the Ax, and Knife,
> 'Tis there the worm makes all things hot,
> And wearies out the life.
>
> Here then is execution done,
> On body and on soul,
> For conscience will be brib'd of none,
> But gives to all their doul.¹²⁷

In *A Confession of My Faith* (1672), Bunyan yet again considered his conscience the devil's abattoir, but he set against it the finished work of Christ:

> But if nothing will do, unless I make of my conscience a continual butchery, and slaughter-shop, unless putting out my own eyes I commit me to the blind to lead me, (as I doubt is desired by some) I have determined the Almighty God being my help, and shield, yet to suffer, if frail life might continue so long, even till the moss shall grow on mine eye-browes rather then thus to violate my faith and principles.¹²⁸

Yet how had Bunyan himself overcome the fear of hell? A passage from *The Pilgrim's Progress* helps to illumine the threat of hell that lies beneath one of Bunyan's recurring fears in *Grace Abounding* – namely, that he, following Esau, had sinfully sold his birthright to a heavenly inheritance and could not win it back with any amount of tears. When Christian asks the shepherds of the Delectable Mountains to explain why a door on the side of Mount Caution leads to a

---

125 Ibid., 81.
126 Bunyan, *The Acceptable Sacrifice*, in *MW*, 12:51. Cf. from the same page: "Conscience and Guilt shall, like *Blood Hounds*, find them out in their Secret Places, and *Roar* against them for their wicked Lives."
127 Bunyan, *MW*, 6:94-95. "Doul" means "grief" or "woe" (Ibid., 324).
128 Bunyan, *A Confession of My Faith*, in *MW*, 4:136.

dark, smoky place from which one can hear tormented cries and crackling brimstone, the shepherds reply, "This is a By-way to Hell, a way that Hypocrites go in at; namely, such as sell their Birthright, with *Esau*; such as sell their Master, with *Judas*."[129] Thus, when Bunyan expressed his concern throughout *Grace Abounding* that he had sold his birthright like Esau (§141, 145, 158, 163, 216, 225-226) or betrayed Jesus like Judas (§154, 158-160), he was revealing nothing other than the dread in his conscience of hell, the sure repository of all hypocrites (cf. §32). He even said at one point that the reprobation of Esau affected him "at my heart" (§178), and, following the usage of Luther and the Bible itself, Bunyan sometimes used "heart" and "conscience" interchangeably.[130]

According to Luther, the *real* hypocrite is the person who, after searching his or her conscience, still will not admit that the old self with its dying gasps continues to wage war there (5:17).[131] Even so, it was expressly through admitting his struggles (recall the permission to *"remember your terrours of conscience, and fear of death and hell"*[132]) that Bunyan could finally hope to survive them. In fact, if he should suspect that his conscience was losing its sense of guilt simply from the passage of time rather than through the blood of Christ, "then I would also strive to fetch it upon my heart again, by bringing the punishment for sin in Hell-fire upon my Spirit; and should cry, *Lord, let it not go off my heart but the right way, but by the Blood of Christ"*

---

129 Bunyan, *PP*, 122.
130 Bunyan, *GA*, 55; Zachman, 22. On Luther, cf. Althaus, 53-54; Pelikan, *The Christian Tradition*, 4:133; Oberman, 227. On Bunyan, cf. Bunyan, *GA*, 48-49 (§160); *The Acceptable Sacrifice*, in *MW*, 12:26-27. In the Old Testament, the Hebrew word *lēb* often took on the meaning of "conscience:" see Hahn, 349; Hans Walter Wolff, *Anthropology of the Old Testament*, trans. Margaret Kohl (Philadelphia: Fortress Press, 1974), 51-53. John Milton also used "conscience" and "heart" interchangeably, such as when he replaced the King James Version's translation of "heart" in 1 John 3:20 with "conscience" in *A Treatise of Civil Power* (John Milton, *The Riverside Milton*, ed. Roy Flannagan [Boston: Houghton Mifflin Company, 1998], 1119-1120).
131 Luther, *CG*, 506. Cf. Luther's comment on Galatians 2:16: "A Christian is not he which hath no sin, or feeleth no sin, but he to whom God imputeth not his sin because of his faith in Christ. This doctrine bringeth strong consolation to afflicted consciences in serious and inward terrors" (Ibid., 138).
132 Bunyan, *GA*, 3.

(§86).¹³³ Thus was Bunyan's seeming display of individualism and introspection in fact a means of control against a still further subjectivism. According to Camden, "Luther insists that the only way for the believer to attain certainty is through an affective response based not on unreliable subjectivity, but on an experience of Christ's intervention."¹³⁴ The same is true for Bunyan, who realized in his spiritual maturity that his journey had not been of his own choosing or strength. "God carried me on, but surely with a strong hand: for neither guilt nor hell could take me off my Work" (§277).¹³⁵

The Emerging Picture of the Self in *Grace Abounding*

John Stachniewski gives special notice to Bunyan's "counting myself far worse than a thousand fools" in *Grace Abounding* (§67):

> [Bunyan's] compounding of "myself" is both rare and significant. There are seven instances up to this paragraph but only four hereafter to the Conclusion. There are countless uses of "my self." The virtual disappearance of the conflation coincides with the growing introspection of the record: Bunyan's self becomes an object of scrutiny and concern; it develops into an important concept which, as we know, carries a complex and culturally important history.¹³⁶

Stachniewski contends that Bunyan's preference to separate the words "my" and "self" when speaking of "myself" showed a modern desire to analyze his own selfhood. Spelling and syntax in seventeenth century texts were highly variable, so the detachment of "self" from "my" may not reflect an intentional editorial decision by either Bunyan or his publisher George Larkin. However, if we con-

---

133 Ibid., 28. In the same paragraph, Bunyan contrasts himself with those who, "seeking rather present Ease from their Trouble, then Pardon for their Sin, cared not how they lost their guilt, so they got it out of their minde." He, instead, looked to Christ "not onely [to] deliver me from the guilt that by these things was laid upon my Conscience, but also from the very filth thereof," (§114), fearing any consequences if his decision "should not come from God" (§173) (Ibid., 36, 52). Cf. U. Milo Kaufmann's comment that Bunyan learned that his variable states of mind did not affect the righteousness which he had through Christ (Kaufmann, "*The Pilgrim's Progress* and *The Pilgrim's Regress*: John Bunyan and C. S. Lewis on the Shape of the Christian Quest," in *Bunyan in Our Time*, ed. Robert G. Collmer [Kent, OH: The Kent State University Press, 1989], 190).
134 Camden, "Most Fit," 834.
135 Bunyan, *GA*, 86.
136 John Stachniewski, ed., in *GAOSA*, 21, 237.

cede Stachniewski's point that *Grace Abounding* was a pioneer text in auto-analysis, then what picture can we develop from a close reading of Bunyan's uses of the word "self" that will fit within the frame of his Lutheran conception of conscience? I believe that there is indeed a marked shift in Bunyan's use of the word "self"over the course of *Grace Abounding*. In the first half of his autobiography, in which he recalled so desperately seeking to diagnose and cure the source of his spiritual malady, Bunyan spoke of his "self"[137] in excoriating terms that correspond to his negative evaluation of the natural conscience both in *Grace Abounding* and the anti-Quaker works. Here are several examples:

> Now you must know, that before this I had taken much delight in ringing, but my Conscience beginning to be tender, I thought that such a practice was but vain, and therefore forced my self to leave it, yet my mind hanckered, wherefore I should go to the Steeple house, and look on: though I durst not ring. But I thought this did not become Religion neither, yet I forced my self and would look on still; but quickly after, I began to think, How, if one of the Bells should fall. (§33)[138]

> I was for a while made afraid to see my want of Faith; but God would not suffer me thus to undo and destroy my *Soul*, but did continually, against this my blinde and sad conclusion, create still within me such suppositions, That I might in this deceive my self; that I could not rest content until I did now come to some certain knowledge whether I had Faith or no. (§49)[139]

---

137 I intentionally split "himself " into "his self " to follow the separation which Stachniewski employs in Bunyan's text of "myself " into "my self." As some of the quotations below make evident, however, Roger Sharrock's "definitive" edition of *Grace Abounding* sometimes does not split "myself " as Stachniewski's edition does. I take that as having no consequence for my project here, however, since I am investigating Bunyan's concept of "self," whether he adjoined it directly to "my" or not.

138 Bunyan, *GA*, 13.

139 Bunyan, *GAOSA*, 17. *GA*, 18, does not include "That I might in this deceive my self " in §49, but it does mention the phrase as a variant reading in the textual apparatus. The certain knowledge of faith for which Bunyan seeks in this paragraph reminds one of John Calvin's definition of faith in his *Institutes*: "Now we shall possess a right definition of faith if we call it a firm and certain knowledge of God's benevolence toward us, founded upon the truth of the freely given promise in Christ, both revealed to our minds and sealed upon our hearts through the Holy Spirit" (III.ii.7) (Calvin, *Institutes of the Christian Religion*, The Library of Christian Classics 20, ed. John T. McNeill, trans. Ford Lewis Battles [Philadelphia: The Westminster Press, 1960], vol. 1, 551).

I went up and down bemoaning my sad condition, counting myself far worse than a thousand fools, for standing off thus long, and spending so many years in sin as I have done; still crying out, Oh that I had turned sooner! Oh that I had turned seven years agoe; it made me also angry with my self, to think that I should have no more wit but to trifle away my time till my Soul and Heaven were lost. (§67)[140]

And *now* was I both a burden and a terror, to my self, nor did I ever so know, as *now*, what it was to be weary of my life, and yet afraid to die. O how gladly *now* would I have been any body but my self, any thing but a man, and in any condition but mine own. (§149)[141]

Once as I was walking to and fro in a good mans Shop, bemoaning to my self in my sad and doleful state, afflicting my self with self abhorrence for this wicked and ungodly thought ... suddenly there was as if there had rushed in at the Window, the noise of Wind upon me, but very pleasant, and as if I had heard a Voice speaking, *Didst* [thou] *ever refuse to be justified by the Blood of Christ?* (§174)[142]

There are many other passages confirming the point that when Bunyan used the term "self" in the first half of *Grace Abounding*, he typically associated it with a verb of violent action: he forced it, deceived it, was angry with it, was a burden and terror to it, and afflicted it. However, when Bunyan considered the blood of Christ – as at the end of the last quotation above – and its power to silence the law, the devil, and the conscience, he began to speak of his self in much milder terms. There was a precursor of this different usage early in *Grace Abounding* when Bunyan said that he took pride in keeping the commandments because then he "had great peace in my Conscience, and should think with my self, God cannot chuse but be now pleased with me" (§35).[143] When Bunyan thought that God was pleased with him, and his conscience was at peace, then he *thought* with his self. But this particular instance brought an illusory peace since, as I have already demonstrated, Bunyan then became preoccupied with the knowledge that only the blood of Christ could cleanse his conscience permanently (cf. Heb 9:14). Yet, when he did finally become convinced that it *was* Christ, and not his own legal (i.e., self-generated) righteousness, who had removed his

---

140 Bunyan, *GA*, 22.
141 Bunyan, *GAOSA*, 42. This paragraph first appeared in the fifth edition of *Grace Abounding* in 1680. *GA*, 45, uses "myself" instead of "my self."
142 Bunyan, *GAOSA*, 48. This paragraph first appeared in the third edition of *Grace Abounding* in 1674(?). *GA*, 52, uses "myself" instead of "my self."
143 Bunyan, *GA*, 14.

burden, he largely exchanged bitter descriptions of the self for calm and rational ones. In the second half of *Grace Abounding*, this new description of self often followed Bunyan's remembrance of past words of divine assurance, to wit:

> Wherefore I began with all seriousness to examine my former comfort, and to consider whether one that have sinned as I have done, might with confidence trust upon the faithfulness of God laid down in those words by which I had been comforted, and on which I had leaned my self. (§196)[144]

> I could recal my self sometimes, and give my self a help. (§199)[145]

> Now I began to consider with my self, that God had a bigger mouth to speak with, than I had heart to conceive with; I thought also with my self, that he spake not his words in haste, or in an unadvised heat, but with infinite wisdom and judgement, and in very truth and faithfulness. (§249)[146]

> Now was I got on high; I saw my self within the arms of Grace and Mercy; and though I was before afraid to think of a dying hour, yet now I cried, Let me die; now death was lovely and beautiful in my sight, for I saw we shall never live indeed till we be gone to the other World. (§259)[147]

When Bunyan viewed his self in relation to the promises of scripture, instead of expressing displeasure with his self, he leaned it on the faithfulness of God, gave it help, thought of it and considered it in relationship to divine promises, and saw it secure in the arms of Grace and Mercy. Notice, as well, that these passages in which Bunyan spoke of his self in this new, more lenient way are all in the second half of the book, *after* recalling the encounter with Luther's *Galatians*. By this I do not intend to suggest that there are *no* irenic references to self in the first half of *Grace Abounding* nor hostile references to self in the second half. But the general pattern still holds because the lenient references in the first half are few and turn out to be false assessments of the self apart from the blood of Christ, and the few belligerent references in the second half are a result of the occasional skirmish with Satan that Bunyan, along with Luther, expected to take place in the Christian conscience.

An example of the latter point occurred when Bunyan revealed why he submitted to imprisonment rather than forego his unli-

---

144 Bunyan, *GAOSA*, 56. *GA*, 61, renders "myself" instead of "my self" and "had sinned" instead of "have sinned."
145 Bunyan, *GAOSA*, 57. *GA*, 62, renders "myself" instead of "my self."
146 Bunyan, *GAOSA*, 70. *GA*, 77, renders "myself" instead of "my self."
147 Bunyan, *GAOSA*, 73. *GA*, 80-81, renders "myself" instead of "my self."

cenced preaching. Bunyan did not *say* that he went to jail for the principle of liberty of conscience, as Roger Pooley, N. H. Keeble, and any number of other Bunyan scholars have claimed.[148] Perhaps the best clue to Bunyan's thinking comes from the title page of an early prison work, *Christian Behaviour* (1663), where Bunyan described himself as "a Prisoner of *Hope.*"[149] Even as "Prisoner" suggests a condition quite different from that of "liberty," so too, was "Hope" for Bunyan something quite different from "conscience." Conscience was the place where he felt distress that he may be disapproved like Esau, but hope was the triumph over fear by the objective word of Christ, such as when Bunyan said in *Grace Abounding*, "I had freely left the Lord Jesus Christ to his choice, whether he would be my Saviour or no, for the wicked words were these, *Let him go if he will*. Then that Scripture gave me hope, *I will never leave thee nor forsake thee*, Heb. 13.5. O Lord, said I, but I have left thee; then it answered again, *but I will not leave thee*. For this I thank God also" (§216).[150] It was on the premise of this objective hope in the liberty of Christ (not natural conscience) that Bunyan did not resist the order for his arrest.

For Bunyan, going to jail was not a statement about civil liberty

---

[148] Pooley, "*Grace Abounding* and the New Sense of Self," 114; N. H. Keeble, "'Till One Greater Man / Restore Us ...': Restoration Images in Bunyan and Milton," in *Awakening Words: John Bunyan and the Language of Community*, ed. David Gay, James G. Randall, and Arlette Zinck (Newark: University of Delaware Press, 2000), 33. Cf. Richard L. Greaves, "Conscience, Liberty, and the Spirit: Bunyan and Nonconformity," in *John Bunyan and English Nonconformity* (London: The Hambledon Press, 1992), 53, 59; Louise Kretzschmar, *Privatization of the Christian Faith: Mission, Social Ethics and the South African Baptists* (Legon, Ghana: Legon Theological Studies Series, 1998), 145; Sim and Walker, 221. To what extent Bunyan's surrender nonetheless *may have been* for the sake of conscience will be the subject of Chapter Four, on Bunyan's contributions to the political debates of his century over liberty of conscience and religious toleration. John Piper claims that Bunyan chose "prison and a clear conscience over freedom and a conscience soiled by the agreement not to preach" (Piper, *The Hidden Smile of God: The Fruit of Affliction in the Lives of John Bunyan, William Cowper, and David Brainerd* [Wheaton, IL: Crossway Books, 2001], 56).

[149] Bunyan, MW, 3:5. As Keeble, "'Till One Greater Man,'" points out (29), "Prisoner of *Hope*" was replaced by "Servant of Christ" in the third edition, but this new title is essentially only a synonym for the former: "Prisoner" and "Servant" are both terms of submission, while Bunyan saw Christ as his only "*Hope*," and thus he speaks of hope in connection with Christ in *Grace Abounding*.

[150] Bunyan, GA, 68.

as much as a statement about self-abnegation and death: "If ever I would suffer rightly, I must first pass a sentence of death upon everything that can properly be called a thing of this life, even to reckon my Self, my Wife, my Children, my health, my enjoyments, and all, as dead to me, and my self as dead to them" (§326).[151] Yet, "notwithstanding these helps, I found my self a man, and compassed with infirmities; the parting with my Wife and poor Children hath oft been to me in this place, as the pulling [of] the flesh from my bones" (§327).[152] Did imprisonment bring a crisis of the self upon Bunyan? Surely it did, and one sees the conflict most vividly where Bunyan described his self as torn between concern for the welfare of his family, particularly his blind daughter Mary, on the one hand, and his divine calling to preach on the other. Yet two things steeled his resolve. Regarding his family, "recalling my self, thought I, I must venture you all with God, though it goeth to the quick to leave you"(§328).[153] And then this:

> I had also another consideration, and that was, The dread of the torments of Hell, which I was sure they must partake of, that for fear of the Cross do shrink from their profession of Christ, his Word and Laws, before the sons of men: I thought also of the glory that he had prepared for those that, in faith, and love, and patience, stood to his ways before them. These things, I say, have helped me, when the thoughts of the misery that both my self and mine might, for the sake of my profession, be exposed to, hath lain pinching on my mind. (§331)[154]

Bunyan feared the negative repercussions of surrendering his principles, not only for his own soul but for those others to whom he was a spiritual model.

> Thus was I tossed for manie weeks, and knew not what to do; at last this consideration fell with weight upon me, That it was for the Word and Way of God that I was in this condition, wherefore I was ingaged not to flinch a hair's breadth from it.... For I am resolved, (God give me strength) never to deny my profession, though I have nothing at all for my pains; and as I was thus considering,

---

151 Ibid., 97. *GA* agrees with *GAOSA*, 89, on the separation of "my" and "self."
152 Bunyan, *GAOSA*, 89. Sharrock's edition, 98 does not segregate "my" from "self." Cf. the similar words of Dr. Rowland Taylor before being led to his execution at Aldham-common in Hadley: "Farewell, my dear wife; be of good comfort, for I am quiet in my conscience. God shall stir up a father for my children" (Foxe, 228).
153 Bunyan, *GA*, 98; *GAOSA*, 89-90.
154 Bunyan, *GA*, 99; *GAOSA*, 90.

that Scripture was set before me, Psa. 44.12. &c. (§337-338)[155]

Thus did Bunyan not explain his behavior with a modern notion of "liberty of conscience." Like Luther's, his conscience was bound to the word of God.

Individualism and Subjectivism in Bunyan and Luther

In demonstrating the indebtedness of Bunyan to Luther's views of conscience, I have already provided some direction for the critical question that now concerns the remainder of this chapter: What is the evidence for and against the argument that their tendencies toward individualism rolled over into something more subjective, resembling the modern *autonomous* self?[156] Here I must reiterate what a distinctive mark Luther left on Bunyan. In the second half of the seventeenth century, very few English Nonconformists held tenaciously to Luther's formula of justification *sola fide* and *sola gratia* as Bunyan did, because leading Puritan thinkers such as Richard Baxter suspected Luther of antinomianism.[157] In short, despite the fact that Bunyan breathed in Puritan air, one can expect that his notions of selfhood – because dependent upon Luther's views of conscience, law, and gospel – would be somewhat different from other currents of thought in England during Bunyan's day, which were moving toward modernity.[158] In Chapter Two, we saw by comparison how Bunyan's individualist tendencies were not as extreme as those of the Quakers. Now we must ask: To what extent *did* Bun-

---

155 Bunyan, *GA*, 100-101. Cf. Vera J. Camden, "Blasphemy and the Problem of the Self in *Grace Abounding*," *Bunyan Studies* 1:2 (Spring 1989): 19.
156 In forthcoming chapters on Bunyan's political views and fictional works, I will address more directly how Bunyan both blended with and challenged various issues within the Puritan theological milieu during the four decades of his professional life.
157 Camden, "Most Fit," 823; Greaves thinks that it is the experiential character of faith which Bunyan absorbed from Luther that enabled his autobiography and imaginative works to retain more lasting appeal than other Puritan works. He further explains that "for Bunyan salvation signified, as it had for Luther, fundamentally escape from the awesome wrath of God. The emphasis of both Luther and Bunyan was on salvation *from* something, whereas most Calvinists, while acknowledging that the elect were saved from sin and divine wrath, nevertheless stressed salvation *to* something, namely, the holy life of a regenerate man" (Greaves, *John Bunyan*, 25, 50). Cf. Vera J. Camden, "Blasphemy and Belief in *Grace Abounding*," *American Baptist Quarterly* 7:4 (December 1988): 462. I will return to Baxter's charge of antinomianism in Chapter Seven.
158 Cf. Greaves, *John Bunyan*, 28, 155.

yan's Lutheranism float with the surging individualist tide toward subjectivism?

Michael G. Baylor restates the classic objection to the doctrine of *sola scriptura* when he says that if there is no objective test for determining the truth content of scripture other than the individual conscience, then the assurance of faith rests only in subjective certainty.[159] Yet, Luther himself apparently saw this danger to true faith in the Anabaptists and other radical groups when he appraised their extreme individualism as the opposite danger from Roman Catholic institutionalism.[160] So he lectured on Romans,

> The vice of pride, the denial of the truthfulness and righteousness of God, [is] the establishment of one's own righteousness and the defense of one's own wisdom, which renders men faithless, heretical, schismatic, full of superstition, individualistic or particularistic. (4:17)[161]

---

159 Michael G. Baylor, *Action and Person: Conscience in Late Scholasticism and the Young Luther*, Studies in Medieval and Reformation Thought 20 (Leiden: E. J. Brill, 1977), 256. Cf. Herreshoff, 169. McGrath suggests that Luther's conception of Christian faith was more individualistic than that of Calvin and Zwingli because concern for the commonweal of the city was much more a part of magisterial Swiss reform than German (81, 165). Meg Lota Brown claims much when she says that "one effect of Luther's emphasis on individual conscience and judgment was that all Christians were encouraged to be their own casuists" (Meg Lota Brown, *Donne and the Politics of Conscience in Early Modern England*, Studies in the History of Christian Thought 61 [Leiden: E. J. Brill, 1995], 37).

160 Pelikan, *The Christian Tradition*, 4:173. Recall that Bunyan, too, warned in *The Heavenly Foot-man* to "be sure thou have a care of *Quakers, Ranters, Free-Willers*: Also do not have too much Company with some *Anabaptists*, though I go under that name my self" (Bunyan, *MW*, 5:153). Further recall his comparison of Catholics and radicals in *A Defence of the Doctrine of Justification, By Faith* (see page 38, above).

161 Martin Luther, *Lectures on Romans: Glosses and Scholia*, ed. Hilton C. Oswald, *Luther's Works*, vol. 25 (Saint Louis: Concordia Publishing House, 1972), 271. Oswald's note 26, in ibid., is worth restating here: "'Individualistic' and 'particularistic' are translations of *moniacus* and *monicus* respectively, both extensions of the thought in the Greek μονιός 'singular.' In his lecture on Ps. 31:2 Luther had named among the self-righteous the *superstitiosi in singularitate* and had described them as people 'who reject obedience and faith and set up their own righteousness, because they are unwilling to have the name of the Lord worshiped above themselves.' In his lectures on 1 Timothy in 1528, Luther said: 'The monks called this fault *singularitas*, that a monk who was dissatisfied with his rule would adopt the hair shirt. In my order the leaders used to oppose "individualism" strenuously, and that was good.'"

Moreover, through the worship of Baal [in ancient Israel] there was depicted a monstrous form of righteousness and superstitious piety which prevails widely to this day. By means of this the Jews, heretics, and monks, that is, arrogant, individualists, worship the true God according to their own ideas with most ridiculous zeal. (11:4)[162]

Baylor perceives that Luther *tried* to resist the subjectivist slide and would not have recognized speech about "freedom of conscience" in the modern sense, but since Luther more than anyone before him closely knitted together conscience and the content of faith, he prepared the way for claims of subjective authority at the dawn of the modern era.[163] Bernhard Lohse, on the other hand, cannot in the end support the idea that modern subjectivity owes its beginning to Luther. He agrees with Baylor that Luther's conjoining of conscience and faith may indeed have brought the curtain down on the Middle Ages, but someone other than Luther, such as Descartes or Locke, had to make the further transition toward individual autonomy.[164] After all, Luther did not grant to Anabaptists the same right of conscience which he claimed for himself at the Diet of Worms, because he did not believe that their consciences were sufficiently grounded in the divine Word, and he even admitted the fallibility of his own conscience when he stood ready to be convinced by scripture or reason that he was in error. Thus does Harold Bloom consider the interiority of Luther to be much less developed than that of Shakespeare's *Hamlet*, and Lohse agrees that "Luther's statements about reason or about the conscience were never intended to assert the autonomy of either in the modern sense."[165] In *Galatians*, Luther himself wrote, "This is the reason why our doctrine is [most sure and] certain: because it carrieth us out of ourselves, that we should not lean to our own strength, our own conscience, our own feeling, our own person, and our own works, but to that which is without us, that is to say, the promise and truth of God which cannot deceive us."[166]

---

162 Ibid., 422. Cf. a similar comparison by Luther of individualists with heretics on Romans 7:8; ibid., 337; and Romans 9:28; ibid., 398.
163 Baylor, 259, 271-272.
164 Lohse, "Conscience," 159, 178-183. Cf. Bainton, 141; Oberman, 204.
165 Harold Bloom, *Shakespeare: The Invention of the Human* (New York: Riverhead Books, 1998), 409; Bernhard Lohse, *Martin Luther: An Introduction to His Life and Work*, trans. Robert C. Schultz (Philadelphia: Fortress Press, 1986), 162.
166 Luther, *CG*, 372 (4:6).

Herein lies the enigma of Bunyan: he struggled to learn with and from Luther that grace, not his variegated experience, determined his salvation, yet he could only confirm such faith through many, many experiences of doubt.[167] He admitted as much in *Grace Abounding*: "I verily thought, and found by experience, that what was taught me by the Word and Spirit of Christ, could be spoken, maintained and stood to, by the soundest and best established Conscience: and though I will not now speak all that I know in this matter; yet my experience hath more interest in that text of Scripture, *Gal*. 1.11,12 than many amongst men are aware" (§285).[168] Because of such admissions, Haskin concludes that Bunyan was "long imprisoned in self-centeredness," and John N. Morris says in agreement that Bunyan's failure even to mention his first wife's name or his baptism in *Grace Abounding* proves his complete absorption with interiority.[169] As Baylor does for Luther, so Stachniewski thinks that Bunyan's desire to establish that he is not a reprobate cannot avoid becoming an occasion for self-formation of the subject.[170] Moreover, Roger Pooley adds that "the authority of the Bible, and the authority of the called individual's reading of it that so pervades *Grace Abounding* means that Bunyan's sense of self is radically subjective in the new sense, to do with self-recognition and self-regulation."[171]

Do such assessments of *Grace Abounding* reckon adequately with Bunyan's purpose, which this chapter identifies and explains – to pass along to his readers the same conscience-soothing remedy that he received from Luther, along with the instructions that one should take this medicine with a sanguine dose of the memory of past sins

---

167 Greaves, *John Bunyan*, 53-54, believes that the personal experience of the grace of God influenced the doctrines of election which Luther and Bunyan formulated. Cf. Bunyan, *GAOSA*, xiii; Sim and Walker, 220. Hill, *Tinker*, comments that "Bunyan was driven back to the individualistic foundations of Protestantism, to Luther" (74).

168 Bunyan, *GA*, 87-88. Cf. Luther on Galatians 1:11: "Moreover, the matter of justification is brittle: not of itself, for of itself it is most sure and certain, but in respect of us. Whereof I myself have good experience. For I know in what hours of darkness I sometimes wrestle" (*CG*, 76). Cf. Camden, "Most Fit," 821-822. Also cf. Sharrock, *John Bunyan*: "The tendency of Puritanism to make the regeneration of the individual soul the central fact of religious experience encouraged the keeping of diaries and the compilation of minute accounts of conversion" (55). It is this impetus toward self-analysis which Sharrock believes became secularized in modernity: ibid., 57.

169 Haskin, "Bunyan's Scriptural Acts," 73; Morris, 91; cf. Jagodzinski, 58.

170 Stachniewski, 85, 128, 154.

171 Pooley, "*Grace Abounding* and the New Sense of Self," 114.

now overcome? Eberhard Jüngel observes that, for Luther, "the inner man is constituted from outside the self."[172] Likewise, while Bunyan's individualism is apparent in *Grace Abounding*, any allegation of his autonomous subjectivity ignores the truth that, for him, the real *subject* of his narrative was not himself but Jesus Christ. And though it may not always be fully evident in *Grace Abounding*, Bunyan was, after all, telling a story about entrance into the church: the impetus for his personal pilgrimage was his desire to stand with the Christians of Bedford on a "Mountain [that] signified the Church of the living God" (§55), and its *telos* was that he be "made a Servant to the Church" (§304).[173] Thus, while most critical readers of *Grace Abounding* have focused on its interiority, its journey inward was actually reversed into a journey outward, for Bunyan was putting his life on display for the public good. As Cecile M. Jagodzinski claims, Bunyan did not write his autobiography for its own sake; it was the meaning of that individual life for the Christian community that made it worthy of retelling.[174] This must be seen as the corrective to any notion that Bunyan relegated his religion entirely to the private sphere.[175]

Conclusion

Mark E. Dever observes that while the Puritan theologian Richard Sibbes remained a conformist, his talk of "educating" the conscience inspired later generations of dissenters. Bunyan certainly believed that the conscience requires proper education.[176] What

---

172 Eberhard Jüngel, *The Freedom of a Christian: Luther's Significance for Contemporary Theology*, trans. Roy A. Harrisville (Minneapolis: Augsburg Publishing House, 1988), 61. Cf. Jüngel's very helpful elaboration on Luther's distinction of the "outer" and "inner" persons and how the "inner" person properly matures as a Christian only as turned outside itself to God's Word (62-65).
173 Bunyan, *GA*, 20, 92.
174 Jagodzinski, 58-65.
175 I will argue when treating *The Pilgrim's Progress* in Chapter Five that Part II shows Bunyan's full intention to bring doubting souls into the reassuring community.
176 Hill, *World*, 407. Cf. the telling observation by Sharrock, "Bunyan Studies Today:" "The biggest shift in our post-war attitude to Bunyan might be defined like this. He has come to be seen, not as an isolated heroic individual, a Carlylean figure, the mechanick preacher as hero after the pattern laid down by John Brown, but as an exemplar of the Puritan culture, someone in a group with contemporaries whose works have analogues and rub together with the works of other men" (53).

Dever says of Sibbes's understanding of conscience is thus also relevant to Bunyan:

> While the importance of conscience has not gone unnoticed in the secondary literature on the seventeenth century, "conscience" tends to occur in connection with the words "liberty" and "freedom," whereas in Sibbes and his contemporaries, ... it occurs more typically in conjunction with the concepts of "obligation" and "judgment." Where the twentieth-century writer has often seen the ground of a civil liberty to come, the seventeenth-century divine saw a remnant of God's law. What is one to make of this difference? Is this a misunderstanding concerning the conscience by later more secular writers, or was Sibbes's teaching on conscience in fact allowing for, even encouraging, social implications that lay unforeseen to him? Furthermore, did Sibbes present conscience as an unerring guide to eternity, or is this the understanding of a more individualistic age cast backwards?[177]

As Dever argues for Sibbes, so do I contend that interpretations of Bunyan's autobiography, when predicated upon his allegedly modern advocacy of liberty of conscience, are anachronistic, retrojecting contemporary concerns onto Bunyan. Since conscience was *not* an autonomous and unerring guide for Bunyan or Luther, it is a misunderstanding of Bunyan's Lutheran conception of conscience to regard *Grace Abounding* as a wholly subjectivist work.[178] There are individualist tendencies present, but there is also a Luther-influenced growth in self-understanding that is not autonomous.

---

177 Mark E. Dever, *Richard Sibbes: Puritanism and Calvinism in Late Elizabethan and Early Stuart England* (Macon, GA: Mercer University Press, 2000), 187. Cf. Hill, *World*, 372.

178 I will demonstrate in the next chapter how Bunyan's resistance against allowing individual conscience to degenerate into subjective anarchy dictated his political views. Cf. Hill, *Century*, 145; *World*, 42.

Chapter Four

Conflicts of Conscience in Bunyan's Political Writings

In his study of the Italian Renaissance, Jacob Burckhardt suggests that a heightened sense of the individual demarcates modern from medieval times. Difficult life under despotic rulers forced medieval persons who had previously looked to race or nation for self-understanding to turn to "inward resources" instead, and they eventually came to think of themselves in individual rather than collective terms.[1] A definite political corollary of the new individualism in Europe was the growing call, especially by the time of the Enlightenment, for toleration and freedom of conscience in the public sphere, with perhaps the quintessential example being John Locke. Locke said that because all persons must construct their lives individually without the foundation of innate ideas, they should also have civil liberties conducive for them doing so. Since the introspective writings of John Bunyan (who was Locke's slightly older contemporary) reflected and, to a degree, furthered the individualist ethos of his era, one might easily assume that Bunyan would have petitioned the state to permit free exercise of conscience to religious nonconformists like himself. However, as Christopher Hill points out, "Unlike Levellers, Cromwell, and Locke, Bunyan contributed nothing to the theory of toleration, proclaimed no principles of natural right."[2] I believe that Bunyan's failure to construct a systematic theory of toleration and free exercise of conscience – remarkable enough from someone whose legacy is "the great seventeenth-century religious writer and contender for religious conscience"[3] – was not a result of neglect but rather of his conflicted Puritan heritage on the relationship between church and state.

---

1   Jacob Burckhardt, *The Civilisation of the Renaissance in Italy*; trans. S. G. C. Middlemore (New York: Harper and Row, 1958), 143.
2   Hill, *Tinker*, 340. For an analysis of how John Locke at the end of the seventeenth century argued as had Gerard Winstanley and the radical Levellers during the Interregnum for toleration based on individual sovereignty, cf. Sim and Walker, 22-25, 32.
3   Robert G. Collmer, ed., *Bunyan in Our Time* (Kent, OH: The Kent State University Press, 1989), inside front sleeve.

The classic Puritan statements on liberty of conscience were made by William Perkins (1558-1602) and his student at Cambridge, William Ames (1576-1633). Yet their writings assumed that the Calvinistic worship for which they desired liberty would also become the religion of the state church and thus have the support and protection of the crown. However, when their disciples found themselves in an adversarial relationship with the unsympathetic Stuart kings James I and Charles I, the Perkins-Ames linking of liberty of conscience with established religion could no longer hold. Nowhere was this tension more evident than in America, where Puritan immigrants who were dissatisfied with Caroline England tried to establish new governments of their own. Was the most important goal of society, as John Cotton believed, the establishment of a single state religion that could maintain public order, or instead, as Roger Williams argued, that liberty of conscience be unfolded to its fullest extent so that even Catholics and Anabaptists could worship freely? Both Cotton and Williams could appeal to the Perkins-Ames tradition to argue their position. With Bunyan, however, the debate became internalized. Having been imprisoned for over twelve years after the Restoration of Charles II in 1660, Bunyan vigorously desired religious liberty for his nonconformist congregation, and he showed no serious belief that Nonconformity could ever be the religion of all. And yet, in his overtly political writings, he assumed a role for magistrates in contending for true religion that seems to be a holdover of the older, establishment kind of Puritanism. The juxtaposition of his individualist tendencies and his nostalgia for a king who would be a Protestant *defensor pacis* left Bunyan at a halting post on the bridge between the pre-modern and modern world views.

Liberty of Conscience in William Perkins and William Ames

According to Perkins in *A Discourse of Conscience* (1596), "Conscience is appointed of God to declare and put in execution his just judgement against sinners: and as God cannot possibly be overcome of man, so neither can the judgement of Conscience being the judgement of God be wholly extinguished."[4] Perkins's emphasis on the conscience as the testimony of God to believers became the basis

---

4   William Perkins, *William Perkins (1558-1602), English Puritanist: His Pioneer Works on Casuistry: "A Discourse of Conscience" and "The Whole Treatise of Cases of Conscience,"* ed. Thomas F. Merrill (Nieuwkoop, The Netherlands: B. DeGraaf, 1966), 3.

for the later Puritan idea that individual conscience *must* be obeyed. Perkins himself did not believe that the conscience was infallible, however: since the conscience was affected by original sin, persons should properly educate their consciences by the Scriptures, which are *in*fallible (when interpreted by Calvinistic orthodoxy). If properly instructed, the conscience could then accurately judge for a person whether his or her actions were godly or ungodly. And since such a conscience spoke for God directly to the person's understanding, and the will of God must always supersede the will of human beings, conscience was *de facto* a superior authority to all human institutions. In sum, Perkins said, "God hath now in the new testament given a liberty to the conscience, whereby it is freed from all laws of his own whatsoever, excepting such laws and doctrines as are necessary to salvation."[5]

If the conscience's liberty for Perkins was superior to all human authority, to what extent did he think a Christian should have been subject to earthly powers, both civil and ecclesiastical? Perkins believed that a Christian should obey these powers, not because of their inherent authority, but because their authority also derived from God: "And it is God onely that gives liberty to the conscience, in regard to his owne lawes. Upon this it followeth, that no mans commandment or Law can of it self, and by its owne soveraigne power bind conscience, but doth it onely by the authoritie and vertue of the written word of God, or some part thereof."[6] Thus would a Christian conscience dictate obedience to civil and ecclesiastical laws, at least insofar as they were consistent with Scripture – and Perkins believed that the church and state of Elizabethan England were indeed consonant. Perkins had little regard for Anabaptists and other sectarian groups which did not accommodate themselves to the Church of England, for the Church's authority was divinely given. Moreover, Perkins believed that the teachings of the Roman Catholic Church were not in agreement with Scripture, and therefore Catholic claims for authority could not have come from God and should not be obeyed. This was because human beings were to obey earthly authorities only insofar as their consciences told them they were obeying God in so doing. This meant that "if it should fall out that men's laws be made of things evil, and forbid-

---

5 William Perkins, *Works* I (London: 1612-1618), 529; quoted in L. John Van Til, *Liberty of Conscience: The History of a Puritan Idea* (Nutley, NJ: Craig Press, 1972), 20.
6 Perkins, 100.

den by God, then there is no bond of conscience at all: but contrariwise men are bound in conscience not to obey."⁷

As L. John Van Til points out, Perkins's conception of conscience was different from that of his monarch, Queen Elizabeth. The Elizabethan Settlement presumed that the monarch had the prerogative to dictate to the consciences of her subjects: only those who worshiped according to her measures would be officially tolerated, let them think in private what they would. Perkins, however, was not interested in a toleration of this sort, because he did not concede that the crown should enforce private opinions as the pragmatic political basis for keeping the peace. Yet, because he nonetheless observed that the teachings of Elizabethan *divines* were consistent with Scripture, Perkins remained a staunch Anglican who could write, "Men therefore must consider that they are Christians, and live in a Christian Commonwealth,"⁸ and he could not have known that his theology of conscience would be turned *against* the state church by nonconformists during the Stuart period. Yet Perkins's exaltation of conscience also contributed mightily to the individualist element of Puritanism. By removing societal and communal barriers between the individual conscience and God, Perkins left the individual to stand alone before God to work out his or her salvation with fear and trembling. This was perpetuated by Perkins's friends at Cambridge, whose "attraction to liberty of conscience inherently assumed the sovereignty of the individual."⁹

Ames played Elisha to Perkins's Elijah: if Perkins was the most influential Puritan writer of his day in England, his student Ames could have claimed the same after Perkins's death, and Ames certainly had a very significant influence in America. While Ames himself was never able to fulfill his desire to join his friend John Winthrop in Massachusetts, virtually every new ship which arrived at the Bay colony brought new editions of Ames's works, so that in John Dykstra Eusden's opinion, "in early American theological and intellectual history, William Ames was without peer."¹⁰ Perry Miller also calls Ames "the father of the New England church polity."¹¹ Ames desired to leave England in reaction to the Laudian persecu-

---

7   Perkins, Works I, 530; quoted in Van Til, *Liberty of Conscience*, 22.
8   Perkins, Works II, quoted in *Puritan Political Ideas, 1558-1794*, ed. Edmund S. Morgan (Indianapolis: The Bobbs-Merrill Company, Inc., 1965), 71.
9   Van Til, *Liberty of Conscience*, 42.
10 John Dykstra Eusden, trans., in William Ames, *The Marrow of Theology* (Grand Rapids: Baker Books, 1997), 11.
11 Perry Miller, *Errand Into the Wilderness* (Cambridge, MA: Harvard University Press, 1993), 58.

tion of the Puritans during the reign of King Charles I. Yet while his high view of conscience was very similar to that of Perkins – "The Conscience is immediately subject to God, and his will, and therefore it cannot submit it self unto any creature without Idolatry"[12] – he pled for godlier magistrates rather than insist that liberty of conscience permitted separation from a church that had become oppressive. Therefore, Ames was unwilling to relinquish the medieval idea that the magistrate was responsible for promoting the laws of God. Even when the magistrates were ungodly, Ames believed, they must be obeyed because they had nonetheless been established by God; in this, he was consistent with John Calvin. On the other hand, should a magistrate discover that certain citizens held erroneous theological beliefs, Ames suggested that the magistrate had a responsibility to coerce their consciences for the good of society and the glory of God. It was this idea that John Cotton defended and Roger Williams rejected – both in the name of conscience – in Massachusetts. And it was this legacy of political subservience that Bunyan in good conscience could not entirely relinquish.

From Ames's perspective, since Paul summoned the Christian to put off the old self, sometimes external force was necessary to induce this change in heretics. In *Conscience, with the Power and Cases Thereof* (1639), Ames stated that Catholics, Anabaptists, Arminians, and even Lutherans were all potentially heretical. To the question, *"Whether are Heretikes to be punished by the civil Magistrate?"* Ames's answer, for its historic importance, is worth quoting in full:

A. 1. That Heretikes are to be resisted by every one that is godly, according to the calling and power which he hath received from God, it appears sufficiently from the nature of the thing: because all the godly are called to a christian warfare, and are in their stations every one to oppose themselves to the kingdome of darknesse.

A. 2. The place and office of a Magistrate requires, that he represse wicked men that trouble the Church, even with the sword, or with publike and externall power if there be need, Rom. 13.4, 1 Tim. 2.2.

A. 3. If therefore Heretikes be manifestly knowne and publikely hurtfull, they are to be restrained of the Magistrate by publike power.

A. 4. And if they be manifestly blasphemous, and pertenacious, and stubborne in those blasphemies, may suffer capitall punishment. For that Law Lev. 24.15,16. although it bind not

---

12 William Ames, *Conscience, with the Power and Cases Thereof* (Amsterdam: Theatrum Orbis Terrarum, Ltd., 1975), I.ii.12, p. 6. Cf. Thomas, 34.

Christians as it is a Law, yet as it is a doctrin comming from God, it doth belong to the direction of Christians in cares of the like nature. When therefore the glory of God, and the safetie of the Church requireth such a punishment, it may, and if other remedies have been used in vain, it ought to be inflicted by the Christian Magistrate.[13]

Later in *Conscience*, Ames added: "The chiefe care of the Magistrate ought to bee, that hee promote true Religion, and represse impiety, *Esa.* 49.23. *Psalm* 2, 11."[14] Van Til overstates the matter when he says that "the similarity between what Perkins and Ames had to say about conscience all but ended with the word *conscience*,"[15] but he nevertheless correctly claims that Ames elevated the politically conservative side of Perkins to such a degree that the statements they shared on the liberty of the conscience could no longer be taken at face value in Ames.

Van Til explains Ames's move by way of his indebtedness to Ramist philosophy. Petrus Ramus (1515-1572) was a French humanist and Calvinist who set against the Aristotelianism of medieval scholasticism a scientific method based upon deduction from the general to the particular. The primary tool for such a method in matters of philosophy was the practical syllogism, or dialectic method. The influence of Ramist thought on Ames is very evident in this selection from Ames:

The Major of that Syllogisme, wherein the whole judgement of Conscience is layd open, treateth alwaies of the Law, the Minor of the fact and state; and the Conclusion of the relation that ariseth from our fact or state, by reason of that Law; which is either guilt, or spiritual Joy. For example, He that liveth in sinne, shall dye, / I live in sinne: / Therefore I shall dye. Or thus, Whosoever beleeveth in Christ, shall not dye, / But I beleeve in Christ: / Therefore I shall not dye, but live, Rom. 8.13.33.34. I Ioh. 3.19.20.[16]

Van Til contends that Ames's identification of conscience with dialectic "eliminated the need to think in terms of conscience as something that could have liberty," for if all moral and philosophical problems could be solved by dialectic, then the conscience was

---

13 Ames, *Conscience*, IV.iv.12-15; pp. 12-13.
14 Ibid., V.xxv.8.3, p. 165.
15 Van Til, *Liberty of Conscience*, 43.
16 Ames, *Conscience*, I.7, p. 50. Perkins also stated, "Conscience gives judgement in or by a kind of reasoning or disputing, called a *practical syllogisme*. Rom. 2.15" (38).

not free but bound to the superiority of dialectic "law" (which for Ames included the Decalogue and other biblical statements that would regulate behavior).[17]

Furthermore, Ames believed that the state had a responsibility to enforce religious law. Prefiguring Locke, Ames said that a people could adopt the government of their own choosing. In this regard, they were at liberty. But once installed, the government had a regulative function in religious matters: it was to act "for the establishment of religion and justice" because "hee which is superior in power, is the Minister of God for good to others, *Rom.* 13.4."[18] As Edmund S. Morgan has said, this was the context for subsequent Puritan debates on both sides of the Atlantic over whether the state had the authority to determine if a conscience was in error and, if so, then to coerce it.[19] In America, both John Cotton and Roger Williams examined the relationship between magistracy and liberty of conscience by in fact appealing to conscience, with Williams saying that conscience must not be constrained and Cotton trying to demonstrate that Williams *violated* conscience with such a belief. Although Bunyan probably was not aware of their dispute, their opposing interpretations of the classic Puritan statements on conscience gave overt expression to – and thus serve to illustrate – the same inner conflict which Bunyan revealed in his political writings.

In sum, the two most frequently cited early Puritans, William Perkins and William Ames, dealt with the conscience and its liberty at the center of their political theology. The differing interpretations of their writings by their Reformed heirs constituted a very important chapter in the rise of modern individualism. Since each person was expected to stand before God alone to work out his or her salvation, for some, says E. M. W. Tillyard, the new emphasis on fidelity to conscience produced "the desire of the individual to stand alone and accept responsibility, and a belittling of all material and adventitious props in exercising this responsibility."[20] But even as Puritanism was beginning to unleash this individualist spirit upon some, the high Calvinist sense of original sin, human depravity, and the need for prevenient grace led others to cling to institutional structures that could keep fallible consciences in check. Williams and Cotton typified these diverging trends.

---

17 Van Til, *Liberty of Conscience*, 50.
18 Ames, *Marrow*, II.xvii.7, p. 308; *Conscience*, V.xx.1, p. 154.
19 Edmund S. Morgan, *Roger Williams*, 133.
20 E. M. W. Tillyard, *The Miltonic Setting Past and Present* (Cambridge: Cambridge University Press, 1938), 78.

The Debate Over Liberty of Conscience Between John Cotton and Roger Williams

The founders of the Massachusetts Bay colony, who were heavily influenced by Ames, believed that they should organize society according to God's law in order to constrain its citizens to live for the glory of God. Of course, most biblically derived civil laws came from the Old Testament since the New Testament does not address the people of God as a political entity holding worldly power. Governor John Winthrop conceived of Massachusetts Bay as a Christian commonwealth, and it did not make sense to him to permit such wide liberty to conscience that one could choose not to participate in the colony's common worship. Liberty not subservient to the commands of God (as mediated through the community) could only be a license for sin. Perry Miller and Thomas H. Johnson say of the American Puritans that,

> When they could not succeed at home, they came to America, where they could establish a society in which the one and only truth should reign forever. There is nothing so idle as to praise the Puritans for being in any sense conscious or deliberate pioneers of religious liberty .... Those who did not hold with the ideals entertained by the righteous ... had every liberty, as Nathaniel Ward said, to stay away from New England.[21]

The conflicted heritage of Puritan teachings on conscience, adds William Haller, was that "it made the individual experience of God in the soul all-important, enormously stimulating individual spiritual experience, and then denied any freedom to the individual will."[22] The divide was between emphasis on the covenant community on one hand and the calling and rights of the individual on the other.[23] Winthrop's reading of Perkins and Ames exalted the common good of the society over individual rights, and he believed that he as magistrate had the power to make this theory a reality at Massachusetts Bay.[24] This is why Perry Miller thinks of the Massachusetts Puritans still as *medieval* men and women.[25]

---

21 Perry Miller and Thomas H. Johnson, *The Puritans* (New York: American Book Company, 1938), 184, 261.
22 William Haller, *The Rise of Puritanism* (New York: Harper Torchbooks, 1957), 193.
23 Carla Gardina Pestana, *Quakers and Baptists in Colonial Massachusetts* (Cambridge: Cambridge University Press, 1991), 84.
24 George L. Mosse, *The Holy Pretence: A Study in Christianity and Reason of State from William Perkins to John Winthrop* (Oxford: Basil Blackwell, 1957), 92, 106.
25 Miller, *Errand*, 218.

Roger Williams (1604-1683) arrived in Massachusetts in 1631 and soon thereafter received an invitation to preach at the church in Boston in the absence of John Wilson, who had returned to England. However, Williams declined the offer because the church had not renounced ties with the Church of England, which he viewed as apostate and hardly better than the Catholic Church. Indeed, the Massachusetts Christians saw themselves as conformists despite the fact they had adopted a congregational church polity. They hoped that their example of purified worship would influence the mother church to follow, and it was for the freedom to embody that example that they came to America. But once they erected their "city set on a hill," why should anyone, they thought, require the freedom to separate from it? Like John Calvin, Williams did not reject the responsibility of magistrates to coerce individuals who in the name of religion committed patently immoral acts. In other words, conscience was not a sufficient authority for violating public standards of morality: human sacrifice or ritual prostitution, for example, should be forbidden.[26] But so long as religious expression did not offend public decency, Williams believed, religious conscience was to be inviolable, even if its precepts seemed to contradict the Bible.

Williams left Boston for Salem, and then he moved on to Plymouth before eventually returning to Salem in 1634. By this time, Winthrop's friend John Cotton (1584-1652), who held the preaching of William Perkins as instrumental in his conversion, had come to the Bay colony and was serving as a teacher in the Boston church. Although Cotton at first saw nothing particularly harmful in what he had read of Williams's political writings, when colony leaders banished Williams for (among other charges) denying that magistrates could enforce religion, Cotton subsequently defended that decision in an exchange of polemical writings. Williams stated his convictions definitively in 1644 with *The Bloudy Tenent of Persecution, for cause of Conscience*, which announced its intention that "Satisfactorie Answers are given to *Scriptures*, and objections produced by Mr. *Calvin*, *Beza*, Mr. *Cotton*, and the Ministers of the New English Churches and others former and later, tending to prove the *Doctrine*

---

26 Edmund S. Morgan, *Roger Williams*, 134.

of persecution for cause of *Conscience.*"²⁷ While Williams conceded that the human conscience was fallible, he denied the inference that it should therefore be coerced in religious matters, for the magistrates were likely no purer in religious habits than their subjects. If the Puritans had not been satisfied with mere toleration in England but came to America to have a greater liberty with which to seek God, then all others should have the same opportunity to worship in freedom, including pagans, Jews, Turks, and unorthodox Christians.²⁸ On this same basis could Williams also say that Emperor Constantine *"ecclipsed"* true Christianity in the fourth century when he tried to exterminate the Arian party with the civil sword.²⁹ Besides, religious coercion had historically been "far from" producing sincere conversions.³⁰

Cotton, incredulous, responded with *The Bloudy Tenent, Washed, And made white in the bloud of the Lambe* in 1647. Cotton denied charges of intolerance in Massachusetts Bay, citing that Indians were allowed to remain pagans without coercion. His interest, he said, was in not allowing subversive ideas to fester *among Christians*. Building his response upon Proverbs 29:2, which speaks of the joy that comes to a land when the righteous are in authority, Cotton said that Christian men are best qualified to preserve a state and its freedoms, and the most lasting freedom is a limited freedom: "If there be power given to speak great things, then look for great blasphemies, look for a licentious abuse of it."³¹ In a godly society, the Christian magistrate could detect whether or not a person's defense of conscience was consistent with divine law and where it was erro-

---

27 Roger Williams, *The Complete Writings of Roger Williams*, vol. 3, *The Bloudy Tenent of Persecution*, ed. Samuel L. Caldwell (New York: Russell and Russell, Inc., 1963), 3. Calvin wished that "less liberty will be taken in the principles of religion, in which God would have the minds of his people to be especially unanimous" (Calvin, *Calvin's Commentaries*, vol. 19, *Commentaries on the Epistle of Paul the Apostle to the Romans*, "The Epistle Dedicatory to Simon Grynæus," trans. John Owen [Grand Rapids: Baker Book House, 1993], xxvii).
28 Gaustad, 70.
29 Roger Williams, 184.
30 Roger Williams, *The Bloudy Tenent yet More Bloudy*; cited in Edmund S. Morgan, *Puritan*, 217.
31 John Cotton, *An Exposition Upon the Thirteenth Chapter of the Revelation* (London: Livewel Chapman, 1655); quoted in Edmund S. Morgan, *Puritan*, 175. Perry Miller documents that this attitude was typical of *The New England Mind from Colony to Province* (Cambridge, MA: Harvard University Press, 1953), 9, 122-123.

neous – and there was no one, he thought, better qualified to do that than the "American Nehemiah," Governor Winthrop.[32] This was, in the end, the brunt of Cotton's charge against Williams: magistrates did not punish individuals for misinformed consciences but rather for persisting in false opinion after being warned. Williams's arguments, said Cotton, allowed that heretics could be free to subvert the Christian commonwealth, and such a notion was so blatantly dishonoring to God that Williams could only be sinning *against* conscience rather than honoring it.[33]

For Cotton, then, one was free only to live according to orthodoxy and was self-evidently corrupt if one chose not do so. And whereas Van Til claims that it was Williams who remained closer to the spirit of Perkins's writings on liberty of conscience,[34] Cotton, too, could claim Perkins's inheritance as his own: "I am very apt to believe, what Mr. Perkins hath [said], ... [that] it is very suitable to Gods all-sufficient wisdome, and to the fulness and perfection of Holy Scriptures, not only to prescribe perfect rules for the right ordering of a private mans soule to everlasting blessednes with himselfe, but also for the right ordering of a mans family, yea, of the commonwealth, too."[35] Indeed, Perkins prefigured Cotton's censure of Williams's "misuse" of conscience when he wrote, "Hence wee see also what notorious rebels those are, that beeing borne subjects of this land, yet choose rather to die then to acknowledge (as they are bound in conscience) the Kings Majestie to bee supreme governour under God in all causes and over all persons."[36]

Williams's final salvo against Cotton was *The Bloudy Tenent Yet More Bloudy*, published in 1652. It had been sixteen years at that point since Williams had founded his own settlement, Providence, which granted religious liberty to all – even anti-Christians, but especially the Quakers, against whose teaching of the inner light Williams responded sharply.[37] Williams's personal adoption of an individualist religion is evident by his spending most of the rest of

---

32 Cf. Bercovitch, 30.
33 Cf. Edmund S. Morgan, *Roger Williams*, 130-131. For a study of the influence of Ames's writings on the rationale for Williams's dismissal from Massachusetts, see Perry Miller, *Orthodoxy in Massachusetts, 1630-1650* (Gloucester, MA: Peter Smith, 1965), 157-159.
34 Van Til, *Liberty of Conscience*, 69.
35 Cotton, "Copy of a Letter from Mr. Cotton to Lord Say and Seal in the Year 1636," quoted in Edmund S. Morgan, *Puritan*, 169.
36 Perkins, 37-38.
37 Cf. Christopher Hill, *Antichrist in Seventeenth-Century England* (London: Verso, 1990), 93.

his life as a "Seeker" who thought there was as yet no "true" church to join. His legacy in America is an important one, for although his political ideas were grounded in Puritanism and not the Enlightenment, he stood in continuity with the constitutional framers a century later: "Williams's Rhode Island, with its stress on freedom, individualism, and being a place 'where no man should be molested for his conscience' – and not Puritan New England with its emphasis on order, community and the mission of a 'city on a hill' – was the prototype of the future American republic."[38]

John Cotton would no doubt have felt vindicated, however, by Sydney Ahlstrom's evaluation that the "passionate little movements [that took advantage of Rhode Island's policy of liberty] soon lost their intensity and frittered away ... [so that] the colony became a kind of composite dead-end street for its founding churches."[39] Dwight A. Moody, perhaps unwittingly but no less shockingly, confesses the completely secular ends of Williams's Rhode Island and William Penn's Pennsylvania when he hails as their ideological heir the decidedly anti-Christian French Revolution! Moody writes, "The success and popularity of their experiments with religious liberty led to its enshrinement in the political documents of the American and French Revolutions, and in this [the twentieth] century, the United Nations."[40] Yet Perry Miller ironically notes that Cotton, too, despite his conservative defense of the role of the magistrate in coercing conscience, also fostered "a marked individuality" through his use and development of covenant theology.[41] According to this school of Puritan thought, God first established a covenant with the human race through Adam (as the representative of the human race, Adam by his sin forfeited eternal life for all humanity) and then a new covenant with humanity through Abraham (Gen 17). Cotton took this to mean that God "takes *Abraham* for ever, and *Abraham* takes God as his friend for ever; and this league of friend-

---

38 Robert D. Linder, "Williams, Roger (1603-1683)," in *Dictionary of Christianity in America*, ed. Daniel G. Reid, Robert D. Linder, Bruce L. Shelley, and Harry S. Stout (Downers Grove, IL: InterVarsity Press, 1990), 1259.
39 Ahlstrom, 182. The legacy of religious individualism in America, says E. B. Holifield, has been the valuing of "Christian teachings only insofar as they promise richer forms of self-realization for autonomous individuals" (Holifield, "Individualism," in *Dictionary of Christianity in America*, ed. Daniel G. Reid, Robert D. Linder, Bruce L. Shelley, and Harry S. Stout [Downers Grove, IL: InterVarsity Press, 1990], 574).
40 Dwight A. Moody, "Trickle of Freedom; Wave of Liberty," *Baptist Standard* (10 December 2001), 4.
41 Miller, *Errand*, 60.

ship implies not only preservation of affection, but it requires a kinde of secret communication one to another, and a doing one for another."[42] The fulfillment of this new covenant was by the grace of Christ, faith in whom brings God's friendship to the believer. Unfortunately, however, Miller does not fully explain why he thinks covenant theology encouraged individualism, but he seems to allude to those Puritan sermons which, in order to encourage the hearer to evaluate whether he or she was in the covenant, fostered a high degree of introspection about subjective experience. Indeed, diary-keeping became a virtual Puritan mandate.

Yet, Ahlstrom argues the opposite conclusion that covenantal ideas "put a curb on purely individualistic endeavors, while an underlying conception of government by social compact gave further strength to the feeling of solidarity."[43] Our historical overview to this point establishes that both Miller and Ahlstrom can be correct because both the germ and the counteragent of individualist religion were present in Puritan attempts to interpret Perkins's talk of liberty of conscience.[44] The differing interpretations of that heritage in the seventeenth century, which favored magisterial authority and communal religion on one hand, and complete religious liberty and individual religion on the other, were enough to divide communities when advocated by capable debaters like Cotton and Williams. This conflicted political inheritance was internalized by John Bunyan.

Individualism and Traditionalism in Bunyan's Political Theory

In describing why Bunyan's political theory has received relatively little scholarly attention, Michael Mullett unintentionally demonstrates the continuing need:

---

42 John Cotton, *Christ the Foundation of Life* (London: 1651), 35; quoted in Miller, *Errand*, 61.
43 Ahlstrom, 135.
44 "H. R. McAdoo, writing on seventeenth-century moral theology, says that 'Conscience has two parts, *synteresis*, or the power by which we hold and understand general principles of morality, and *conscientia*, by which we apply these principles to specific actions in order to assess their rightness and wrongness. Conscience is a function of the practical intellect. It is the mind of man passing moral judgments.' *Conscientia* is the method by which these casuists apply the law to the particular situation, and as they face *conscientia*, they face the problem of the kind of logic employed in the cases of conscience" (Dwight Cathcart, *Doubting Conscience: Donne and the Poetry of Moral Argument* [Ann Arbor: The University of Michigan Press, 1975], 106).

It is worth noting that, of his nearly sixty published works, none directly concerns politics, and that one early production, the 1663 *Christian Behaviour* 'illustrates the conservatism of Bunyan's social views.' Conservative or not, there is every indication that Bunyan was not deeply interested in political questions, in view of the overwhelming priority of spiritual and religious issues in his scheme of things. However, he was a leader in a church which had taken a consistent radical line on political questions.[45]

Mullett's evaluation reflects the very conflict between two strands of Puritan tradition which this essay is tracing: how could it simultaneously be that Bunyan's church toed a "consistent radical line on political questions" while Bunyan's writings remained politically traditional? Mullett is correct that Bunyan did not write a treatise strictly on politics as such (though neither did Perkins or Ames), but his opinions about the state, particularly in the posthumously published works, occur frequently enough that a reconstruction of Bunyan's political views is possible. Before illustrating the two sides of Bunyan's thought, however, it is germane to establish that Bunyan worked within the Perkinsian tradition.

Like most Puritans, Bunyan was a covenant or federal theologian. This is most evident in *An Exposition on the Ten First Chapters of Genesis* (1692): "Wherefore those that think it enough to attain to the state of *Adam* in Innocency, think it sufficient to be meer Naturalists; think themselves well, without being made Spiritual: yea, let me add, they think it safe standing by a Covenant of Works; they think themselves happy, though not concerned in a Covenant of Grace."[46] Richard Muller believes that Bunyan emphasized predestination more than did Perkins or Ames,[47] and Christopher Hill says that the major difference between Bunyan's covenantalism and Perkins's was that Bunyan did not assume a state church,[48] but neither scholar doubts that Bunyan was one of Perkins's theological heirs. Richard Greaves joins Hill in also placing Bunyan alongside Perkins and Ames in the category of "strict Calvinists" who argued that the "law has a rightful and necessary place in the life of a Christian."[49]

---

45 Mullett, 52-53.
46 Bunyan, *MW*, 12:124-125. Cf. Bunyan, *The Advocateship of Jesus Christ*, in *MW*, 11:131.
47 Muller, 320.
48 Hill, *Tinker*, 179.
49 Richard Greaves, "John Bunyan and Covenant Thought in the Seventeenth Century," *Church History* 36:2 (June 1967): 152. Cf. Greaves, *John Bunyan*, 104-118. Hill, *Tinker*, notes, "Bunyan shares to the full what to modern ways of thinking seems the rather disagreeable legalism of the covenant theologians" (178).

Furthermore, Bunyan could hardly have drawn *A Mapp Shewing the Order and Causes of Salvation and Damnation* (1692), which diagrams the doctrine of double predestination from the divine decrees through many intermediary steps to ultimate salvation and reprobation, without knowledge of Perkins's "ocular Catechisme," *A Golden Chain, or, The Description of Theology: Containing the Order of the Causes of Salvation and Damnation, According to God's Word*.[50] Martyn Lloyd-Jones and C. E. Hambrick-Stowe also liken the stages of conversion in *Grace Abounding* and *The Pilgrim's Progress* to those described in Perkins's sermons, with Hambrick-Stowe even suggesting that "the correspondence between the two presentations is so close that it may be surmised that Bunyan was consciously working from Perkins's earlier scheme."[51] Thus is the influence upon Bunyan not only of Puritanism generally but even of Perkins particularly evident.

But how did Bunyan appropriate that influence – with emphasis on liberty of conscience, promoting what would later become liberal individualism, or with emphasis on the right of the magistrate to constrain conscience, the inherited traditionalism of his Puritan forebears? I will present the evidence for each side, beginning with the strand of Bunyan's political writings that tends toward complete liberty of religious expression and which would ally him in this regard with an erstwhile Baptist, Roger Williams.

Religious Liberty

The strongest individualistic language in Bunyan's political writings came in *A Relation of My Imprisonment*, which was not released

---

50 Perkins, "Golden Chain," in *Introduction to Puritan Theology: A Reader*, ed. Edward Hindson (Grand Rapids: Baker Book House, 1976), insert after p. 138. Gordon Campbell makes a convincing case that Bunyan relied on Perkins in "The Source of Bunyan's *Mapp of Salvation*," *Journal of the Warburg and Courtauld Institutes* 44 (1981): 240-241. For more speculation about Perkins's influence on Bunyan's covenant theology, cf. Richard L. Greaves, *John Bunyan and English Nonconformity* (London: The Hambledon Press, 1992), 40.

51 Martyn Lloyd-Jones, *Romans*, vol. 6, *The Law: Its Function and Limits* (Edinburgh: Banner of Truth Trust, 1973), 261, 357 ff.; C. E. Hambrick-Stowe, *The Practice of Piety: Puritan Devotional Disciplines in Seventeenth-Century New England* (Chapel Hill: The University of North Carolina Press, 1985), 77. Likewise does Maurice Hussey say, "We experience little surprise in finding by comparison how closely related Bunyan is to William Perkins, the 'apostle of practical divinity'" (Hussey, "Christian Conduct in Bunyan and Baxter," *The Baptist Quarterly* 14:2 [April 1951]: 75).

by Bunyan's descendants for publication until 1765, one hundred and five years after the events that prompted it. There Bunyan recounted his interrogation before various justices concerning the following charge:

> That John Bunyan of the town of Bedford, labourer, being a person of such and such conditions, he hath (since such a time) devilishly and perniciously abstained from coming to church to hear divine service, and is a common upholder of several unlawful meetings and conventicles, to the great disturbance and distraction of the good subjects of this kingdom, contrary to the laws of our sovereign lord the king, &c.[52]

When offered the exchange of his freedom for his agreement to stop preaching, Bunyan replied that he would have to violate such terms of release since his conscience would not allow him to resist his calling. If it was a sin to preach at conventicles, then, he said, "I should sin still."[53] Bunyan had become a man against his culture in the sense that, with Williams, he had cut any necessary tie between individual religiosity and ecclesial conformity. Such was the impetus of Separatism, that "extreme expression of the religious individualism of Puritan faith and doctrine."[54]

Nowhere in *A Relation* did Bunyan better demonstrate his superior allegiance to soul over society – and at the same time demonstrate his casuistic skill – than in responding to Paul Cobb, Clerk of the Peace, who entreated him, "Pray be ruled." Upon the example of Jesus and Paul, Bunyan said, he certainly intended to obey the civil magistrate. But "the law hath provided two ways of obeying: The one to do that which I in my conscience do believe that I am bound to do, actively; and where I cannot obey actively, there I am

---

52 Bunyan, *A Relation of the Imprisonment of Mr. John Bunyan*, in *GA*, 113.
53 Ibid., 110.
54 Haller, 181. Mark R. Bell offers a healthy caution: "Often it is unacceptable for historians to look to the past for modern concepts, but in the case of Baptists it is tempting. Words like democracy, liberty, individualism, plurality, and tolerance come to mind. Applying these ideas to the earliest Baptists is anachronistic and, as the Levellers discovered, outright dangerous; but there is the suggestion of some connection" (Bell, *Apocalypse How? Baptist Movements During the English Revolution* [Macon, GA: Mercer University Press, 2000], 257).

willing to lie down, and to suffer what they shall do unto me."[55] Here, Bunyan exalted the authority of conscience over the authority of magistracy, so that the former dictated to what degree Bunyan could honor the latter. And when he professed elsewhere, "I shall not force or compel any man to hear me," he suggested, as did Williams shortly before him and Locke shortly after him, that religious conviction should result only from persuasion, not coercion.[56] Thus could Bunyan not in good conscience attend the services of the Church of England since he did not feel an inner persuasion to honor any outward *civil* requirement to do so. He told Justice Keelin [John Kelyng] that he neither attended the parish church nor used the Book of Common Prayer because the Bible did not expressly command him to do so, but he saw nothing treasonous in this since he did not believe that civil harmony was in the balance. Those who desired to use the Prayer Book, he conceded, "have their liberty; that is, I would not keep them from it, but for our parts, we can pray to God without it."[57]

At issue in Bunyan's responses to Clerk Cobb was the intent of an act to suppress dissenters passed by Parliament in 1593 with the support of Queen Elizabeth. Cobb interpreted the act to support the distinction between toleration and liberty of conscience: the act tolerated only public worship services, and so Bunyan was not at liberty to worship in private meetings. But "I am no heretic," Bunyan replied, and explained that the act was only meant to punish any who, unlike him, used religious assemblies as a pretext for working mischief.[58] His insinuation was that religious nonconformists should be given a berth, at least in private conventicles, in which to practice their

---

55 Bunyan, *A Relation*, in *GA*, 124-125. John R. Knott provides two examples of Bunyan's view toward unjust suffering: In the *Commentary on the Ten First Chapters of Genesis*, Bunyan says, "The Voice of Blood is a very *killing voice*, and will one day speak such Thunder and terror in the Consciences of all the brood of *Cain*, that their pain and burthen will be for ever unsupportable," and in *Seasonable Counsel*, he writes, "The way 'to imbolden thy face against the faces of thine enemies,' he advises, is to be willing to accept any amount of suffering; one can thus assure a 'quiet conscience' and provoke God to 'appear for thy rescue, or to avenge thy blood when thou art gone'" (John R. Knott, "Bunyan and the City of Blood," in *Awakening Words: John Bunyan and the Language of Community*, ed. David Gay, James G. Randall, and Arlette Zinck [Newark: University of Delaware Press, 2000], 59, 61).
56 Bunyan, *A Relation of My Imprisonment*, in *GA*, 110.
57 Ibid., 117.
58 Ibid., 122.

peaceable principles, for they and Bunyan would "walk according to all righteous laws, and that whether there was a King or no."[59] William York Tindall contends that such statements betray how radical Bunyan truly was: "He saw and detested the injustice of laws, jails, magistrates, and governors, between whom and the saints was a perpetual war."[60] Like Roger Williams, Bunyan also traced the entrance of the spirit of Antichrist into the world to the time of Constantine in *Of Antichrist, and His Ruine* (1692), and in that same document he applauded King Artaxerxes of Persia for *not* imposing religion on freed Judean exiles. He also wished that "all Kings would but give such liberty," even if "contrary (if he had any) to his own National Worship."[61] In *The House of the Forest of Lebanon* (1692), Bunyan stated that the kingdom of Jesus Christ makes "no infringement on any mans Liberties," again calling for magistrates to reward the peaceableness of most nonconformists with religious liberty.[62]

"Fear God, and Honour the King"

Yet there is a considerable strand of Bunyan's political writings that was not woven into the banner of a new, more libertarian pattern. For example, despite his disagreements with the repressive policy of the Church of England toward evangelical preachers like himself, Bunyan did not follow Roger Williams in refusing all fellowship with conformists. Perhaps influenced by the pleasant memory of his church in Bedford actually being part of the church establishment during the Cromwellian period, Bunyan may have had his children baptized as infants in the parish church and, in *A Defence of Justification, by Faith* (1672), he also defended the Anglican Church's Thirty-Nine Articles against their latitudinarian detractor, Edward Fowler.[63] Whereas Williams found the "reformation" of King Henry

---

59 Ibid., 124.
60 Tindall, 137.
61 Bunyan, *MW*, 13:xxiv, 497, 487, 425-426.
62 Bunyan, *The Miscellaneous Works of John Bunyan*, vol. 7, ed. Graham Midgley (Oxford: Clarendon Press, 1989), xl, 153; cf. Mullett, 283.
63 Mullett 44, 101; Sharrock, *John Bunyan*, 35-36; Bunyan, *MW*, 4:123-124. Compare Bunyan's traditionalism to the early English Baptist Christopher Blackwood, who wrote in 1644 *The Storming of Antichrist in his two last and strongest Garrisons, of Compulsion of Conscience and Infant Baptism*. Bell says that for many early Baptists, "Religious persecution and infant baptism were the two surest signs of the Beast, but at the same time, they were also his two strongest fortresses" (26). Cf. Hill, *Antichrist*, 95; Timothy George, "Between Pacifism and Coercion: The English Baptist Doctrine of Religious

VIII to be no more laudable than the medieval papacy, since Henry's marital machinations overstepped all lawful bounds,[64] Bunyan approved that "the Noble King, King *Henry* VIII. did cast down the Antichristian-worship; so he cast down the Laws that held it up: So also did the good King *Edward* his Son. The brave Queen also, the Sister to King *Edward*, hath left of things of this nature, to her lasting Fame, behind her."[65]

As W. R. Owens notes, Bunyan rather obviously omitted the Stuart kings from his praise,[66] and he no doubt did so because of their Catholic sympathies. But Bunyan hailed past Protestant monarchs, though he surely knew that "good King *Edward* " introduced the Prayer Book and "the brave Queen" Elizabeth had little tolerance for dissenters. Since he argued in *Of Antichrist* that the Protestant Tudors each did successively more to resist "Antichristian-Worship," one can deduce that Bunyan expected any future Protestant kings to move even further toward supporting what he believed to be the full development of Protestantism, which lay in separating Puritanism. Tindall supports his arguments for Bunyan's political radicalism by citing a letter from Bunyan's congregation to Oliver Cromwell in 1653, encouraging him not to accept kingship. Yet Bunyan was a deacon in 1659 when the Bedford church members permitted Cromwell to appoint John Burton as their new pastor, and there Bunyan expressed a clear nostalgia for Protestant monarchs in *Of Antichrist*, where, as Roger Sharrock says, "the last days are forecast as being heralded by an alliance of Protestant kingdoms but not in terms of social revolution."[67] Bunyan's emphasis on the word

---

Toleration," *The Mennonite Quarterly Review* 58:1 (January 1984): 43. By contrast, in Bunyan's *The Life and Death of Mr. Badman*, Mr. Wiseman offers a typically Reformed defense of infant baptism when he speaks of "the advantage of *Election* for their fathers sakes" which the children of ungodly parents do not have (Bunyan, *The Life and Death of Mr. Badman*, ed. James F. Forrest and Roger Sharrock [Oxford: Clarendon Press, 1988], 77). Wiseman also reminisces about *"Olivers* dayes" (Ibid., 54).

64 Roger Williams, 309.
65 Bunyan, *Of Antichrist and His Ruine*, in *MW*, 13:441.
66 W. R. Owens, in ibid., 526, 528.
67 Tindall, 138; G. B. Harrison, ed., *The Church Book of Bunyan Meeting, 1650-1821* (London: J. M. Dent and Sons Limited, 1928), vi; Roger Sharrock, "*The Life and Death of Mr. Badman*: Facts and Problems," *The Modern Language Review* 82:1 (January 1987): 24. Bunyan likely shared the conservative reaction of the Presbyterians that the best check against increasing episodes of religious enthusiasm at the end of the Interregnum – most notably the Quaker James Nayler's "triumphal entry" into Bristol in 1657 – was a monarchy.

"protest" in another quotation from *Of Antichrist* supports this contention: "Thus when the Synagogue of Satan, of old, had Taken Christ, and Accused him, they made *Pontius Pilate* to Condemn and hang him. But God has begun to shew to some of the Kings this Wickedness, and has prevail'd with them to *PROTEST against her*."[68]

Bunyan's professions of monarchical loyalty were plentiful, especially in his late and posthumous works. I will survey them here by way of proceeding to the more critical issue for this chapter, which is whether Bunyan ceded to the monarch any right to coerce religious conscience. In *A Confession of My Faith* (1672), Bunyan called the magistracy "Gods ordinance" for putting "*wickedness to shame*."[69] In *Israel's Hope Encouraged* (1692), despite the occasion of his writing being the encouragement of beleaguered dissenters, he still could say that "we had a gracious King [Charles II and] brave Parliaments" for protecting citizens from potential Catholic violence during the Popish Plot of 1678.[70] And in *Christ a Compleat Saviour* (1692), Bunyan encouraged prayer for magistrates "to hate the Whore [=the papal Antichrist], to eat her Flesh, to make her desolate, and burn her with Fire."[71] John Cotton would surely have agreed with Bunyan's statement in *Seasonable Counsel* (1682):

> Tho' the Christian as a Christian is the only man at liberty, as called thereunto of God, yet his liberty is limited to things that are good: he is not licensed thereby to indulge the flesh. Holiness and liberty are joyned together, yea our call to liberty, is a call to holiness. See, and you shall find, that a quiet and peaceable life, in our respective places, under the Government, is that which we should pray for.[72]

With the relatively early *The Holy City* (1665), in which he urged subjection to magistrates "*for conscience sake*," Bunyan established a theme which reappeared in some of the works published posthumously in 1692: the expectation that the destruction of Antichrist

---

68 Bunyan, *MW*, 13:496.
69 Bunyan, *MW*, 4:153.
70 Bunyan, *MW*, 13:21.
71 Ibid., 306.
72 Bunyan, *MW*, 10:32-33. Coincidentally, George Offor notes that "Dr. John Cotton of New England, in his 'True Constitution of a Visible Church,' fully concurs with Bunyan" in his view of the church as a congregation of the faithful which should strictly follow biblical injunctions toward each other and government (Offor, *The Whole Works of John Bunyan* [Grand Rapids: Baker Book House, 1977], 2:577).

would be accomplished by kings.⁷³ I have already cited some of the individualist tendencies in *Of Antichrist, and His Ruine*, but this is also the work where Bunyan praised the Tudor kings and avowed that "to testifie my Loyalty to my King, my Love to my Brethren, and Service for my Countrey, has been the cause of this my present Scribble."⁷⁴ He again emphasized the divine installation of monarchs and remained convinced that future Protestant kings would arise who would be *"Bout-Hammers"* against Antichrist, and if the Stuarts "go not on in the Work of Reformation so fast as thou wouldest they should, the fault may be thine; know that thou also hast thy cold and chill frames of heart."⁷⁵ Thus, in the same document, we see the dual inheritance of English Puritan political theory – one radical and calling for a new era, the other more Erastian and quiescent.

The same duality is true of *The Saints Knowledge of Christs Love*, which argued for the divine right of kings alongside not "suffering the Law to rule but over my outward man."⁷⁶ It is also in *The House of the Forest of Lebanon*, which, notwithstanding its plea for toleration mentioned earlier, said that "even in Gospel times, Kings [in the iconoclastic mold of Jehu and Josiah] shall hate the Whore, make *her desolate, and naked, and shall eat her Flesh, and burn her with Fire."⁷⁷* While *An Exposition of the Ten First Chapters of Genesis* probably alluded to King James II when it said that Nimrod in Genesis 10:8 was the first who ever "sought after Absolute Monarchy," by no

---

73 Bunyan, *MW*, 3:40, 166-168. Glen Bowman speaks of how obedience for "conscience's sake" is a common refrain of early Protestant reformers (Bowman, "Every Man is a Church in Himself: The Development of Donne's Ideas on the Relationship between Individual Conscience and Human Authority," *Fides et Historia* 29:1 [Winter/Spring 1997]: 47). Cf. the opposite view of Jonathan Edwards, who, while endorsing the idea of a Christian magistracy, said, "This great work [of destroying Antichrist] shall be accomplished, not by the authority of princes, nor by the wisdom of learned men, but by God's Holy Spirit, Zech. 4:6-7" (Edwards, *The Works of Jonathan Edwards*, vol. 9, *A History of the Work of Redemption*, ed. John F. Wilson [New Haven: Yale University Press, 1989], 460).
74 Bunyan, *MW*, 13:429. Cf. Richard L. Greaves: "Bunyan's willingness to adopt a policy of cautious co-operation with the Government was an outgrowth of his shift to a more conservative political ideology" (In Bunyan, *MW*, 11:xix).
75 Bunyan, *MW*, 13:481, 488-489.
76 Mullett, 281-282; Bunyan, *MW*, 13:392.
77 Bunyan, *MW*, 7:164. Note that the quotation of Revelation 17:12,16 is precisely the same as that which Bunyan used in *Seasonable Counsel*, above.

means is Tindall's assertion plausible that this aside confirms Bunyan's merely "specious loyalty."[78] For in *An Exposition*, Bunyan dreamed of a church where there was "Oneness," hailed the work of Josiah in promoting religion, and – if Christopher Hill is correct – was even conciliatory toward tolerationist ideas meant by James II principally for the benefit of Catholics.[79] Tindall adduces no evidence for his assertion that Bunyan's loyalist comments covered up his real interest in sedition.[80] Instead, they reveal that two strands of Puritan thought could operate on Bunyan's mind simultaneously and with roughly equal force. Indeed, the conflict between liberty of conscience on one hand and political traditionalism on the other was endemic to the Baptist situation in England after the middle of the seventeenth century, when Baptists tried to toe a middle line between Anabaptistic separatism and accommodation to Puritan society for the sake of preserving the movement.[81]

Owen C. Watkins, in his introduction to *Seasonable Counsel*, warns that no easy assumption should be made that nonconformists such as Bunyan would automatically prefer complete liberty of conscience for all in order to guarantee their own freedom of worship. Instead, says Watkins, "Few of the Nonconformists who protested about being persecuted thought that all beliefs should be tolerated by a Christian state."[82] Yet, he adds, Bunyan "had little to say about toleration as a principle."[83] I would amend Watkins's assessment by saying that although Bunyan wrote many statements about the role of government in religion, he said little that could formally reconcile the inherent tensions among them. In *A Discourse of the Building ... of the House of God* (1688), for example, Bunyan's left hand seemed not to know what his right was doing:

For those that have *private* opinions too
We must make room, or shall the Church undo;
Provided they be such as don't impair

---

78 Tindall, 140-141.
79 Bunyan, *MW*, 12:267, 276, 227; Hill, cited in ibid., xlvi. In "A Continuation of Mr. Bunyan's Life," added to the 1692 (7th) edition of *Grace Abounding*, George Cokayne said that even though Bunyan took advantage of toleration since "God is the only Lord of Conscience," his "piercing wit penetrated the Veil" and saw that this was really for Catholic benefit (See Bunyan, *GA*, 169-170).
80 Tindall, 136.
81 Bell, 80, 91.
82 Owen C. Watkins, in Bunyan, *MW*, 10:xx.
83 Ibid.

Faith, Holiness, nor with good Conscience jarr;
Provided also those that hold them shall
Such Faith hold to themselves, and not let fall
Their fruitless Notions in their Brothers way,
Do thus, and Faith and Love will not decay.[84]

It is not easy to determine from this passage whether Bunyan would have felt more at home in Roger Williams's Rhode Island or John Cotton's Massachusetts.

This brings us to the very important question of whether Bunyan, though himself a dissenter, conceded the right of magistrates to coerce to any degree the religious conscience of individuals. Bunyan's belief that Christian unity is more important than private opinions – especially in light of his saying in *Of Antichrist* that Babylon (cf. Rev 18) is the home of sects, and kings have the divinely ordained task to destroy it[85] – could be read as endorsing some form of coercion, though obviously not against orthodox nonconformists like himself.[86] *The Life and Death of Mr. Badman* and *The Holy War* further seem to reflect this side of Bunyan, with Mr. Wiseman in the former wanting to report to a magistrate that he heard someone blaspheming the Holy Spirit, and Emanuel in the latter leaving a standing order to the Mansoulians to execute captured Diabolonians.[87] Yet Bunyan's call in *A Discourse of the House of God* to "*make room*" for private opinions was certainly individualistic; communalism was not the same as collectivism. Bunyan found it difficult

---

84 Bunyan, *A Discourse of the Building, Nature, Excellency and Government of the House of God with Counsels and Directions to the Inhabitants Thereof*, in *MW*, 6:311. Greaves calls this a call for "a reasonable degree of toleration," but what does "reasonable" mean? (Greaves, *John Bunyan and English Nonconformity*, 70).

85 Bunyan, *MW*, 13:466. Bunyan could have had in mind for destruction the Quakers, whom he called in *A Vindication of Some Gospel-Truths Opened* "a new upstart sect" (Bunyan, *MW*, 1:184). In the same work, he referred to the Quakers as heretics or committers of heresy nine times (Ibid., 124-125, 134-135, 146, 150, 190, 213).

86 Cf. George: "By admitting the possibility of a Christian magistrate and by so positively affirming the coercive powers of the state in matters temporal and civil, the independence of the spiritual realm is undermined and its freedom from *religious* coercion thereby threatened" (49).

87 Bunyan, *Badman*, 54-55; *HW*, 134-135. Among those for whose execution Emanuel leaves a standing order is Mr. Heresie (145). When Clip-promise is hanged at the end of the allegory, Bunyan as narrator remarks, "And truly my judgment is that all those of his name and life should be served even as he" (243).

to choose between the two models I have described. So there are unresolved tensions in Bunyan's political thought regarding the relation of his soteriology to his ecclesiology: he never worked out a way whereby an objective reliance upon Christ's righteousness could become the religious law of the land. But then, despite the reputation he has won as a champion of conscience, he never wanted to consider himself an innovator: "I do confess my self one of the old-fashion Professors, that *covet to fear God, and honour the King.*"[88]

Bunyan's Political Conservatism in Comparison to Milton

For conclusive evidence that Bunyan was not the ardent agitator for liberty of conscience whom commentators have reconstructed from *Grace Abounding to the Chief of Sinners* and its epilogue on Bunyan's trial and imprisonment, one need only compare his political writings with those of the seventeenth century's other great epic writer, John Milton. Though of disparate educational backgrounds, social classes, and opinions about Calvinism, these two writers both supported the Parliamentary cause during the Civil Wars (though Bunyan much less vocally so) and suffered ill effects from the Restoration of Charles II in 1660. Bunyan, of course, was confined to the Bedford jail from 1660-1672 for his nonconformist preaching; Milton escaped the most dire reprisals for his vocal endorsement of Charles I's execution because of Andrew Marvell's activities in the House of Commons, but he did endure a brief imprisonment. Both also wrote at length on the role of conscience in the Christian life. But whereas Bunyan believed that he should retain his civil liberty because he in good conscience could preach only scriptural orthodoxy, Milton argued for civil liberty because God had left all human consciences free. Thus, while Bunyan's argument for religious liberty was really an expression of his commitment to a theological standard, Milton's was more modern and individualistic in that it took into consideration no communal or historic standard of belief. For Bunyan, liberty of conscience lay in the freedom to voice "old-fashioned" Reformation ideas in the new setting of the conventicle: as the Westminster Confession suggests when it says that "God alone is Lord of the conscience, and hath left it free from the doctrines and commandments of men which are in any thing contrary to His Word," conscience in this way of thinking was not privatized but "free"

---

88 Bunyan, *Of Antichrist and His Ruine*, in MW, 13:489. Cf. Bunyan's *A Few Sighs from Hell*: "I exercise my self, to have always a Conscience void of offence, both towards God, and towards man" (*MW*, 1:58).

only in relation to God.⁸⁹ But for Milton, liberty of conscience was constituted by the freedom for any Protestant to voice even "heretical" ideas without threat of persecution.⁹⁰ And insofar as Milton's emphasis on the natural liberty of conscience – in contrast with Bunyan's emphasis on the natural *bondage* of conscience prior to conversion (and even after, in a certain sense) – coincided with the forward-looking political libertarianism of his one-time student Roger Williams, Bunyan's political thought by contrast fell more toward the more magisterial Puritan paradigm of William Ames and John Cotton.

Religious Liberty vs. Orthodoxy in Milton's Political Writings

Whereas Bunyan's most explicitly political considerations came largely in the last sixteen years of his life after the Declaration of Indulgence freed him from jail in 1672, Milton's political treatises spanned the three most tumultuous decades of his era, from 1641 (*Of Reformation in England*), a year before the start of the Civil Wars, to 1673 (*Of True Religion*), a year after the Declaration emancipated Bunyan and other dissenters. Throughout these works, Milton refused to link theological orthodoxy with religious liberty; if anything, he widened the distinction between church and state as the years progressed.

In *Of Reformation in England*, Milton gave only an ambiguous report of the ancient Arians and Pelagians, whose respective diminution of the eternality and elective work of Christ Bunyan strongly reproved:

> Witnes the *Arians* and *Pelagians* which were slaine by the Heathen for *Christs* sake; yet we take both these for no true friends of *Christ*. If the *Martyrs* (saith *Cyprian* in his 30. Epistle) decree one thing, and the *Gospel* another, either the *Martyrs* must lose their Crowne by not observing the *Gospel* for which they are *Martyrs*; or the Majestie of the *Gospel* must be broken and lie flat, if it can be overtopt by the *novelty* of any other *Decree*.⁹¹

By the time he wrote *Of True Religion* over thirty years later, Milton boldly declared Arians, Socinians (who denied the Trinity),

---

89 The Westminster Confession, Article 20.02, in Gerald Bray, ed., *Documents of the English Reformation* (Minneapolis: Fortress Press, 1994), 502.
90 For a contemporary Christian critique of invoking "liberty of conscience" to protect privatized theological innovation, see Robert P. Mills, "The Myth of Private Conscience," *The Presbyterian Layman* (May/June 2001): 2.
91 Milton, 878.

and Arminians (who, like the Pelagians, rejected an Augustinian view of predestination) to be equal heirs of the Protestant vision alongside Lutherans and Calvinists. Milton's explanation was that the Arians and Socinians "dispute the satisfaction of Christ, or rather the word *Satisfaction*, as not Scriptural: but they acknowledge him both God and their Saviour," and "the Arminian lastly is condemn'd for setting up free will against free grace; but that Imputation he disclaims in all his writings, and grounds himself largely upon Scripture only."[92] Such defenses must be admitted as personally relevant for Milton, considering his own denial of the co-eternality of the three persons of the Godhead[93] and his rejection of any elective decrees by God[94] both in his polit-

---

92 Ibid., 1152.
93 As evidence for Milton's Arianism, observe God's declaration in *Paradise Lost*, 5.603-605, not of Jesus' earthly baptism but of the Son's heavenly generation: "This day I have begot whom I declare / My onely Son, and on this holy Hill / Him hath anointed, whom ye now behold / At my right hand" (ibid., 495). The suggestion that there was a "time" before which the Son did not exist coincides with Arius's own declaration of the Son that "There was when He was not." See J. N. D. Kelly, *Early Christian Doctrines* (San Francisco: Harper and Row, 1978), 228. Compare Milton's statement in *On Christian Doctrine*: "So God begot the Son as a result of his own decree. Therefore it took place within the bounds of time, for the decree itself must have preceded its execution .... As for those who maintain that the Son's generation was from eternity, I cannot discover on what passage in the scriptures they ground their belief" (Milton, 1169). Milton seemed conscientiously to avoid calling God's Spirit the "Holy Spirit" in *Paradise Lost* (e.g., 7.165; 12.488); while he does refer properly to the Holy Spirit in *On Christian Doctrine*, he said that this Spirit is "not any particular person" (ibid., 1176).
94 In *Paradise Lost*, 5.525-534, the angel Raphael informs Adam: "And good he [God] made thee, but to persevere / He left it in thy power, ordained thy will / By nature free, nor over-rul'd by Fate / Inextricable, or strict necessity; Our voluntarie service he requires, / Not our necessitated, such with him / Findes no acceptance, nor can find, for how / Can hearts, not free, be tri'd whether they serve / Willing or not, who will but what they must / By Destinie, and can no other choose?" (ibid., 492). Curiously, in *Of Reformation*, Milton spoke of "the strict necessity of Conscience" itself as being constituted by "free choyce" (ibid., 892). This coincides with *Areopagitica*: "Many there be that complain of divin Providence for suffering *Adam* to transgresse, foolish tongues! when God gave him reason, he gave him freedom to choose, for reason is but choosing" (ibid., 1010). Compare *On Christian Doctrine*, where Milton offered the quintessential Arminian apology that biblical language of predestination alludes only to God's foreknowledge of free belief: "Suffice it to know, without investigating the matter any

ical writings and in *Paradise Lost*. Milton's discarding of orthodoxy also shows him in full step with the Enlightenment. But even more critically for the argument here, Milton in defending the free expression of "heretical" doctrines in opposition to which Bunyan understood his life's work took the Reformation notion of *sola scriptura* to the individualist extreme that Martin Luther had so dreaded: he exalted the *process* of personal Bible interpretation over any interpretation of itself.[95]

For Milton, this process, not the objective faith of Christ that availed for Luther and Bunyan, was *the* content of true Christian faith. This explains why Milton became increasingly protective of those radical religionists of his century who claimed a right of conscience to interpret the Bible in non-standard ways.[96] Such advocacy is thinly veiled in *Paradise Lost*, where Abdiel, the only angel to hear Satan's call for rebellion who does not conform to it, addresses his conspiratorial colleague:

---

further, that God, out of his supreme mercy and grace in Christ, has predestined to salvation all who shall believe" (ibid., 1168).

95 Cf. Charles R. Geisst: "The unorthodoxy of these religious ideas gives perhaps the best illustration of what Milton meant by inward liberty: the free expression of an idea in accordance with reason, no matter how heretical" (Geisst, *The Political Thought of John Milton* [London: The Macmillan Press Limited, 1984], 23).

96 *A Treatise of Civil Power in Ecclesiastical Causes* (1659): "First, it cannot be deni'd, being the main foundation of our protestant religion, that we of these ages, having no other divine rule or authoritie from without us warrantable to one another as a common ground but the holy scripture, and no other within us but the illumination of the Holy Spirit so interpreting that scripture as warrantable only to our selves and to such whose consciences we can so perswade, can have no other ground in matters of religion but only from the scriptures" (Milton, 1122).

The Readie and Easie Way to Establish a Free Commonwealth (1660): "That this is best pleasing to God, and that the whole Protestant Church allows no supream judge or rule in matters of religion, but the scriptures, and these to be interpreted by the scriptures themselves, which necessarily inferrs liberty of conscience, I have heretofore prov'd at large in another treatise, and might yet furder by the public declarations, confessions and admonitions of whole churches and states, obvious in all historie since the Reformation" (Ibid., 1146). While the Protestant Reformers agreed that scripture interprets scripture, they denied the conclusion that this entails liberty of conscience.

Of True Religion: "How shall we prove ... all things at least founded on Scripture, unless we not only tolerate them, but patiently hear them, and seriously read them?" (Ibid., 1155).

> There be [those] who Faith
> Prefer, and Pietie to God, though then
> To thee not visible, when I alone
> Seemd in thy World erroneous to dissent
> From all: my Sect thou seest, now learn too late
> How few somtimes may know, when thousands err.[97]

Abdiel's acceptance of the term "sect" to describe his unpopular loyalty to God contrasts with Bunyan's *distancing* of himself from sectarian appearances, at least in his pejorative use of that term in reference to the Quakers.[98]

In *Of Antichrist, and His Ruine,* Bunyan set his political loyalty in opposition to the sects who dwelled in proverbial Babylon, and in *A Vindication of Some Gospel-Truths Opened,* he established his theological orthodoxy in opposition to the teachings of the Quakers, that "new upstart sect."[99] Bunyan also called the Quakers "heretics" on numerous occasions. But "sect" and "heresy" were not terms of disdain according to Milton, for they lacked specific content. "Sects may be in a true Church as well as in a false," wrote Milton in *Of True Religion,* and someone "may be a heretick in the truth," he claimed in *Areopagitica.*[100] "Heresy" for Milton was "no word of evil note" but meant simply to believe a doctrine that someone else – whether a pastor, a council, a church father, or a pope – approves.[101]

---

97 Ibid., 512 (6.143-148). The bold print is my own added emphasis. Satan's reply to Abdiel (6.156) reveals that his followers meet "in Synod," an allusion either to the Anglican or Presbyterian establishments. In *A Treatise of Civil Power in Ecclesiastical Causes* (1659), Milton stated that "no man, no synod, no session of men, though calld the church, can judge definitively the sense of scripture to another mans conscience" (Ibid., 1124).

98 See Chapter Four, ft. 85, above.

99 Bunyan, *MW*, 13:466; 1:184.

100 Milton, 1151, 1015. Milton's claim in *Areopagitica* that writings of "heretics" should not be banned from publication has a soft parallel in Bunyan's *A Vindication of Some Gospel-Truths Opened,* where, although Bunyan did not address licensed printing, he did say, "It is very expedient that there should be heresies among us, that thereby those which are indeed of the truth might be made manifest; and also that the doctrine of GOD, and his son JESUS CHRIST, might the more cast forth its lustre and glory" (Bunyan, *MW*, 1:34).

101 Milton (*A Treatise of Civil Power*), 1124. Cf. "He then [who] to his best apprehension follows the scripture, though against any point of doctrine by the whole church receivd, is not the heretic; but he who follows the church against his conscience and perswasion grounded on the scripture" (Ibid.); "He [is] the only heretic, who counts all heretics but himself" (Ibid., 1125); and *Of True Religion*: "Heresie therefore is a Religion taken up and believ'd from the traditions of men and additions to the word of God" (Ibid., 1151).

He gave as an example in *Of Reformation in England* the unique authority which some had afforded the Marian martyrs Thomas Cranmer, Hugh Latimer, and Nicholas Ridley: "More tolerable it were for the *Church* of GOD that all these names were utterly abolisht, like the *Brazen Serpent*; then that mens fond opinions should thus idolize them, and the Heavenly *Truth* be thus captivated."[102] Bunyan could, of course, speak in similar terms about the qualitative inferiority of the most skilled scriptural commentators to scripture itself, such as when he addresses the "learned reader" in *The Holy City*: "I honour the Godly, as Christians, but I prefer the BIBLE before them; and having that still with me, I count my self far better furnished than if I had (without it) all the Libraries of the two Universities: Besides, I am for *drinking Water out of my own Cistern*; what GOD makes mine by the evidence of his Word and Spirit, that I dare make bold with."[103] Yet Bunyan nonetheless regulated his reading of scripture according to ancient and Reformation formulations of Trinity, Christology, soteriology, and the like. Milton did not.

If Bunyan's concern was to defend orthodoxy, or right belief, then Milton's concern was to defend right principles. He stated these principles most explicitly in *Of True Religion*: "The Rule of true Religion is the Word of God only: and that ... Faith ought not to be an implicit faith, that is, to believe, though as the Church believes, against or without express authority of Scripture."[104] In Milton's perspective, the Roman Catholics did not practice true religion because they worshiped according to customs and traditions which had no biblical basis, and so Milton, like John Locke, believed that Catholics forfeited their right to toleration on that basis.[105] Obviously, therefore, Milton's conception of religious liberty predated modern notions of freedom of religion based on natural rights and not on the preference for the Bible over custom.[106] But at least under the

---

102 Ibid (*Of Reformation*), 879.
103 Bunyan, *MW*, 3:72. Bunyan did add in the same work, however, that the Protestant Reformers and Marian martyrs laid the foundation upon which his work was building (134).
104 Milton, 1151.
105 Ibid., 1153; (*Areopagitica*), 1022. Bunyan also wrote, "'Tis not custom, but good conscience that will help at Gods Tribunal" (*Badman*, 106).
106 Cf. Virginia R. Mollenkott, "Relativism in *Samson Agonistes*," *Studies in Philology* 67:1 (January 1970): 89; Susanne Woods, "Elective Poetics and Milton's Prose: *A Treatise of Civil Power* and *Considerations Touching the Likeliest Means to Remove Hirelings Out of the Church*," in *Politics, Poetics, and Hermeneutics in Milton's Prose*, ed. David Loewenstein and James Grantham Turner (Cambridge: Cambridge University Press, 1990), 202.

broad umbrella of a Protestant nation, Milton's advocacy of complete freedom from coercion was certainly more liberal in the modern sense than Bunyan's traditionalist desire for a Christian king who could fight against Antichrist. "No true Protestant can persecute," Milton believed, "or not tolerate his fellow Protestant, though dissenting from him in som opinions, but he must flatly deny and Renounce these two his own main Principles."[107] With Roger Williams and a good number of English Baptists, Milton argued for something that apparently did not concern Bunyan – blanket liberty of conscience that would hopefully not rend but unite English Christendom. Moreover, Milton said in *A Treatise of Civil Power* that mutual toleration is "the common sect" in which all true Protestants agree.[108] Protestant principles, according to Milton, have more authority over the individual than does codified law, and so, as Locke also wrote, it is both presumptuous and injurious to Christian liberty for either secular or ecclesiastical leaders to exert force on a person in order to obtain confessional agreement.[109]

Herein lay an important transitional moment to the modern period. Whereas Bunyan invoked the sanctity of conscience for continuing his unlicenced preaching because his conscience was captive to Christ through a creedally mediated understanding of scripture, Milton made each individual the arbiter of a subjective orthodoxy.[110]

---

107 Milton (*Of True Religion*), 1151.
108 Ibid., 1126; George, 42-45. In *Doctrine and Discipline of Divorce*, Milton, as something of a proto-Freudian, contended that the threat of repression is responsible for the alleged licentiousness of Antinomians and Familists (Milton, 949).
109 Milton, 1123. Milton added that force does not change consciences anyway (Ibid., 1129, 1131). In *Paradise Lost*, 12.520-533, the archangel Michael reveals to the fallen Adam that in the postlapsarian world, some by "pretense, / Spiritual Lawes by carnal power shall force / On every conscience; Laws, which none shall finde / Left them inrould, or what the Spirit within / Shall on the heart engrave. What will they then / But force the Spirit of Grace it self, and binde / His consort Libertie; what, but unbuild / His living Temples, built by Faith to stand, / Thir own Faith not anothers: for on Earth / Who against Faith and Conscience can be heard / Infallible? yet many will presume: / Whence heavie persecution shall arise / On all who in the worship persevere / Of Spirit and Truth" (Ibid., 705-706). Likewise in *Paradise Regain'd*, 1.222-223, Jesus reflects that he will assume his kingdom "By winning words to conquer willing hearts, / And make perswasion do the work of fear" (Ibid., 728).
110 In *A Treatise of Civil Power*, Milton defined conscience as "that full perswasion whereby we are assur'd that our beleef and practice, as far as we are able to apprehend and probably make appeer, is according to the will of

Milton scholars readily confess that he was, in John T. Shawcross's words, "amazingly modern in his views."[111] And for my purpose here, such easy admission to modernity makes modernity in *Bunyan*'s political thought less obvious to understand. Milton's reliance on the inner light in religious matters actually became the mirror image of Catholic tradition: rather than allow itself to be *dictated to* by the scripture, the conscience according to Milton exercised authority *over* scripture by determining scripture's interpretation.[112] But unlike Catholicism, the individual authority of the conscience swelled so large for Milton that the institutional church and its

---

God & his Holy Spirit within us, which we ought to follow much rather then any law of man, as not only his word every where bids us, but the very dictate of reason tells us" (Milton, 1122). Cf. Perez Zagorin: "Milton's radical individualism thus made the mind and conscience of each believer the sole and ultimate judge of religious truth" (Zagorin, *Milton, Aristocrat and Rebel: The Poet and His Politics* [Rochester, NY: D. S. Brewer, 1992], 100).

111 John T. Shawcross, "The Higher Wisdom of *The Tenure of Kings and Magistrates*," in *Achievements of the Left Hand: Essays on the Prose of John Milton*, ed. Michael Lieb and John T. Shawcross (Amherst: The University of Massachusetts Press, 1974), 143. Cf. ibid., 157; Stanley E. Fish, *Self-Consuming Artifacts: The Experience of Seventeenth Century Literature* (Pittsburgh: Duquesne University Press, 1994), 279; Christopher Hill, *Milton and the English Revolution* (New York: The Viking Press, 1977), 458; and the influence of Milton on Henry David Thoreau in James Duban, "Conscience and Consciousness: The Liberal Christian Context of Thoreau's Political Ethics," *The New England Quarterly* 60:2 (June 1987): 208.

112 In *Paradise Lost*, 3.194-197, Milton's God emphasizes against Bunyan's predestinarianism and Christ-freed conscience that the heavenly pilgrimage begins with autonomous human use of an inward light: "And I will place within them as a guide / My Umpire *Conscience*, whom if they will hear, / Light after light well us'd they shall attain, / And to the end persisting, safe arrive" (Milton, 422). Cf. *Paradise Regain'd*, 4.288-290, where Jesus admits, "He who receives / Light from above, from the fountain of light, / No other doctrine needs, though granted true" (Ibid., 772). Coincidentally, Quakers helped Milton to edit *Paradise Lost* since his blindness prevented him doing so alone, and the Quaker Thomas Ellwood believed that he had suggested to Milton *Paradise Regain'd* (Ibid., 327; John T. Shawcross, *John Milton: The Self and the World* [Lexington, KY: The University Press of Kentucky, 1993], 147-153; A. L. Rowse, *Milton the Puritan: Portrait of a Mind* [New York: University Press of America, 1977], 243). Cf. Armand Himy, "*Paradise Lost* as a Republican 'Tractatus theologico-politicus," in *Milton and Republicanism*, ed. David Armitage, Armand Himy, and Quentin Skinner (Cambridge: Cambridge University Press, 1995), 126. Roy Flannagan even compares Jesus in *Paradise Regain'd* to a Quaker lay-preacher (In Milton, 714).

administration of the sacraments retained no central purpose. Bunyan would never have admitted this last step, even when his interpretation of scripture seemed most individualistic.[113] Stephen R. Honeygosky and Thomas N. Corns especially emphasize the heightened individualism that Milton's prose shared with Bunyan's primal adversaries, the Quakers, and other radical religionists to the left of Bunyan's own Baptist group.[114] According to Terry Eagleton, English literature and culture under Milton's influence was well on its way toward – rather, he says, they "degenerated into" – the Romanticism and Victorianism "which lost collective belief, and declined into an errant individualism."[115]

Milton's Antimonarchicalism

In *The Second Defence of the English People* (1654), Milton recalled that when some Presbyterian ministers had claimed that the writings of the Protestant Reformers would not support regicide, he felt an inward compulsion to correct them in print. He had not intended this defense to have direct application to Charles I, he said, though he did advocate that "Queen Truth should be preferred to King Charles."[116] This earlier defense was probably *The Tenure of Kings and Magistrates* (1649?), in which Milton contended that Luther, Zwingli, Calvin, and Peter Martyr all were in favor of the deposition of evil magistrates.[117] In *The Tenure*, Milton again anticipated

---

113 Cf. Shawcross, *John Milton*, 255.
114 Stephen R. Honeygosky, *Milton's House of God: The Invisible and Visible Church* (Columbia, MO: University of Missouri Press, 1993), 93-95, 103, 139-145, 169, 187; Thomas N. Corns, "Bunyan, Milton and the Diversity of Radical Protestant Writing," in *John Bunyan: Reading Dissenting Writing*, ed. N. H. Keeble (Oxford: Peter Lang, 2002), 32-36. Compare, however, the evaluation of Christopher Hill on *Paradise Lost*: "Adam's fall was due not to pride or intellectual curiosity, as it well might have been if Milton had followed Genesis and the commentators. It was due to love, love for woman; and to a preference for society rather than a lonely rectitude in individual isolation. It is not quite what we should expect from the poet traditionally seen as the high priest of self-righteous protestant individualism" (Hill, *World*, 398).
115 Terry Eagleton, *Literary Theory: An Introduction* (Minneapolis: The University of Minnesota Press, 1998), 33.
116 Milton, 1118.
117 Ibid., 1071-1072, 1075. Milton's positive use of the Reformers here served his purpose but contrasted with his opinion in *Areopagitica* that if England had listened to John Wyclif, it might never have heard of Luther or Calvin.

Locke by saying that government rules according to the consent of the governed, and hence, private citizens have the right to remove the king they installed, especially if the king does not conduct his office honorably.[118] The magisterial Reformers in fact advocated no possibility for a popular coup, even against an unjust ruler. For Luther in *Secular Authority: To What Extent it Should be Obeyed*, and for Calvin in *Institutes of the Christian Religion*, there were no such insurrectionist tendencies:[119] "Although leading Protestant Reformers seem at first sight to be arguing for a novel and subjectivist individual liberty of conscience, they prove on further scrutiny to be resolute defenders of the right and duty of the ecclesiastical and civil powers to co-operate in the extirpation of heresy within the area of their joint jurisdiction."[120] For Milton, however, the monarchy played no role in the advancement of Christ's kingdom on earth except for the maintenance of religious liberty[121] – regarding which he had practically no hope in the Stuart kings. In *The Readie and Easie Way*, he asked if the moderate Queen Elizabeth did not protect full liberty of conscience, then what hope was there for any Stuart monarch doing so?[122]

So yet again by contrast, despite the individualist dimension of Bunyan's political thought, the political views of the Bedford

---

Also, "We have lookt so long upon the blaze that *Zuinglius* and *Calvin* hath beacon'd up to us, that we are stark blind," he says, adding that a reforming of the Reformation is necessary in order to move beyond the strictures of Geneva and Westminster (Ibid., 1018-1019, 1021,1023). In *Doctrine and Discipline of Divorce*, Milton conveniently overlooked his usual separation of church and state when he hailed England as God's prime bearer of reformation to the world – beginning with "our English *Constantine* that baptiz'd the Roman Empire" (Ibid., 933)!

118 Cf. Perez Zagorin, *A History of Political Thought in the English Revolution* (Bristol, England: Thoemmes Press, 1997), 114.

119 Martin Luther, in Dillenberger, 398; Galen Johnson, "John Calvin, Huguenot?" *Koinonia* 11:2 (Fall 1999): 198. In my article, I provide primary documentation to overturn the popular conception that Calvin advocated violent resistance against anti-Christian monarchs. Cf. Felipe Fernández-Armesto and Derek Wilson, *Reformations: A Radical Interpretation of Christianity and the World, 1500-2000* (New York: Scribner, 1996), 287.

120 F. L. Cross and E. A. Livingstone, eds., "Toleration, Religious," *The Oxford Dictionary of the Christian Church*, 3rd ed. (Oxford: Oxford University Press, 1997), 1629.

121 In *A Treatise of Civil Power*, Milton said that the magistrate should be the defender but not the enforcer of the two tables of the Mosaic law (Milton, 1133).

122 Ibid., 1146-1147.

preacher looked aft in comparison to Milton's. In *Of Antichrist, and His Ruine, The Holy City, Seasonable Counsel,* and other writings, Bunyan worked to establish his loyalty to the same Stuart king whose government imprisoned him and to distance himself from any who might plot the overthrow of God's agent. He even avowed in *A Relation of My Imprisonment,* "They charged me also, that I went thither to plot and raise division, and make insurrection, which, God knows, was a slander."[123] One can further contrast Bunyan's own nostalgic recollection of "noble" King Henry VIII and his two Protestant heirs in *Of Antichrist* with Milton's speech about the Tudors in *Of Reformation in England,* where Milton could only lament the shortcomings of reformation during their reigns.[124] And whereas Bunyan could implore readers in *The Holy City,* appealing to Romans 13:5, that they be subject to magistrates *"for conscience sake,"* Milton explained the same verse quite differently in *A Treatise of Civil Power*: *"Be subject not only for wrath, but for conscience sake*: how for conscience sake against conscience? ... It appears plainly that the apostle in this place gives no judgment or coercive power to magistrates."[125]

A New View of Freedom

Milton's excision of the state from religious matters closely resembled the position of Roger Williams, who interpreted the early Puritans' teaching on liberty of conscience to mean that each conscience

---

123 Bunyan, *GA,* 130.
124 Milton, 877-878. Again, Milton's evaluation of Henry VIII's "faultinesse" (877) served his republican purpose here, but in *Doctrine and Discipline of Divorce* (1644), where Milton argued for divorce on the basis of incompatibility, he said that "it pleas'd God make him [Henry] see all the tyranny of *Rome,* by discovering this which they exercis'd over divorce; and to make him the beginner of a reformation to this whole Kingdome, by first asserting into his *familiary* power the right of just divorce" (Ibid., 973).
125 Ibid., 1121. During the civil wars and the Interregnum, Milton urged Parliament and Oliver Cromwell not to repress free consciences as prior monarchs had done, not only in *A Treatise of Civil Power* but also in the sonnets "On the New Forcers of Conscience" (1646), "To Sir Henry Vane the Younger" (1652), and "To the Lord Generall Cromwell" (1652), where he contrasted "free Conscience" with "secular chaines" (Ibid., 265, 291). In *Paradise Regain'd,* Jesus speaks what Roy Flannagan calls "a dangerous sentiment in an age of monarchy": "Yet he who reigns within himself, and rules / Passions, Desires, and Fears, is more a King; / Which every wise and vertuous man attains" (Ibid., 750).

should be left free from any coercion other than the persuasion of God. James Holly Hanford suggests that Milton's consistent endorsement of the separation of church and state may owe itself in some measure to the example of his friend Williams, who had already been expelled from Massachusetts before Milton wrote *Areopagitica*. With Milton's treatises on printing, divorce, and politics all espousing a new degree of freedom, there can be no doubt, Hanford says, that Milton had "enrolled himself as an individualist in doctrine, parting company once and for all" with the establishment communitarian strand of Puritanism represented in the writings of William Ames and John Cotton.[126]

Although Perez Zagorin finds *Areopagitica* rhetorically inferior to Williams's *The Bloudy Tenent of Persecution*, "no account of political thought in the English revolution may overlook Milton," he contends, because of Milton's strategic role in the modern shift toward the individual subject.[127] As did Williams in America, so Milton reconciled what most people had previously considered to be irreconcilable – Protestant theology and complete liberty. Both he and Williams took from William Perkins's seminal writings on conscience the hope for separatism based on liberty, even as they rejected the fear of William Ames that separatism brought fragmentation.[128] Milton revealed a keen awareness that his chief contribution was for the sake of the individual rather than the church, as in "To Mr. *CYRIACK SKINNER* Upon His Blindness" (1655):

> What supports me, dost thou ask?
> The Conscience, Friend, to have lost them [his eyes] over ply'd
> In Liberties Defence, my noble task;
> Of which all *Europe* rings from side to side.
> This thought might lead me through this World's vain mask
> Content, though blind, had I no other guide.[129]

Freedom for Milton and Williams was no longer the liberty to uphold

---

126 James Holly Hanford, *John Milton, Englishman* (New York: Crown Publishers, 1949), 121. Cf. Shawcross, *John Milton*, 133: "Clearly Milton is not in agreement with William Perkins ... or William Ames on many of these issues." Here one might compare the equation of conscience and self in *Samson Agonistes*, where Samson answers his friends' advice to "Regard thy self" with, "My self? my conscience and internal peace" (Milton, 834 [ll. 1333-1334]). Mollenkott notes that *Samson Agonistes* has "an immediate appeal to the modern mind" because of its "unusually modern emphasis upon the partial validity of everyone's point of view" (102, 91).
127 Zagorin, *History*, 106-107.
128 Honeygosky, 105, 39.
129 Milton, 29 (ll. 9-14).

the public order of the commonwealth but to follow the inward and individual persuasion of God against the laws of any king or governing body.[130] This is precisely the right that Bunyan claimed when resisting the Book of Common Prayer and continuing his preaching in conventicles – and so, to some degree, Bunyan certainly joined Milton in being "an embattled individual at odds with his age."[131] Yet the belief that the power of scripture and Spirit to form an individual's conscience apart from all other individuals person made Milton – as a model of his own conception of Protestantism – "a church of one in which he was his own minister."[132] By contrast, Bunyan retained a more traditional hope that doctrinal orthodoxy and even loyalty to the king could still be the sources of national unity.

Conclusion

Patrick Crutwell believes that, after the English Civil War, literature became fully "modern" by exalting argumentation over cultural consensus, thereby severing ties with the Middle Ages.[133] Milton certainly helped to conceive this new political philosophy with his plea in *Areopagitica*: "Give me the liberty to know, to utter and to argue freely according to conscience, above all liberties."[134] John F. Danby offers as a model of this new individualism the character Edmund from Shakespeare's *King Lear*, who casts off traditional beliefs in human nature, the state, and God "to recognize no limits save those coming from incapacity to get one's way."[135] Edmund in turn embodied the philosophy of Thomas Hobbes, who saw human beings as by nature in competition rather than community. In *Leviathan* (1651), investigation of scripture and appeal to the godly king played no role in Hobbes's utilitarian political program. So

---

130 Woods, 203; Honeygosky, 143.
131 Keeble, "Till one greater man," 35. Cf. Hill, *World*, 409; Bunyan, *Milton*, 49.
132 Zagorin, *Milton*, 101. Cf. Shawcross, *John Milton*, 256; Anthony Low, *The Reinvention of Love: Poetry, Politics and Culture from Sidney to Milton* (Cambridge: Cambridge University Press, 1993), 169-170; Honeygosky, 143; Denis Saurat, *Milton: Man and Thinker* (New York: The Dial Press, 1925), 182. Note *Paradise Regain'd*, 1.463-464, where Jesus decides he will send his spirit to dwell "In pious Hearts, an inward Oracle / To all truth requisite for me to know" (Milton, 735).
133 Patrick Crutwell, *The Shakespearean Moment and its Place in the Poetry of the Seventeenth Century* (New York: Columbia University Press, 1955), 206-207.
134 Milton, 1021.
135 John F. Danby, *Shakespeare's Doctrine of Nature: A Study of King Lear* (London: Faber and Faber, 1949), 46.

although Hobbes was certainly no libertarian, he took government out of the purview of theologians and thus took political theory a giant step toward modernity by making it entirely a subject of human debate and resolution.[136] Hobbes left all casuistical matters not determined by the sovereign entirely up to the conscience of individuals, with the only qualification being not theological orthodoxy but sincere intention.[137] Perhaps the full flower on the modern bloom of political philosophy was John Stuart Mill's *On Liberty* (1859). "This, then, is the appropriate region of human liberty," Mill wrote: "It comprises, first, the inward domain of consciousness; demanding liberty of conscience in the most comprehensive sense; liberty of thought and feeling; absolute freedom of opinion and sentiment on all subjects, practical or speculative, scientific, moral, or theological."[138] Like Milton, Mill saw his concern with the tyranny of tradition or custom in all its forms, including Christianity, to be in line ideologically with the Reformation.[139] Judged by the standard of Hobbes or Mill, John Bunyan was not the modern man that John Milton was becoming.

Bunyan's political writings did come after the Civil War, and they often reflected a new cultural ethos that emphasized the individual. But the grounding of his thought was in a previous age. While Martin Schmidt's claim that the development of modern Western consciousness ran through Perkins, Ames, and Bunyan is accurate,[140] this is to tell only part of the story. The other part, now only a vestigial remain of the modern body politick in the West, was the hope they placed in the magistrate who would establish Puritan religion according to the scriptures. Few would now prefer the limited conception of civil freedom held by Bunyan to the fuller freedoms espoused by Milton and Williams. Yet the part of Bunyan's thought still demanding our attention is that private revelation and individual experience should never completely trump the life of the community, whether political or ecclesial. This conviction reached maturity in the allegories from the last decade of Bunyan's life: *The Pilgrim's Progress*, Parts I and II, *The Life and Death of Mr. Badman*, and *The Holy War*. These writings are the concern of my next two chapters.

---

136 Cf. Hill, *Century*, 163.
137 Cf. Thomas, 45-46, 52.
138 John Stuart Mill, *On Liberty*, in *Mill: Texts, Commentaries*, ed. Alan Ryan (New York: W. W. Norton and Company, 1975), 50.
139 Ibid., 62-63.
140 Schmidt, 85.

CHAPTER FIVE

Christian Selfhood in *The Pilgrim's Progress*, Parts I and II

After one encounters the stirring adventures of *The Pilgrim's Progress*, Part I, perhaps the "walking tour" that is Part II – so Monsignor Ronald Knox called it – seems both less entertaining and less artful.[1] Indeed, the evaluation by James Anthony Froude over a century ago – that Part II's sluggishness, lack of drama, and apparent misogyny render it a "feeble reverberation" of the original – still dominates critical opinion of a work that Bunyan wrote to combat apocryphal sequels to his *magnum opus*.[2] But while the staid character of Part II may be less artistically interesting even for its admirers, I believe that it offers a more compelling portrait of the deeper Christian life than does Part I. For once one reads both parts of *The Pilgrim's Progress* within the categories of conscience and Christian selfhood that I have thus far established in Bunyan's larger corpus, then one discovers that Part II contains Bunyan's more developed thought *apropos* individualism and subjectivism.

While some have taken Coleridge's dictum that *The Pilgrim's Progress* was produced by the Bunyan of Parnassus and not the Bunyan of the Conventicle to the extreme, saying that one should not look for Bunyan's theology there,[3] I contend on the contrary that

---

1 Ronald Knox, *Essays in Satire* (London: Sheed and Ward, 1928), 206.
2 James Anthony Froude, *Bunyan* (London: Macmillan and Company, 1895), 171. For an overview of some of the common criticisms of Part II since Froude, see N. H. Keeble, "Christiana's Key: The Unity of *The Pilgrim's Progress*," in *The Pilgrim's Progress: Critical and Historical Views*, ed. Vincent Newey (Totowa, NJ: Barnes and Noble Books, 1980), 1-2.
3 E.g., in his introduction to Bunyan's *The Pilgrim's Progress*, N. H. Keeble says that Bunyan's greatest allegory won a wide readership "because its inspired author was liberated from the constraints of his theology" (N. H. Keeble, in John Bunyan, *The Pilgrim's Progress* [Oxford: Oxford University Press, 1991], xi). F. R. Leavis, in his afterword to *The Pilgrim's Progress*, says that Bunyan's insights into human nature remain when "we may find wholly unprofitable the theology with which Bunyan accompanies it" (298). Likewise does I. M. Green say that "Bunyan was not always such a high Calvinist in practice as he was in principle, especially in his most

one should read his few fictional works most properly within the context of Bunyan's many doctrinal and confessional treatises. As Geoffrey Nuttall writes, Bunyan himself would not have thought of *The Pilgrim's Progress*, *The Life and Death of Mr. Badman*, and *The Holy War* as "imaginative" works of art but as metaphorical vehicles for honoring the Pauline-Lutheran conception of God.[4] As Bunyan himself explained near the end of his Apology for *The Pilgrim's Progress*, Part I, "*It seems a Novelty, and yet contains / Nothing but sound and honest Gospel-strains.*"[5] One finds explicitly present throughout *The Pilgrim's Progress* the same doctrinal emphases that we have seen at work in Bunyan's dogmatic works as well as *Grace Abounding*: the blood-bought satisfaction for sins, the opposition of law and gospel, justification by faith, the "alien" righteousness of Christ, the two-natures Christology, the doctrine of the Trinity, and even the Lutheran notion of *simul iustus et peccator*.[6]

Bunyan's spiritual exemplar Martin Luther once wrote in a letter, "I am persuaded that without skill in literature genuine theology cannot stand," and in his *Commentary on Galatians*, which Bunyan knew so very well, Luther advocated the seemliness of allegory for embodying theology into a form easily digestible by laypeople:

> For the people are greatly delighted with allegories and similitudes, and therefore Christ himself oftentimes useth them. For they are, as it were, certain pictures which set forth things as if they were painted before the eyes of the simple, and therefore

---

forcefully evangelical works, such as *Come and Welcome* [*to Jesus Christ*] and *Good News for the Vilest of Men*, and in his imaginative writings, such as *A Book for Boys and Girls* and *The Pilgrim's Progress*, as opposed to technical treatises like *The Doctrine of the Law and Grace* [*Unfolded*]" (Green, "Bunyan in Context: The Changing Face of Protestantism in Seventeenth-Century England," in *Bunyan in England and Abroad*, ed. M. van Os and G. J. Schutte [Amsterdam: Vrije Universiteit University Press, 1990], 13). Gordon Campbell advises that it is not only futile but obstructive to search for Bunyan's theology in "The Theology of *The Pilgrim's Progress*," in *The Pilgrim's Progress: Critical and Historical Views*, ed. Vincent Newey (Totowa, NJ: Barnes and Noble Books, 1980), 258-259, 261, and "Fishing in Other Men's Waters: Bunyan Among the Theologians," in *John Bunyan: Conventicle and Parnassus* (Oxford: Clarendon Press, 1988), 151. In "Be Not Extream," I challenge Campbell's assumption as a self-fulfilling prophecy in which whoever assumes that Bunyan's theology will be an obstacle to reading his novel will inevitably find it to be one (460). Cf. Mullett, 200-201.

4 Geoffrey F. Nuttall, "The Heart of *The Pilgrim's Progress*," *American Baptist Quarterly* 7:4 (December 1988): 473.
5 Bunyan, *PP*, 7.
6 Ibid., 139, 143, 148, 209-211, 225, 255.

they move and persuade very much, especially the simple and ignorant. (Gal 4:21)

For it is a seemly thing sometimes to add an allegory when the foundation is well laid and the matter thoroughly proved. For as painting is an ornament to set forth and garnish an house already builded, so is an allegory the light of a matter which is already otherwise proved and confirmed. (Gal 4:24)[7]

While Luther did not think that allegory was the appropriate arena for *constructive* theology, he believed that allegory *was* an appropriate medium by which to convey dogma to the masses on matters which the church had already decided. Allegorical literature served for Luther, then, a function roughly equivalent to that of stained-glassed windows in medieval cathedrals or woodcuts during the Reformation, which was to impart the basic Christian narratives and doctrines to the laity.

Bunyan explained that when he *"Fell suddenly into an Allegory,"* he had no premeditation to write for anyone other than *"mine own self to gratifie."* But when some of his friends read what he had produced and encouraged its printing, he explained its publication with a defense that could have been culled from Luther: Christ himself (along with the apostles and prophets) wrapped his message in metaphors. Following such a holy example, Bunyan averred that his *"Book is writ in such a Dialect, / As may the minds of listless men affect."*[8] Bunyan had actually said as early as *Some Gospel-Truths Opened* that Christ's use of similitudes made their usage permissible for his followers, thus revealing that, in the fictional works, Bunyan

---

7   Martin Luther, "Letter to Eoban Hess, March 29, 1523," quoted in Roland Mushat Frye, *God, Man, and Satan: Patterns of Christian Thought and Life in Paradise Lost, Pilgrim's Progress, and the Great Theologians* (Princeton: Princeton University Press, 1960), 7; Luther, *CG*, 414, 417. Jaroslav Pelikan translates *parabolis* in Luther's commentary on Galatians 4:21 as "parables" whereas the older English translation uses "similitudes" (Luther, *Lectures on Galatians*, 433). Contrast Luther's approval of allegory with John Calvin, who believed that allegory is usually a tool of the devil to weaken sound biblical teachings (David L. Puckett, *John Calvin's Exegesis of the Old Testament* [Louisville: Westminster John Knox Press, 1995], 107).

8   Bunyan, *PP*, 1, 2, 4, 7. I find the comment of George W. Walton to be generally true, even if overstated: "For Bunyan the proverb was a rhetorical figure more suitable to fictional than to doctrinal truth, that is, more fitting for persuasive embellishment than for authoritative demonstration of his faith" (Walton, "Bunyan's Proverbial Language," in *Bunyan in Our Time*, ed. Robert G. Collmer [Kent, OH: The Kent State University Press, 1989], 26).

was pursuing the same line of theological thought on which he embarked in the early anti-Quaker writings.[9] Bunyan lamented in the preface to Part II that some interpreters misread Part I as a romance, but he refused to "slight them as they slight me."[10]

The "doctrine" of *The Pilgrim's Progress*, Part I, is to show why some individuals attain all the way to *"the Gate of Glory"* and receive *"the everlasting Prize,"* while others set out for eternal life but *"loose their labour, and like fools do die."*[11] Clearly, therefore, Part I is a dramatization of Bunyan's own concern over election in *Grace Abounding*.[12] It also offers a narrative expression of his later diagram, *A Mapp Shewing the Order and Causes of Salvation and Damnation*, which explicates why some people are saved and some people are damned. Bunyan thus remained very close to the approach that John Calvin took toward his doctrine of double predestination: Calvin did not derive election and reprobation from a prior notion of God's sovereignty but instead deduced from his entire theological and exegetical work that an absolute decree was a more satisfactory arbiter between the saved and the damned than either good works or free choice.[13] While it may sometimes appear that Christian's various trials place his election in jeopardy, one must recall that Bunyan was illustrating the difference between the saved and the damned for a popular audience – a difference based not upon human will or exertion, but rather the nature of God's mercy (Rom 9:16).[14] Christian requires unmerited grace to continue the journey

---

9   N. H. Keeble, in Bunyan, *The Pilgrim's Progress*, ed. Keeble, x.
10 Bunyan, *PP*, 171. *The Holy War* describes life in Mansoul during Diabolus's temporary reign as including "Odious Atheistical Pamphlets and filthy Ballads & Romances full of [ri]baldry" (Bunyan, *HW*, 31). Cf. Mullett for a contention that *The Pilgrim's Progress was* a romance (Mullett, 192) but Michael Davies for the belief that it is not a romance at all but a conversion of romance into doctrine (Michael Davies, 'Stout & Valiant Champions for God': The Radical Reformation of Romance in *The Pilgrim's Progress*," in *John Bunyan: Reading Dissenting Writing*, ed. N. H. Keeble (Oxford: Peter Lang, 2002), 110.
11 Bunyan, *PP*, 6.
12 Cf. Bunyan, *GA*: "For that the Elect only attained eternal life, that I without scruple did hearily close withall: but that my self was one of them, there lay all the question" (§61; p. 21).
13 McGrath, 167.
14 Cf. Bunyan, *GA*: "Therefore, this would still stick with me, How can you tell you are Elected? and what if you should not? how then? O Lord, thought I, what if I should not indeed? It may be you are not, said the Tempter: it may be so indeed, thought I. Why then, said Satan, you had as

he concludes at the River of Death no less than when he began in the City of Destruction.[15] In a similar vein, the eighteenth-century hymn-writer and preacher John Newton reacted to John Wesley's doctrine of perfectionism by saying that he expected to be saved in the end as a sinner and not as a saint.[16]

If *The Pilgrim's Progress*, Part I, is indeed a recasting of Bunyan's Reformation conception of how people come to salvation or damnation, then Part II is no less a theological work but one that focuses quite differently on the nature of the Christian life. Any number of commentators have observed that if Part I is about an individual pilgrimage, then Part II is about the corporate journey of the church.[17] Yet I contend further that, insofar as Part II reflects the spiritual seasoning of Bunyan himself (which we saw in an initial stage at the end of *Grace Abounding*), then Part II reveals Bunyan's most mature perspectives on human individuality, subjectivity, and selfhood. I read Part II not as a mere sequel to Part I, as Mullett and Sharrock also insist,[18] but as a continuation and completion of a story half-told. If Part I explains how some fall away while others do not, then Part II explains how the Christian life is meant to be lived. To think that Part I is an independent tale only because Christian arrives at the Celestial City wrongly assumes that Bunyan really had no new wisdom left to impart but had to vary the landscape

---

good leave off, and strive no further; for if indeed you should not be Elected and chosen of God, there is no talke of your being saved: *For it is neither in him that willeth, nor in him that runneth, but in God that sheweth mercy*" (§59-60; p. 21). Hopeful's words to Christian in the River of Death that the waves and billows demonstrate not God's abandonment of Christian but a desire to try him appears to amount to a confirmation of Christian's election (Bunyan, *PP*, 158). Cf. the words of Hugh Latimer to Nicholas Ridley shortly before their execution by burning: "Be of good comfort, Master Ridley, and play the man. We shall this day light such a candle, by God's grace, in England, as I trust shall never be put out" (Foxe, 309).

15 In Part II, after Mr. Honest sings about how, by grace, one must die to sin in order to live, Gaius responds, "It is right ...; good Doctrine, and Experience teaches this" (Bunyan, *PP*, 265).

16 D. Bruce Hindmarsh, *John Newton and the English Evangelical Tradition* (Grand Rapids: William B. Eerdmans Publishing Company, 1996), 129.

17 See N. H. Keeble, "'Here is her Glory, even to be under Him': The Feminine in the Thought and Work of John Bunyan," in *John Bunyan and His England, 1628-88*, ed. Anne Laurence, W. R. Owens, and Stuart Sim (London: The Hambledon Press, 1990), 147.

18 Mullett, 243; Sharrock, in John Bunyan, *The Pilgrim's Progress*, ed. Roger Sharrock (London: Penguin Books, 1987), 24.

and the characters in Part II to achieve any dramatic effect at all.[19] Yet, Bunyan indicated in "The Author's Way of Sending Forth His Second Part of the Pilgrim" that he expected Part II to win even greater esteem than Part I. He sent Part II *"To Friends, not foes: to Friends that will give place / To thee,"* so he intended his book, as he did *Grace Abounding,* for other Christians.[20] And he further revealed that Christiana would instruct them more fully than did Christian:

Besides, what my first Pilgrim *left conceal'd,*
Thou my brave Second Pilgrim *hast reveal'd;*
What Christian *left lock't up and went his way,*
Sweet Christiana *opens with her Key.*[21]

What previously hidden secrets does Part II unlock? A comparative study of the use of "conscience" and "self" in Parts I and II reveals that Bunyan knew the subjectivist dangers lurking in the individualism of Part I, and thus provided a necessary ecclesial and even sacramental corrective in Part II.

The Role of Conscience in *The Pilgrim's Progress,* Parts I and II

Since Bunyan alluded to conscience throughout his autobiography, one should expect that he would do the same in the story of his fictive alter-ego. As we saw in Chapter Three, Bunyan's understanding of conscience in *Grace Abounding* followed a pattern that he learned from Luther's *Commentary on Galatians*: the natural conscience is aware of its impurity before God's law; it tries to exonerate itself by performing good works but only creates a false god in the process; it becomes "tender" when it hears the proclamation of the gospel, and finally, it becomes "good" only when it ceases to listen to its own voice and trusts in the imputed righteousness of Jesus Christ for salvation. This process that the redeemed conscience undergoes is again evident in *The Pilgrim's Progress,* Part I.

Although Bunyan does not use the word "conscience" when describing the Slow of Dispond, the Slow certainly serves for Christian the same function as does the conscience in *Grace Abounding.*

---

19   Cf. Keeble: "Even for R. M. Frye, who sees the individualism of Part I and the communalism of Part II as constituting, together, a 'stereoscopic view' of the complete Christian life, the parts remain distinct wholes, juxtaposed and complementary narratives, but 'each complete in itself '" ("Christiana's Key," 3).
20   Bunyan, *PP*, 171.
21   Ibid.

Following Luther, Bunyan constantly linked the natural conscience in *Grace Abounding* with the severe punishment that follows all violations of the Mosaic law: that law itself is a expression of God's holy will, but because original sin has rendered nugatory the human ability to keep the law in every point, it serves only to condemn. Likewise, in the bottom of the Slow of Dispond there are stepping stones "by the direction of the Law-giver" to help pilgrims gain their footing, but they are so encrusted with mire as to be practically useless. The marginalia explain that it is here that "the sinner is awakened about his lost condition" just as the soul's fears, doubts, and apprehensions also settle here.[22] This corresponds to the first awakening of the conscience to its damnable condition described by both Luther and *Grace Abounding*. Even as Luther and Bunyan expected the troubled conscience to try to rid itself of its guilt through works righteousness, as Christian goes immediately from the Slow of Dispond to the village of Morality, heeding the advice of Mr. Worldly-Wiseman that Mr. Legality can remove the burden of his sin. Another marginal note at the conclusion of Evangelist's chastisement of Christian offers this warning against works-righteousness: *"There is no deliverance from the guilt, and burden of sin, but by the death and blood of Christ."*[23] Coincidentally, Evangelist also identifies Legality as "the Son of the Bond woman" Hagar from Galatians 4, the same chapter from which Luther's commentary seeks permission to use allegory to convey established doctrine to the unversed.[24] Christian's anguished "What shall I do to be saved?" at the beginning of the story, followed by the episodes at the Slow and at Sinai, are certainly enough to reject the rebuttal of Thomas Sherman, who wrote his own sequel to *The Pilgrim's Progress* in 1682 because he thought Bunyan's original did not show the full misery of a person's preconverted state.[25]

At the House of the Interpreter, immediately before Christian's burden falls away before the cross,[26] Christian sees a dust-filled room that a man with a broom cannot wipe clean, but then a woman with a pail of water settles it easily. Interpreter explains that the dust is original sin, and the room in which it dwells is the human heart;

---

22 Ibid., 15-16.
23 Ibid., 28.
24 Ibid., 23. Cf. Maxine Hancock, *The Key in the Window: Marginal Notes in Bunyan's Narratives* (Vancouver: Regent College Publishing, 2000), 82.
25 James F. Forrest and Roger Sharrock, eds., in Bunyan, *Badman*, xii.
26 Cf. Mullett: "The 'discovery' of Christ aligned Bunyan with Luther, for Luther had found the key to the removal of sin in the Cross" (35).

the broom denotes the futile effort to clear original sin by the law, whereas the woman with water pours nothing else but the gospel.[27] Considering the occasional interchangeability of "heart" and "conscience" in both Bunyan and Luther, perhaps the dusty room is yet another figure of conscience.[28] But there are many other explicit references to the conscience aside from the Slow of Dispond and the dusty room. Also in Interpreter's house, a man recounts a frightening dream to Christian in which he could not escape the wrath of God: "I also sought to hide my self, but I could not; for the Man that sat upon the Cloud, still kept his eye upon me: my sins also came into mind, and my Conscience did accuse me on every side."[29] Then, when Christian encounters Formalist and Hypocrisy after leaving Interpreter, the narrator sees "that they went on every man in his way, without much conference one with another; save that these two told *Christian*, That, as to *Laws and Ordinances*, they doubted not, but they should as conscientiously do them as he."[30] The careful observer of Bunyan's theology knows that this "conscientious," and thus idolatrous, effort to be saved by keeping the moral law earns these two travelers their miserable names.

It is interesting to note that Bunyan singles out the solitary manner of Formalist and Hypocrisy: whereas Christian welcomes the companionship that he later receives from Faithful and grieves deeply that his wife and children do not accompany him on his journey,[31] Formalist, Hypocrisy, and other acquaintances along the narrow way are more determined to keep to themselves. Therefore, even while Christian earns his reputation as an individualist hero, he seeks all along to break out of his loneliness, probably because Bunyan could remember a time when "I counted my self alone, and

---

27 Bunyan, PP, 29-30. Cf. Bunyan, GA: "But my Original and inward pollution, that, that was my plague and my affliction, that I saw at a dreadfull rate all ways putting forth it selfe within me, that I had the guilt of to amazement" (§84, p. 27).
28 See Chapter Three, ft. 130, above.
29 Bunyan, PP, 37. After declaring that he also saw the pit of Hell open, the dream-haunted man repeats, "My Conscience too within afflicted me" (Ibid).
30 Ibid., 40.
31 In *The Life and Death of Mr. Badman*, Badman's godly wife takes an attitude similar to that of Christian, as reflected by her death speech: "My prayers are not lost, my tears are yet in Gods bottle; I would have had a Crown, and Glory for my husband, and for those of my children that follow his steps; but so far as I can see yet, I must rest in the hope of having all my self" (Bunyan, *Badman*, 141).

above the most of men unblest."[32] Christian reaches the Celestial City in the end only by the aid of his two companions, first Faithful and then Hopeful. Here already is an indication that Part II is a more "complete" work than Part I because its protagonists find the full community of saints for which Christian so desperately yearns. It is in Part II that Christian, without even appearing as a character, finally gets his wish, for Part II provides an opportunity for readers to meet and actually travel with Christian, as it were, through his family representatives – *"To have his Company, and hear him tell / Those* Pilgrim *storyes which he knows so well."*[33] It is as if Part II "is *still* Christian's story," says N. H. Keeble. "The apparent narrative completeness of Part I, we realize, was as illusory as Christian's seeming isolation."[34] Indeed, Part II is a continuation, not a sequel.

After the removal of Christian's burden, many of Christian's experiences amount to the kind of post-conversion disturbances of conscience that Bunyan mentioned in *Grace Abounding*.[35] Apollyon, for example, seems to play the role of the natural conscience when he reminds Christian that he will not receive heaven's wage because he fumbled his roll of salvation on Hill Difficulty. But when Christian hears Faithful recount his conversion narrative on the other side of the Valley of the Shadow of Death and responds to Faithful's escape from the seductress Wanton, *"She did not promise you the content of a good conscience,"* he seems from that moment no longer responsible for explaining his bouts of conscience to his friends.[36]

---

32 Bunyan, *GA*, 28 (§87). In his table talks, Martin Luther warned that the solitary person is particularly vulnerable to melancholy and the assaults of devil (Marius, 121-122, 217).
33 Bunyan, *PP*, 170.
34 Keeble, "Christiana's Key," 11.
35 Cf. Henri Talon: "The direct source of *The Pilgrim's Progress* is Bunyan's own experience. The hero of the book is fashioned in his author's image. The spiritual development found in the autobiography, *Grace Abounding*, appears again in the allegory; but the growth of a conscience has become a pilgrimage, the inward action has taken a concrete form, and the invisible ways of the understanding have built a road and paths like those of seventeenth-century England" (Talon, ed., *God's Knotty Log: Selected Writings of John Bunyan* [Cleveland: The World Publishing Company, 1961], 11). Yet, Walton cautions that Bunyan is "reluctant to allow his own private experiences to be more authoritative than Scripture" (28).
36 Bunyan, *PP*, 68. Stauffer observes that Christian's motto of "the just shall live by faith" corresponds to Luther's Reformation breakthrough (713) and that Faithful's full conversion narrative sounds like it could have come from Martin Luther (716). Indeed, Stauffer finds all of Part I to be Lutheran in its agenda (722).

For instance, it is Faithful who reports of Shame, "He said that a tender conscience was an unmanly thing," who explains that "God prefers a tender Conscience," and who advises Talkative to his displeasure that he speak no more than *"what your Conscience can justifie you in."*[37] Later, Hopeful's relation of his conversion in Vanity Fair also follows the now-familiar Lutheran pattern. Hopeful tells how he felt the threat of God's wrath, thought of how to ease his anxiety by his own works while his sins only "got faster hold of my Conscience," and felt peace only after he realized that salvation is not by works.[38] These experiences qualify him to explain why Temporary from the town of Graceless quit his pilgrimage: "Though the Consciences of such men are awakened, yet their minds are not changed: therefore when the power of guilt weareth away, that which provoked them to be Religious, ceaseth."[39]

Faithful's talk about a tender conscience evokes Bunyan's recollection in *Grace Abounding* of the godly women whose conversation helped produce in him "a very great softness and tenderness of heart, which caused me to fall under the conviction of what by Scripture they asserted." This in turn emphasizes how Bunyan could look to women to exemplify Christian devotion.[40] Christiana and Mercie in Part II, by welcoming the assistance of Great-heart on their pilgrimage, show not their stereotyped inferiority to Christian but their actualization of that which Christian realizes but does not always carry out when he cautions Faithful not to "be tickled at the thoughts of our own manhood, for such commonly come by the worst when tried."[41] Here, too, Christiana will teach a better lesson than Christian, as the preface to Part II reveals:

---

37 Bunyan, *PP*, 72, 73, 84. Parenthetically, the author of the apocryphal work, *The Pilgrim's Progress*, Part III, introduced a new character named Tender Conscience (Cf. Susan Cook, "Pilgrim's Progresses: Derivative Texts and the Seventeenth-Century Reader," in *Awakening Words: John Bunyan and the Language of Community*, ed. David Gay, James G. Randall, and Arlette Zinck [Newark: University of Delaware Press, 2000], 189).
38 Bunyan, *PP*, 139-140.
39 Ibid., 152. Luther's *CG* has a section on Galatians 5:5 which explains the difference between faith and hope while insisting on their common purpose in soothing the law-afflicted conscience (459-464). It is likely no coincidence that Christian's two companions in Part I are Faithful and Hopeful.
40 Bunyan, *GA*, 15 (§41). Cf. Camden, "Most Fit," 831.
41 Bunyan, *PP*, 131. In Part II, Timorous shows her misunderstanding of Christiana's desire to go on pilgrimage by saying, "Do not so unwomanly cast away your self " (Ibid., 181).

Go then, I say, tell all men who thou art,
Say, I am Christiana, *and my part*
Is now with my four Sons, to tell you what
It is for men to take a Pilgrims *lot.*[42]

While Christiana's journey lacks the intensity of Christian's, John R. Knott is correct to say that its spirituality is all the richer than her husband's because it becomes increasingly located within the Christian community.[43]

Christiana experiences a burdened conscience at the beginning of Part II when she thinks of her past unwillingness to accompany her husband on pilgrimage. "And upon this, came into her mind by *swarms*, all her unkind, unnatural, and ungodly Carriages to her dear Friend: Which also clogged her Conscience, and did load her with guilt."[44] She then reveals her anguish to her four sons: "I have also been much affected with the thoughts of mine own State and yours, which I verily believe is by nature miserable: My Carriages also to your Father in his distress, is a great load to my Conscience. For I hardened both mine own heart and yours against him, and refused to go with him on Pilgrimage."[45] Some time later, when the new pilgrimage is well underway, Christiana's eldest son Mathew falls sick to his stomach at the Palace Beautiful. The physician Skill diagnoses Mathew's condition as "the Gripes" (which a marginal gloss explains as *"Gripes of Conscience"*) and cures him with some medicine compounded *"ex Carne & Sanguine Christi"* ("from the body and blood of Christ").[46] The Latinate phrasing points to a

---

42 Ibid., 172.
43 John R. Knott, Jr., "Bunyan and the Holy Community" (*Studies in Philology* 80:2 (Spring 1982): 208.
44 Bunyan, *PP*, 177. Sim and Walker misunderstand Bunyan's typically critical description of conscience when they say that Christiana's "conscience cannot allow her blindly to follow social norms and conventions in the manner of her neighbors" (156). In Bunyan's perspective, when a person first feels pangs of conscience, the conscience tries to persuade the person of what it *should do* to absolve itself, not what social norms it *should avoid*.
45 Bunyan, *PP*, 180-181.
46 Ibid., 228, 229. Bunyan apologizes in the margin: *"The Lattine I borrow."* Compare his *HW*, where he knows that "Mors" means "death" (2), uses the Latin "Diabolus" for the name of Satan, and even has Diabolus say, "Probatus est" (172). By contrast, God the Father and God the Son go by Hebrew names, "Shaddai" and "Emanuel." After Mathew's case of the gripes, Christiana's son James also begins to feel sick shortly thereafter, but because he takes some of Skill's pills, he quickly revives (Bunyan, *PP*, 241). Compare the reference to the doctrine of justification as a medicine against a wounded in conscience in *Saved by Grace*, in *MW*, 8:218-219.

sacramentalism yet to come. Occasionally after this, Part II has reminders that the way to salvation begins in contrition,[47] but there is a near-complete lack of the continual struggles of conscience that punctuate Part I.

The most notable contrast between the two books in this regard is the death scene of Mr. Honest in Part II. "In his Life time [he] had spoken to one *Good-conscience* to meet him there [at the River of Death], the which he also did, and lent him his Hand, and so helped him over. The last Words of Mr. *Honest* were, *Grace Reigns.* So he left the World."[48] Whereas the narrator justifies Christian's near-drowning at the end of Part I with the forewarning that the depth of the River of Death is proportional to the depth of the person's faith, there is no sense in Part II that death *must* present a crisis of conscience, and the river ebbs and flows as naturally as the tide.[49] Not only does this change reflect an evolution in Bunyan's thought, but it has drawn artistic praise from religious and secular readers alike:

> *The Pilgrim's Progress*, Part Two, impressed me as a gem. Perhaps it is easier to write about family and children than about the wrestling of one's own soul. In any case, the final section of Part Two, recounting the ways in which each pilgrim went through the river, strikes as deep a chord as anything in the English language.[50]

> But who with any wisdom to offer, worth listening to, could have published [a negative] reaction to the incomparable end of Part Two of *The Pilgrim's Progress*, where the pilgrims, waiting by the river, receive one by one the summons to cross? – Incomparable, for where else in prose can a like sustained exaltation be found?[51]

Since there is far less preoccupation with the problems of conscience

---

47 E.g., Great-heart says, "I care not at all for that Profession that begins not in heaviness of Mind," and Christiana's son James summarizes, "No fears, no Grace" (Bunyan, *PP*, 253-254).
48 Ibid., 309.
49 Ibid., 157, 304. Cf. Marius: "In Luther's particular case, the Christian was not required to have such faith that horror at death and annihilation and corruption could be considered a sign of unbelief and damnation" (205) In Bunyan's *Badman*, Mr. Wiseman explains, "Suppose one man should die quietly, another should die suddenly, and a third should die under great consternation of spirit; no man can Judge of their eternall condition by the manner of any of these kinds of deaths" (157).
50 F. W. Dillistone, "The Bunyan Tercentenary," *Theology Today* 55:2 (July 1988): 165.
51 F. R. Leavis, "Bunyan Through Modern Eyes," *The Common Pursuit* (New York: New York University Press, 1964), 210. Leavis, I might add, was a thorough-going humanist who claimed no Christian affiliation.

in Part II than in Part I, does this reflect a corresponding shift in Bunyan's perceptions of selfhood?

The Emerging View of "Self" in *The Pilgrim's Progress*, Parts I and II

Even as there are more references to "conscience" in Part I of *The Pilgrim's Progress* than in Part II, there are considerably more uses of the word "self" in Part I as well. Stanley Fish says that *all* of Christian's conflicts in Part I are conflicts of self and memory,[52] but this only begs the further question: if Bunyan was less preoccupied with "conscience" and "self" in Part II, then to what did he turn his attention in the latter part?

A concern for the "selfhood" of his reader was an important consideration in Bunyan's consent to publish Part I. Consistent with what we have already discovered about the theological purpose of Part I as illustrating the difference between the saved and the damned, we find these claims in its opening Apology:

Wouldest thou loose thy self, and catch no harm?
And find thy self again without a charm?
Would'st read thy self, and read thou know'st not what
And yet know whether thou art blest or not,
By reading the same lines? O then come hither,
And lay my Book, thy Head and Heart together.[53]

Part I famously begins with burdened Christian standing alone, reading his book, the Bible. He is one of those who needs to know whether he is "blest or not." And so, he confides to his wife that he is *"in my self undone."*[54] Once Christian is upon his journey, he is unable to remove his burden by himself, and Evangelist tells him to "abhor thy self for hearkening" to Worldly-Wiseman.[55] This means

---

52 Fish, *Self-Consuming Artifacts*, 233.
53 Bunyan, *PP*, 7 (emphases mine). Again recall when reading the final line Bunyan's occasional equation of "heart" with "conscience." Vincent van Gogh apparently took Bunyan's advice to lose and find oneself through reading *The Pilgrim's Progress* very much to his own heart. Van Gogh highly commended Bunyan's classic – even saying in his only printed sermon, "Our life is a pilgrim's progress – as an example of a life of Christian self-denial that finds itself through its labors for the Celestial City" (See Kathleen Powers Erickson, "Pilgrims and Strangers: The Role of *The Pilgrim's Progress* and *The Imitation of Christ* in Shaping the Piety of Vincent van Gogh," *Bunyan Studies* 4 [Spring 1991]: 8, 12, 29).
54 Bunyan, *PP*, 8.
55 Ibid., 17, 23.

that Christian can make it to the Celestial City on his own no more than can Christiana and her train; the only difference is that Christiana's guide Great-heart, unlike Evangelist in Part I, travels alongside rather than appearing to her from time to time.[56] Christian can then in turn scold Formalist and Hypocrisy for entering the narrow way "by your selves without his [Christ's] direction."[57] When Christian renders an account of his life to Charity at the Palace Beautiful, he admits, "I am conscious to my self of many failings."[58] Hopeful exhibits a similar awareness much later in Part I when he verifies Christian's own account of facing a demonic reprise against his self: "I know something of this my self; for before I knew my self it was so with me."[59]

There is the beginning of something individualistic in the words of Bunyan's protagonists, but it is a birth that must quickly lead to death in order, paradoxically, to find life again. Individualism is modern only when the person is defined over against (and as having precedence over) the community. Christian says to Apollyon that while he formerly tried to "mend my self," now "I have let my self to another," and to Ignorance he explains, *"Then we have right thoughts of God, when we think that he knows us better then we know our selves."*[60] The budding self-awareness in *The Pilgrim's Progress* can indeed lead to an autonomous inward authority, as Stuart Sim and David Walker suggest, *if* one's knowledge of one's self is solitary, self-generated, and thus autonomous.[61] But Christian knows that it is not, and also that the primal sin of the human race is to seek one's own autonomy. By contrast, this is what Mr. Temporary does not understand, for one Save-self persuades him to reject Christian's company.[62]

In Part II, there is nothing to compare to the many references to "self" in Part I; indeed, the word "self" appears only a handful of times, and only once in the indicting manner made against Christian in Part I and against Bunyan himself in *Grace Abounding*. That one time is early in Part II when the character Secret informs Chris-

---

56 In Part I, Christian says to Hopeful, "'Tis good also that we desire of the King a Convoy yea that he will go with us himself " (Ibid., 132). This is exactly the role that Great-heart serves for the pilgrims in Part II.
57 Ibid., 40.
58 Ibid., 51.
59 Ibid., 151.
60 Ibid., 57, 147.
61 Sim and Walker, 131-140. Cf. Muller, 324.
62 Bunyan, *PP*, 152. There is an equivalent character to Save-self in Part II called Self-will (Ibid., 255-257).

tiana that God is ready to forgive her and welcome her alongside Christian, and the narrator tells the reader that *"Christiana at this was greatly abashed in her self "* upon hearing this.[63] After this episode, there is veritably *no* proclivity for autonomous selfhood in Part II. In contrast, Great-heart speaks for all the pilgrims when he assures Mr. Feeble-Mind, "We will deny our selves of some things, both *Opinionative* and *Practical*, for your sake."[64]

Monica Furlong and Roger Sharrock contend that Great-heart is Bunyan's own fatherly, pastoral *persona* in Part II.[65] If so, then we have an author who by 1684, the year of Part II's publication, spoke about "conscience" and "self" much less frequently than before because he had finally escaped the subjectivist agony over his own condition and felt assured in expressing the kind of communal Christian life that he had sought ever since his vision of a wall separating him from the church.[66] The emerging view of the self in *The Pilgrim's Progress*, Part II, is one defined within Christian community.

Individualism and Subjectivism in *The Pilgrim's Progress*, Parts I and II

Patricia Caldwell comments that, "Every reader of *The Pilgrim's Progress* must have noticed that as Christian and Hopeful approached the Celestial City the promise of free and true communication became more and more imminent."[67] In truth, the importance of communal relationships in *The Pilgrim's Progress* has been often ignored, even by the best of Bunyan scholars. While I do not deny Bunyan's individualist tendencies there, I reject the direction of scholarly studies that plot *The Pilgrim's Progress* far along the road toward individual *autonomy* and *subjectivity*, especially since Part II so obviously and intentionally pursues an entirely different path. But it is rare to find a work tracing the extreme individualism of *The Pilgrim's Progress* that attempts to treat Part II at any length.

---

63 Ibid., 180.
64 Ibid., 271. Great-heart is characteristically self-denying, saying elsewhere, "I would not boast, for that I am not mine own Saviour," and, "It is my duty, said he, to distrust mine own ability, that I may have reliance on him that is stronger then all" (Ibid., 243, 246). While in the Delectable Mountains, Mercie hears a voice say through the doorway to Hell, *"If I were to live again, how would I deny my self rather then come to this place"* (Ibid., 287).
65 Furlong, 117; Sharrock, *John Bunyan*, 144.
66 Bunyan, *GA*, §53-55, pp. 19-20.
67 Patricia Caldwell, *The Puritan Conversion Narrative: The Beginnings of American Expression* (Cambridge: Cambridge University Press, 1983), 135.

Gaius Glenn Atkins states the case for Bunyan's modernity most starkly: "'Pilgrim's Progress' is nothing other than the history of the lonely adventures of a soul which has assumed responsibility of its own salvation."[68] No less a Bunyan scholar than Roger Sharrock agrees that Part I "depicts the lonely drama of the individual soul," and Michael A. Mullett contributes that it has an "individualistic emphasis on effort on the part of the lone contender."[69] Charles Taylor speaks of a Puritan tradition of "leaving home," regarding Bunyan's Christian as the pioneer who made a significant contribution to individualism in early America.[70] David Herreshoff spends much time addressing Marxist objections to Bunyan's individualism, beginning with Christopher Hill's confirmation of Taylor's point that Christian shows his rugged individuality by placing his fingers in his ears to drown out the cries of his family.[71] Vincent Newey finds in the escape from Doubting Castle in Part I a quintessentially individualistic episode in which Christian realizes that the key to unlocking the doors of the castle lies entirely within himself ("in my bosom").[72]

What is often neglected about Christian's moments of isolation in Part I is how much he would prefer to have company.[73] For instance, when Pliable returns to the City of Destruction after accompanying Christian for a little while, "*Christian* was left to tumble in the Slow of *Dispond* alone," and then at the Wicket-gate Christian explains to Good Will that he comes alone "because none of my Neighbours saw their danger as I saw mine."[74] Later, Formalist and Hypocrisy laugh at Christian's discourse about law and grace, leaving him to "talk but with himself."[75] Then, both By-ends and Ignorance profess their preference for walking alone to keeping the company of Christian and Hopeful, to which Hopeful laments, "I perceive that thou and I must walk by our selves again."[76] Christian's individualism

---

68 Gaius Glenn Atkins, "Bunyan's Pilgrim's Progress," *Pilgrims of the Lonely Road* (Freeport, NY: Books for Libraries Press, Inc., 1967), 192.
69 Sharrock, *John Bunyan*, 74; Mullett, 187.
70 Taylor, 39.
71 Herreshoff, 173-185.
72 Newey, "Bunyan and the Confines of the Mind," 24.
73 As David Seed says, "Critics have commented frequently on Christian's isolation in Part I, but this has been rather over-stated" (Seed, "Dialogue and Debate in *The Pilgrim's Progress*," in *The Pilgrim's Progress: Critical and Historical Views*, ed. Vincent Newey [Totowa, NJ: Barnes and Noble Books, 1980]: 75).
74 Bunyan, *PP*, 15, 26.
75 Ibid., 41.
76 Ibid., 100, 149.

seems quite forced upon him: the very reason he naively, but mistakenly, accepts Worldly-Wiseman's advice is that Wiseman offers his friendship along with it. In the midst of the Valley of the Shadow of Death, where the demons howl so loudly that Christian cannot recognize his own voice, the hope that sustains him is that he might "have company by and by."[77] Henri Talon makes the disputable claim about Part I "that on the mystical pilgrimage, 'one cannot possibly have company,' as Kierkegaard says." Yet it is not for lack of desire that Christian's journey is often a lonely one. [78] By contrast, it is the ever-expanding "company" which Christiana keeps and for which Christian so often pines that demonstrates most completely the "new" perspective on the Christian life in Part II that Bunyan offers as a corrective to the lonely way of Part I.

The Desire for Company

Although Christian and Faithful meet for the first time after the Valley of the Shadow of Death, their mutual desire for companionship has been so strong that they immediately address each other as closest friends:

> **Chr.** *My honoured and well beloved Brother* **Faithful**, *I am glad that I have overtaken you; and that God has so tempered our spirits, that we can walk as Companions in this so pleasant a path.*
>
> *Faith.* I had thought dear friend, to have had your company quite from our Town, but you did get the start of me; wherefore I was forced to come thus much of the way alone.[79]

Christian discovers that Faithful's way has been as undesirably lonely as his own, and their joint misery makes for good company as soon as they meet. Faithful later expresses their mutual desire that Evangelist would also be in their company on a permanent basis.[80] After Faithful's martyrdom in Vanity Fair, the narrator is glad to report that Hopeful pursues Christian and agrees to be his new companion, to their mutual benefit: Hopeful's encouragement helps to spare Christian from thorough-going despair in Doubting Castle and the River of Death. So does Hopeful profess in the

---

77 Ibid., 64.
78 Henri Talon, *John Bunyan*, Writers and Their Works 73 (London: Longmans, Green & Co., 1956), 26.
79 Bunyan, *PP*, 66-67.
80 Ibid., 86. In Part II, Mercie has a dream in which she "sat all alone in a Solitary place, and was bemoaning the hardness of my Heart." If solitariness is a corollary to hardness of heart, then company is a corollary to salvation.

Inchanted ground that, "I see it is true that the wise man saith, *Two are better then one*. Hitherto hath thy Company been my mercy."[81] By contrast, fated Ignorance approaches the Celestial City quite alone.[82]

The opening pages of Part II indicate that a significant part of heaven's compensation for Christian's troubles is the company he will come to keep there: Secret informs Christiana that Christian, "with Legions more his Companions," enjoys the beatific vision of God. Then Christiana repeats to Mrs. Timorous, "He dwelleth in the presence of the King of the Country, he sits and eats with him at his Table, he is become a Companion of *Immortals*, and has a House now given him to dwell in."[83] Christiana is glad that she does not have to begin her journey alone as her husband did, "not only that she had a Companion [Mercie], but also for that she had prevailed with this poor Maid to fall in love with her own Salvation."[84] Despite Bunyan's defensiveness in Part II for borrowing *ex Carne & Sanguine Christi* from Latin, his frequent conjunction of companionship with sitting at table suggests that Bunyan may have known the Latin etymology of "company" as meaning "[to have] bread together." It is no coincidence, therefore, that there are many more sacramental images in Part II (as I shall explore below) to correspond with its companionate character, and nearly every companion extols the *virtue* of company:

Christiana to Mercie: Thou shalt be a sharer in all the good that I have, because thou so willingly didst become my Companion.[85]

Mercie to Great-heart: O that we might have thy Company to our Journeys end![86]

At the house of Gaius: For *Gaius* and they were such sutable Company, that they could not tell how to part.[87]

Feeble-mind to Ready-to-hault: Man! how camest thou hither? I was but just now complaining that I had not a sutable Companion, but thou art according to my Wish.[88]

Ready-to-hault to Feeble-mind: I shall be glad of thy Company.[89]

Honest to Mnason: Our great Want, a while since, was Harbor, and

---

81 Ibid., 98, 136. Bunyan as narrator interjects at this point, "*Saints fellowship, if it be manag'd well, / Keeps them awake, and that in spite of hell*" (Ibid., 137).
82 Ibid., 162.
83 Ibid., 179, 182.
84 Ibid., 186.
85 Ibid., 217. The emphases in this and subsequent quotations are my own.
86 Ibid., 220.
87 Ibid., 264.
88 Ibid., 271. I continue to follow Bunyan's own italicization here and below.
89 Ibid.

> *good Company, and now I hope we have both.*[90]
>
> *Shepherds of the Delectable Mountains to Great-heart*: This is a comfortable Company, you are welcome to us.[91]
>
> *Great-heart to Standfast*: So-ho, Friend, let us have your Company, if you go, as I suppose you do, to the Celestial City.[92]

That the much greater emphasis on community in Part II is not merely a complement but a corrective to the extreme individualism of Part I reflects J. P. Kenyon's observation that Puritan religiosity was much more of a group phenomenon than Part I of *The Pilgrim's Progress* might suggest when read alone.[93] This is also a large part of the reason why Bunyan speaks in Part II of "the Advantage that this Company had over the other."[94]

The Church. In Part I of *The Pilgrim's Progress*, Christian's book, the Bible, is the visitors' guide of Heaven but not its map.[95] It beckons Christian to leave the City of Destruction for the Celestial City and tells him what he will find once he arrives there ("an *Inheritance, incorruptible, undefiled, and that fadeth not away*"), but it does not tell him *how* to get there. Christian must ask Evangelist for directions, and yet he still gets lost several times along the way.[96] Bunyan is apparently reticent to use the word "church" in Part I – doing so only once, and that negatively, when he says that Worldly-Wiseman attends church in the town of Legality.[97] Granted, various stations along the way, such as the Wicket-gate, the House of Interpreter, the Palace Beautiful, and the Delectable Mountains, provide Christian with points of fellowship that allegorize nonconformist congregations,[98] but he does not stay for very long at any

---

90 Ibid., 273.
91 Ibid., 284.
92 Ibid., 299.
93 Kenyon, 33-34.
94 Bunyan, *PP*, 288.
95 By contrast, in Part II, the conductor Great-heart carries a map in his pocket (Ibid., 297).
96 Ibid., 8-13.
97 Ibid., 22. Cf. Bunyan's *HW*, where Mr. Forget-good speaks of the burdensomeness of goodness "In *Flesh*-lane right opposite to the Church" (124).
98 At the Palace Beautiful, Prudence, Piety, and Charity welcome Christian "in to the Family"(Bunyan, *PP*, 47). Cf. in Part II, where those who "belonged to the Family" bid Christiana and her party godspeed on their way to the Palace (Ibid., 208). Cf. B. R. White: "Bunyan learned lessons [in Bedford] about submission within the family of the local church" (White, "The Fellowship of Believers: Bunyan and Puritanism," in *John Bunyan: Conventicle and Parnassus*, ed. N. H. Keeble [Oxford: Clarendon Press, 1988], 19).

of them.[99] Faithful even bypasses the Palace Beautiful altogether. This may explain Ken Simpson's claim that readers of only *The Pilgrim's Progress*, Part I, may ignore Bunyan's larger conception of the church.[100]

Conversely, Christiana does not begin her pilgrimage after reading the Bible; in fact, although Bunyan mentions his own book (*The Pilgrim's Progress*, Part I) nine times in "The Authors Way of Sending Forth His Second Part of the Pilgrim," he uses the word "book" as a clear reference to the Bible only twice in the entirety of Part II. This occurs when Prudence teaches Christiana's sons, "Especially be much in the Meditation of that Book that was the cause of your Fathers becoming a Pilgrim," and later, when Great-heart consults a book – precisely as a map – in an arbor outside the Enchanted Ground.[101] The pilgrims of Part II do not neglect God's Word, of course, but they learn from it not on the road, as does Christian, but at the stations along the way – which Bunyan is now prepared to identify ecclesially. At both the Palace Beautiful and the inn of Gaius (a new character), Christiana and her companions stay for more than a month.[102] From Gaius's inn, they arrive immediately at the house of Mnason (another new character), who now provides relief for pilgrims in Vanity Fair, and they stay there "a great while" as well.[103] Yet it is at Gaius's inn, above all, that Bunyan's appreciation for the church in the Christian life becomes most evident. Gaius welcomes his visitors with food and "a Bottle of Wine, red as Blood" and then invokes Song of Solomon 2:5, which is traditionally an allegory of Christ and the church: *"Drink of his Flagons then, thou,*

---

99 The shepherds of the Delectable Mountains ask Christian and Hopeful to "stay here a while," and they "were content to stay," but within a very short time, "the Pilgrims had a desire to go forwards, and the Shepherds a desire they should" (Bunyan, *PP*, 120, 122). Atkins summarizes Part I: "No one of Bunyan's pilgrims has ever learnt in whatsoever state he is in therein to be content" (242). Yet in Part II, Great-heart commends to those in his care the song of the shepherd boy: *"I am content with what I have, / Little be it, or much: / And, Lord, Contentment still I crave, / Because thou savest such"* (Bunyan, *PP*, 238).

100 Ken Simpson, "'For the Best Improvement of Time:' *Pilgrim's Progress* and the Liturgies of Nonconformity," in *Awakening Words: John Bunyan and the Language of Community*, ed. David Gay, James G. Randall, and Arlette Zinck (Newark: University of Delaware Press, 2000), 113.

101 Bunyan, *PP*, 226, 297. Cf. Knott, "Bunyan and the Holy Community," 210.

102 Bunyan, *PP*, 224, 264. During the stay with Gaius, Mathew marries Mercie, and James marries Gaius's daughter, Phebe.

103 Ibid., 277. During this stay, Christiana's sons Samuel and Joseph marry Mnason's daughters, Grace and Martha, respectively.

Church, his Dove, / And eat his Apples, who art sick of Love."[104] Greatheart, in turn, thanks Gaius for *"thy Charity before the Church"* and calls him *"mine Host, and of the whole Church."*[105] After reading Part II, it is possible to say with Geoffrey F. Nuttall that *The Pilgrim's Progress* is a good deal *less* centered upon the individual than the great medieval allegory, Dante's *Divine Comedy*. Even in Part I, Nuttall says, "one has much more the sense of company, of Christian *with* Faithful and *with* Hopeful," than in the *Comedy*.[106]

Gordon Wakefield argues that there is a very clear presence of the church in *The Pilgrim's Progress*, but readers miss it if they think of the church in episcopal or presbyterian, not nonconformist, congregational, Baptist terms.[107] Karen Smith's study of community life among certain Calvinistic Baptists in eighteenth-century England begins with observations about their seventeenth-century predecessors which frames Wakefield's comment even more precisely. "The idea," Smith says, "that an individual's experience of faith is nurtured and shaped within the context of the wider covenant community" has always been a basic tenet of Baptist belief, regardless of the sub-denominational variety.[108] In this religious context, Baptistic Christian faith was never a bond only between the believer and Christ; it required the other believers of the community as well. So, then, *The Pilgrim's Progress*, Part I, cannot stand alone without Part II. Christian has individual importance only as he represents the progress that all the believers in Part II make together.[109]

If *The Pilgrim's Progress*, Part I, relies on *Grace Abounding* for its real-to-life storytelling, we do not have an equivalent autobiographical work on which Bunyan could have based Part II. Unfortunately, Bunyan left little personal information about himself from the years 1678-1684, between the publications of *The Pilgrim's Progress*, Parts I and II.[110] To some degree, then, the assumption that

---

104 Ibid., 262.
105 Ibid., 270, 276. Cf. 3 John 6.
106 Nuttall, "Heart," 479.
107 Gordon Wakefield, *Bunyan the Christian* (London: HarperCollins, 1992), 67.
108 Karen Smith, "The Covenant Life of Some Eighteenth-Century Calvinistic Baptists in Hampshire and Wiltshire," in *Pilgrim Pathways: Essays in Baptist History in Honour of B. R. White*, ed. William H. Brackney and Paul S. Fiddes with John H. Y. Briggs (Macon, GA: Mercer University Press, 1999), 166; cf. 167, 175.
109 Cf. Simpson, 116.
110 G. B. Harrison observes that the records of the Bedford congregation during Bunyan's ministry were also "scanty" and "very badly kept" (*Church Book*, viii).

the more communal approach to pilgrimage in Part II is based upon Bunyan's experiences as a full-time pastor and father is speculative, but there seems little reason to doubt it.[111] Some church records are extant from this period in which Bunyan mentioned various actions that required his pastoral attention.[112] We know that Bunyan also published *The Life and Death of Mr. Badman* (1680) and *The Holy War* (1682) during this period, as well as *A Treatise of the Fear of God* (1679), *The Greatness of the Soul* (1682), *A Holy Life, the Beauty of Christianity* (1683), and *A Case of Conscience Resolved* (1683).

The Holy War and *A Case of Conscience Resolved* bear most directly upon Bunyan's expanded portrayal of the church in *The Pilgrim's Progress*, Part II, because of their relevance for Bunyan's depiction of women. In *Grace Abounding*, Bunyan admitted his shyness around women, which was largely a reaction to slanderous and deeply wounding accusations that he had used his pastoral office as a pretense for adultery.[113] *The Holy War* has no named female characters at all,[114] and *A Case of Conscience Resolved* deals with and rejects the notion that women could meet for separate Bible studies without men. To a number of observers, all this reflects a condescending attitude toward women that carries over into Part II of the *Progress*. Mullett, for instance, believes that the sexist program of *Conscience* is the proper foundation for understanding the women of *The Pil-*

---

111 Cf. Roger Sharrock, ed., in Bunyan, *The Pilgrim's Progress* (Penguin), 400 (ft. 7, 16); Keeble, "Christiana's Key," 8; Furlong, 117, 124-125. In their introduction to Bunyan's *The Holy War*, Roger Sharrock and James F. Forrest observe that "these are the years in which he acquired the nickname of 'Bishop Bunyan' and in which he poured out his energies in strenuous preaching tours into the countryside; there were also visits to London" (ix). Yet "during these years of activity hardly anything is known of his personal life except that he continued to live with his family in a cottage in St. Cuthbert Street, Bedford. There is only the evidence, chronologically vague, in the brief contemporary accounts of his journeys and his sermons" (xiii). Perhaps such anonymity befitted a more communally-minded Bunyan.
112 John Brown, 302.
113 Bunyan, GA, §309, 315-316, pp. 93-95. Note particularly the embarrassment Bunyan must have felt after his allowing Agnes Beaumont to ride behind him on horseback to a church meeting became grist for scandalous rumors. See Vera J. Camden, ed., *The Narrative of the Persecutions of Agnes Beaumont* (East Lansing: Michigan State University Press, 1998), 1-33.
114 Furlong believes that Bunyan realized after writing *The Holy War* "how dull, mechanical and unimaginative" his fiction was without female characters and so wrote Christiana to preside "over the whole enterprise" in *The Pilgrim's Progress*, Part II (178-179). Cf. Galen Johnson, "Be Not Extream," 453-454.

grim's Progress, Part II, as spiritually enervated and thus in need of a male guide, Great-heart.[115] In his reading, Part II is no less "manly" (owing to Great-heart) than Part I, though he does not give notice to Christian's wish in Part I that he would not be so "tickled at the thoughts" of his masculinity. A chorus of critics take positions similar to Mullett on the women in Part II: Margaret Olofson Thickstun, Tamsin Spargo, and N. H. Keeble think Bunyan's portrayal of Christiana to be so patronizing that Christian's wife can only be the pattern for *female* believers and not Christians universally, while Thomas H. Luxon says even more forcefully that the women are too simple-minded to stand equally elect alongside Christian.[116] These authors are quick to point out that the most commonly used modifier for the female sex in Part II is "weak." What does it betoken for Bunyan's view of the church to describe a large percentage of its members in this fashion?

The Pilgrim's Progress, Part II, does indeed consider women (usually along with children) to be "weak" at least half a dozen times.[117] And *A Case of Conscience Resolved* confirms that Bunyan delimited the role of women in the church in comparison with men, although I agree with Sim and Walker that Bunyan's perception of women lay trapped somewhere between his traditional interpretation of gender roles and his belief that God is no respecter of persons.[118] But even if Bunyan were not simply referring to the comparative *physical* weakness of women, in truth, women are not the only "weak" characters in either part of *The Pilgrim's Progress*, nor does Bunyan

---

115 Mullett, 247-248.
116 Margaret Olofson Thickstun, *Fictions of the Feminine: Puritan Doctrine and the Representation of Women* (Ithaca, NY: Cornell University Press, 1988), 104; Spargo, 118; Keeble, "Here is her Glory," 147; Luxon, 203-205. Luxon holds that in early Protestant thought, only men were spiritually mature enough to be the bride of Christ (93).
117 Bunyan, *PP*, 196, 202, 214, 219, 279, 296. Cf. 2 Timothy 3:6.
118 Sim and Walker, 170. Cf. Aileen Ross: "*A Case of Conscience Resolved* is a stinging enough rebuke to bring the devout 'godly sisters' around to Bunyan's way of thinking, but Bunyan's pastoral care for them is plain enough. It is shown to even more advantage in the second part of *The Pilgrim's Progress*, which is often said to be a compliment to the women of Bedford Meeting after the remonstrance in the earlier tract" (Ross, "'Baffled and Befooled': Misogyny in the Works of John Bunyan," in *Awakening Words: John Bunyan and the Language of Community*, ed. David Gay, James G. Randall, and Arlette Zinck [Newark: University of Delaware Press, 2000], 161; cf. 166).

forego sometimes praising the faith of women over that of men.[119] Evangelist reminds Christian and Faithful that they have "many weaknesses" in Part I, and Great-heart confesses to Valiant-for-truth in Part II that his company includes both women and men who are "feeble and weak."[120] Indeed, at the conclusion of a long speech in *The Pilgrim's Progress*, Part II, extolling the virtues of female believers who ministered to Christ when the male disciples did not, Gaius explains, "Women therefore are highly favoured, and shew by these things that they are sharers with us in the Grace of Life."[121] Physical or emotional weakness puts no one at a disadvantage in Bunyan's church, for the church includes not only "weak" women and children but also men like Ready-to-hault on his crutches,[122] Feeble-mind with his doubts, Dispondencie with his fears, or even Little-faith from Part I. Since the essential character traits of these last two men also belong to Christian in Part I – indeed, Dispondencie also gets trapped in Doubting Castle – then does not Christiana speak words of implicit admonition *against* the kind of pilgrim her husband was when she advises Dispondencie to "cast away Fear" and Feeble-mind to "repent thee of thy aptness to fear and doubt" before they cross the River of Death?[123]

Christiana is not only the exemplary *female* Christian, then, as Thickstun and Spargo argue, but a type for *all* obedient Christians.[124]

---

119 *A Case of Conscience Resolved* ends with a warning not directed toward women but toward men: "Morning-Closet-Prayers, are now by most *London*-Professors, thrown away; and what kind of ones they make at night, God doth now (and their Conscience when awake will) know; however I have cause, as to this, to Look at home" (Bunyan, *MW*, 4:330).
120 Bunyan, *PP*, 86, 291. T. L. Underwood compares Great-heart's magnanimity to Bunyan's tract, *Peaceable Principles and True* (In Bunyan, *MW*, 4:xxxvi). Bunyan styled his *Instruction for the Ignorant* (1675) as "fitted for the capacity of the weakest")Roger Sharrock and James F. Forrest, eds., in Bunyan, *HW*, xiv).
121 Bunyan, *PP*, 261.
122 Compare Captain Experience in Bunyan's *HW*, who continues to fight for Emanuel though he is forced to go on crutches. Diabolus reacts, "What spirit has possessed these *Mansoulians* that they fight me upon their Crutches" (220)?
123 Bunyan, *PP*, 306.
124 Cf. Sim and Walker: "We should not regard submissiveness, therefore, as a wholly feminine trait. It is required of both sexes as part of the election process. ... Male guidance need not be thought always to equal male domination: Christian too is the recipient of much directive male guidance on his pilgrimage, and we do not tend to think of *him* as the victim of patri-

She may, in fact, be an even more complete type than Christian himself. Bunyan expresses his belief in *The Greatness of the Soul*, one of the works published between *The Pilgrim's Progress*, Parts I and II, that "God hath appointed, that those that come into his Royal presence, should first go to the House of the Women, the Church."[125] "Christiana is thus revealed as a type of the Church," says Melissa D. Aaron: "Bunyan knew that the Church ought to be female."[126] Aaron's main idea is that the representative figure of the church *should* be weak because the church on earth – particularly of the dissenting variety that Bunyan embraced during his adulthood – is weak and paradoxically triumphs only through its humility. Bunyan believed as such already in the early *Profitable Meditations* (1661), in which he observed,

> This is the state of Saints, both weak and strong,
> They have this Help, this Profit and this Stay:
> For Christ doth walk his Candlesticks among,
> To keep his Weak-ones, lest they pine away.[127]

Women typify the church for Bunyan not simply because of their comparative physical weakness, however, but because that weakness prompts them to a constant confession of their spiritual dependence on God's grace. It was precisely John Milton's inability to see the institutional church as the communally "weak" bride of Christ (cf. 1 Peter 3:7), writes Anthony Low, that committed the great poet to an isolated individualism and made him "an early precursor of Modernist and – more notably – Postmodernist ideo-

---

archy. We should also note that Christian is the recipient of female guidance as well" (168). Also note George B. Cheever: "Perhaps the Second Part of this pilgrimage comes nearer to the ordinary experience of the great multitude of Christians than the First Part .... The First Part shows, as in Christian, Faithful, and Hopeful, the great examples and strong lights of this pilgrimage; it is as if Paul and Luther were passing over the scene. The Second Part shows a variety of pilgrims, whose stature and experience are more on a level with our own" (Cited in Offor, 3:171).

125 John Bunyan, *The Greatness of the Soul*, cited by Roger Sharrock, ed., in Bunyan, *The Pilgrim's Progress* (Penguin), 391.

126 Melissa D. Aaron, "'Christiana and her train': Bunyan and the Alternative Society in the Second Part of *The Pilgrim's Progress*," in *Awakening Words: John Bunyan and the Language of Community*, ed. David Gay, James G. Randall, and Arlette Zinck (Newark: University of Delaware Press, 2000), 182.

127 Bunyan, *Profitable Meditations*, in *MW* 6:11 (§XLI).

logical zeal and political commitment."[128] Bunyan, by contrast, was not *so* sectarian as to give up on the institutional church, deeply flawed though it was. In that sense, he remained closer to the older Puritanical Anglicanism of John Donne and George Herbert than his fellow dissenter Milton.[129]

Bunyan envisioned the church not as withdrawing into the soul of each individual but as expanding communally on earth until the eschaton. For Christiana's band is composed not only of those who are blessed with the kingdom of heaven because they have been persecuted for righteousness' sake, but also of those meek who will inherit the earth (Matt 5:5,10).[130] Christiana's four sons and their wives do not cross the river at the same time as she and most of the others do at the end of Part II; the narrator reports, "I did not stay where I was, till they were gone over. Also since I came away, I heard one say, that they were yet alive, and so would be for the Increase of the Church in that Place where they were for a time."[131] How very different this is from the individualistic Milton, who himself attended no church in his later years but came to believe that the church, wholly unattractive in its weakness, played a minimal role if any at all in mediating God's love for humanity.[132] Yet the shepherds of the Delectable Mountains in Bunyan's *The Pilgrim's Progress*, Part II, "have [regard] for the *Feeble*, as for the *Strong*," for

---

128 Low, 5, 169. Achsah Guibbory notes, however, that Milton made the physically weak but spiritually resilient Lady of his masque, *Comus*, a figure of the true church, in opposition to the title character, a male villain (Guibbory, *Ceremony and Community from Herbert to Milton: Literature, Religion, and Cultural Conflict in Seventeenth-Century England* [Cambridge: Cambridge University Press, 1998], 168). Cf. a similar point made by Horace Sams, Jr., "Temptation in Imaginative Literature of Milton and Bunyan: Two Faces of the Puritan Persona" (Ph. D. diss., University of South Florida, 1985), 220. Perhaps the seemingly contrasting opinions of Low and Guibbory can be reconciled by observing that while the Lady may indeed be a figure of the individual Christian, it would not fit within Milton's increasing disgust with all institutional forms of the church to see her as a type of the church universal. Christiana seems to represent both.
129 Cf. Low, 162-170.
130 Though there are no martyrdoms in Part II akin to that of Faithful in Part I, examples of persecution in Part II include the attempted assault on Christiana's virtue by two "ill-favoured ones," the aggressions by the Giants Grim, Maul, Slay-good, and Despair, and the attack of thieves upon Valiant-for-truth. Cf. Sim and Walker: "There is no suggestion that 'weak women' can be spared such trials" (159).
131 Bunyan, *PP*, 311.
132 Cf. Low, 169.

they reveal that "our Prince has an Eye to what is done to the least of these."[133]

Church Ordinances. If the church in Bunyan's conception is to increase on earth, then it will require the administration of church ordinances, which signify the divine sustenance of the Christian life. The increased use of sacramental imagery in Part II further demonstrates Bunyan's restriction of the seemingly normative individualism in Part I. What was the background to Bunyan's thought on baptism and the Lord's Supper prior to *The Pilgrim's Progress*, Part II? In *Differences in Judgment About Water-Baptism, No Bar to Communion* (1673), his primary intention was to refute the notion of William Kiffin and the majority of seventeenth-century Baptists that infant baptism is necessarily a sin.[134] He argued there that he did not *encourage* infant baptism but bore with it as the infirmity of some fellow Christians.[135] He then distinguished an "ordinance" from a "church ordinance:" "Water-baptism, and all God's Ordinances, are to be used to Edification," but, "The act of Water-baptism hath not place in Church-worship, neither in whole nor in part; wherefore pressing it upon the Church is to no purpose at all."[136] Water baptism is a command of Christ, Bunyan said, but it is "no Church-Ordinance."[137] It is a command for individuals as individuals and not for the church as a whole. "The Lord's Supper," on the other

---

133 Bunyan, *PP*, 284. Cf. T. L. Underwood's linking of the ecumenicity of this passage to Bunyan's later doctrinal works in his introduction to Bunyan, *MW*, 4:xxxvi. Compare Bunyan's *A Discourse of the Building of the House of God*: "This place, as *Hospitals*, will entertain / Those which the lofty of this World *disdain*: / The *Poor*, the *Lame*, the *Maimed*, *Halt* and *Blind*, / The *Leprous*, and *Possessed* too, may find / Free welcome here, as also much relief / As ease them will of Trouble, Pain and Grief " (*MW*, 6:280).

134 On the other hand, in *The Doctrine of the Law and Grace Unfolded* (1659), Bunyan criticized those who believe that infant baptism is necessary for salvation (Bunyan, *MW*, 2:182).

135 Bunyan's Bedford congregation had a long history of receptiveness to infant baptism. Its first pastor John Gifford discouraged disputes over baptism and received those baptized as infants as church members without rebaptism. Bunyan's immediate successor as pastor in Bedford, Ebenezer Chandler, also insisted that infant baptism be no bar to communion. Not until a hundred years after Bunyan's death did a pastor of the congregation, Joshua Symonds, declare that baptism should be only for believers by immersion (G. B. Harrison, *Church Book*, vi, ix, xii).

136 Bunyan, *Differences in Judgment About Water-Baptism, No Bar to Communion*, in *MW*, 4:222.

137 Ibid., 226.

hand, "not Baptism, is for the Church, as a Church."[138] Because baptism is not a simultaneous act for all church members as a body, its mode was ultimately indifferent to Bunyan in *Differences*. The proper administration of baptism is a matter of individual conscience and thus should not curtail open communion.

Richard Greaves has done the most extensive work on Bunyan's understanding of baptism. In his 1969 biography, he asserts that Bunyan's de-emphasis on baptism as an initiatory rite into the church brought his position fairly close to the position of the Quakers, whose theology he contemned, and in a more recent article, he contends even more strongly that water baptism for Bunyan was an optional expression of a person's conversion experience.[139] Yet what are we to make of Bunyan's convoluted statement in *A Defence of the Doctrine of Justification, By Faith* (1672), where he criticized a false attack on the ordinances in Edward Fowler's *Design of Christianity*?

> He must put a difference between those Laws of the Gospel that are Essential to Holiness, and those Positive Precepts that in themselves are indifferent, & absolutely considered neither good nor evil; but must know also that of those Positive Precepts he alloweth but three in the Gospel, but three that are purely such; to wit, *that of coming to God by Christ*, the Institutions of Baptism, and the Lord's Supper.[140]

It appears that Bunyan thus rejected any idea that coming to God by Christ, baptism, and the Lord's Supper are indifferent (though the *mode* of baptism may be indifferent). Even so, as Sharrock says, there is still no representation of baptism in *The Pilgrim's Progress*, Part I.[141]

---

138 Ibid., 223.
139 Greaves, *John Bunyan*, 138-139; "Introduction," 10. Cf. Mullett, 179; Karen Smith, 175-178. Ken Simpson writes, "Conversion narratives, public professions of faith, and church covenant ceremonies replace baptism as rites of initiation while preaching, prayer, and the Lord's Supper edify, sustain, and nourish faith rather than convey grace immediately" (115).
140 Bunyan, *A Defence of the Doctrine of Justification, By Faith*, in MW, 4:93. Cf. Bunyan's *A Confession of My Faith*: "I believe therefore, that election doth not forestall or prevent the means which are of God appointed to bring us to Christ, to grace and glory" (Ibid., 147).
141 Roger Sharrock, ed., in Bunyan, *The Pilgrim's Progress* (Penguin), 402. Cf. Simpson, 120-121. Paul S. Fiddes writes: "The story of eternal purpose, temporal actualization, and renewal is the story of a 'Pilgrim's Progress'[:] in John Bunyan's allegory, the Pilgrim enters the earthly journey of faith through the narrow gate of conversion, but it is only later by a wayside cross that 'his burden loosed from off his shoulders and fell from off his back.' This reflects the typical Calvinist stage of inner assurance, but it also

In Part II, however, there is a possible representation of water baptism at the House of Interpreter, immediately before Interpreter assigns Great-heart as the pilgrims' guide.

> In the Morning they arose with the *Sun*, and prepared themselves for their departure: But the *Interpreter* would have them tarry a while, for, said he, you must orderly go from hence. Then said he to the Damsel that at first opened unto them, Take them and have them into the Garden, to the *Bath*, and there wash them, and make them clean from the soil which they have gathered by travelling. Then *Innocent* the Damsel took them and had them into the Garden, and brought them to the *Bath*, so she told them that there they must wash and be clean, for so her Master would have the Women to do that called at his House as they were going on *Pilgrimage*. They then went in and washed, yea they and the Boys and all, and they came out of that *Bath* not only sweet and clean; but also much enlivened and strengthened in their Joynts: So when they came in, they looked fairer a deal, then when they went out to the washing.
>
> When they were returned out of the Garden from the *Bath*, the *Interpreter* took them and looked upon them and said unto them, *fair as the Moon*. Then he called for the *Seal* wherewith they used to be *Sealed* that were washed in his *Bath*. So the *Seal* was brought, and he set his Mark upon them, that they might be known in the Places whither they were yet to go: Now the seal was the contents and sum of the Passover which the Children of *Israel* did eat when they came out from the Land of *Egypt*: and the mark was set between their Eyes. This seal greatly added to their Beauty, for it was an Ornament to their Faces. It also added to their gravity, and made their Countenances more like them of Angels.[142]

Sharrock comments that this passage represents adult baptism by immersion, possibly Bunyan's concession to Baptists who may have decried the lack of such imagery in Part I.[143] I agree that the Bath is a baptistery, mainly because the passage compares it to the exodus of the ancient Israelites from Egypt, and Bunyan knew that 1

---

fits with the Baptists' placing of assurance in the context of covenant-making and baptism" (Fiddes, "'Walking Together:' The Place of Covenant Theology in Baptist Life Yesterday and Today," in *Pilgrim Pathways: Essays in Baptist History in Honour of B. R. White*, ed. William H. Brackney and Paul S. Fiddes with John H. Y. Briggs [Macon, GA: Mercer University Press, 1999], 66).

142 Bunyan, *PP*, 207-208.
143 Roger Sharrock, in ibid., 343-344. Cf. N. H. Keeble, ed., in Bunyan, *The Pilgrim's Progress* (Oxford), 279; Hill, *Tinker*, 294; Frye, 152-158; Knott, "Bunyan and the Holy Community," 219.

Corinthians 10:1-4 likens the exodus to Christian baptism – a point that Martin Luther also made in *The Babylonian Captivity of the Church*.[144] In his commentary on Galatians 3:6, Luther even wrote of baptism as a laver (bath) of the new birth and renewal by the Holy Spirit (sanctification).[145] But is Bunyan's bath really a baptism for *adult* believers only? The narrator says quite clearly that not only Christiana and Mercie, but Christiana's "boys" also are washed, and they are baptized together at the same time as the adults.

Some might contend that since Christiana's sons all cry out to pursue their father and cry further for joy when their mother commits to doing so, this constitutes an "age of accountability" on their part by which they may enter the bath voluntarily subsequent to individual profession of faith.[146] Yet the narrator does not state that the children's desire for pilgrimage is born of a sense of personal sin and instead mentions their desire to be reunited with their absentee father. Nor does the ability of the youngest child, James, to respond to Prudence's catechesis at the Porter's Lodge suggest that he was of an "accountable" age at the bath, for there is no record of any of the children speaking *before* the bath. In any event, there is no conclusive evidence that Christiana's children – her "sweet babes," as she calls them at the beginning of the journey – had each made a personal decision of faith before entering the sanctifying bath of baptism.[147] Even if one is unconvinced that the Bath denotes infant baptism – though this still seems a possibility – Bunyan's attitude toward baptism here is nonetheless noticeably different from that in *Differences in Water-Baptism*, written over a decade earlier, that baptism is strictly an individual act. In *The Pilgrim's Progress*, Part II, baptism appears to be not merely a personal choice but a holy act in the communal life of the church. One might even call the imagery of the Bath sacramental since those who entered it received a seal of grace. This would actually serve to bring Bunyan's theology of baptism in line with his insistent theological emphasis on the objectivity of Christ's salvific work as having precedence to any human response. Thus did Bunyan's teachings on the sacraments remain a part of his soteriology, in contrast with subsequent generations of Baptists, for whom the physical elements could only symbolically convey the presence of Christ.[148]

---

144 Bunyan, *Differences in Water-Baptism No Bar to Communion*, in MW 4:213-214; Luther, in Dillenberger, 294.
145 Luther, CG, 222.
146 Bunyan, PP, 178, 181.
147 Ibid., 189.
148 Thompson, 294-297. Stanley K. Fowler has explored the surprising sacra-

Bunyan's incipient sacramentalism may have been a stunning disappointment to his great admirer Charles Spurgeon, the eighteenth century Baptist evangelist. In *Pictures from "Pilgrim's Progress": A Commentary on Portions of John Bunyan's Immortal Allegory*, Spurgeon criticized a "Romanized" adaptation that he had seen of *The Pilgrim's Progress*, Part I, where Christian's burden falls off not before the cross but in the bath of baptism. "According to this doctored edition of the allegory," Spurgeon recalled, "Christian was washed in the laver of baptism, and all his sins were thus removed. That is the High Church mode of getting rid of sin. The true way is to lose it at the cross."[149] Yet, in *The Pilgrim's Progress*, Part II, Interpreter's bath does serve the functional equivalent of the cross in Part I. Bunyan did not displace the cross, of course; he still mentioned it nine times in Part II as the very *raison d'etre* of the Christian life.[150] The bath in Part II does not obviate the salvific assurance won by Jesus on the cross but precisely conveys and seals it. This is a sacramental understanding of the Christian life. Perhaps Spurgeon might even consider it "High Church"!

Nor did Bunyan hesitate in *A Book for Boys and Girls* (1686) to use the very word "sacraments" to describe baptism and the Lord's Supper, which are "Both Mysteries divine, which do to me, / By Gods appointment, benefit afford."[151] Moreover, when Innocent enters the Bath in Part II, she declares that this is what the Master (Christ) expects *women* to do. This surely cannot mean that only women and not men should undertake baptism; none of the four males who enter the Bath are adult men, but Bunyan believed in *The Advocateship of Jesus Christ* (1688) that under the term "little children" (1 John 2:12-14) could be "comprehended all Men."[152] *The Pilgrim's Progress*, Part II, is not simply a retelling of the Christian life for the particular instruction of women and children.[153] Its female protagonist is a model for *all* pilgrims, and she is a woman who, like Lydia of Thyatira, leads her family in household baptism (Acts

---

mentalism of some early Baptist writers (not including Bunyan nor certainly his possible allowance of sacramental infant baptism) in *More Than a Symbol: The British Baptist Recovery of Baptismal Sacramentalism*, Studies in Baptist History and Thought 2 (Carlisle, UK: Paternoster Press, 2002), 10-32.

149 Charles H. Spurgeon, *Pictures from "Pilgrim's Progress": A Commentary on Portions of John Bunyan's Immortal Allegory*, in *The Pilgrim's Progress* [CD-ROM] (Greenville, SC: Media-Book, 1999), 86.
150 Bunyan, *PP*, 172, 209, 212, 228, 251, 261, 269, 279, 289.
151 Bunyan, *MW*, 6:212.
152 Bunyan, *MW*, 11:146.
153 Cf. Knott, "Bunyan and the Holy Community," 224.

16:14-15). Nor is this baptism optional; it is something which Interpreter says the pilgrims "must" do.

A later episode in Part II also challenges the view that Bunyan always retained an individualist, non-sacramental view of water baptism that relegated its administration to optional status. It occurs after the pilgrims leave Mnason's house in Vanity Fair and come upon a river that flows from the Delectable Mountains.

> By this River side in the Medow, there were Cotes and Folds for Sheep, an House built for the *nourishing* and bringing up of those Lambs, the Babes of those Women that go on Pilgrimage. Also there was here one that was intrusted with them, who could have compassion, and that could gather these Lambs with his Arm, and carry them in his Bosom, and that could gently lead those that were with young. Now to the Care of *this Man, Christiana* admonished her four Daughters to commit their little ones; that by these Waters they might be housed, harbored, suckered and nourished, and that none of them might *be lacking in time to come*. This man, if any of them go astray, or be lost, he will bring them again, he will also bind up that which was broken, and will strengthen them that are sick. Here they will never want Meat, and Drink and Cloathing, here they will be kept from Thieves and Robbers, for this man will dye before one of those committed to his Trust, shall be lost. Besides, here they shall be sure to have good *Nurture* and Admonition, and shall be taught to walk in right Paths, and that you know is a Favour of no small account. Also here, as you see, are delicate *Waters*, pleasant *Medows*, dainty *Flowers*, variety of *Trees*, and such as bear *wholsom Fruit*. Fruit, not like that that *Matthew* eat of, that fell over the Wall out of *Belzebubs* Garden, but Fruit that procureth Health where there is none, and that continueth and increaseth it where it is.
>
> So they were content to commit their little Ones to him; and that which was also an Incouragement to them so to do, was, for that all this was to be at the Charge of the King, and so was an Hospital to young Children, and *Orphans*.[154]

Provocative questions arise from this passage, but none of the recent scholarly editions of *The Pilgrim's Progress* offers any commentary upon it. If the daughters-in-law agree to leave their chil-

---

154 Bunyan, *PP*, 280-281. Cf. Bunyan's *Come, and Welcome, to Jesus Christ*: "The Lord also leads some by the Waters of Comfort" (*MW*, 8:356). Also compare the description of Captain Charity in Bunyan's *HW*: "For his Scutcheon, he had three *naked Orphans imbraced in the bosom*" (68). Roger Sharrock and James F. Forrest note, "Charity is often depicted in medieval and Renaissance iconography as a mother-figure surrounded by infants" (In ibid., 260).

dren at this house on the presumption that the children will need an orphanage, then why do the daughters-in-law and their husbands *not* cross the River of Death but settle in the Land of Beulah precisely to populate the church? Although the man who operates the house is surely a Christ-like figure who welcomes little ones and rescues them when they are lost (Matt 18:14, 19:14; John 10:11,28), does he perform an *institutional service* for the church?[155]

In any case, it is possible that the nearness of the orphanage to water and the health-giving meat and drink served there betoken baptism and the Lord's Supper.[156] If so, then one sees Bunyan here at his most Reformed and least subjective: if grace visits the helpless, then it comes to babes. That Bunyan came to consider children an important part of Christ's church is confirmed by *A Book for Boys and Girls*, published two years after *The Pilgrim's Progress*, Part II, in 1686. There Bunyan taught the boys and girls who read his theological primer a rhymed paraphrase of the Nicene Creed, concluding as follows:

Moreover I believe
In God the Holy Ghost;
And that there is an Holy Church,
An universal Host.

Also I do believe,
That sin shall be forgiven;
And that the dead shall rise; and that
The Saints shall dwell in Heaven.[157]

Seemingly exchanging a model of church membership based upon adult profession only for one in which children were nurtured as part of the fellowship from the beginning, Bunyan believed that children should share fully in the fellowship of the church. Again he emphasized in *A Discourse of the Building of the House of God* that in the church, "Alas here's *Children*, here are great with Young; Here are the *Sick* and *Weak*, as well as *Strong*."[158]

As the act of baptism in *The Pilgrim's Progress*, Part II, is a com-

---

155 In Bunyan's *Badman*, when Badman's wife senses that her death is near, she entrusts the care of her children to her minister: "Ask counsel of good men, and do nothing therein, if he lives, without my Ministers advice. I have also my self desired him to look after thee" (144).

156 In the seventeenth century, the word "meat" could be used as a synonym for "food" and found specific reference to the bread of the Eucharist in George Herbert's poem, "Love (III)."

157 Bunyan, *MW*, 6:208. Note, of course, that the adjective "universal" comes from a Greek root, "catholic."

158 Ibid., 292.

munal event, so, too, is the Lord's Supper. This may seem hardly a noteworthy fact, except that the one communion image in Part I is a solitary event. Before Christian leaves the Palace Beautiful, which represents according to Sharrock the communal life of the church, the "good Companions" there provide him with a loaf of bread and a bottle of wine, which he uses to refresh himself after his narrow victory over Apollyon in the Valley of Humiliation.[159] He does not require a minster or even a second pilgrim gathered with him in Christ's name to partake of the eucharistic elements. In Part II, by contrast, the pilgrims dine together at nearly every stop along the way. A cook at the house of Gaius provides a supper of bread and "Juice of the true Vine, that makes glad the Heart of God and Man," which Gaius blesses in this way:

> So let all ministring Doctrines *to* thee in this Life, beget *in* thee a greater desire to sit at the Supper of the great King in his Kingdom; for all Preaching, Books, and Ordinances here, are but as the laying of the Trenshers, and as setting of Salt upon the Board, when compared with the Feast that our Lord will make for us when we come to his House.[160]

Mnason, the shepherds of the Delectable Mountains, and a *"Victualling-House"* in the Inchanted ground also provide meals for the pilgrims.[161] Christiana's "walking tour" obviously includes fine, even divine, dining!

Again, we do not have autobiographical data from Bunyan after his second imprisonment (1677-1678) that might help to explain developments in Bunyan's thought about means of grace. But if Martin Luther is again any precedent, perhaps it took the quieting of Bunyan's restless conscience by Christ for him finally and fully to appreciate baptism and the Lord's Supper as signifiers of the unmerited grace which alone could save him. Luther, for instance, hardly mentioned the sacraments before 1519, but after his Reformation breakthrough of justification *sola gratia*, *sola fide*, the conjoining of word and sacrament became common in his theology.[162] Walter E. Conn observes how important the sacramental life of the worshiping community (*koinonia*) became for Luther as the "validating context for conscience."[163] We see something similar to this at the end of *Grace Abounding* when Bunyan says that Christ's words of

---

159 Sharrock, *John Bunyan*, 145; Bunyan, *PP*, 56, 60-61.
160 Bunyan, *PP*, 261-262.
161 Ibid., 274, 277, 285, 296.
162 Marius, 206-207.
163 Walter E. Conn, *Conscience: Development and Self-Transcendence* (Birmingham, AL: Religious Education Press, 1981), 16-17.

institution at the last supper became "very precious" to him.¹⁶⁴ While Milton and the Quakers so disdained "outward forms" in worship that they indeed interiorized the sacraments completely, we see enough emphasis on church and sacrament in *The Pilgrim's Progress*, Part II, to disagree with James F. Forrest, who says that the individualist scheme of *The Pilgrim's Progress* obviates the need for sacraments. Likewise is Peter Goldman incorrect in arguing that the individualistic pattern of Puritan conversion shown in Part I and *Grace Abounding* really *became* Bunyan's only sacrament.¹⁶⁵ Instead, Bunyan's increasing appreciation for means of grace prompted his assertion in *The Advocateship of Jesus Christ* (1688), "Go to Ordinances with Expectation to hear from thy *Advocate* there."¹⁶⁶

The Pilgrim's Progress and Modernity

Those who find *The Pilgrim's Progress* to be a modern work typically base their evaluation on their understanding of its individualism since, as Charles Taylor argues, the location of authority within oneself defines the modern, as opposed to medieval, man or woman.¹⁶⁷ This is also how Christopher Hill, Vincent Newey, and Thomas Docherty understand *The Pilgrim's Progress*.¹⁶⁸ Indeed, Hill sees *The Pilgrim's Progress* as the grand predecessor of the novel, what he considers "the most individualistic of all literary forms."¹⁶⁹ Aileen

---

164 Bunyan, *GA*, 79 (§253). Cf. John Calvin's definition of a sacrament: "First, we must consider what a sacrament is. It seems to me that a simple and proper definition would be to say that it is an outward sign by which the Lord seals on our consciences the promises of his good will toward us in order to sustain the weakness of our faith; and we in turn attest our piety toward him in the presence of the Lord and of his angels and before men" (Calvin, *Institutes*, 2:1277 [IV.xiv.1]).

165 James F. Forrest, "Allegory as Sacred Sport: Manipulation of the Reader in Spenser and Bunyan," in *Bunyan in Our Time*, ed. Robert G. Collmer (Kent, OH: The Kent State University Press, 1989), 109; Peter Goldman, "'The Alien Word': Puritan Conversion Narratives and the Early Modern Crisis of Representation," (Ph. D. diss., University of California, Irvine, 2000), 70-79, 122. Cf. Guibbory, 152-154.

166 Bunyan, *MW*, 11:156.

167 Taylor, 35-36.

168 Hill, *Century*, 217; Newey, "Bunyan and the Confines of the Mind," 32-33; Thomas Docherty, *John Donne, Undone* (London: Methuen, 1986), 172.

169 Hill, *Century*, 218. If Hill is correct, this was a remarkable achievement by Bunyan, since he had practically no influence on – nor influence from, for that matter – the elite literary circles of the late seventeenth century. Cf. Taylor, 287; N. H. Keeble, ed., in Bunyan, *The Pilgrim's Progress* (Oxford), xii.

D. Ross sees in Part II "a fictive work of remarkable power" *despite* its emphasis on the group rather than the individual.[170] Her assumption, however, capsulizes an attitude toward Part II that I have sought to address and correct. Part II flourishes precisely *because* of its emphasis on the community and its placing of individual Christianity within a community context. It reflects the conventicler Bunyan's own mature appreciation for the institutional church and its sacraments, as also seen in *A Holy Life* (1683): "He that religiously professeth the name of Christ, has put himself into the Church of Christ, though not into a particular one, yet into the universal one. Now that is holy."[171] And the communal, even universal, accent of Part II checks the secularized, wildly individualistic reading of Part I that has controlled Bunyan studies since Coleridge.

N. H. Keeble is one of the few scholars who allows the tension between Parts I and II to stand without demeaning Part II as inferior because it is not as "modern," but he does not go as far as do I to argue that Bunyan quite likely envisioned Part II as being *superior*. For while Part I is a superbly dramatic account of how one *becomes* a Christian, Part II excels as a largely undramatic account of how one *remains* a Christian.[172] *The Pilgrim's Progress* is "an ambivalent work," Keeble says: "not only our first novel, but our last allegory, a bridge between two worlds, the medieval and modern. In this, it exactly reflects the paradoxical temper of the Puritan, whose religious tradition encouraged him to be not merely a shrewd observer of men and their environment but also to detect significance in what he observed."[173] I concur with Keeble that the Puritan mind could hold together the individual and the community, whereas the contemporary mind often separates them. Take John Donne, for instance. He once preached of Jesus Christ, "And though in our interest in him who is also a King and a Priest, we are all *regale Sacerdotium*, Kings and Priests too, yet let us accept the name, and execute the office of a Deacon, of ministration, especially upon our selves: for as every man is a world in himself, so every man is a Church in himself too."[174] And in "Satyre III," he said that the path

---

170 Aileen Ross, 154.
171 Bunyan, *MW*, 9:300.
172 Cf. Knott: "Bunyan's sequel lacks the dramatic force of the first part and will never be as widely read, yet it presents dimensions of spiritual life that he was unable to explore in his account of Christian's solitary pilgrimage" ("Bunyan and the Holy Community," 200).
173 N. H. Keeble, ed., in Bunyan, *The Pilgrim's Progress* (Oxford), xxi.
174 John Donne, Sermon 7 (29 February 1627), in *The Sermons of John Donne*,

up the mountain of Religion is an individual one: "At the last day? Oh, will it then boot thee / To say a Philip, or a Gregory, / A Harry, or a Martin taught thee this?"[175] Like Bunyan's Christian, Donne also had an introspective fear that his sins would overwhelm him at death: "I have a sinne of feare, that when I have spunne / My last thred, I shall perish on the shore."[176] But in *Devotions Upon Emergent Occasions*, Meditation 17, Donne also penned the immortal words of *non*-individuality, ecclesial corporeality, and finding in God's grace "our onely securitie:" "No man is an *Iland*, intire of it selfe; every man is a peece of the *Continent*, a part of the *maine*."[177]

Donne wrote the *Devotions* while recovering from a serious fever in late 1623. He used his personal experiences with illness and pain ("emergent occasions") to reflect upon the relationship of all humanity to God. Kate Gartner Frost, probably the foremost expert on that work, warns against reading Donne's self-scrutiny as an early modern manifestation of subjectivist self-interest. "The modern reader approaches the subject of autobiography equipped with presuppositions that do not always serve her well in the seventeenth century," Frost contends. The self-inspection of the *Devotions*, she adds, was intended for communal Christian edification and thus to deflect the reader's gaze from its human author to its divine

---

vol. 8, ed. Evelyn M. Simpson and George R. Potter (Berkeley: University of California Press, 1956), 184.

175 Donne, "Satyre III," in *The Complete Poetry and Selected Prose of John Donne*, ed. Charles M. Coffin (New York: The Modern Library, 1994), 98 (ll. 95-97). Cf. Hill, *Century*, 80, and Meg Lota Brown: "It is appropriate that 'Satyre III' never specifies which religion is the true one, since Donne's point is that the readers must decide for themselves" (57).

176 Donne, "A Hymne to God the Father," in *The Complete Poetry*, 271 (ll. 13-14).

177 Donne, *Devotions Upon Emergent Occasions*, in ibid., 441. Meditation 17 of the *Devotions* is also where Donne warns, "And therefore never send to know for whom the *bell* tolls; It tolls for *thee*." Compare Hopeful's confession that his past sins formerly came to mind "If I heard the Bell Toull for some that were dead" (Bunyan, *PP*, 138), as well as Bunyan's advice in *The Heavenly Footman*, "Do not say, I have time enough to get to heaven seven years hence; for I tell thee, the bell may toll for thee before seven days more be ended; and when death comes, away thou must go, whether thou art provided or not"(In Talon, ed., *God's Knotty Log*, 30). In Bunyan's *Badman*, Mr. Wiseman sighs "at the remembrance of the death of that man for whom the Bell tolled at our Town yesterday" (14). For more on the similarities between Bunyan and Donne, see Galen Johnson, "Suicide and the Keys of Escape in Bunyan and Donne," *Bunyan Studies* 10 (2002): 51-53; for the relationship between individual and church in Donne, cf. Bercovitch, 11.

Author.[178] Likewise in *The Pilgrim's Progress*, Bunyan did not intend his own conversion and growth narrative to be the model for all other Christians but instead as a witness to the transformation which the objective pattern of providential history had worked in him.[179]

The Eastern Orthodox tradition has never lost sight of the fact that Christ's justification of persons is not actuated *individually* but in relation to God, the world, and the church.[180] It is precisely when one *forgets* that one's neighbor "belongs to the same organism as yourself," wrote C. S. Lewis, that "you will become an Individualist."[181] Likewise, perhaps it is again the bias of our own individualistic age which assumes that any self-reflective writing by Bunyan *must* be subjectivist and autonomy-forecasting.[182]

Conclusion

I do not deny that Bunyan stood astride the premodern and modern eras; indeed, I have asserted as much in previous chapters. But I also believe that once *The Pilgrim's Progress*, Part II, is read in light of Bunyan's larger thought on conscience, individuality, and selfhood, it shows Bunyan retreating from a modern, subjective interiority that undermined an objective view of Christ's person and work, toward a deeper submersion into the communal Christian life.[183] Henri Talon says, "Without the Second Part of *The Pilgrim's Progress* we would only have an unfinished portrait of the Puritan

---

178 Kate Gartner Frost, *Holy Delight: Typology, Numerology, and Autobiography in Donne's "Devotions Upon Emergent Occasions"* (Princeton: Princeton University Press, 1990), 16. For a fuller explanation of Donne's emphasis on the communal Christianity, see Jeffrey Johnson, *The Theology of John Donne* (Cambridge: D. S. Brewer, 1999), *passim*. For a differing view on Donne's relationship to modern notions of subjectivity, see Low, 59-60.
179 I make this point in response to Hans Frei, who argues that both Bunyan and English Methodism ran the risk of subjugating biblical narrative to personal experience rather than the reverse (Frei, *The Eclipse of Biblical Narrative: A Study in Eighteenth and Nineteenth Century Hermeneutics* [New Haven: Yale University Press, 1974], 153).
180 John D. Zizioulas, *Being as Communion: Studies in Personhood and the Church* (Crestwood, NJ: St. Vladimir's Seminary Press, 1985), 15, 64.
181 C. S. Lewis, *Mere Christianity* (New York: Macmillan Publishing Co., Inc., 1952), 159.
182 Cf. Sharrock, *John Bunyan*, 156; Margaret Miles, "Pilgrimage as Metaphor in a Nuclear Age," *Theology Today* 45:2 (July 1988): 177.
183 Cf. Bunyan, *PP*, 42.

and of Man as a religious being."[184] The primary reason for this is that Bunyan fully intuited what John Calvin knew from his facility with Latin: "*Con-scientia* is a knowing-with, or joint knowing. It cannot remain private."[185]

---

184 Talon, ed., *God's Knotty Log*, 18.
185 Edward A. Dowey, *The Knowledge of God in Calvin's Theology*, 3rd ed. (Grand Rapids: William B. Eerdmans Publishing Company, 1994), 59.

CHAPTER SIX

Conscience and Citizenship in *The Life and Death of Mr. Badman* and *The Holy War*

The Life and Death of Mr. Badman (1680) and *The Holy War* (1682) are symbolically and literally the "middle children" of Bunyan's four major fictional works. The first and favorite "child," *The Pilgrim's Progress*, Part I (1678), still garners international recognition. The last "child," *The Pilgrim's Progress*, Part II (1684), has achieved a certain renown based on its resemblance to its famous eldest sibling. *The Life and Death of Mr. Badman* and *The Holy War* are still known and occasionally read, but mainly because they come from the writer of the two greater allegories and not so much for their own intrinsic attractions. With rare exceptions, such as Maurice Hussey's endorsement of *Mr. Badman* as the "undoubted peak in the author's literary achievement" and G. B. Harrison's praise of *The Holy War* as "the greatest English allegory" – evaluations now more than half a century old – most observers point out that these two works bear a paler image of Bunyan's own genius than the two parts of *The Pilgrim's Progress*.[1] Such is the evaluation of Horace Sams, Jr., for example, who states plainly that "*Mr. Badman* and *The Holy War* deserve the neglect subsequent generations have accorded them, whereas *Grace Abounding* and *The Pilgrim's Progress* have lasting and universal qualities that merit retention."[2]

Even those who have found *Mr. Badman* worthy of study for its place in the genealogy of the English novel are quick to observe its

---

1 Maurice Hussey, "Bunyan's 'The Life and Death of Mr. Badman,'" *The Congregational Quarterly* 28:4 (October 1950): 359; cf. 366; G. B. Harrison, *John Bunyan*, 199. Frank Mott Harrison also calls *The Holy War* "a literary triumph," though he actually writes more from an evangelical than a literary perspective (Frank Mott Harrison, *John Bunyan: A Story of His Life* [Edinburgh: The Banner of Truth Trust, 1964], 166). George Bernard Shaw found *The Holy War* "hardly readable," but he did write about *The Life and Death of Mr. Badman*, "Unfashionable as the book was when I bought it, I am satisfied that it was a sound investment as a work of art" (McMillin, 91, 93).
2 Sams, 233.

flaws.³ Scholars say that it lacks real drama and artistry and spends too much time moralizing.⁴ Roger Sharrock even strips from *Badman* its single honor as proto-novel and declares regretfully that it is, "profoundly, a *lower* book."⁵ Beth Lynch has found enough material for an article-length treatment of the many reproofs of *The Holy War* over the years, ranging from artificiality to predictability to inferiority to simple lack of beauty.⁶ Yet Lynch believes about *The Holy War* what I have argued elsewhere concerning Bunyan's larger body of writings: "Much of the critical resistance to, and dismissal of, *The Holy War* lies precisely in the enlightened reader's refusal to accept Bunyan's Reformed soteriology as the very substance of his narrative art."⁷ About *The Holy War* and *Mr. Badman*, I make an even bolder claim: not only do these two works demonstrate Bunyan's soteriology (which is actually more Lutheran than Reformed), but they also reveal, even more fully than Bunyan's two better known allegories, a concern for Christian citizenship in the world that could hardly be labeled subjectivist.

The Life and Death of Mr. Badman

The notions of "conscience" and "self" that Bunyan employs in *The Life and Death of Mr. Badman* are consistent with the characteristically Lutheran emphases which permeate his other doctrinal and fictional works. One reads in a conversation between Mr. Wiseman

---

3   E.g., Jack Lindsay, *John Bunyan: Maker of Myths* (London: Methuen Publishers, 1937), 209; James F. Forrest and Roger Sharrock, eds., in Bunyan, *Badman*, xii, xxx, xliii. Forrest and Sharrock point out that, contrary to the idea that *Mr. Badman* was a pioneer of the novel, Bunyan's assumption therein that sicknesses and accidents are divine punishments on the wicked form "a late representative of an increasingly old-fashioned genre" (Ibid., xxiv-xxv).
4   E.g., John Brown, 308; Hill, *Tinker*, 231; Mullett, 213.
5   Roger Sharrock, "*The Life and Death of Mr. Badman*: Facts and Problems," 25, 17. In the introduction to *The Holy War*, Sharrock and James F. Forrest also say that *Mr. Badman* "does not look forward very keenly or very far to the new novel" (Sharrock and Forrest, eds., in Bunyan, HW, xx).
6   Beth Lynch, "'Rather Dark to Readers in General': Some Critical Casualties of John Bunyan's *The Holy War* (1682)," *Bunyan Studies* 9 (1999/2000): 25-26, 32-33; Hill, *Tinker*, 252-253; Arlette Marie Zinck, "Of Arms and the Heroic Reader: The Concept of Psychomachy in Spenser, Milton and Bunyan" (Ph. D. diss., University of Alberta, 1993), 172; Roger Sharrock and James F. Forrest, in Bunyan, HW, xxxv; Talon, *John Bunyan: The Man and His Works*, 256.
7   Galen Johnson, "Be Not Extreme," 447-464; Lynch, 34.

and Attentive about Mr. Badman the same equation of the conscience with "the light of nature" that Bunyan turned against the Quakers, and the same linking of this natural conscience with the law, death, the devil and hell that undergirds *Grace Abounding to the Chief of Sinners*. When Wiseman says on several occasions that Badman committed his many business and marital outrages against the light or law of nature, he does not suggest that this light is an autonomous authority that offered Badman the means to save himself.[8] The light of nature could have shown Badman only his crimes; it could not have saved him from them. Thus does Wiseman explain that Badman could have realized by this light how wicked his life had been, how horrific his cursing and swearing had been (as Bunyan himself had once learned), and particularly in his habit of "breaking" (declaring bankruptcy to defraud his creditors), how he had committed "a thing odious to Reason and Conscience, and contrary to the Law of nature."[9] In such a condition, Badman is the antitype of Christian and Christiana, who constantly seek godly company: all but three of thirty-seven uses of "company" or "companion" refer to Badman's disreputable acquaintances, including one who asks, "*What would the Devil do for company, if it was not for such as I*[?]"[10] Attentive compares all such ruffians to a drunken man who lives according to the law of nature less than does a horse, for the horse only drinks to his refreshment and not to his harm.[11]

By not heeding the warnings of his conscience to seek a redeemer, Badman confirms his reprobation.[12] Wiseman also tells of several perpetrators of sexual misconduct who confessed their acts because of afflicted consciences, but Badman outranks them all in vileness because he does not feel even basic guilt.[13] Attentive concludes,

> I say, it cannot be, but that the man that is such as this Mr. Badman, must be a rank and stinking Atheist; for he that believes that there is either God or Devil, Heaven or Hell, or Death, and

---

8   Badman's belief that he has control over his life is but an illusion: "Now I enjoy my self, and am Master of mine own wayes, and not they of me" (Bunyan, *The Life and Death of Mr. Badman*, 85).
9   Ibid., 21, 32, 91.
10 Ibid., 41. Cf. Bunyan, *GA*, §43, p. 16.
11 Bunyan, *Badman*, 45.
12 Wiseman says that Badman "was one that never was good, therefore such an one who is not dead only, but damned" (Ibid., 14). Bunyan also compared Badman with Judas (9) and Esau (76), the representatives of reprobation whose league he so dreaded in *Grace Abounding*.
13 Ibid., 53-56.

Judgment after, cannot doe as Mr. Badman did; I mean, if he could do these things without reluctancy and check of Conscience; yea, if he had not sorrow and remorse for such abominable sins as these.[14]

Wiseman confirms Attentive's evaluation, saying that Badman's extraordinarily high estimation of his own wit and worldly achievements choked any remorse that his conscience might otherwise have felt.[15] Much less did Badman ever express a desire for the righteousness of Christ to clothe him or the Holy Spirit to sanctify him.[16] Wiseman and Attentive thus become the preachers of the gospel which Bunyan announces in his preface to the religiously wayward reader: "*Let thy conscience speak, I say, is it* [Bunyan's book] *not prepared for thee, thou being an ungodly man?*"[17] Bunyan's frank purpose "*is to stop an hellish Course of Life, and to save a soul from death.*"[18] He hopes that the example of Mr. Badman will prick the consciences of the unregenerate to become "alive *to the* Pilgrims Progress" rather than to take their conceit with them to hell, where the worm that does not die, as Bunyan interprets Mark 9:48, is the worm of a guilty conscience.[19] Thus, although the audience within the narrative itself is Attentive, who is already a professing Christian, Bunyan's intended reading audience for this work was certainly not limited to believers alone.[20]

Bunyan hoped by giving negative examples to approximate the person in *The Pilgrim's Progress* who settles a clogged and dusty conscience by pouring water on it. According to Wiseman, there was an abundance of "ungodly" persons in England at the time, and Bunyan understandably counted on his authorial reputation as the most likely incentive for such persons to read his book.[21] Perhaps Bunyan also held out hope that godly wives would share *The Life and Death of Mr. Badman* with roughneck husbands in the same manner that his own first wife shared Arthur Dent's *The Plain Man's Path-way to*

---

14 Ibid., 84. Cf. similar statements *passim*, but especially 16.
15 Ibid.
16 Ibid., 139.
17 Ibid., 6.
18 Ibid., 5.
19 Ibid., 2, 6, 151. Note a similar interpretation in Bunyan's *One Thing is Needful*: "This ghastly worm is guilt for sin, / Which on the Conscience feeds, / With vipers teeth both sharp and keen, / Whereat it sorely bleeds" (*MW*, 6:94).
20 *Contra* James F. Forrest and Roger Sharrock, in Bunyan, *Badman*, xiii.
21 Ibid., 85.

Heaven and Lewis Bayly's *The Practice of Piety* with him.[22] Bunyan was particularly disturbed by men who mixed religious language into their daily conversation – as Badman does to woo his wife and maintain customers – in order to sanction unholy lives. "But as *Luther says*" in his *Commentary on Galatians*, "*In the name of God begins all mischief.*"[23]

The last fifty pages of *Mr. Badman* are replete with warnings against the stifling of conscience. When Badman breaks his leg and then becomes sick, the pains of conscience and the associated fear of death, hell, and judgment suddenly crash down upon him, and he begins "to roar out of his ill-spent Life," but his conscience, says Wiseman, is so "besotted," "benummed," "senceless and ignorant" that it cannot long remain sensitive to "its miserable state."[24] Thus does Badman die peacefully without any anguish in his conscience.[25] Henri Talon's evaluation of Bunyan's technique is accurate: "Teach, go ahead, lay siege to consciences and then take them by storm – those are his aims."[26]

Stuart Sim and David Walker claim too much, however, when they say that Bunyan's negative casuistry forces Christians "into a process of self-authorisation."[27] Everything that we have seen so far about Bunyan's use of "conscience" in *The Life and Death of Mr. Badman* is consistent with his larger corpus of writings: the conscience is the location where awareness of personal sin occurs; in response, it either forsakes all for Christ or else cuts itself off from the gospel and dies in its own filth, *but it cannot cleanse itself*. Badman willfully and persistently stifles conscience; therefore, says Attentive, "*This argueth that Mr.* Badman *had but little conscience.*" Rather, corrects Wiseman, "This argued that Mr. *Badman* had *No* Conscience at all."[28] In Bunyan's way of thinking, whether *The Life and Death of Mr. Badman* produced repentance and a new authority in its reader was

---

22 Bunyan, *GA*, §15, p. 8. Bunyan would have read from Dent a similar condemnation of exploiting the poor as that which he himself would eventually write not only in *Mr. Badman* but also *A Few Sighs from Hell* (James F. Forrest and Roger Sharrock, in Bunyan, *Badman*, xvii; T. L. Underwood and Roger Sharrock, in Bunyan, *MW*, 1:xxxviii).
23 Bunyan, *Badman*, 105.
24 Ibid., 128, 135, 137, 139, 160, 166.
25 Vittorio Gabrieli compares Badman's remorseless death to Shakespeare's *Henry V* in "Falstaff and Mr. Badman: Libertine and Puritan," *Notes and Queries* 35:2 (June 1988): 167.
26 Talon, *John Bunyan: The Man and His Works*, 238.
27 Sim and Walker, 173.
28 Bunyan, *Badman*, 90.

solely due to God's elective will. He offered his work only as an instrument: *"How many it will kill to Mr. Badmans course ... that is not in me to determine; this secret is with the Lord our God only, and he alone knows to whom he will bless it to so good and so blessed an end."*[29]

"Good Conscience" and Christian Economic Ethics

For nearly thirty pages, Wiseman lectures Attentive on the content of a *good* conscience, and he does so specifically within the context of business ethics. Though Bunyan certainly believed that the intervention of Christ within the natural conscience could redeem it and make it a center of communication between Christ and the person, he rarely used the term "good conscience" outside this section in *Mr. Badman*. Examples we have already seen come from *Grace Abounding*, where Bunyan revealed that he had "a good Conscience" despite some slanderous things said against him; *The Pilgrim's Progress*, where Christian says that Wanton could not have afforded Faithful *"the content of a good conscience,"* and *A Discourse of the House of God*, where Bunyan declared that there is room in the church for private opinions so long as they do not "with good Conscience jarr."[30] In *Prison Meditations*, Bunyan described the Bedford prison as "very sweet to me" because, through divine comfort, "Here dwells good Conscience, also Peace."[31] Bunyan explained his hesitancy to use the term "good conscience" in *The Water of Life*: "There are good Men, good Consciences, good Works, good Days, good Angels, &c. but none so good as Grace, for 'tis Grace that has made them so."[32] In all of Bunyan's corpus outside of *Mr. Badman*, the most uses of the term "good conscience" in any single work were four times in *Paul's Departure and Crown*.[33] In *Mr. Badman*, however, Bunyan used the phrase "good conscience" twenty-four times over twenty-six pages. What accounts for this atypically frequent invocation of the "good conscience"? I believe that it was the logical outworking of Bunyan's disavowal of sectarianism in his political writings, in which he began to prescribe how persons should conduct themselves in mundane civil affairs.

---

29 Ibid., 2.
30 Bunyan, *GA*, 93 (§310); *PP*, 68; *A Discourse of the Building, Nature, Excellency and Government of the House of God with Counsels and Directions to the Inhabitants Thereof*, in *MW*, 6:311.
31 Bunyan, in *MW*, 6:45 (ll.76, 80).
32 Bunyan, in *MW*, 7:209.
33 Bunyan, *MW*, 12:392 (three times), 395.

Badman's practice of "breaking" becomes the occasion for extended advice by Wiseman on proper economic conduct. Certain economic decisions can be performed with a good conscience, Wiseman says, and others cannot. In the latter category, he lists the further accumulation of debt by someone who cannot repay what he already owes, lavish spending on food and clothing, and extortion.[34] He focuses particularly on the dishonest gain of wealth by charging too much money for staple goods. Badman is quite skillful at this. He uses different weights and scales for buying and selling so that he always pays less and profits more than he justly should. He charges the greatest price for the worst wheat, and he often makes poor buyers pay twice for the same goods if they cannot produce proof of payment for the original purchase. To this crime, Attentive responds, "*He must sink, there is no remedy.*"[35] Wiseman then takes the occasion to speak at length on the evil of selling commodities at exorbitant prices. In so doing, he elucidates the basic principle of ethical business practice by those whose consciences have been formed by Christian practices:

> First, If it be lawful for me alway[s] to sell my commodity as dear, or for as much as I can, then 'tis lawful for me to lay aside in my dealing with others, good conscience, to them, and to God: but it is not lawful for me, in my dealing with others, to lay aside good conscience, &c. Therefore it is not lawful for me always to sell my commodity as dear, or for as much as I can.[36]

On the basis of 1 Thessalonians 4:6, which says that God will avenge the defrauded, Wiseman elaborates that selling commodities for the maximum possible earnings takes advantage of the customer's ignorance, need, and fondness for the good.[37] Individual autonomy in Bunyan's mind became increasingly linked with market capitalism, and here he rejected both. A Christian approach to business involves good conscience to God and charity toward one's neighbor. For the sake of these two things, a merchant should undersell the market value of his good if the buyer is poor and needy.[38] The person who does not exercise good conscience and charity, Wise-

---

34 Bunyan, *Badman*, 92-93, 108.
35 Ibid., 108.
36 Ibid., 110.
37 Ibid., 111.
38 Ibid., 117.

man says, is next of kin to Mr. Badman, the quintessential Hobbesian motivated only by his own economic good.[39]

Bunyan's emphasis on commodities invokes the trade of Vanity Fair in *The Pilgrim's Progress*. In Part I, there is a lengthy description of the merchandise for sale there, and because Vanity Fair was built by Beelzebub, Apollyon, and Legion, even such good things as houses and spouses are considered as vain as honors and bauds. The rows of the fair are divided by nationality – Britain Row, French Row, Italian Row, Spanish Row, German Row. "But as in other *fairs*, some one Commodity is as the chief of all the *fair*, so the Ware of *Rome* and her Merchandize is greatly promoted in *this fair*: Only our *English* Nation, with some others, have taken a dislike thereat."[40] This is more a religious than an economic condemnation to be sure, but Faithful's martyrdom in Vanity Fair because he was not interested in any of the dealers' wares still illustrates the great otherworldliness of Part I. However, in *The Pilgrim's Progress*, Part II, Christiana and her party are welcomed to the town by Mnason, "an old Disciple" who provides food and lodging for pilgrims. Mnason describes the change in the town since Faithful's martyrdom: "In *those* days we were afraid to walk the Streets, but *now* we can shew our Heads. *Then* the Name of a Professor was odious, *now*, specially in some parts of our Town (for you know our Town is large) Religion is counted Honourable."[41]

The change is very significant. Part I sarcastically associates "honourable religion" with the social elites and hypocrites, such as the pretentious Mr. By-ends and his wife.[42] But Part II welcomes social honor for Christianity. In Vanity Fair, Christiana's sons Samuel and Joseph marry Mnason's daughters Grace and Martha, respectively. Moreover, the pilgrims stay in the town for a long period, during which time they seek its welfare and raise families. The reason for this is to make an active Christian witness in the secular world:

> Wherefore the *Pilgrims* grew acquainted with many of the good people of the Town, and did them what Service they could. *Mercie*, as she was wont, laboured much for the Poor, wherefore their

---

39 Ibid., 114-115; David Hawkes, *Idols of the Marketplace: Idolatry and Commodity Fetishism in English Literature, 1580-1680* (New York: Palgrave, 2001), 230; and "Master of His Ways? Determinism and the Market in *The Life and Death of Mr. Badman*," in *John Bunyan: Reading Dissenting Writing*, ed. N. H. Keeble (Oxford: Peter Lang, 2002), 214.
40 Bunyan, *PP*, 89.
41 Ibid., 275.
42 Ibid., 99.

Bellys and Backs blessed her, and she was there an Ornament to her Profession. And to say the truth, for *Grace, Phebe* [wife of James], and *Martha*, they were all of a very good Nature, and did much good in their place. They were also all of them very Fruitful, so that *Christian's* Name, as was said before, was like to live in the World.[43]

In Part II, therefore, the world is not something to be hurriedly fled but faithfully occupied as the real (though not final) home of Christians, where they live as salt and light (Matt 5:13-14). This was also Bunyan's working assumption in *The Life and Death of Mr. Badman*. A Christian has responsibilities of right conduct in the world, especially in business matters, since the welfare of others and public regard for the gospel are at stake. Thus should one sell commodities with a concern for the welfare of the *polis*, but if one sells them for maximum profit, they then become objects of evil.

Wiseman says that persons by flattering speech alone cannot make themselves "fit for the Kingdom of Heaven, or men of good conscience on earth."[44] The stress on fair dealings with customers in his discourse shows the importance of community and the role of Christians in seeking its good. Indeed, Bunyan foresaw the concern of Wendell Berry that the "community alone, as principle and as fact, can raise the standards of local health (ecological, economic, social, and spiritual) without which [public and private] interests will destroy one another."[45] Mr. Badman does not seek the good of his community but only the preservation of his own "rights" by doing as he pleases, greedily ruining others' lives in the process. But Christians would be the ideal business dealers in Bunyan's view since their consciences are captive to Christ, and a relationship with their Lord manifests itself in righteous deeds.[46] There is little bite to Christopher Hill's critique that Bunyan came, "perhaps too late, to emphasize community, charity, the rights of the poor."[47] These emphases were

---

43 Ibid., 277. In *Good News for the Vilest of Men*, Bunyan spoke of charity as a means of evangelism: "Why not go to the poor Man's House, and give him a *Penny*, and a Scripture to think upon? Why not send for the Poor to fetch away, at least, the Fragments of thy Table, that the Bowels of thy fellow-sinner may be refresht as well as thine?" (Bunyan, *MW*, 11:81).
44 Bunyan, *Badman*, 98.
45 Wendell Berry, *Sex, Economy, Freedom and Community: Eight Essays* (New York: Pantheon Books, 1993), 119; cf. 120-121.
46 Cf. J. G. Randall, "Against the Backdrop of Eternity: Narrative and the Negative Casuistry of John Bunyan's *The Life and Death of Mr. Badman*," *The Baptist Quarterly* 35:7 (July 1994): 347-348.
47 Hill, *Tinker*, 22.

the inheritance of Bunyan's long-held dedication to Lutheran conceptions of conscience and law, whence he derived his belief that natural law is binding even on non-Christians in the secular sphere. Badman's failure to act out of good conscience not only seals his damnation, but it also violates the moral law on which society stands.

In play here also is Luther's understanding of the two uses of the moral law. For both Luther and Calvin, moral law after the advent of Christ has two primary uses: it reveals to human beings their utter inability to live righteously before God, and, as the insuperable basis of civil law, it punishes individuals who will desist from public crimes only by compulsion. Calvin, however, explicitly added a "third use" of the law, which he actually considered its most important use. Though Christ has written the law on believers' hearts, Calvin said, Christians are still to strive to keep the law as a guide for purposeful growth in sanctification.[48] Calvin's adjoining of the law to the life of converted Christians has led to charges of legalism, while Luther's insistence that the Christian has no *need* of law has led to charges of antinomianism. Bunyan did not advocate Calvin's "third use," and so he was targeted with the same accusation as was Luther.[49] Yet together with the magisterial Reformers and unlike the Anabaptists, Bunyan believed biblical law to be binding on all citizens of the state, and in *The Life and Death of Mr. Badman*, he conveyed this belief by condemning unfair business transactions done against the law of nature and good conscience.[50]

It is impossible in this view of citizenship for the conscience to legitimate actions conducted only in the best interests of one's own self. At the same time Bunyan expressed his care of individual souls, therefore, he also expressed care for his nation. It was only in the beginning of the twentieth century, as D. W. Bebbington demon-

---

48 François Wendel, *Calvin: Origins and Development of His Religious Thought*, trans. Philip Mairet (Grand Rapids: Baker Books, 1997), 198-201.

49 Anjov Ahenakaa says that Bunyan followed Calvin's third use of the law, but Ahenakaa misunderstands the law's third use as the role of guiding society as a whole. Certainly, both Bunyan and Luther did believe in this use of the law, but that was actually the Reformers' *second* use (Ahenakaa, "Justification and the Christian Life in John Bunyan: A Vindication of Bunyan from the Charge of Antinomianism" [Ph. D., diss., Westminster Theological Seminary, 1997], 263-268).

50 E.g., Bunyan, *Badman*, 112-113. Kretzschmar renders a contemporary appreciation of *Mr. Badman* when she holds up Bunyan's condemnation of unscrupulous business practices as an example to white South African Baptists who must still deal with a long history in their country of racial discrimination (146).

strates, that British nonconformity jettisoned its program for a national morality.[51] It would thus be myopic to expect that Bunyan did so. No less than nine times in *Mr. Badman*, either the narrator or one of the characters specifically expresses a desire for a more moral England.[52] Indeed, in his introduction, Bunyan compared his program for moral reform to a king's messenger who apprehends traitors; there can be no question, then, that he offered *Mr. Badman* to the service of the commonweal no less than to God.[53] Wiseman maintains, of course, that social reform will only happen insofar as God will "smite" the proud person "in his conscience by the Word."[54] This means that the common grace that God gives to all people to guide their conduct in the world with a good conscience is *still grace*, though not the same as elective grace.[55] The result of such social concern is a deflection from the self-preoccupation that sometimes characterizes *Grace Abounding*. After the preface of *Mr. Badman*, where Bunyan recalled *"considering with my self,"* defended the dialogue format as *"more easie to my self,"* hoped his words *"might not only deliver my self,"* and hid how he came to write the book as *"best known to my self,"* his uses of the term "self" became almost all synonyms for "person" and not a detached object for observation in the modern sense.[56]

---

51 D. W. Bebbington, *The Nonconformist Conscience: Chapel and Politics, 1870-1914* (London: George Allen and Unwin, 1982), 159-160.
52 Bunyan, *Badman*, 2 (twice), 7, 10, 29, 66, 82, 125 (twice).
53 Ibid., 2.
54 Ibid., 119.
55 Wiseman and Attentive say that the children of godly parents receive a special advantage from the sovereign will of God that makes them more likely to act in the world with a good conscience, and so does Mrs. Badman hope before her death that she has had such an influence on her children (Ibid., 77-78, 143). Wiseman denies that the children of godly parents are automatically elect (so did Calvin), but the argument that children of believers are specially blessed by God was precisely the Presbyterian argument for infant baptism, and so by adopting this line, Bunyan again showed an openness to a sacramental notion of the Christian life, coinciding with the pedobaptisms at Interpreter's Bath in *The Pilgrim's Progress*, Part II. Anne Dunan reads *The Life and Death of Mr. Badman* within the context of other seventeenth-century writings which addressed young adults and concludes that "they invite us to read Bunyan's text as one where growing up healthily is associated with saving grace" (Dunan, "*The Life and Death of Mr. Badman* as a 'Compassionate Counsel to All Young Men': John Bunyan and Nonconformist Writings on Youth," *Bunyan Studies* 9 [1999/2000]: 50; cf. 65).
56 Bunyan, *Badman*, 1, 8.

Bunyan advised readers to "*continue thou in the things that thou hast learned, not of wanton men, not of licentious times, but of the Word and Doctrine of God, that is according to Godliness; and thou shalt walk with Christ in white.*"[57] Trust in the objective "Word" of God is a commonplace in *The Life and Death of Mr. Badman*: it appears at least twenty-five times. Yes, the result is preachy and even moralistic. Yes, by forcing his readers to be sensitive to their own mortality, as Mullett points out, Bunyan perhaps encouraged individualistic introspection.[58] But whatever else it may be, *Mr. Badman* is not subjectivist in its outlook; it stands, as David Hawkes claims, in opposition to the autonomous, egocentric pursuit of self-interest.[59] It is an allegorical disputation for a biblically-derived communal morality.

The Holy War

Arlette Zinck summarizes the obstacles one must overcome in understanding *The Holy War* when she describes it as "the most complex and, arguably, the least engaging of Bunyan's fictions."[60] The allegory is so complex because it is difficult to determine on how many levels Bunyan intended his text to operate, and on which of several possible readings he placed the most emphasis. Scholars have contended that *The Holy War* is either another rendition of Bunyan's personal religious maturity told not as pilgrimage but as protracted war, a diagnosis for the struggles that all human souls undergo, a rehearsal of the collective fall of the human race, or a political commentary on the Restoration of Charles II and its effects on nonconformists. There is undoubtedly some truth in all these interpretations.

Frank Mott Harrison argues that the first reading, concerning the autobiographical nature of *The Holy War*, should be the primary one since the original edition contained a folding plate with the town of Mansoul superimposed over a portrait of Bunyan, and King Shaddai's castle sitting above Bunyan's heart.[61] Michael Mullett sees *The Holy War* as "a Puritan religious metaphor for the struggle for the possession of the individual human soul," and Daniel Lamont agrees that the allegory is mainly about the "individual soul."[62]

---

57 Ibid., 10.
58 Mullett, 160.
59 Hawkes, "Master," 223, 227-228.
60 Zinck, "Of Arms," 214.
61 Frank Mott Harrison, 167.
62 Mullett, 235; Daniel Lamont, "Bunyan's *Holy War*: A Study in Christian Experience," *Theology Today* 3:4 (January 1947): 459.

There is also a sense in which Mansoul's succumbing to Diabolus retells how the original sin affects the human race universally, and it is very similar in that regard to Milton's *Paradise Lost*, first published only fifteen years before *The Holy War*.[63] Roger Sharrock believes that Mansoul is simultaneously corporate *and* individual.[64] But while he concedes the spiritual purpose of *The Holy War*, Sharrock also observes that the political divisions in the text have a basis in the real world of seventeenth century England.[65]

Indeed, several commentators have observed that Diabolus's replacement of Mansoul's Lord Mayor and Recorder (Lustings for Understanding and Forget-good for Conscience, respectively) reflects actual changes in the municipality of Bedford. In November 1681, only a few months before the publication of *The Holy War*, King Charles II tried to strengthen royalist support in corporate towns by drafting new charters that ousted Whigs and nonconformists from government offices. The Recorder was in charge of local elections and enforcing new regulations and so was an important person in the king's plan to attenuate nonconformist fervor. In Bedford, the Deputy Recorder, Robert Audley, was removed from his post for being an enemy to the state because he tolerated separatists such as Bunyan, and the mayor who ordered Audley's dismissal was Paul Cobb, one of Bunyan's interrogators shortly into his first imprisonment (1661). In a public speech, Audley rebuked

---

63 Scholars such as Edmund Arbuthnott Knox (97), William York Tindall (200-202, 281 [ft. 37], and Monica Furlong (134) have entertained the possibility that Bunyan had something of *Paradise Lost* in mind when writing *The Holy War*; others like Henri Talon (*John Bunyan: The Man and His Works*, 240, 242 [ft. 3]), Gordon Wakefield (*Bunyan the Christian*, 98), and N. H. Keeble ("Till one greater Man," 27) simply note the similarities between the two texts but are cautious to suggest that Bunyan had actually read Milton. Talon and Tindall further point out that Bunyan may not have known Milton but could have known the adaptation of *Paradise Lost* by the Baptist Benjamin Keach called *The Glorious Lover* (1679). Michael A. Mullett also joins Knox and Hill in suggesting that the English Civil Wars could have provided a common experience from which both men drew illustrative material (243-244).

64 Sharrock, *John Bunyan*, 122. Cf. Roger Sharrock and James F. Forrest, in Bunyan, *HW*, xxix.

65 Roger Sharrock and James F. Forrest, in Bunyan, *HW*, xxii. Richard L. Greaves finds in *The Holy War* a "secondary level of political criticism" (Greaves, "John Bunyan and the Ethic of Suffering," in *John Bunyan and His England, 1628-88*, ed. Anne Laurence, W. R. Owens, and Stuart Sim [London: The Hambledon Press, 1990], 68).

civil officials who operated according to "ill principles" without justice. Thus is it no surprise that the rightful Recorder of Mansoul would be Mr. Conscience, for at the exact time when Bunyan was completing *The Holy War*, "the Recorder's voice was indeed that of a troubled and tried conscience, whether in Mansoul, Bedford, or many another English town."[66]

I believe that an informed understanding of Bunyan's general conception of conscience, when applied particularly to Mansoul's Recorder, offers an answer for those who find *The Holy War* both uninspiring and uninspired. For some, it is precisely because Bunyan tried to manage so much at once that *The Holy War* fails to capture and hold its readers' imaginations. Even G. B. Harrison, whose praise of the book is virtually unstinted, believes that the allegory is so elaborate and overextended that it makes a less successful appeal to conscience than does *The Pilgrim's Progress*.[67] Jack Lindsay finds contradictory Bunyan's attempted combination of individualism with an interest in the social whole, but his Marxist ideological agenda clouds his judgment. Lindsay claims that by defining the individual in terms of a social organism, Bunyan intuits a basically Marxist philosophy,[68] but Lindsay forgets that Marx's categories of covenant and community are actually secularized derivatives of Old Testament ideals that balanced individual and community on the fulcrum of God's elective grace and covenant faithfulness. Henri Talon thinks that the intertwining of so many layers of meaning in *The Holy War* moved Bunyan audaciously beyond *The Pilgrim's Progress* in his individualism: "From detailed sketches to sweeping frescoes, from an intimate private narrative to a generalisation of personal experience, from the pilgrimage of a single man to the struggles of a populous city that is watched by the whole universe – what a proud exaltation of self!"[69] But the "self" of *The Holy War*, and its full capacity for engaging the reader, cannot be so cursorily assessed without a full understanding of its central character, Mr. Conscience, and the pattern for godly citizenship which he espouses.

---

66 Roger Sharrock and James F. Forrest, in Bunyan, HW, xxii-xxv. Cf. John Brown, 316-318; Talon, *John Bunyan: The Man and His Works*, 245-246; Lindsay, 216; Mullett, 232, 235.
67 G. B. Harrison, *John Bunyan*, 198-199.
68 Lindsay, 224-225.
69 Talon, *John Bunyan: The Man and His Works*, 243.

The Role of Conscience in The Holy War

Mr. Conscience is the Recorder of the town of Mansoul in the country of Universe. After the forces of Diabolus – having been evicted from Heaven for daring to seize power from King Shaddai and his son Emanuel – win their way into Mansoul through the Ear-gate and then slay Lord Innocency (this is Bunyan's account of the fall), Diabolus puts out of office both Conscience and Lord Mayor Understanding and replaces them with his own henchmen. Bunyan's description of Conscience's skills and behavior is notable for its consistency with Bunyan's understanding of conscience since his earliest writings:

> As for Mr. *Recorder*, before the Town was taken, he was a man well read in the Laws of his King, and also a man of courage and faithfulness to speak truth at every occasion: And he had a tongue as bravely hung, as he had an head filled with judgement. Now this man, *Diabolus* could by no means abide, because, though he gave his consent to his coming into the Town, yet he could not, by all wiles, trials, Stratagems, and devices that he could use, make him wholly his own. True, he was much degenerated from his former King, and also much pleased with many of the Giants Laws, and service: but all this would not do for as much as he was not wholly his. He would now and then think upon *Shaddai*, and have dread of his Law upon him, and then he would speak with a voice, as great against *Diabolus*, as when a Lyon roareth. Yea, and would also at certain times when his fits were upon him (for you must know that some times he had terrible fits) make the whole Town of *Mansoul* shake with his voice: and therefore the now King of *Mansoul* could not abide him.
>
> *Diabolus* therefore feared the *Recorder* more than any that was left alive in the Town of *Mansoul*, because, as I said his words did shake the whole Town; they were like the ratling-thunder, and also like Thunder-claps. Since therefore the *Giant* could not make him wholly his own, what doth he do but studies all that he could, to debauch the old Gentleman, and by debauchery, to stupifie his mind, and more harden his heart in ways of vanity. And as he attempted, so he accomplished his design: He debauched the man, and by little and little, so drew him into sin and wickedness, that at last he was not only debauched as at first: and so by consequence defiled, but was almost (at last, I say) past all Conscience of sin.[70] And this was the farthest *Diabolus* could go.

---

70 Compare the ending of *Piers Plowman*, where Conscience leaves Unity Holy Church after a monk drugs Contrition, leaving him unable to shed tears for sin (William Langland, *Piers Plowman*, trans. A. V. C. Schmidt [Oxford: Oxford University Press, 1992], 254).

Wherefore he be-thinks him of an other project, and that was to perswade the men of the Town that Mr. Recorder was mad, and so not to be regarded. And for this he urged his fits, and said, if he be himself, why doth he not do thus always? but, quoth he, as all mad folk have their fits, and in them their raving language; so hath this old and doating Gentleman. Thus by one means or another, he quickly got *Mansoul* to slight, neglect, and despise what ever Mr. *Recorder* could say.[71]

Mr. Conscience's expertise is the law of King Shaddai and so, in fact, he is the "voice" of Shaddai for Mansoul. However, Conscience's knowledge is no match for the wiles of the one who could persuade angels to join his doomed cause. Knowing that he must stifle Conscience in order to assume full control of the town, Diabolus tricks Conscience into subservience. Yet from time to time, Conscience falls into "fits" during which he cannot help but to speak the commandments of Shaddai, and he does so with the sound of thunder or a roaring lion. On such occasions, Diabolus berates Conscience before his fellow citizens as a madman, and so Conscience's prattling becomes to them a great annoyance. Bunyan's marginal gloss explains, "Men [are] sometimes angry with their Consciences."[72] Diabolus names as the new Recorder one Forget-good, "a very sorry fellow" who "could remember nothing but mischief, and to do it with delight."[73] When Conscience's occasional outbursts set the town in "a hubbub" – even as does the preaching of Faithful in Vanity Fair – he is twice beaten down by one Mr. Benumming, and then Diabolus places him under house arrest along with Lord Understanding.[74]

It seems quite natural to compare this presentation of Conscience and his troubles to *Grace Abounding to the Chief of Sinners*. There, following Luther, Bunyan told how the devil's silencing of the law's censure prohibits the soul from moving toward Christ. The conscience may still yell and roar when it considers its just condemnation for betraying God's law, but the devil convinces persons to dismiss such outbursts as those of madness. Christian's wife and children also respond this way to his spiritual pangs at the beginning of *The Pilgrim's Progress*, Part I, though they convert in Part II; Mr. Badman, however, dies under such delusions about himself. Indeed, Bunyan's marginal gloss, "*Diabolus* has no conscience to God," is

---

71 Bunyan, *HW*, 18-19.
72 Ibid., 21.
73 Ibid., 25.
74 Ibid., 58, 61-62; cf. Bunyan, *PP*, 90.

also Mr. Wiseman's evaluation of Mr. Badman.[75] And Mr. Benumming's battering of Conscience illustrates Bunyan's belief in *Grace Abounding* "that this temptation of the Devil is more than usual amongst poor creatures than many are aware of, even to over-run their spirits with a scurvie and seared frame of heart, and benumming of conscience."[76]

When Emanuel designs to regain Mansoul and, after some initial assaults, makes strategy that "the next Battel would issue in his being made master of the place," he commands his military captains Boanerges, Conviction, and Judgment to liberate Mr. Conscience.[77] When they knock down his door with a battering ram, however, Conscience cannot discern whether the captains are friends or foes. All Conscience can talk about is death and destruction, to the astonishment of all who are present, but as in *Grace Abounding*, this preoccupation with death is an initial step to new life, for Bunyan interprets in the margin: "The office of Conscience when he is awakened."[78] Conscience informs those who come to witness the eerie scene that they all are traitors against Prince Emanuel, but much as in the Lukan story of Zacchaeus the publican (Luke 19:1-10), such self-condemnation sways Emanuel to visit Conscience's house.[79] As Emanuel makes his way there, glistening in his golden armor, the townspeople tremble in fear of their certain punishment from him, yet in this humbled position, they profess their desire that he should again be their sovereign. Emanuel makes Conscience's house the permanent station of Captains Boanerges and Conviction, orders Diabolus to be taken in chains from the town castle, and summons the citizens of Mansoul to gather in the castle yard.[80] Rather than deliver a speech to the crowds, however, Emanuel orders the protective custody of Conscience, Understanding, and Lord Wilbewill. As it turns out, the imprisonment of Conscience to the lordship of Emanuel will prove his safest refuge.

The three hostages send a message to Emanuel, asking him to spare their lives and those of the townspeople. At first, Emanuel will not even receive their messenger, Mr. Desires-awake, and when

---

75 Bunyan, *HW*, 84; *Badman*, 90.
76 Bunyan, *GA*, 11 (§25).
77 Compare the sixteenth century Catholic mystic Teresa of Ávila, who likens the preachers and theologians of the church to captains defending a castle or city (Teresa of Ávila, *The Way of Perfection*, trans. E. Allison Peers [New York: Image Books, 1991], 46).
78 Bunyan, *HW*, 87-88.
79 Ibid., 89.
80 Ibid., 91, 93-94.

he does respond, it is only to say that he will consider the request. Conscience interprets for the rest that the prince's curt response is an omen of death.[81] Yet, their anxiety prompts them to petition Emanuel again. Some want Mr. Good-deed to carry the letter, but Conscience vetoes the idea because he realizes that not *"a thousand of old* Good-deeds," but only mercy, can save Mansoul.[82] So Desires-awake bears their second request, accompanied by Mr. Wet-eyes, but Emanuel again delays his answer, and so Conscience feels that he should prepare himself to die. The next day, the three captives appear before Emanuel at his bidding. He asks them what their punishment should be for having submitted to Diabolus, and they suggest execution. But when Emanuel asks them to stand before him for sentencing, rather than condemning them, he not only pardons all three but also pronounces clemency for the entire town. He then charges Conscience to proclaim this good news, and Conscience immediately calls for a town meeting to be held in the market place the next day. Conscience and Understanding stutter together in their relief, "Oh! Tidings! glad tidings! good tidings of good! and of great joy to poor *Mansoul!*" Bunyan's capitalization further emphasizes Conscience's exultation in being exonerated of a capital crime: "the *Recorder* delivered it in these words, PARDON, PARDON, PARDON for *Mansoul.*"[83] Imprisoned Conscience has become free Conscience.

Emanuel's control over Conscience is symbolically complete when he makes Conscience's house his permanent residence, for the house lies adjacent to the castle. Boanerges, Conviction, and their soldiers also arrange quarters in this same, apparently large, house. But shortly after Emanuel takes up residence in Conscience's house, he orders Conscience to prepare to assume a different office than that of Recorder.[84] The reassignment is not a demerit but a change that puts Conscience's skills in legal matters to even better use. Emanuel's announcement of Conscience's new duties forms a pivotal moment in the story:

> Then did the Prince call unto him the *Old Gentleman*, who afore had been the *Recorder* of *Mansoul*, Mr. *Conscience* by name, and

---

81 Ibid., 94-97.
82 Ibid., 98-99.
83 Ibid., 99-108. Cf. Roger Sharrock and James F. Forrest: "The doctrine of free grace is effectively illustrated when Emmanuel, after the rejection of numerous petitions, grants an entirely undeserved mercy to the rebel town" (In ibid., xxxvii).
84 Ibid., 114, 118.

told him, That for as much as he was well skilled in the Law and Government of the Town of *Mansoul*, and was also well spoken, and could pertinently deliver to them his Masters will in all terrene & domestick matters, therefore he would also make him a Minister *for*, *in*, and *to* the goodly Town of *Mansoul*; in all the Laws, Statutes and Judgments of the famous Town of *Mansoul*. And thou must (said the Prince) confine thy self to the teaching of Moral Vertues, to Civil and Natural duties, but thou must not attempt to presume to be a revealer of those most high and supernatural Mysteries that are kept close in the bosome of *Shaddai* my Father: for those things know no man, nor can any reveal them but my Fathers *Secretary* only.[85]

Of Conscience's confinement to moral virtues and natural duties, a note in the margin explains that these are "His limits." Of Conscience's prohibition against presuming to reveal supernatural mysteries, Bunyan further annotates his meaning to the reader: "His Caution." This suggests that Conscience does not have autonomous authority. Christ-pardoned Conscience must operate according to limits and caution; for the remainder of the book, therefore, Mr. Conscience goes by the title of "Subordinate Preacher."[86]

Emanuel informs Conscience that he must stay low and humble, be content with his station, and not presume to overstep the bounds of what a citizen of Mansoul may properly know. He must be the scholar of everything the Father's Secretary (the Holy Spirit) teaches and must consult this Secretary before making his pronouncements.[87] In contrast to Milton, who in *The Reason of Church-Government* referred to the human conscience as God's secretary, Bunyan demarcated the two so that the conscience itself is *not* God's secretary and so cannot operate autonomously.[88] This is proper since Conscience still expresses occasional doubts that Mansoul will survive, and he trembles from a sense of his own sin while preaching

---

85 Ibid., 140.
86 Ibid., 148; cf. 149, 156-159.
87 Ibid., 141-142. The Secretary's identity as the Holy Spirit is made certain in a statement by Emanuel that agrees with the ecumenical councils of Nicea (325) and Constantinople (381), which affirmed that Christ and the Holy Spirit are of the "same substance" as God: "He that is from the Court, said he, is a person of no less quality and dignity than is my Father and I: and he is the Lord chief *Secretary* of my Fathers house, for he is, and always has been the chief dictator of all my Fathers Laws, a person altogether well skill'd in all mysteries, and knowledg [sic] of mysteries as is my Father, or as my self is. Indeed he is one with us in nature, also as to loving, and being faithful to, and in, the eternal concerns of the Town of *Mansoul*" (Ibid., 139).
88 Milton, 925.

to others.[89] This means that Conscience is the authentic voice of Bunyan, who wrote in *Grace Abounding*, "It is far better that thou do judge thy self, even by preaching plainly to others, then that thou, to save thyself, imprison the truth in unrighteousness: Blessed be God for his help also in this."[90]

When Diabolus launches his counter-attack to regain Mansoul, he gives Conscience "a shot not far off the heart:" Conscience is left "so wounded, yea, and his wounds so festered, that he could have no ease day or night, but lay as if continually upon a rack." Indeed, "but that *Shaddai* rules all, certainly they had slain him out-right."[91] Emanuel later commends Conscience for continuing to exhort the town according to Shaddai's laws, even as all of Mansoul is under attack.[92] Thus, Conscience in *The Holy War* is not simply an "abstracted individual soul" as Daniel Lamont claims but the liaison of divine law for humanity.[93]

Conscience's responsibilities as Subordinate Preacher intersect with several of the concerns that I have traced throughout Bunyan's writings, making *The Holy War* gather the various strands of evidence that I have brought together in opposition to allegations of Bunyan's subjectivism. For instance, in the early theological writings against the Quakers, Bunyan set objective doctrines against the Quakers' inner light. In *The Holy War*, Conscience has the responsibility, both as Recorder and as Subordinate Preacher, to proclaim such historic Christian teachings as Emanuel's gracious election (a "*most wholsom Doctrine*" and "a great Doctrine of the Gospel") and the plenary satisfaction for sin by Christ's blood on the cross.[94] And Conscience must hear and receive his doctrine from Shaddai's Secretary, the Holy Spirit. While there is certainly something mystical and individualistic in this, it is not nearly so subjective as the Quakerish/Miltonic notion that illumination comes entirely from within. We have already witnessed several close parallels between *The Holy War* and *Grace Abounding*, for in both, Bunyan revealed a Lutheran equation of conscience and law that eliminated from the conscience any sense of sinless autonomy. Moreover, one of Emanuel's declarations to Conscience parallels the sacramentalism of *The Pilgrim's Progress*, Part II:

---

89 Bunyan, *HW*, 156, 158.
90 Bunyan, *GA*, 90 (§295).
91 Bunyan, *HW*, 198, 205.
92 Ibid., 212.
93 See this chapter, footnote 62.
94 Bunyan, *HW*, 241, 245; cf. 142, 145, 150, 186-187, 238, 240-241, on the importance of doctrine.

> Because thou art old, and through many abuses made feeble; therefore I give leave and license to go when thou wilt to my fountain, my conduit, and there to drink freely of the blood of my Grape, for my conduit doth always run Wine. Thus doing, thou shalt drive from thy heart and stomach all foul, gross, and hurtful rumours. It will also lighten thine eyes, and will strengthen thy memory for the reception and keeping of all that the Kings most noble *Secretary* teacheth.[95]

This speech shows Bunyan's developed belief that an objective eucharistic sign is a sufficient means of divine grace.

Citizenship in The Holy War

We also discover in The Holy War an often neglected emphasis on responsible citizenship in the secular sphere, much as one finds in *The Life and Death of Mr. Badman*. Rather than placing the ultimate future of Mansoul in doubt, Emanuel's leaving of some Diabolonians in the town demonstrates that Christians cannot be sectarians only. The role of Conscience in Mansoul is to call all its citizens to moral virtue and legal obedience in "civil and domestick matters" – a virtue that can have no salvific value in Bunyan's thought, even though its neglect in civil and domestic matters can be harmful to the Christian witness. So while The Holy War certainly is another depiction of Bunyan's personal religious crisis and maturation, its broader setting is not a nonconformist church but the wider culture, where righteous and unrighteous coexist as wheat and tares. In the *polis*, governing officials such as the town Recorder teach God's law as a sumptuary duty which all must obey, and they have the power to exact penalties of those who do not. Only God, his Son, or his Spirit can reveal the holy mystery of salvation (though this mystery has objective reality in word and sacrament).[96] As Isabel Rivers says, Bunyan believed that the Quakers and Edward Fowler the Latitudinarian could not understand this crucial distinction between the

---

95 Ibid., 141. On this passage, see Gordon S. Wakefield, "'To be a Pilgrim': Bunyan and the Christian Life," in *John Bunyan: Conventicle and Parnassus*, ed. N. H. Keeble (Oxford: Clarendon Press, 1988), 122. Elsewhere, the citizens of Mansoul eat wine and bread and wash their garments white at Emanuel's castle (Bunyan, HW, 115, 225).

96 Brainerd P. Stranahan compares this to Hopeful's words in *The Pilgrim's Progress* that fleshly nature cannot know God (Stranahan, "Bunyan's Satire and its Biblical Sources," in *Bunyan in Our Time*, ed. Robert G. Collmer [Kent, OH: The Kent State University Press, 1989], 54).

natural duties that Conscience can oversee from within and the higher teaching of grace that comes only from without.[97] But Coleridge understood: "We are told by Bunyan, that the Conscience can never find relief for its *disobedience* to the Law in the Law itself – and this is as true of the Moral as of the Mosaic Law."[98] Bunyan followed the "two spheres" theory of Luther: both civil law and spiritual truth come from God, who grants to human beings the capacity to enforce the former but reserves control of the latter solely for himself. Christians continue to obey civil law because it is from God, though they realize that they cannot obtain saving mercy by doing so.[99]

It is Diabolus who speaks with the clearly subjectivist voice of modernity when he boasts to the Mansoulians, "I have granted you to live, each man like a Prince in his own [self], even with as little controul from me, as I my self have from you."[100] A life that is *only* inwardly controlled will not desire to be rid of its carnal nature: that is why subjection to the Secretary is one's only hope in spiritual matters, even for Mr. Conscience.[101] But Diabolus is frustrated with Conscience precisely because he cannot persuade Conscience to blur the different uses of the law. This prompts Emanuel's rebuke of Diabolus when Diabolus proposes becoming Emanuel's deputy in order to reform the town religiously according to moral law:

> Thou talkest now of a reformation in *Mansoul*, and that thou thy self if I will please, will be at the head of that reformation, all the while knowing that the greatest proficiency that man can make in the Law, and the righteousness thereof, will amount to no more for the taking away of the curse from *Mansoul*, *than just nothing at all*, for a Law being broken by *Mansoul*, that had before upon a supposition of the breach thereof, a curse pronounced against him for it of God, can never by his obeying of the Law deliver himself therefrom.[102]

Diabolus misses the Lutheran distinction of law and gospel. The law is indeed a divinely-given instrument for maintaining order in

---

97 Isabel Rivers, "Grace, Holiness, and the Pursuit of Happiness: Bunyan and Restoration Latitudinarianism," in *John Bunyan: Conventicle and Parnassus*, ed. N. H. Keeble (Oxford: Clarendon Press, 1988), 61 (ft. 67).
98 Samuel Taylor Coleridge, *Samuel Taylor Coleridge*, The Oxford Authors, ed. H. J. Jackson (Oxford: Oxford University Press, 1985), 578.
99 Bunyan, HW, 85. Cf. Luther's *The Freedom of a Christian* (1520).
100 Bunyan, HW, 20-21.
101 Ibid., 44-45; cf. 56-57, 60.
102 Ibid., 84-85.

the secular sphere, but it cannot produce the kind of saving righteousness that only the gospel gives.

The Perseverance of the Saints through Gospel-Informed Conscience

The confidence of both Conscience and Credence that the final mastery over Mansoul belongs to Emanuel, and this despite their own personal infirmities (Credence is struck in battle as is Conscience), belies the complaint of some observers that *The Holy War* ends without a satisfactory resolution. The apparent open-endedness of the novel, argue some, reveals Bunyan's ultimate subjective uncertainty about his religious claims. The basis for such a contention is that after Emanuel thwarts Diabolus's protracted attempt at a coup and orders the execution of a number of Diabolonian operatives in the town, he delivers a speech to the townspeople in which he says that he has left some of their enemies alive for their own good, and then he concludes the allegory with these words:

> *Remember therefore, O my* **Mansoul,** *that thou art beloved of me; as I have therefore taught thee to watch, to fight, to pray, and to make war against my foes, so now I command thee to believe that my love is constant to thee. O my* **Mansoul,** *how have I set my heart, my love upon thee, watch. Behold, I lay none other burden upon thee, than what thou hast already, hold fast till I come.*[103]

Sharrock and Forrest mention twice in their critical edition of *The Holy War* that "nothing is concluded" by this conclusion, and that it resembles the fourteenth-century allegory *Piers Plowman*, where the reader does not learn if the character Conscience will find the Christ-figure Piers.[104] Jack Lindsay says that Bunyan forgets his Calvinism if he is suggesting that it is really possible for Mansoul to fall completely away from Emanuel.[105] Christopher Hill flatly calls the ending "unsatisfactory."[106] And Beth Lynch asserts that the "utter uncertainty" of *The Holy War* is all that a Puritan can expect in this life.[107] But these observers may forget Emanuel's assurance that, even when the Mansoulians sense that he is absent, they should yet know that he is really not far away. The future of Mansoul is not open-ended, for it stands under the constant guard of an omnipresent Lord.

---

103 Bunyan, *HW*, 249-250.
104 Roger Sharrock and James F. Forrest, in ibid., xxxvi, 277.
105 Lindsay, 223.
106 Hill, *Tinker*, 253.
107 Lynch, 35.

Old and feeble though he is, God-supported Conscience can actually forecast the conclusion of Mansoul's history so unmistakably that it would be superfluous for Bunyan to portray its actual fruition: "Their *Subordinate Preacher* too made a Sermon about it, and he took that theme for his Text, *Gad, a troop shall overcome him, but he shall overcome at the last* [Gen 49:19]. Whence he shewed that though *Mansoul* should be sorely put to it at the first, yet the victory should most certainly be *Mansouls* at the last."[108] Even though Emanuel appears slow to defend his territory during Diabolus's second onslaught, during which time many Doubters move into Conscience's house, he later reveals, "*I left thee not.*"[109] Again, the story follows Bunyan's own experience in *Grace Abounding*: "God did not utterly leave me, but followed me still, not now with convictions, but Judgements, yet such as were mixed with mercy."[110]

As evidence of this divine protection in *The Holy War*, Diabolus is unable to enter the castle of Mansoul (the "Heart," notes Bunyan in the margin) – which he must control to become undisputed ruler of Mansoul – though he besieges it for two and one-half years.[111] According to *Grace Abounding*, Bunyan himself received diabolical assaults "well-nigh two years and an half," but "*many days*," he learned with relief from Daniel 10:14, "are not for ever."[112] Diabolus's employment of the "Bloodmen" is "his last and sure card" to play against Mansoul, but the Bloodmen are captured and brought to Emanuel.[113] Indeed, Edmund Arbuthnott Knox notes that the lack of heroic dignity of Diabolus, in contrast to Milton's Satan, eliminates all concern that Emanuel might not be the victor.[114] Credence, like Conscience, also knows that the final triumph is certain. In language reminiscent of Julian of Norwich that also recalls Hopeful's words to Christian in the River of Death, Credence declares to Mayor Understanding, "Cheer up, my Lord, for all will be well in time."[115]

---

108 Bunyan, *HW*, 197.
109 Ibid., 204, 245.
110 Bunyan, *GA*, 7 (§12).
111 Bunyan, *HW*, 206.
112 Bunyan, *GA*, 62 (§198).
113 Bunyan, *HW*, 233.
114 Edmund Arbuthnott Knox, 107.
115 Bunyan, *HW*, 211. Cf. Julian of Norwich: "And thus pain, *it* is something, as to my sight, for a time; for it purgeth, and maketh us to know ourselves and to ask mercy. For the Passion of our Lord is comfort to us against all this, and so is His blessed will. And for the tender love that our good Lord hath to all that shall be saved, He comforteth readily and sweetly, signifying thus: *It is sooth that sin is cause of all this pain; but all shall be well, and all*

Stuart Sim and David Walker have offered the most provocative interpretation yet of the ending of *The Holy War*. Employing the cultural theory of Jean-François Lyotard, they argue that *The Holy War* is not simply a modern but a postmodern book. Lyotard expostulates that postmodernism is not a recent occurrence but that, in fact, history has long rotated between "modernisms" and "postmodernisms." "Modernism" occurs, he says, when a single "grand narrative" provides a society with a common vision and coherence; however, when various individuals or groups begin competing to define what that "grand narrative" should be, then disputes, or "differends," arise that cannot be resolved, and this is the primary feature of "postmodernism."[116] Sim and Walker believe that Bunyan was a man caught on the cusp of transition between modernism and postmodernism. He lived in a time when Puritanism had splintered into so many types – Presbyterian, Independent, Baptist, not to mention the radical Nonconformists such as Quakers and Levellers – that the more vehemently he argued for his own vision of a godly England, the more he demonstrated how impossible it was that any one Puritan paradigm would find support from a majority of the population. The authors conclude that, in *The Holy War*, "Bunyan is trying to impose a modern solution on a postmodern dilemma."[117]

This thesis is provocative, but does it really "work" – that is, do Sim and Walker adequately defend why Bunyan *should* or even *can* be interpreted by Lyotardian theory? Even they implicitly recognize the liability of doing so when they say, "*If* [my emphasis] we backdate such a theory as Lyotard's onto seventeenth-century England, what we find is a cultural context ... where the problem of legitimacy, or more precisely how you *secure* legitimacy, is becoming acute."[118] The authors accept that any refusal to compromise individual hopes for society in order to achieve a "grand narrative" is

---

shall be well, and all manner [of] thing[s] shall be well" (Julian of Norwich, *Revelations of Divine Love*, ed. Grace Warrack [London: Methuen and Company Limited, 1901], 56-57 [Chapter 27]). James F. Forrest has a mellifluent description of Captain Credence: "Captain Credence is indeed the glad genius of his tongue, and he tunes its use to judgement in a manner fit to outsing the bootless burdens that escaped the choked mouths of Diabolus's captive advocates" (Forrest, "Milton and the Divine Art of Weaponry: 'That Two-Handed Engine' and Bunyan's 'Nameless Terrible Instrument' at Mouthgate," *Milton Studies* 16, ed. James D. Simmonds [Pittsburgh: University of Pittsburgh Press, 1982], 138).

116 Sim and Walker, 12-14.
117 Ibid., 215.
118 Ibid., 15.

quintessentially postmodern, but does this mean that the biblical injunctions toward purity which inspired Bunyan not to compromise his faith should then be considered postmodern also? The rotating jurisdiction over Mansoul between Emanuel and Diabolus might seem to play into their hands, but their central argument is not convincing. They take Emanuel's final counsel, "Hold fast," as evidence that Mansoul must learn "to exist in a pluralist world whether she likes it or not,"[119] but Emanuel's advice actually comes from Revelation 2:25 and 3:11, which anticipate not an indefinite rotation of cultural visions but the final triumph of Christ over all the earth.[120] Bunyan knew that Christians have no worldly or political guarantee of success and thus agreed that their struggle will continue until the end of the age, but unlike the postmodernist, who can only watch the pendulum of history swing without any conviction that one way is better than another, Christians fight the good fight in confidence and eschatological hope that the kingdom of God will prevail and inaugurate a state of glory.[121]

Conclusion

If Sim and Walker were correct to say that *The Holy War* depicts Mansoul as open to endless oscillation, then it could hardly be anything but a dull story. As Søren Kierkegaard taught in his pseudonymous book *Repetition* (1843), it takes eschatology to redeem such banal existence, for "*Eternity is indeed the true repetition*, in which history comes to an end and all things are explained."[122] Bunyan could

---

119 Ibid., 214. Bunyan himself refers to Mansoul with feminine metaphors three times in *HW*, 54.
120 Arlette Zinck recognizes the allusion to Revelation in "From Apocalypse to Prophecy: The Didactic Strategies of *The Holy War*," in *John Bunyan: Reading Dissenting Writing*, ed. N. H. Keeble (Oxford: Peter Lang, 2002), 197. So does Richard L. Greaves in *Glimpses of Glory*, 427.
121 *Contra* Thomas H. Luxon, this eschatological hope does not invalidate the concern Bunyan showed for the present world in *The Holy War* and other late works. Cf. Luxon, 37, 43, *et passim*, and refer to my sustained response to Luxon's failure to appreciate Bunyan's eschatology in "Be Not Extream," 456-458.
122 Søren Kierkegaard, *Fear and Trembling / Repetition*, Kierkegaard's Writings 6, ed. Howard V. Hong and Edna H. Hong (Princeton: Princeton University Press, 1983), 148, 327. For an application of Kierkegaard's *Repetition* to Bunyan's *Grace Abounding*, see Vera J. Camden, "'That of Esau': Hebrews xii.16,17 in *Grace Abounding*," in *John Bunyan: Reading Dissenting Writing*, ed. N. H. Keeble (Oxford: Peter Lang, 2002), 153-154.

leave an open ending to *The Holy War* precisely because the outcome of Mansoul is assured within his eschatological scheme. *"I shall come and fetch thee to my self,"* Emanuel promises, *"according as it is related in the Scriptures of truth."*[123] It was Bunyan's eschatological assurance that enabled him to set out a confident vision for the transformation of his society in both *The Holy War* and *The Life and Death of Mr. Badman*.

---

123 Bunyan, *HW*, 248. Emanuel also promises that Mansoul will have continual communion with him, Shaddai, and the Lord Secretary, and that it shall no longer harbor fear of death or Diabolonian threats (Ibid., 247).

CHAPTER SEVEN

A Test Case for Bunyan's Subjectivism: Bunyan and Richard Baxter

Jeffrey Stout summarizes the case for the subjectivist trend of early Protestantism:

> The Protestant appeal to the individual conscience and inner persuasion in effect produces yet another version of the problem of many authorities. But now we have far more authorities than before, for *every* man recognizes his own inner light. Every conscience constitutes a separate authority. We are left with no means to settle disagreements about matters of public importance. What started out as an appeal to the single authority of scriptural revelation now seems to recognize, implicitly at least, ten authorities in every pew. The potential for anarchy did not go unnoticed by the Catholic critics.[1]

Stout believes that the Reformation's failure to ground biblical truth in a single common authority opened the way for the skepticism of Descartes. Yet Bunyan did not think that every person should rely on a highly individualized inner light, nor did he believe that every person's conscience constitute a separate authority, though the first allegation is true of the Quakers and the second true of Milton, thus showing the *partial* accuracy of Stout's claim. Bunyan was an exception to their pattern. In *The Holy War*, a single Conscience speaks the same word to everyone in the town of Mansoul, and all the citizens must listen to him, who in turn must listen to the Holy Spirit.

Although I have offered evidence that Bunyan resisted the completely inward turn of the modern self, David Lyle Jeffrey extrapolates from Bunyan's reading of the Bible a rather different conclusion. In *People of the Book: Christian Identity and Literary Culture*, Jeffrey cites a passage from Bunyan's *The Holy City* to expose Bunyan's subjectivist tendency: "Having [the Bible] still with me, I count myself far better furnished than if I had [without it] all the Libraries of the two Universities: Besides, I am for drinking water out of my own Cistern: what GOD makes mine by the evidence of his Word

---

1   Jeffrey Stout, *The Flight from Authority: Religion, Morality, and the Quest for Autonomy* (Notre Dame: University of Notre Dame Press, 1981), 44.

and Spirit, that dare I make bold with."[2] *The Holy City* is a comparatively early work (1665) and so perhaps cannot bear the full weight of the case that Jeffrey places upon it; I believe that Bunyan later became aware of how his writings might be exploited for individualist purposes and wrote especially *The Pilgrim's Progress*, Part II, as a corrective to this and to reflect the mature theological position he had worked out in the meantime. While the early Bunyan did indeed glean the scriptures and perhaps even Luther and Christian tradition for confirmation of views at which he had already arrived, the later Bunyan agreed to have his theological outlook shaped by the creedal tradition of the church catholic. Yet, other writers also charge that *The Holy War*, a late work, was no less subjectivist than *The Holy City*. Daniel Lamont, for example, calls *The Holy War* a "sheer[ly] subjective" encounter; Beth Lynch also sees in the book "a shift inwards."[3]

Jeffrey's argument, based on *The Holy City*, is that when Bunyan said he needed no help other than the Holy Spirit in interpreting the Bible, he invested himself with an inward authority that actually conflated scripture with self. This claim is certainly relevant to *The Holy War* as well, since Mr. Conscience there receives instruction directly from Shaddai's secretary, the Holy Spirit (which Sim and Walker also call a process of self-authorization).[4] In opposition to Bunyan, Jeffrey sets Richard Baxter (1615-1691), the venerable Puritan pastor and prolific author. Jeffrey cites Baxter as a "moderate" Puritan who perceived the dangers of relying upon the Bible only: "He that will have no books but his creed and the Bible, may follow that sectary, who, when he had burnt all his other books as human inventions, at last burnt the Bible, when he grew learned enough to understand that the translation of that was human too." But does Jeffrey via Baxter correctly diagnose Bunyan's apparent anti-intellectualism as "spiritually counterproductive" for finding the objective ground of faith that Bunyan sought?[5]

I will respond to Jeffrey's indictment of Bunyan's subjectivism in two ways. First, I will explore Bunyan's view of non-biblical sources to test Jeffrey's characterization of Bunyan as a largely anti-intellectual "independent Bible reader." Then, I will examine the respective theological emphases of Bunyan and Baxter to determine which were more individualistic or subjectivist.

---

2 Jeffrey, 265.
3 Daniel Lamont, 36; Lynch, 28.
4 Sim and Walker, 210.
5 Jeffrey, 275.

Bunyan's Opinion of "Church Fathers"

Jeffrey's quotation from *The Holy City* appears to establish Bunyan as someone who thought that the only truly important interpretation of the Bible was his own. Other selections from Bunyan might also seem to support Jeffrey's claim:

> Reader, if thou do find this book empty of Fantastical expressions, and without light, vain, whimsical Scholar-like terms, thou must understand, it is because I never went to School to *Aristotle* or *Plato*, but was brought up at my fathers house, in a very mean condition, among a company of poor Countrey-men.[6]

> As for your saying, That *Calvin, Peter Martyr, Musculus, Zanchy*, and *others*, did not question, but that God could have Pardoned sin, without *any other* Satisfaction, then the Repentance of the Sinner …, it matters nothing to me, I have neither made my Creed out of them, nor other, then the Holy Scriptures of God.[7]

> *I have not writ at a venture, nor borrowed my Doctrine from libraries. I depend upon the sayings of no man: I found it in the Scriptures of Truth, among the true sayings of God.*[8]

At other times, Bunyan slightly tempered his independence in biblical interpretation with an admission of fallibility, much as Luther said before the Diet of Worms that he would recant his writings if someone could demonstrate that his exegesis was incorrect.

> I dare not presume to say, That I *know* I have hit right in every thing, but this I can say, I have endeavoured so to do. True, I have not for these things fished in other mens *Waters*, my Bible and Concordance are my only Library in my writings. Wherefore, Courteous Reader, if thou findest any thing, either in word or matter, that thou shalt judge doth vary from God's truth, let it be counted no mans else but mine.[9]

But Bunyan did not completely berate those who did borrow from "other men's lines":

> I never endeavoured to, nor durst make use of other men's lines, *Rom.* 15.18, (though I condemn not all that do) for I verily thought, and found by experience, that what was taught me by the Word

---

6 Bunyan, *The Doctrine of the Law and Grace Unfolded*, in *MW*, 2:16.
7 Bunyan, *A Defence of the Doctrine of Justification, By Faith*, in *MW*, 4:38.
8 Bunyan, *Light for Them That Sit in Darkness*, in *MW*, 8:51.
9 Bunyan, *Solomon's Temple Spiritualized*, in *MW*, 7:9. Cf. Dayton Haskin, "Bunyan, Luther, and the Struggle," *University of Toronto Quarterly* 50:3 (Spring 1981): 303.

and Spirit of Christ, could be spoken, maintained, and stood to, by the soundest and best established Conscience.[10]

In the same paragraph of *The Holy City* where Jeffrey finds evidence of Bunyan's subjectivism, Bunyan elaborated on what non-biblical "lines" were "usable." Here is a fuller quotation than Jeffrey provides:

> Sir, What you find suiting with Scriptures, take; though it should not suit with Authors: but that which you find against the Scriptures, slight; though it should be confined by Multitudes of them. Yea further, Where you find the Scriptures and your Authors jump [disagree], yet believe it for the sake of Scriptures Authority. I honour the Godly, as Christians, but I prefer the BIBLE before them; and having that still with me, I count my self far better furnished than if I had (without it) all the Libraries of the two Universities.[11]

Bunyan recognized the value of Christian tradition, though he refused to grant it equal authority alongside the Bible. To do so would be to relinquish the very *raison d'être* for the Reformation's rejection of papism.[12] This is precisely the distinction that Luther first made, which Bunyan also appropriated. By purposely claiming the legacy of the early creeds and confessions, without the taint of papal accretions, "Luther bequeathed to Protestantism the mechanism of dividing the patristic legacy from the Roman tradition. The former was of the Spirit, the latter of human artifice. One could accept the authority of one without the other."[13] Within this same framework, Bunyan could be quite appreciative of earlier Christian writers.

Bunyan's indebtedness to Luther, Dent, and Bayly was explicit in *Grace Abounding*; in *The Life and Death of Mr. Badman*, he borrowed freely from Samuel Clarke's *A Mirror or Looking-Glass both for Saints, and Sinners* (1671); his admiration for the early Christians Ignatius, Romanus, and Polycarp is made clear in *The Pilgrim's Progress*, Part

---

10 Bunyan, *GA*, §285, pp. 87-88.
11 Bunyan, *The Holy City*, in *MW*, 3:72.
12 Cf. John Milton in *Of True Religion*: "I will not now enter into the Labyrinth of Councels and Fathers, an intangl'd wood which the Papist loves to fight in, not with hope of Victory, but to obscure the shame of an open overthrow" (Milton, 1151).
13 D. H. Williams, *Retrieving the Tradition and Renewing Evangelicalism: A Primer for Suspicious Protestants* (Grand Rapids: William B. Eerdmans Publishing Company, 1999), 187. Williams demonstrates how Luther, Calvin, and the Protestant Reformers saw reclamation of the patristic tradition as an integral part of a belief in *sola scriptura*.

II, and he praised the Marian martyrs in *A Holy Life*, whose stories he derived from John Foxe's *Book of Martyrs*.[14] In *Seasonable Counsel*, Bunyan even aligned himself with Origen, Jerome of Prague, Thomas Cranmer, James Baynham, and Cicely Ormis – all persons whom he called "good folk" despite recanting their faith under duress.[15] Wiseman explains in *Mr. Badman* that "saints of old time were the best," a statement that reflects Bunyan's desire in *Grace Abounding* "to see some ancient Godly man's Experience, who had writ some hundred[s] of years before I was born."[16] That desire was in fact prompted in part by recalling a verse of the Apocrypha: *"Look at the generations of old, and see, did ever any trust in God and were confounded?"*[17] When Bunyan realized after a year of searching that the verse was from Ecclesiasticus 2:10, he wrote, "Though it was not in those Texts that we call holy and Canonical, yet forasmuch as this sentence was the sum and substance of many of the promises, it was my duty to take the comfort of it, and I bless God for that word, for it was of God to me: that word doth still, at times, shine before my face."[18] Throughout my project, I have shown how Bunyan, as had Luther, also defended the formulations of Christology and Trinity conceived at Nicea and the early ecumenical councils because they, too, were the "sum and substance" of scriptural teachings. This is a far different approach from radical religionists such as the anti-trinitarian Socinus, who called Athanasius "Antichrist" for his role in settling the orthodox definition of the two natures of Christ, or the Anabaptist Sebastian Franck, who said that of the "foolish" ancient doctors of the church – Ambrose, Augustine, Jerome, and Gregory – "not even one knew the Lord, so help me God."[19] Again one may also set in opposition to Bunyan the great heterodox poet John Mil-

---

14 Bunyan, *PP*, 260; Bunyan, *MW*, 9:345. Cf. the note by Roger Sharrock, in Bunyan, *GA*, 154; Thomas S. Freeman, "A Library in Three Volumes: Foxe's 'Book of Martyrs' in the Writings of John Bunyan," *Bunyan Studies* 5 (Autumn 1994): 47-57. Bunyan also mentioned the martyrology of Foxe in *A Few Sighs from Hell* (*MW*, 1:358).
15 Bunyan, *MW*, 10:64.
16 Bunyan, *Badman*, 124; *GA*, §129, p. 40. Of course, to Bunyan, "old Christians" could be Puritans, *"for so the godly were called in time past"* (Bunyan, *Badman*, 144).
17 Bunyan, *GA*, §62, p. 21.
18 Ibid., §65, p.22.
19 Bunyan, *PP*, 210; Pelikan, *The Christian Tradition*, 4:323-324; Sebastian Franck, "A Letter to John Campanus," in *Spiritual and Anabaptist Writers*, ed. George Hunston Williams and Angel M. Mergal (Philadelphia: The Westminster Press, 1957), 151.

ton, who was wary of the study of the church fathers for their employment of a rhetorical style that was pagan in origin.[20]

The many examples that show Bunyan's reliance on non-biblical, theological sources mitigate his early boast in *The Holy City* that he had not read the books of the learned. Richard Greaves, Christopher Hill, and Gordon Campbell thus warn against taking literally Bunyan's claims to have relied solely on the Bible, for he also borrowed from other biblically sound writings.[21] On the other hand, many university-trained intellectuals have found much to instruct them in the works of the tinker. For, as C. S. Lewis explains, "Anyone who is honestly trying to be a Christian will soon find his intelligence being sharpened: one of the reasons why it needs no special education to be a Christian is that Christianity is an education itself. That is why an uneducated believer like Bunyan was able to write a book that has astonished the whole world."[22] In Bunyan's own lifetime, the Independent preacher John Owen told King Charles II that he would swap his Cambridge education for Bunyan's communicative abilities. Two centuries later, Coleridge mocked the elitism of James Sedgwick by saying, "*John Bunyan!* – Why, thou miserable Barrister, it would take an Angel an eternity a post to tinker thee into a Skull of half his Capacity!"[23] Cecile M. Jagodzinski and John Piper have also observed the importance of books in Bunyan's own spiritual life, and how his own immortal books were always meant for the public good, whether his readers were Christian or non-Christian.[24]

In *The Holy City*, Bunyan proved his perceptiveness by anticipating Jeffrey's concern:

> My second Word is to my wise and learned Reader. Sir, I suppose in your reading of this DISCOURSE, you will be apt to blame me for two things: first, because I have not so beautified my Matter with acuteness of Language as you could wish or desire: Secondly, because also I have not given you, either in the Line, or in the Margent, a Cloud of Sentences from the Learned FATHERS, that have according to their Wisdom (possibly) handled these Matters long before me.[25]

---

20 Jameela Lares, *Milton and the Preaching Arts* (Pittsburgh: Duquesne University Press, 2001), 136-137.
21 Greaves, *John Bunyan and English Nonconformity*, 39-41; Hill, *Tinker*, 157-169; Campbell, "Fishing," 137-151.
22 Lewis, *Mere Christianity*, 75. Cf. Piper, 75.
23 John Owen, *Works*, in Bunyan, *The Pilgrim's Progress*, ed. Sharrock (Penguin), 399 (ft. 5); Coleridge, *Samuel Taylor Coleridge*, 578.
24 Jagodzinski, 59; Piper, 60.
25 Bunyan, *The Holy City*, in *MW*, 3:71.

Martin Luther, too, had to face the objection that he had erected his private interpretation of scripture against that of the whole church over the centuries. Jeffrey does not deal with Luther in *People of the Book* except to label him an "independent Bible reader."[26] But Luther responded to a charge similar to the one that Jeffrey makes against Bunyan in his *Commentary on Galatians* (1:11), which Bunyan knew well.

> This argument therefore of the false apostles had a goodly shew, and seemed to be very strong. Which also at this day prevaileth with many, namely, that the Apostles, the holy fathers and their successors have so taught; that the Church so thinketh and believeth. Moreover, that it is impossible that Christ should suffer his Church so long time to err. Art thou alone, say they, wiser than so many men, wiser than the whole Church? After this manner the devil, being changed into an angel of light, setteth upon us craftily at this day by certain pestiferous hypocrites, who say: ... The Church hath thus believed and taught this [for a] long time. So have all the doctors of the primitive Church, holy men, more ancient and better learned than thou. Who art thou, that darest dissent from all these, and bring us into a contrary doctrine? When Satan reasoneth thus, conspiring with the flesh and reason, then is thy conscience terrified and utterly despaireth, unless thou constantly return to thyself again, and say: Whether it be St. Cyprian, Ambrose, Augustine, either St. Peter, Paul, or John, yea or an angel from heaven, that teacheth otherwise, yet this I know assuredly, that I teach not the things of men, but of God: that is to say, I attribute all things to God alone, and nothing to men.[27]

The regulative principle for Luther's exegesis was to look for what sets forth Christ. If the church fathers or angels or even the apostles do not set forth Christ, they are not to be believed. "Whatever does not teach Christ is certainly not yet apostolic, even though St. Peter or St. Paul does the teaching," Luther wrote. "Whatever preaches Christ would be apostolic, even if Judas, Annas [John 18], Pilate, and Herod were doing it."[28] So when Jerome and other patris-

---

26 Jeffrey, 92, 367. Luther's *Lectures on Genesis* gives apparent support for Jeffrey's case: "If I were the only one in the entire world to adhere to the Word, I alone would be the church and would properly judge about the rest of the world that it is not the church" (Martin Luther, *Lectures on Genesis, Chapters 6-14*, ed. Jaroslav Pelikan, *Luther's Works*, vol. 2 [Saint Louis: Concordia Publishing House, 1960], 102).

27 Luther, *CG*, 77.

28 Luther, "Preface to the Epistles of St. James and St. Jude," in *Word and Sacrament I*, ed. E. Theodore Bachmann, *Luther's Works*, vol. 35 (Philadelphia: Muhlenberg Press, 1960), 396.

tic writers failed to distinguish law and gospel, Luther admitted that they "brought men's consciences into great danger."[29]

Likewise, Bunyan acknowledged in *The Holy City* that it is grace and not human acclaim that makes someone a "church father," and on that basis could he appropriate secondary works. Indeed, Bunyan aligned his own interpretation of the Bible with the doctrines of the magisterial Reformers, particularly when against the radically individualized biblical interpretation of the Quakers and others. Maxine Hancock observes how the encounter with Lot's wife in *The Pilgrim's Progress*, Part I, counters such readings: when Hopeful ("he being no Scholar," the narrator says) cannot understand the inscription on the head of a monument, he calls on Christian ("for he was learned") to aid his interpretation, and together they conclude that the monument is the pillar of salt into which Lots's wife was transformed.[30] In *A Book for Boys and Girls*, Bunyan was very critical of theologically uneducated Bible readers. After describing the distastefulness of music played by an unskillful musician, he explained,

> The unlearn'd Novices in things Divine,
> With this unskill'd Musician I compare.
> For such, instead of making Truth to shine,
> Abuse the Bible, and unsavoury are.[31]

In *The Holy City*, Bunyan elaborated further on the tradition in which he had become trained:

> Wherefore these Altar-men [Ezra and Nehemiah], or these men in their Altar-work, did figure-out for us our famous and holy Worthies, that before us have risen up in their place, and shook off those Reliques of Antichrist that intrenched upon the Priestly Office of our Lord and Saviour, even worthy *Wickliff, Hus, Luther, Melancton, Calvin*, and the blessed Martyrs in Q. *Maries* dayes, &c. with the rest of their companions: these in their day were stout & valiant Champions for God, according to their light, and did upon the Altar of God, which is *Christ* our Lord, offer up many strong cries, with groans and tears, as every day required, for the compleat recovering of the Church of God; the benefit of whose Offering we have felt and enjoyed to this day.[32]

---

29 Luther, *Commentary on Galatians* in Dillenberger, 145.
30 Bunyan, *PP*, 108-109; Hancock, 19. Hancock points for an influence on Bunyan to seventeenth-century guides to Bible reading which would have been available to him that encouraged seeking the interpretive guidance of more learned readers (19, 34-35).
31 Bunyan, *MW*, 6:243.
32 Bunyan, *The Holy City*, in *MW*, 3:134. Cf. Roger Sharrock and James F. Forrest, in Bunyan, *HW*, 265.

Note well Bunyan's desire for the "compleat" recovering of the Church of God. Bunyan realized all the more acutely in the final years of his life and ministry that Christian catholicity did not entail a particular ecclesiastical polity but the union of all saints in doctrine and practice under the Lordship of Christ and the direction of the Holy Spirit. This unity transcended Bunyan's or anyone else's subjective particularity. Note, too, that this is a unity in which "alter men" play a significant role. Bunyan did not view individual Bible reading as unconnected to its authoritative interpretation as revealed by the Holy Spirit in the orthodox tradition of the church. In 1413, John Hus wrote in *The Church* that "Every pilgrim ought faithfully to believe the holy, catholic church."[33] Bunyan, the immortal pilgrim, did so. His faith and practice bound him to "ancient" Christians.

In the 1999 "Joint Statement on the Doctrine of Justification" by the Lutheran World Federation and the Roman Catholic Church, the Catholic signatories acknowledged that Luther's grounding of faith on the objective word of Christ alone was not a heresy of modernity but a reclamation of the ancient belief of the church.[34] Rather than eliminating tradition, Luther honored it in a rightful manner. Did Richard Baxter understand the similar hope of Luther's disciple Bunyan?

Bunyan and Baxter on Justification by Faith

Richard Baxter was born thirteen years before Bunyan and died three years after Bunyan. There is no conclusive evidence that the two ever met, although they each preached at various times at Pinners Hall, London.[35] Forrest and Sharrock suggest that Baxter's *A Christian Directory* (1673) and *The Poor Man's Family-Book* (1674) may have been sources for Bunyan's dialogical manner of analyzing sins in *The Life and Death of Mr. Badman*.[36] Like Richard Sibbes, Baxter

---

33 John Hus, in D. H. Williams, 227.
34 "Joint Declaration on the Doctrine of Justification," 1999 [on-line]; available from http://www.elca.org/ea/jddj/jddj.html.
35 Edmund Arbuthnott Knox, 40; Irvonwy Morgan, *The Nonconformity of Richard Baxter* (London: The Epworth Press, 1946), 87; Roger Sharrock and James F. Forrest, in Bunyan, *HW*, ix.
36 James F. Forrest and Roger Sharrock, in Bunyan, *Badman*, xviii, xxxii; cf. 180-182. See supporting evidence in Dunan, 50-51, 59-60, 62, 66; Randall, 347-349, 351; Hussey, "Christian Conduct," 79-81. For other comparisons between Bunyan and Baxter, cf. Roger Pooley, "Plain and Simple: Bunyan and Style," in *John Bunyan: Conventicle and Parnassus*, ed. N. H. Keeble (Oxford: Clarendon Press, 1988), 94; Vincent Newey, "'With the Eyes of My Understanding': Bunyan, Experience, and Acts of Interpretation," in ibid., 193; Muller, 334.

never withdrew from the communion of the Church of England, but with Bunyan, he preferred open communion for all professing Christians.[37] Indeed, he once lamented the "many holy, excellent ministers" such as Bunyan who were imprisoned for nonconformity in 1660.[38] The most unusual linking of Bunyan and Baxter was made by Max Weber, who said that Baxter's rejection of Luther's emphasis on mutual confession among Christians [the priesthood of all believers] closed an outlet for the discharge of guilt, which then spilled over into the Puritan work ethic undergirding *The Pilgrim's Progress*.[39]

Only in one work did Baxter specifically name Bunyan in print, though one wonders if he was aware of Bunyan's first vocation, since he numbered tinkers among the enemies of "knowledge and religion."[40] Baxter believed Bunyan otherwise to be an "honest, Godly man," but he agreed with Edward Fowler that Bunyan should be castigated as an antinomian.[41] Bunyan also mentioned Baxter only once as well – a passing comment in *Peaceable Principles and True* that appears to evaluate Baxter favorably, though Bunyan disagreed with Baxter on a minor point about baptism.[42] Fowler's *The Design of Christianity* (1671), of course, was the target of Bunyan's *A Defence of the Doctrine of Justification, by Faith*, as well as portions of *Light for Them That Sit in Darkness*. Though Fowler was an Arminian and a Latitudinarian, and Baxter was a Calvinist, the two conducted a friendly correspondence on their common opposition to antinomianism, the opinion that grace frees Christians from having to observe moral law. Since Arminians believed that justification and its maintenance depend in part on humans' use of their autonomous free will, and Latitudinarians emphasized good works in accordance with human reason, it is obvious why Fowler would

---

37 Marcus L. Loane, *Makers of Religious Freedom in the Seventeenth Century: Henderson – Rutherford – Bunyan – Baxter* (Grand Rapids: William B. Eerdmans Publishing Company, 1961), 204; N. H. Keeble and Geoffrey Nuttall, eds., *Calendar of the Correspondence of Richard Baxter* (Oxford: Clarendon Press, 1991), 2:224.
38 Richard Baxter, in John Nicholson, *John Bunyan and the Visionary Search for an English Conscience* (London: BOZO, 1983), 18.
39 Max Weber, *The Protestant Ethic and the Spirit of Capitalism*, trans. Talcott Parsons (New York: Charles Scribner's Sons, 1958), 106-107. Cf. McGrath, 244.
40 Stachniewski, 143-144.
41 Keeble and Nuttall, 2:201; William M. Lamont, *Richard Baxter and the Millennium* (London: Crook Helm, 1979), 128, 267.
42 Bunyan, *MW*, 4:284.

object to antinomianism: he rejected the doctrine of justification by faith alone for not insisting on moral duties.[43] Baxter belonged to a group of moderate Calvinists in the late seventeenth century, including Samuel Rutherford, Anthony Burgess, and Henry Burton, who strongly emphasized the keeping of the moral law by Christians. He wrote in *The Scripture Gospel Defended* that Bunyan's *The Doctrine of the Law and Grace Unfolded* "ignorantly subverted the Gospel of Christ" through its antinomian tendencies.[44]

On the contrary, as Richard Greaves observes, Bunyan's *Doctrine* described the eternal covenant between God the Father and God the Son in such a way as "to assure struggling Christians of the permanence of their faith and the unquestionable reality of their ultimate salvation."[45] Nothing could have been further from Bunyan's mind than proclaiming a doctrine that could promote moral laxity. He anticipated the objection that justification by Christ's imputed righteousness alone could become a license for sin: "If I was to point out one that is under the power of the devil, and going poste haste to hell (for my life) I would look no further for such a man, then to him that would make such a use as this of the grace of God."[46] In *Of the Law and a Christian*, he emphasized that the elect believer, "to the comfort of his conscience and the bowing of his heart, ... though he be without Law to God, as it is considered the first or old Covenant, yet even he is not without Law to him as considered under grace, not without Law go God, but under the Law to Christ."[47] In *Christian Behaviour*, Bunyan responded strongly against those who accused his doctrine of justification of permitting "*looseness of Life.*"[48] And in *The Jerusalem Sinner Saved: or, Good News for the Vilest of Men*, he encouraged believers not to let the charge of antinomianism blunt their reliance on Christ's objective atonement:

---

43   T. L. Underwood, ed., in Bunyan, *MW*, 4:xxi.
44   Richard L. Greaves, ed., in Bunyan, *MW*, 2:xxv, xxx. Cf. Muller, 327. The anonymous *Dirt Wip't Off* (1672) also accuses Bunyan of being a "*Ranting Antinomian*" full of "gross ignorance" whose doctrine of Christ's imputed righteousness produced "the most outrageous Fury, the most turbulent Spirit, the most reviling and defaming Pen and Tongue, and consequently the most malicious Spirit" (T. L. Underwood, ed., in Bunyan, *MW*, 4:xxiv). One Gilbert Clerke wrote to Baxter to explain that he should accept Socinianism since the Socinians, like himself, rejected antinomianism (Keeble and Nuttall, 2.227).
45   Richard L. Greaves, ed., in Bunyan, *MW*, 2:xxvi.
46   Bunyan, *MW*, 2:170.
47   Bunyan, *MW*, 12:411.
48   Bunyan, *MW*, 3:9.

> The World, when they hear the Doctrine that I have asserted and handled in this little Book, to wit, that *Jesus Christ* would have Mercy offered in the *first place to the biggest Sinners*; will be apt, because themselves are Unbelievers, to think that this is a Doctrine that leads to Loosness, and that gives liberty to the Flesh; but if you that Believe, love your Brethren, and your Neighbours truly, and as you should, you will put to silence the ignorance of such foolish Men, and stop their mouths from speaking Evil of you.[49]

Greaves says that it was in such assertions that Bunyan "shied from Antinomian subjectivity."[50] Tim Cooper even more boldly claims that they prove Baxter's accusations against Bunyan to have been rhetorical weapons that did not accurately appraise Bunyan's theology.[51]

Bunyan was only "antinomian" in the sense that the Mosaic or moral law could not save. He was no libertine. On the contrary, he separated himself from Lawrence Clarkson, a Ranter who held in direct contradiction to Bunyan that liberty in Christ meant to sin against the law without guilt, even as he aligned himself closer to "moderate" antinomians like William Dell, Tobias Crisp, and John Saltmarsh.[52] Once again, his real example was Luther, whose castigation of the law in no way invalidated the role of the law in *civil* life. Yet Baxter's tendency that the Christian must carefully observe the moral law *as a guarantor of salvation* was certainly a departure from Luther's theology of the two spheres as well as his concept of

---

49 Bunyan, *MW*, 11:82.
50 Richard L. Greaves, in Bunyan, *MW*, 12:xxx.
51 Tim Cooper, *Fear and Polemic in Seventeenth-Century England: Richard Baxter and Antinomianism* (Aldershot, England: Ashgate Publishing Limited, 2001), 169. Cooper contends that Baxter made of the Antinomians a scapegoat for the failures of Puritan government after the English Civil Wars. He also gives a very helpful review of how Luther's antinomianism was wrongly interpreted as licentiousness, and how Baxter's own opinion about the issue came nearly to mirror the extremism he imagined in his opponents. Ahenakaa says that the inspiration of his dissertation, which argues forcefully against Bunyan's antinomianism, is the antinomian reading of *The Pilgrim's Progress* and *Grace Abounding* common in his native Nigeria (vii, 286).
52 John Stachniewski, ed., in Bunyan, *GA*, xxxvi-xxxvii; Greaves, *John Bunyan and English Nonconformity*, 41-42; Hill, *Tinker*, 190-191, 292-293. The eighteenth century hymn-writer and preacher John Newton observed of Crisp, "This author is branded an antinomian by many, but I know not why unless for exalting the power and grace of Christ" (Hindmarsh, 336).

simul iustus et peccator.⁵³ Baxter accused Luther himself of being careless in his formulation of justification, but was Luther's frank recognition that sin continues to attack Christians truly opposed to the continued observation of moral law?⁵⁴ Luther responded to this accusation in *The Freedom of a Christian* (1520) and *Against the Antinomians* (1539). His belief was that "we do not ... reject good works; on the contrary, we cherish and teach them as much as possible. We do not condemn them for their own sake but on account of this ... perverse idea that righteousness is to be sought through them."⁵⁵ B. A. Gerrish concludes that to label Luther an antinomian, considering his emphasis on good works *post* salvation, would require an absurd amount of qualification.⁵⁶ The same was true of Bunyan.

I have already demonstrated from *The Life and Death of Mr. Badman* and *The Holy War* how the moral law for Bunyan was good of itself (indeed, it is the role of Conscience to uphold it) but nonetheless unequipped to save sinners. Charges of antinomianism against Bunyan do not hold because they do not consider his Lutheran conception of law and gospel. By thinking that the moral law could actually make one holy before God, Fowler failed to understand that God intends this law to have jurisdiction only in *earthly* affairs. Fowler tended to equate social virtues with saving righteousness, and Baxter tended to ground justification in the actual righteousness of the Christian.⁵⁷ In *Aphorismes of Justification*, Baxter, not unlike the Quakers, explicitly denied that Christ's justification of the sinner was an action performed *outside* that person, and he confirmed in *Of Justification* that saving righteousness is, to some degree, "performed" by the individual.⁵⁸ Both Fowler and Baxter thus forfeited the emphasis by both Luther, and Calvin too, on justification *external* to the individual in the person of Jesus Christ. Before Bunyan visualized his righteousness at the right hand of God in *Grace Abounding*, Calvin wrote in the *Institutes*, "You see that our righteousness is not in us but in Christ, that we possess it only because we are partakers in

---

53 J. Wayne Baker, "*Sola Fide, Sola Gratia*: The Battle for Luther in Seventeenth-Century England," *The Sixteenth Century Journal* 16:1 (Spring 1985): 119; Camden, "Most Fit," 823.
54 Baker, 129.
55 Martin Luther, *The Freedom of a Christian*, in Dillenberger, 72. Cf. Gerrish, *Grace and Reason*, 88-90, 118.
56 Gerrish, *Grace and Reason*, 136.
57 Rivers, 61.
58 Ahenakaa, 34, 178; cf. ibid., 14, 32, for similarities between Baxter's understandings of justification and that of the Roman Catholic Council of Trent.

Christ; indeed, with him, we possess all its riches."[59] William Lamont believes that Baxter's theology, unlike Bunyan's, was "self-consciously distancing itself from its Calvinist roots."[60]

In an essay entitled, "Bunyan, Baxter, and Franklin," Karl Joachim Weintraub suggests that Baxter's desire to confirm his salvation by something internal was conducive to Benjamin Franklin's secularized Puritan desire for moral perfection: no longer requiring the God of Christian orthodoxy, Franklin's ethic relied solely on personal qualities.[61] J. Wayne Baker concludes that Baxter and Fowler even reintroduced the works righteousness that Luther and Bunyan abhorred into Protestantism.[62] Because few in the late seventeenth century still understood freedom from the law in the Lutheran sense as Bunyan did, Protestantism begot at that time, says George Lindbeck, "a chaotically permissive individualism."[63] Such so-called antinomians as Bunyan were really the only ones who understood Luther, Baker adds.[64] But Bunyan was really "neither mystic nor antinomian," insists N. H. Keeble, who has also catalogued Baxter's works.[65] In fact, Bunyan's grasp of Lutheran distinctions allowed him to appreciate the epistle of James in a manner that even Luther himself never did: Bunyan's alter-ego Christian declares, in reference to James 1:22-27, that "the Soul of Religion is the practick part," yet this in no way mitigates the emphasis in *The*

---

59 Calvin, *Institutes*, 1:753 (III.xi.23).
60 William Lamont, "Bunyan and Baxter: Millennium and Magistrate," in *John Bunyan: Reading Dissenting Writing*, ed. N. H. Keeble (Oxford: Peter Lang, 2002), 43.
61 Karl Joachim Weintraub, *The Value of the Individual: Self and Circumstance in Autobiography* (Chicago: The University of Chicago Press, 1978), 228-260. Although Bellah, 32, believes Franklin's *Autobiography* is "a secular version" of *The Pilgrim's Progress*, there is rich symbolism in Franklin's confession that while Bunyan's writings were among the first he ever purchased, he later wished that he had sold these and other works of "polemic divinity" for "more proper books" – Franklin's turn *away* from Bunyan's divinity was a decisive turn *toward* modern individualism (Benjamin Franklin, *Autobiography of Benjamin Franklin*, ed. John Bigelow [Garden City, NY: Doubleday Dolphin Books, n.d.], 73).
62 Baker, 125, 130.
63 George A. Lindbeck, "Modernity and Luther's Understanding of the Freedom of a Christian," in *Martin Luther and the Modern Mind: Freedom, Conscience, Toleration, Rights*, Toronto Studies in Theology 22, ed. Manfred Hoffman (New York: The Edwin Mellen Press, 1985), 19.
64 Baker, 133.
65 N. H. Keeble, "Christiana's Key," 13. Cf. Roger Sharrock and James F. Forrest, eds., in Bunyan, *HW*, xxx.

Pilgrim's Progress and throughout Bunyan's works on justification by faith.⁶⁶ "I believe," wrote Bunyan in *A Confession of My Faith*, "that to effectual Calling, the holy Ghost must accompany the word of the Gospel, and that with mighty power: I mean that calling, which of God is made to be the fruit of electing love."⁶⁷ Bunyan's doctrine of justification did not neglect but properly framed his notion of sanctification as a life-long process of improvement that nevertheless would never reach perfection, lest the Christian believe that he or she should enter Heaven on the basis of merit.⁶⁸

So to David Lyle Jeffrey's comparison of Baxter and Bunyan, one must ask: which of the two was really more subjective? Baxter said that most Christians can never be assured of their salvation, but that their best evidence lies in good works.⁶⁹ As Daniel Lamont describes such a view, "a good man is now defined as a man who does 'good things,' though God is not at all in his thoughts."⁷⁰ On the other hand, though Bunyan struggled for many years to find assurance of salvation in his own goodness, he eventually consented with Luther to ground his assurance on the objective work of Christ, which included historic Christianity's theology and sacraments. By contrast, Baxter came increasingly like Milton or Desiderius Erasmus to have less interest in the theological doctrines that kept Bunyan and Luther from being fully absorbed into the ethos of modernity.⁷¹ John Newton, the eighteenth century admirer of Bunyan who penned the hymn "Amazing Grace," perceived this truth when he observed that while Baxter could be very useful for spiritual edification, his "rather cloudy" theology was quite expendable.⁷²

---

66   Bunyan, *PP*, 79.
67   Bunyan, *A Confession of My Faith*, in *MW*, 4:147.
68   Richard L. Greaves, "John Bunyan: The Present State of Historical Scholarship," in *Bunyan in England and Abroad*, ed. M. van Os and G. J. Schutte (Amsterdam: Vrije Universiteit Press, 1990), 31. Cf. Bunyan, *John Bunyan*, 49; Arlette M. Zinck, "'Doctrine by ensample': Sanctification through Literature in Milton and Bunyan," *Bunyan Studies* 6 (1995/1996): 45; Kaufmann, 193; Camden, "Most Fit," 819-820; Mullett, 183; Roger Sharrock and James F. Forrest, eds., in Bunyan, *HW*, xxxii.
69   Richard Baxter, *Select Practical Writings of Richard Baxter, with a Life of the Author*, ed. Leonard Bacon (New Haven: Durrie and Peck, 1835), 1.310-311; Muller, 332-333.
70   Daniel Lamont, 464.
71   Weintraub, 248-250.
72   Hindmarsh, 81; cf. 122.

Conclusion

Once again, I concede the nascent individualism of Bunyan's writings: personal experience undoubtedly played a very large part in Bunyan's religious self-perception. For Bunyan, as for Luther, there was an intense personal interest in the religious subject, and B. A. Gerrish is right that the debate over the degree of subjectiv*ism* in Lutheran thought will never entirely go away.[73] But Baxter's fixation on the moral law *could not* finally bring him to find objective assurance in the alien righteousness of Christ, whereas such assurance was the very hope of Bunyan and Luther.[74] In fact, Bunyan's Lutheran conceptions of conscience, selfhood, law and gospel formed a barrier that kept his individualism from becoming autonomous in the fully modern sense. He was a writer and pastor and theologian whose conscience remained imprisoned to the same Jesus Christ who made it free. My hope, therefore, has been to reclaim Bunyan not only as an important cultural and literary figure but as a prominent spokesman of Christian ecclesial tradition.

---

73 B. A. Gerrish, "Doctor Martin Luther: Subjectivity and Doctrine in the Lutheran Reformation," in *Continuing the Reformation: Essays on Modern Religious Thought* (Chicago: The University of Chicago Press, 1993), 46-47, 51-52, 56.
74 Cf. Bercovitch, 28.

Bibliography

Primary Sources

Ames, William. *Conscience, with the Power and Cases Thereof*. Amsterdam: Theatrum Orbis Terrarum, Ltd., 1975.

———. *The Marrow of Theology*. Translated by John Dykstra Eusden. Grand Rapids: Baker Books, 1997.

Barbour, Hugh, and Arthur O. Roberts, eds. *Early Quaker Writings 1650-1700*. Grand Rapids: William B. Eerdmans Publishing Company, 1973.

Baxter, Richard. *Select Practical Writings of Richard Baxter, with a Life of the Author*, 2 vols. Edited by Leonard Bacon. New Haven: Durrie & Peck, 1835.

Bray, Gerald, ed. *Documents of the English Reformation*. Minneapolis: Fortress Press, 1994.

Bultmann, Rudolf. *Jesus Christ and Mythology*. New York: Charles Scribner's Sons, 1958.

Bunyan, John. *Grace Abounding to the Chief of Sinners*. Edited by Roger Sharrock. Oxford: Clarendon Press, 1962.

———. *Grace Abounding with Other Spiritual Autobiographies*. Edited by John Stachniewski with Anita Pacheco. Oxford: Oxford University Press, 1998.

———. *The Holy War*. Edited by Roger Sharrock and James F. Forrest. Oxford: Clarendon Press, 1980.

———. *The Life and Death of Mr. Badman*. Edited by James F. Forrest and Roger Sharrock. Oxford: Clarendon Press, 1988.

———. *The Miscellaneous Works of John Bunyan*. Vol. 1: *Some Gospel-Truths Opened*; *A Vindication of Some Gospel-Truths Opened*; *A Few Sighs from Hell*. Edited by T. L. Underwood and Roger Sharrock. Oxford: Clarendon Press, 1980.

———. *The Miscellaneous Works of John Bunyan*. Vol. 2: *The Doctrine of the Law and Grace Unfolded*; *I Will Pray with the Spirit*. Edited by Richard L. Greaves. Oxford: Clarendon Press, 1976.

———. *The Miscellaneous Works of John Bunyan*. Vol. 3: *Christian Behaviour*; *The Holy City*; *The Resurrection of the Dead*. Edited by J. Sears McGee. Oxford: Clarendon Press, 1987.

———. *The Miscellaneous Works of John Bunyan*. Vol. 4: *A Defence of the Doctrine of Justification, By Faith*; *A Confession of My Faith, and A Reason of My Practice*; *Differences in Judgment About Water-Baptism, No Bar to Communion*; *Peaceable Principles and True*; *A Case of Conscience Resolved*; *Questions About the Nature and Perpetuity of the Seventh-Day-Sabbath*. Edited by T. L. Underwood. Oxford: Clarendon Press, 1989.

———. *The Miscellaneous Works of John Bunyan*. Vol. 5: *The Barren Fig Tree*; *The Strait Gate*; *The Heavenly Foot-man*. Edited by Graham Midgley. Oxford: Clarendon Press, 1986.

———. *The Miscellaneous Works of John Bunyan*. Vol. 6: *Poems*. Edited by Graham Midgley. Oxford: Clarendon Press, 1980.

———. *The Miscellaneous Works of John Bunyan*. Vol. 7: *Solomon's Temple Spiritualized; The House of the Forest of Lebanon; The Water of Life*. Edited by Graham Midgley. Oxford: Clarendon Press, 1989.

———. *The Miscellaneous Works of John Bunyan*. Vol. 8: *Instruction for the Ignorant; Light for Them that Sit in Darkness; Saved by Grace; Come, and Welcome, to Jesus Christ*. Edited by Richard L. Greaves. Oxford: Clarendon Press, 1979.

———. *The Miscellaneous Works of John Bunyan*. Vol. 9: *A Treatise of the Fear of God; The Greatness of the Soul; A Holy Life*. Edited by Richard L. Greaves. Oxford: Clarendon Press, 1981.

———. *The Miscellaneous Works of John Bunyan*. Vol. 10: *Seasonable Counsel; A Discourse Upon the Pharisee and the Publicane*. Edited by Owen C. Watkins. Oxford: Clarendon Press, 1988.

———. *The Miscellaneous Works of John Bunyan*. Vol. 11: *Good News for the Vilest of Men; The Advocateship of Jesus Christ*. Edited by Richard L. Greaves. Oxford: Clarendon Press, 1985.

———. *The Miscellaneous Works of John Bunyan*. Vol. 12: *The Acceptable Sacrifice; Last Sermon; An Exposition on the Ten First Chapters of Genesis; Of Justification By an Imputed Righteousness; Paul's Departure and Crown; Of the Trinity and a Christian; Of the Law and a Christian; A Mapp Shewing the Order & Causes of Salvation & Damnation*. Edited by W. R. Owens. Oxford: Clarendon Press, 1994.

———. *The Miscellaneous Works of John Bunyan*. Vol. 13: *Israel's Hope Encouraged; The Desire of the Righteous Granted; The Saints Privilege and Profit; Christ a Compleat Savior; The Saints Knowledge of Christ's Love; Of Antichrist, and His Ruine*. Edited by W. R. Owens. Oxford: Clarendon Press, 1994.

———. *The Pilgrim's Progress*. Afterword by F. R. Leavis. New York: Signet Classics, 1991.

———. *The Pilgrim's Progress*. Edited by N. H. Keeble. Oxford: Oxford University Press, 1991.

———. *The Pilgrim's Progress*. Edited by Roger Sharrock. London: Penguin Books, 1987.

———. *The Pilgrim's Progress*. Edited by James Blanton Wharey and Roger Sharrock. Oxford: Clarendon Press, 1960.

Bushnell, Horace. *Christian Nurture*. Grand Rapids: Baker Book House, 1979.

Calvin, John. *Commentaries on the Epistle of Paul the Apostle to the Romans*. Translated by John Owen. Grand Rapids: Baker Book House, 1993.

———. *Institutes of the Christian Religion*. The Library of Christian Classics 20-21. Edited by John T. McNeill. Translated by Ford Lewis Battles. Philadelphia: The Westminster Press, 1960.

Coleridge, Samuel Taylor. *Coleridge on the Seventeenth Century*. Edited by Roberta Florence Brinkley. Durham, NC: Duke University Press, 1955.

———. *Samuel Taylor Coleridge*. The Oxford Authors. Edited by H. J. Jackson. Oxford: Oxford University Press, 1985.

Dillenberger, John, ed. *Martin Luther: Selections From His Writings*. New York: Anchor Press/Doubleday, 1961.

Donne, John. *The Complete Poetry and Selected Prose of John Donne.* Edited by Charles M. Coffin. New York: The Modern Library, 1994.

———. *The Sermons of John Donne.* Vol. 8. Edited by Evelyn M. Simpson and George R. Potter. Berkeley: University of California Press, 1956.

Edwards, Jonathan. *The Works of Jonathan Edwards.* Vol. 9: *A History of the Work of Redemption.* Edited by John F. Wilson. New Haven: Yale University Press, 1989.

Emerson, Ralph Waldo. *Selected Writings of Emerson.* Edited by Brooks Atkinson. New York: The Modern Library, 1940

Feuerbach, Ludwig. *The Essence of Christianity.* Translated by George Eliot. Amherst, NY: Prometheus Books, 1989.

Fosdick, Harry Emerson. *On Being a Real Person.* New York: Harper and Row, 1943.

Fox, George. *The Journal.* Edited by Nigel Smith. London: Penguin Books, 1998.

———. *The Works of George Fox.* Vol. 3: *The Great Mystery of the Great Whore Unfolded.* New York: AMS Press, 1975.

Foxe, John. *Foxe's Book of Martyrs.* Springdale, PA: Whitaker House, 1981.

Franklin, Benjamin. *Autobiography of Benjamin Franklin.* Edited by John Bigelow. Garden City, NY: Doubleday Dolphin Books, n.d.

Harnack, Adolf von. *What is Christianity?* Translated by Thomas Bailey Saunders. Philadelphia: Fortress Press, 1986.

Hawthorne, Nathaniel. *The Blithedale Romance.* Edited by William E. Cain. Boston: Bedford Books of St. Martin's Press, 1996.

Herbert, George. *George Herbert: The Complete English Poems.* Edited by John Tobin. London: Penguin Books, 1991.

Julian of Norwich. *Revelations of Divine Love.* Edited by Grace Warrack. London: Methuen and Company Limited, 1901.

———. *Revelations of Divine Love.* Translated by Clifton Wolters. London: Penguin, 1966.

"Joint Declaration on the Doctrine of Justification." 1999 [on-line]. Available from http://www.elca.org/ea/jddj/jddj.html; Internet; accessed 26 April 2001.

Kant, Immanuel. *Religion Within the Boundaries of Mere Reason, and Other Writings.* Edited by Allen Wood and George di Giovanni. Cambridge: Cambridge University Press, 1998.

Kierkegaard, Søren. *Fear and Trembling / Repetition.* Kierkegaard's Writings 6. Edited by Howard V. Hong and Edna H. Hong. Princeton: Princeton University Press, 1983.

Langland, William. *Piers Plowman.* Translated by A. V. C. Schmidt. Oxford: Oxford University Press, 1992.

Lewis, C. S. *Mere Christianity.* New York: Macmillan Publishing Co., Inc., 1952.

Locke, John. *An Essay Concerning Human Understanding.* In *The English Philosophers from Bacon to Mill.* Edited by Edwin A. Burtt, 238-402. New York: The Modern Library, 1967.

———. *The Reasonableness of Christianity.* Edited by George W. Ewing. Washington, D.C.: Regnery Publishing, Inc. Gateway Editions, 1965.

Luther, Martin. *The Christian in Society* I. Edited by James Atkinson. *Luther's Works*, Vol. 44. Philadelphia: Fortress Press, 1966.

_____. *A Commentary on St. Paul's Epistle to the Galatians.* Edited by Philip S. Watson. Westwood, NJ: Fleming H. Revell Company, 1953.

_____. *Lectures on Galatians, 1535: Chapters 1-4.* Edited and translated by Jaroslav Pelikan. *Luther's Works*, Vol. 26. Saint Louis: Concordia Publishing House, 1963.

_____. *Lectures on Genesis, Chapters 6-14.* Edited by Jaroslav Pelikan. *Luther's Works*, Vol. 2. Saint Louis: Concordia Publishing House, 1960.

_____. *Lectures on Romans: Glosses and Scholia.* Edited by Hilton C. Oswald. *Luther's Works*, Vol. 25. Saint Louis: Concordia Publishing House, 1972.

_____. *Word and Sacrament I.* Edited by Theodore Bachmann. *Luther's Works*, Vol. 35. Philadelphia: Muhlenberg Press, 1960.

Mill, John Stuart. *Mill: Texts, Commentaries.* Edited by Alan Ryan. New York: W. W. Norton and Company, 1975.

Milton, John. *The Riverside Milton.* Edited by Roy Flannagan. Boston: Houghton Mifflin Company, 1998.

Offor, George, ed. *The Whole Works of John Bunyan*, 3 vols. Grand Rapids: Baker Book House, 1977.

Penn, William. *The Peace of Europe, The Fruits of Solitude, and Other Writings.* Edited by Edwin B. Bronner. London: J. M. Dent/Everyman, 1993.

Perkins, William. *William Perkins (1558-1602), English Puritanist: His Pioneer Works on Casuistry: "A Discourse of Conscience" and "The Whole Treatise of Cases of Conscience."* Edited by Thomas F. Merrill. Nieuwkoop, The Netherlands: B. DeGraaf, 1966.

Ross, Hugh McGregor, ed. *George Fox Speaks for Himself: Texts That Reveal His Personality – Many Hitherto Unpublished.* York, England: William Sessions Limited, 1991.

Schaff, Philip, ed. *The Creeds of Christendom with a History and Critical Notes*, 6th ed. Revised by David S. Schaff. 3 vols. Grand Rapids: Baker Books, 1998.

Schleiermacher, Friedrich. *On Religion: Speeches to Its Cultured Despisers.* Translated by Richard Crouter. Cambridge: Cambridge University Press, 1990.

Spurgeon, Charles H. *Pictures from "Pilgrim's Progress": A Commentary on Portions of John Bunyan's Immortal Allegory.* In *The Pilgrim's Progress* [CD-ROM]. Greenville, SC: Media-Book, 1999.

Talon, Henri, ed. *God's Knotty Log: Selected Writings of John Bunyan.* Cleveland: The World Publishing Company, 1961.

Teresa of Ávila. *The Way of Perfection.* Translated by E. Allison Peers. New York: Image Books, 1991.

Whitman, Walt. *Complete Poetry and Collected Prose.* Edited by Justin Kaplan. New York: The Library of America, 1982.

Williams, George Hunston, and Angel M. Mergal, eds. *Spiritual and Anabaptist Writers.* Philadelphia: The Westminster Press, 1957.

Williams, Roger. *The Complete Writings of Roger Williams.* Vol. 3: *The Bloudy Tenent of Persecution.* Edited by Samuel L. Caldwell. New York: Russell and Russell, Inc., 1963.

Secondary Sources

Aaron, Melissa D. "'Christiana and her train': Bunyan and the Alternative Society in the Second Part of *The Pilgrim's Progress.*" In *Awakening Words: John Bunyan and the Language of Community*. Edited by David Gay, James G. Randall, and Arlette Zinck, 169-185. Newark: University of Delaware Press, 2000.

Ahenakaa, Anjov. "Justification and the Christian Life in John Bunyan: A Vindication of Bunyan from the Charge of Antinomianism." Ph. D. diss., Westminster Theological Seminary, 1997.

Ahlstrom, Sydney E. *A Religious History of the American People*. New Haven: Yale University Press, 1972.

Althaus, Paul. *The Theology of Martin Luther*. Translated by Robert C. Schultz. Philadelphia: Fortress Press, 1966.

Atkins, Gaius Glenn. *Pilgrims of the Lonely Road*. Freeport, NY: Books for Libraries Press, Inc., 1967.

Bailey, Richard. *New Light on George Fox and Early Quakerism*. San Francisco: Mellen Research University Press, 1992.

Bainton, Roland H. *Here I Stand: A Life of Martin Luther*. New York: Abingdon-Cokesbury Books, 1950.

Baker, J. Wayne. "*Sola Fide, Sola Gratia*: The Battle for Luther in Seventeenth-Century England." *The Sixteenth Century Journal* 16:1 (Spring 1985): 115-133.

Barclay, Robert. *An Apology for the True Christian Identity*, 14th ed. Glasgow: R. Barclay Murdoch, 1886.

Bartell, Shirley Miller. "Uncertainty in Bunyan versus Assurance in Fox." *Quaker History* 58 (Autumn 1969): 93-103.

Baylor, Michael G. *Action and Person: Conscience in Late Scholasticism and the Young Luther*. Studies in Medieval and Reformation Thought 20. Leiden: E. J. Brill, 1977.

Bebbington, D. W. *The Nonconformist Conscience: Chapel and Politics, 1870-1914*. London: George Allen and Unwin, 1982.

Bell, Mark R. *Apocalypse How? Baptist Movements During the English Revolution*. Macon, GA: Mercer University Press, 2000.

Bellah, Robert N., et al. *Habits of the Heart: Individualism and Commitment in American Life* New York: Harper and Row, 1985.

Bercovitch, Sacvan. *The Puritan Origins of the American Self*. New Haven: Yale University Press, 1975.

Berry, Wendell. *Sex, Economy, Freedom and Community: Eight Essays*. New York: Pantheon Books, 1993.

Bloom, Harold. *Shakespeare: The Invention of the Human*. New York: Riverhead Books, 1998.

Bowman, Glen. "Every Man is a Church in Himself: The Development of Donne's Ideas on the Relationship between Individual Conscience and Human Authority." *Fides et Historia* 29:1 (Winter/Spring 1997): 44-59.

Braithwaite, William C. *The Beginnings of Quakerism*, 2nd ed. Revised by Henry J. Cadbury. Cambridge: Cambridge University Press, 1955.

Brantley, Richard E. *Anglo-American Antiphony: The Late Romanticism of Tennyson and Emerson*. Gainesville, FL: University Press of Florida, 1994.

———. *Coordinates of Anglo-American Romanticism: Wesley, Edwards, Carlyle and Emerson*. Gainesville, FL: University Press of Florida, 1993.

———. *Wordsworth's "Natural Methodism."* New Haven: Yale University Press, 1975.

Brown, John. *John Bunyan (1628-1688): His Life, Times, and Work*. Revised by Frank Mott Harrison. London: The Hulbert Publishing Company (Limited), 1928.

Brown, Meg Lota. *Donne and the Politics of Conscience in Early Modern England*. Studies in the History of Christian Thought 61. Leiden: E. J. Brill, 1995.

Burckhardt, Jacob. *The Civilisation of the Renaissance in Italy*. Translated by S. G. C. Middlemore. New York: Harper and Row, 1958.

Caldwell, Patricia. *The Puritan Conversion Narrative: The Beginnings of American Expression*. Cambridge: Cambridge University Press, 1983.

Camden, Vera J. "Blasphemy and Belief in *Grace Abounding*." *American Baptist Quarterly* 7:4 (December 1988): 460-471.

———. "Blasphemy and the Problem of the Self in *Grace Abounding*." *Bunyan Studies* 1:2 (Spring 1989): 5-21.

———. "'Most Fit For a Wounded Conscience:' The Place of Luther's 'Commentary on Galatians' in *Grace Abounding*." *Renaissance Quarterly* 50:3 (Autumn 1997): 819-849.

———, ed. *The Narrative of the Persecutions of Agnes Beaumont*. East Lansing: Michigan State University Press, 1998.

———. "'That of Esau': Hebrews xii.16,17 in *Grace Abounding*." In *John Bunyan: Reading Dissenting Writing*. Edited by N. H. Keeble, 133-163. Oxford: Peter Lang, 2002.

Campbell, Gordon. "Fishing in Other Men's Waters: Bunyan and the Theologians." In *John Bunyan: Conventicle and Parnassus*. Edited by N. H. Keeble, 137-152. Oxford: Clarendon Press, 1988.

———. "The Source of Bunyan's *Mapp of Salvation*." *Journal of the Warburg and Courtauld Institutes* 44 (1981): 240-241.

———. "The Theology of *The Pilgrim's Progress*." In *The Pilgrim's Progress: Critical and Historical Views*. Edited by Vincent Newey, 251-262. Totowa, NJ: Barnes and Noble Books, 1980.

Cartledge, Tony. "Baptist, Methodist Theologians Debate 'Priestcraft' of the Clergy." *The Presbyterian Layman* (December 2001), 8A.

Cathcart, Dwight. *Doubting Conscience: Donne and the Poetry of Moral Argument*. Ann Arbor: The University of Michigan Press, 1975.

Collmer, Robert G., ed. *Bunyan in Our Time*. Kent, OH: The Kent State University Press, 1989.

Conn, Walter E. *Conscience: Development and Self-Transcendence*. Birmingham, AL: Religious Education Press, 1981.

Cook, Susan. "Pilgrim's Progresses: Derivative Texts and the Seventeenth-Century Reader." In *Awakening Words: John Bunyan and the Language of Community*. Edited by David Gay, James G. Randall, and Arlette Zinck, 186-201. Newark: University of Delaware Press, 2000.

Cooper, Tim. *Fear and Polemic in Seventeenth-Century England: Richard Baxter and Antinomianism*. Aldershot, England: Ashgate Publishing Limited, 2001.

Corns, Thomas N. "Bunyan, Milton and the Diversity of Radical Protestant Writing." In *John Bunyan: Reading Dissenting Writing*. Edited by N. H. Keeble, 21-38. Oxford: Peter Lang, 2002.

Cross, F. L., and E. A. Livingstone, eds. "Toleration, Religious." *The Oxford Dictionary of the Christian Church*, 3rd ed., 1629-1630. Oxford: Oxford University Press, 1997.

Cruttwell, Patrick. *The Shakespearean Moment and its Place in the Poetry of the Seventeenth Century*. New York: Columbia University Press, 1955.

Damrosch, Leo. *The Sorrows of the Quaker Jesus: James Nayler and the Puritan Crackdown on the Free Spirit*. Cambridge, MA: Harvard University Press, 1996.

Danby, John F. *Shakespeare's Doctrine of Nature: A Study of King Lear*. London: Faber and Faber, 1949.

Dandelion, Pink. *A Sociological Analysis of the Theology of Quakers: The Silent Revolution*. Studies in Religion and Society 34. Lewiston, NY: Edwin Mellen Press, 1996.

Davies, Horton. *Worship and Theology in England, I. From Cranmer to Hooker, 1534-1603*. Grand Rapids: William B. Eerdmans Publishing Company, 1996.

Davies, Michael. "Bunyan's Exceeding Maze: *Grace Abounding* and the Labyrinth of Predestination." In *Awakening Words: John Bunyan and the Language of Community*. Edited by David Gay, James G. Randall, and Arlette Zinck, 97-112. Newark: University of Delaware Press, 2000.

_____. "'Stout & Valiant Champions for God': The Radical Reformation of Romance in *The Pilgrim's Progress*." In *John Bunyan: Reading Dissenting Writing*. Edited by N. H. Keeble, 103-132. Oxford: Peter Lang, 2002.

Dever, Mark E. *Richard Sibbes: Puritanism and Calvinism in Late Elizabethan and Early Stuart England*. Macon, GA: Mercer University Press, 2000.

Dickens, A. G. *The English Reformation*. University Park, PA: The Pennsylvania State University Press, 1993.

Dillistone, F. W. "The Bunyan Tercentenary." *Theology Today* 55:2 (July 1988): 159-165.

Dixon, Sandra Lee. *Augustine: The Scattered and Gathered Self*. St. Louis: Chalice Press, 1999.

Docherty, Thomas. *John Donne, Undone*. London: Methuen, 1986.

Douglas, Constance A. "Rebirth Through Narrative: John Bunyan's Autobiographies." Ph. D. diss., Louisiana State University and Agricultural and Mechanical College, 1987.

Dowey, Edward A. *The Knowledge of God in Calvin's Theology*, 3rd ed. Grand Rapids: William B. Eerdmans Publishing Company, 1994.

Duban, James. "Conscience and Consciousness: The Liberal Christian Context of Thoreau's Political Ethics." *The New England Quarterly* 60:2 (June 1987): 208-222.

Dunan, Anne. "*The Life and Death of Mr. Badman* as a 'Compassionate Counsel to All Young Men': John Bunyan and Nonconformist Writings on Youth." *Bunyan Studies* 9 (1999/2000): 50-68.

Dunn, James D. G. "The New Perspective on Paul: Paul and the Law." In *The Romans Debate: Revised and Expanded Edition*. Edited by Karl P. Donfried, 299-308. Peabody, MA: Hendrickson Publisher, Inc., 1991.

Dunn, Richard S. "William Penn's Odyssey: From Child of Light to Absentee Landlord." In *Public Duty and Private Conscience in Seventeenth-Century England: Essays Presented to G. E. Aylmer*. Edited by John Morrill, Paul Slack, and Daniel Woolf, 305-324. Oxford: Clarendon Press, 1993.

Eagleton, Terry. *Literary Theory: An Introduction*. Minneapolis: The University of Minnesota Press, 1998.

Erickson, Kathleen Powers. "Pilgrims and Strangers: The Role of *The Pilgrim's Progress* and *The Imitation of Christ* in Shaping the Piety of Vincent van Gogh." *Bunyan Studies* 4 (1991): 7-36.

Fernández-Armesto, Felipe, and Derek Wilson. *Reformations: A Radical Interpretation of Christianity and the World, 1500-2000*. New York: Scribner, 1996.

Fiddes, Paul S. "'Walking Together:' The Place of Covenant Theology in Baptist Life Yesterday and Today." In *Pilgrim Pathways: Essays in Baptist History in Honour of B. R. White*. Edited by William H. Brackney and Paul S. Fiddes with John H. Y. Briggs, 47-74. Macon, GA: Mercer University Press, 1999.

Fish, Stanley E. *How Milton Works*. Cambridge, MA: The Belknap Press of Harvard University Press, 2001.

―――. *Self-Consuming Artifacts: The Experience of Seventeenth Century Literature*. Pittsburgh: Duquesne University Press, 1994.

Forrest, James F. "Allegory as Sacred Sport: Manipulation of the Reader in Spenser and Bunyan." In *Bunyan in Our Time*. Edited by Robert G. Collmer, 93-112. Kent, OH: The Kent State University Press, 1989.

―――. "Milton and the Divine Art of Weaponry: 'That Two-Handed Engine' and Bunyan's 'Nameless Terrible Instrument' at Mouthgate." In *Milton Studies* 16. Edited by James D. Simmonds, 131-140. Pittsburgh: University of Pittsburgh Press, 1982.

Fowler, Stanley K. *More Than a Symbol: The British Baptist Recovery of Baptist Sacramentalism*. Studies in Baptist History and Thought 2. Carlisle, UK: Paternoster Press, 2002.

Fox, Richard Wightman. "Experience and Explanation in Twentieth-Century American Religious History." In *New Directions in American Religious History*. Edited by Harry S. Stout and D. G. Hart, 394-413. New York: Oxford University Press, 1997.

Freeman, Thomas S. "A Library in Three Volumes: Foxe's 'Book of Martyrs' in the Writings of John Bunyan." *Bunyan Studies* 5 (Autumn 1994): 47-57.

Frei, Hans W. *The Eclipse of Biblical Narrative: A Study in Eighteenth and Nineteenth Century Hermeneutics*. New Haven: Yale University Press, 1974.

Frost, Kate Gartner. *Holy Delight: Typology, Numerology, and Autobiography in Donne's "Devotions Upon Emergent Occasions."* Princeton: Princeton University Press, 1990.

Froude, James Anthony. *Bunyan*. London: Macmillan and Company, 1895.

Frye, Roland Mushat. *God, Man, and Satan: Patterns of Christian Thought and Life in Paradise Lost, Pilgrim's Progress, and the Great Theologians*. Princeton: Princeton University Press, 1960.

Furlong, Monica. *Puritan's Progress*. New York: Coward, McCann and Geoghegan, Inc., 1975.

Gabrieli, Vittorio. "Falstaff and Mr. Badman: Libertine and Puritan." *Notes and Queries* 35:2 (June 1988): 165-167.

Gaustad, Edwin S. *Liberty of Conscience: Roger Williams in America*. Grand Rapids: William B. Eerdmans Publishing Company, 1991.

Geisst, Charles R. *The Political Thought of John Milton*. London: The Macmillan Press Limited, 1984.

George, Timothy. "Between Pacifism and Coercion: The English Baptist Doctrine of Religious Toleration." *The Mennonite Quarterly Review* 58:1 (January 1984): 30-49.

Gerrish, B. A. "Doctor Martin Luther: Subjectivity and Doctrine in the Lutheran Reformation." In *Continuing the Reformation: Essays on Modern Religious Thought*, 38-56. Chicago: The University of Chicago Press, 1993.

_____. *Grace and Reason: A Study in the Theology of Luther*. Oxford: Clarendon Press, 1962.

Goldman, Peter. "'The Alien Word': Puritan Conversion Narratives and the Early Modern Crisis of Representation." Ph. D. diss., University of California, Irvine, 2000.

Greaves, Richard L. *Glimpses of Glory: John Bunyan and English Dissent*. Stanford: Stanford University Press, 2002.

_____. "Introduction: Bunyan, the Shadow of Persecution, and the Power of Awakening Words." In *Awakening Words: John Bunyan and the Language of Community*. Edited by David Gay, James G. Randall, and Arlette Zinck, 9-22. Newark: University of Delaware Press, 2000.

_____. *John Bunyan*. Courtenay Studies in Reformation Theology 2. Grand Rapids: William B. Eerdmans Publishing Company, 1969.

_____. "John Bunyan and Covenant Thought in the Seventeenth Century." *Church History* 36:2 (June 1967): 151-169.

_____. *John Bunyan and English Nonconformity*. London: The Hambledon Press, 1992.

_____. "John Bunyan and the Ethic of Suffering." In *John Bunyan and His England, 1628-88*. Edited by Anne Laurence, W. R. Owens, and Stuart Sim, 63-76. London: The Hambledon Press, 1990.

_____. "John Bunyan: The Present State of Historical Scholarship." In *Bunyan in England and Abroad*. Edited by M. van Os and G. J. Schutte, 29-43. Amsterdam: Vrije Universiteit University Press, 1990.

_____. "John Bunyan's 'Holy War' and London Nonconformity." *The Baptist Quarterly* 26:4 (October 1975): 158-168.

Green, I. M. "Bunyan in Context: The Changing Face of Protestantism in Seventeenth-Century England." In *Bunyan in England and Abroad*. Edited by. M. van Os and G. J. Schutte, 1-27. Amsterdam: Vrije Universiteit University Press, 1990.

Grossman, Cathy Lynn, and Anthony DeBarros. "Still One Nation Under God, But Survey Finds Shifting Beliefs." *USA Today*, 24 December 2001, sec. D, pp. 1,2.

Guibbory, Achsah. *Ceremony and Community from Herbert to Milton: Literature, Religion, and Cultural Conflict in Seventeenth-Century England*. Cambridge: Cambridge University Press, 1998.

Hahn, Hans-Christoph. "Conscience." In *The New International Dictionary of New Testament Theology*. Volume 1: *A-F*. Edited by Colin Brown, 348-351. Grand Rapids: Zondervan Publishing House, 1986.

Haller, William. *The Rise of Puritanism*. New York: Harper Torchbooks, 1957.

Hambrick-Stowe, C. E. *The Practice of Piety: Puritan Devotional Disciplines in Seventeenth-Century New England*. Chapel Hill: The University of North Carolina Press, 1985.

Hancock, Maxine. *The Key in the Window: Marginal Notes in Bunyan's Narratives*. Vancouver: Regent College Publishing, 2000.

Hanford, James Holly. *John Milton, Englishman*. New York: Crown Publishers, 1949.

Hardin, Richard. "Bunyan, Mr. Ignorance, and the Quakers." *Studies in Philology* 69 (1972): 496-508.

Harding, M. Esther. *Journey Into Self*. Boston: Sigo Press, 1993.

Harrison, Frank Mott. *John Bunyan: A Story of His Life*. Edinburgh: The Banner of Truth Trust, 1964.

Harrison, G. B. *John Bunyan: A Study in Personality*. Garden City, NY: Doubleday, Doran & Company, Inc., 1928.

_____, ed. *The Church Book of Bunyan Meeting, 1650-1821*. London: J. M. Dent and Sons Limited, 1928.

Haskin, Dayton. "Bunyan, Luther, and the Struggle with Belatedness in *Grace Abounding*." *University of Toronto Quarterly* 50:3 (Spring 1981): 300-313.

_____. "Bunyan's Scriptural Acts." In *Bunyan in Our Time*. Edited by Robert G. Collmer, 61-92. Kent, OH: The Kent State University Press, 1989.

_____. "*The Pilgrim's Progress* in the Context of Bunyan's Dialogue with the Radicals." *Harvard Theological Review* 77:1 (1984): 73-94.

Hauerwas, Stanley. *Unleashing the Scripture: Freeing the Bible from Captivity to America*. Nashville: Abingdon Press, 1993.

Hawkes, David. *Idols of the Marketplace: Idolatry and Commodity Fetishism in English Literature, 1580-1680*. New York: Palgrave, 2001.

_____. "Master of His Ways? Determinism and the Market in *The Life and Death of Mr. Badman*. In *John Bunyan: Reading Dissenting Writing*. Edited by N. H. Keeble, 211-230. Oxford: Peter Lang, 2002.

Herreshoff, David. "Marxist Perspectives on Bunyan." In *Bunyan in Our Time*. Edited by Robert G. Collmer, 161-185. Kent, OH: The Kent State University Press, 1989.

Hill, Christopher. *Antichrist in Seventeenth-Century England*. London: Verso, 1990.

_____. *The Century of Revolution, 1603-1714*. New York: W. W. Norton and Company, 1980.

_____. *Milton and the English Revolution*. New York: The Viking Press, 1977.

_____. *A Tinker and a Poor Man: John Bunyan and His Church, 1628-1688*. New York: W. W. Norton and Company, 1988.

_____. *The World Turned Upside Down: Radical Ideas During the English Revolution*. London: Penguin Books, 1991.

Himy, Armand. "*Paradise Lost* as a Republican 'Tractatus theologico-politicus'." In *Milton and Republicanism*. Edited by David Armitage, Armand Himy, and Quentin Skinner, 118-134. Cambridge: Cambridge University Press, 1995.

Hindmarsh, D. Bruce. *John Newton and the English Evangelical Tradition.* Grand Rapids: William B. Eerdmans Publishing Company, 1996.

Hindson, Edward, ed. *Introduction to Puritan Theology.* Grand Rapids: Baker Book House, 1976.

Holifield, E. B. "Individualism." In *Dictionary of Christianity in America.* Edited by Daniel G. Reid, Robert D. Linder, Bruce L. Shelley, and Harry S. Stout, 573-574. Downers Grove, IL: InterVarsity Press, 1990.

Honeygosky, Stephen R. *Milton's House of God: The Invisible and Visible Church.* Columbia, MO: University of Missouri Press, 1993.

Hubbard, Geoffrey. *A Quaker by Convincement.* Middlesex, England: Penguin Books, 1974.

Hussey, Maurice. "Bunyan's 'The Life and Death of Mr. Badman.'" *The Congregational Quarterly* 28:4 (October 1950): 359-366.

———. "Christian Conduct in Bunyan and Baxter." *The Baptist Quarterly* 14:2 (April 1951): 75-83.

Ingle, H. Larry. *First Among Friends: George Fox and the Creation of Quakerism.* New York: Oxford University Press, 1994.

Jagodzinski, Cecile M. *Privacy and Print: Reading and Writing in Seventeenth-Century England.* Charlottesville: University Press of Virginia, 1999.

James, William. *The Varieties of Religious Experience.* Introduction by Jaroslav Pelikan. New York: Vintage Books, 1990.

Jeffrey, David Lyle. *People of the Book: Christian Identity and Literary Culture.* Grand Rapids: William B. Eerdmans Publishing Company, 1996.

Jewett, Robert. *Christian Tolerance: Paul's Message to the Modern Church.* Philadelphia: The Westminster Press, 1982.

Johnson, Galen K. "'Be Not Extream:' The Limits of Theory in Reading John Bunyan." *Christianity and Literature* 49:4 (Summer 2000): 447-464.

———. "Church and Conscience in William Langland and Julian of Norwich." *Fides et Historia* 32:2 (Summer/Fall 2000): 51-66.

———. "The Conflicted Puritan Inheritance of John Bunyan's Political Writings", *Baptist History and Heritage* 38:2 (Spring 2003): 103-115

———. "John Calvin, Huguenot?" *Koinonia* 11:1 (Fall 1999): 194-215.

———. "Suicide and the Keys of Escape in Bunyan and Donne." *Bunyan Studies* 10 (2001/2002): 46-64.

Johnson, Jeffrey. *The Theology of John Donne.* Cambridge: D. S. Brewer, 1999.

Jüngel, Eberhard. *The Freedom of a Christian: Luther's Significance for Contemporary Theology.* Translated by Roy A. Harrisville. Minneapolis: Augsburg Publishing House, 1988.

Juster, Susan. "The Spirit and the Flesh: Gender, Language, and Sexuality in American Protestantism." In *New Directions in American Religious History.* Edited by Harry S. Stout and D. G. Hart, 334-361. New York: Oxford University Press, 1997.

Kaufmann, U. Milo. "*The Pilgrim's Progress* and *The Pilgrim's Regress*: John Bunyan and C. S. Lewis on the Shape of the Christian Quest." In *Bunyan in Our Time.* Edited by Robert G. Collmer, 186-199. Kent, OH: The Kent State University Press, 1989.

Keeble, N. H. "Christiana's Key: The Unity of *The Pilgrim's Progress*." In *"The Pilgrim's Progress": Critical and Historical Views*. Edited by Vincent Newey, 1-20. Totowa, NJ: Barnes and Noble Books, 1980.

———. "'Here is her Glory, even to be under Him': The Feminine in the Thought and Work of John Bunyan." In *John Bunyan and His England, 1628-88*. Edited by Anne Laurence, W. R. Owens, and Stuart Sim, 131-147. London: The Hambledon Press, 1990.

———. "'Till One Greater Man / Restore us ...': Restoration Images in Bunyan and Milton." In *Awakening Words: John Bunyan and the Language of Community*. Edited by David Gay, James G. Randall, and Arlette Zinck, 27-50. Newark: University of Delaware Press, 2000.

———, and Geoffrey F. Nuttall, eds. *Calendar of the Correspondence of Richard Baxter*, 2 vols. Oxford: Clarendon Press, 1991.

Kelly, J. N. D. *Early Christian Doctrines*. San Francisco: Harper and Row, 1978.

Kenyon, J. P. *Stuart England*, 2nd ed. The Pelican History of England 6. London: Penguin Books, 1985.

Knott, John R. "Bunyan and the City of Blood." In *Awakening Words: John Bunyan and the Language of Community*. Edited by David Gay, James G. Randall, and Arlette Zinck, 51-67. Newark: University of Delaware Press, 2000.

———. "Bunyan and the Holy Community." *Studies in Philology* 80:2 (Spring 1983): 200-225.

———. *Discourses of Martyrdom in English Literature, 1563-1694*. Cambridge: Cambridge University Press, 1993.

Knox, Edmund Arbuthnott. *John Bunyan in Relation to His Times*. London: Longmans, Green and Company, 1928.

Knox, Ronald. *Essays in Satire*. London: Sheed and Ward, 1928.

Kretzschmar, Louise. *Privatization of the Christian Faith: Mission, Social Ethics and the South African Baptists*. Legon, Ghana: Legon Theological Studies Series, 1998.

Kuenning, Lawrence S. "The Bunyan-Burrough Debate of 1656-1657 Analyzed Using a Computer Hypertext." Ph. D. diss., Westminster Theological Seminary, 2000.

Lamont, Daniel. "Bunyan's *Holy War*: A Study in Christian Experience." *Theology Today* 3:4 (January 1947): 459-472.

Lamont, William M. "Bunyan and Baxter: Millennium and Magistrate." In *John Bunyan: Reading Dissenting Writing*. Edited by N. H. Keeble, 39-58. Oxford: Peter Lang, 2002.

———. *Richard Baxter and the Millennium*. London: Croom Helm, 1979.

Lares, Jameela. *Milton and the Preaching Arts*. Pittsburgh: Duquesne University Press, 2001.

Leavis, F. R. "Bunyan Through Modern Eyes." In *The Common Pursuit*, 204-210. New York: New York University Press, 1964.

Lindbeck, George A. "Modernity and Luther's Understanding of the Freedom of a Christian." In *Martin Luther and the Modern Mind: Freedom, Conscience, Toleration, Rights*. Toronto Studies in Theology 22. Edited by Manfred Hoffman, 1-22. New York: The Edwin Mellen Press, 1985.

Linder, Robert D. "Williams, Roger (1603-1683)." In *Dictionary of Christianity in America*. Edited by Daniel G. Reid, Robert D. Linder, Bruce L. Shelley, and Harry S. Stout, 1258-1260. Downers Grove, IL: InterVarsity Press, 1990.

Lindsay, Jack. *John Bunyan: Maker of Myths*. London: Methuen Publishers, 1937.

Lloyd-Jones, Martyn. *Romans*. Vol. 6: *The Law: Its Function and Limits*. Edinburgh: Banner of Truth Trust, 1973.

Loane, Marcus L. *Makers of Religious Freedom in the Seventeenth Century: Henderson – Rutherford – Bunyan – Baxter*. Grand Rapids: William B. Eerdmans Publishing Company, 1961.

Lohse, Bernhard. "Conscience and Authority in Luther." In *Luther and the Dawn of the Modern Era*. Studies in the History of Christian Thought 8. Edited by Heiko A. Oberman, 158-183. Leiden: E. J. Brill, 1974.

_____. *Martin Luther: An Introduction to His Life and Work*. Translated by Robert C. Schultz. Philadelphia: Fortress Press, 1986.

Low, Anthony. *The Reinvention of Love: Poetry, Politics and Culture from Sidney to Milton*. Cambridge: Cambridge University Press, 1993.

Luxon, Thomas H. *Literal Figures: Puritan Allegory and the Reformation Crisis in Representation*. Chicago: The University of Chicago Press, 1995.

Lynch, Beth. "'Rather Dark to Readers in General': Some Critical Casualties of John Bunyan's *The Holy War* (1682)." *Bunyan Studies* 9 (1999/2000): 25-49.

Marius, Richard. *Martin Luther: The Christian Between God and Death*. Cambridge, MA: The Belknap Press of Harvard University Press, 1999.

Mascuch, Michael. *Origins of the Individualist Self: Autobiography and Self-Identity in England, 1591-1791*. Stanford: Stanford University Press, 1996.

McGrath, Alister E. *A Life of John Calvin: A Study in the Shaping of Western Culture*. Oxford: Blackwell, 1993.

McGraw, Phillip C. *Self Matters: Creating Your Life from the Inside Out*. New York: Simon and Schuster, 2001.

McMillin, Scott. "G. B. S. and Bunyan's *Badman*." *The Shaw Review* 9:3 (September 1966): 90-99.

Miles, Margaret. "Pilgrimage as Metaphor in a Nuclear Age." *Theology Today* 45:2 (July 1988): 166-179.

Miller, Perry. *Errand Into the Wilderness*. Cambridge, MA: Harvard University Press, 1993.

_____. *The New England Mind from Colony to Province*. Cambridge, MA: Harvard University Press, 1953.

_____. *Orthodoxy in Massachusetts, 1630-1650*. Gloucester, MA: Peter Smith, 1965.

_____, and Thomas H. Johnson. *The Puritans*. New York: American Book Company, 1938.

Mills, Robert P. "The Myth of Private Conscience." *The Presbyterian Layman* (May/June 2001): 2.

Mollenkott, Virginia R. "Relativism in *Samson Agonistes*." *Studies in Philology* 67:1 (January 1970): 89-102.

Moody, Dwight A. "Trickle of Freedom; Wave of Liberty." *Baptist Standard*, 10 December 2001, p. 4

Morgan, Edmund S. *Roger Williams: The Church and the State*. New York: Harcourt, Brace and World, Inc., 1967.

_____, ed. *Puritan Political Ideas, 1558-1794*. Indianapolis: The Bobbs-Merrill Company, Inc., 1965.

Morgan, Irvonwy. *The Nonconformity of Richard Baxter*. London: The Epworth Press, 1946.

Moroney, Stephen K. *The Noetic Effects of Sin: A Historical and Contemporary Exploration of How Sin Affects Our Thinking*. Lanham, MD: Lexington Books, 2000.

Morris, John N. *Versions of the Self: Studies in English Autobiography from John Bunyan to John Stuart Mill*. New York: Basic Books, Inc., 1966.

Mosse, George L. *The Holy Pretence: A Study in Christianity and Reason of State from William Perkins to John Winthrop*. Oxford: Basil Blackwell, 1957.

Muller, Richard A. "Covenant and Conscience in English Reformed Theology: Three Variations on a 17th Century Theme." *The Westminster Theological Journal* 42:2 (Spring 1980): 308-334.

Mullett, Michael A. *John Bunyan in Context*. Keele: Keele University Press, 1996.

Nellist, Brian. "*The Pilgrim's Progress* and Allegory." In *The Pilgrim's Progress: Critical and Historical Views*. Edited by Vincent Newey, 132-153. Totowa, NJ: Barnes and Noble Books, 1980.

Newey, Vincent. "Bunyan and the Confines of the Mind." In *The Pilgrim's Progress: Critical and Historical Views*. Edited by Vincent Newey, 21-48. Totowa, NJ: Barnes and Noble Books, 1980.

_____. "'With the Eyes of My Understanding': Bunyan, Experience, and Acts of Interpretation." In *John Bunyan: Conventicle and Parnassus*, 189-216. Edited by N. H. Keeble. Oxford: Clarendon Press, 1988.

Nicholson, John. *John Bunyan and the Visionary Search for an English Conscience*. London: BOZO, 1983.

Nuttall, Geoffrey F. "The Heart of *The Pilgrim's Progress*." *American Baptist Quarterly* 7:4 (December 1988): 472-483.

_____. *The Holy Spirit in Puritan Faith and Experience*. Oxford: Basil Blackwell, 1946.

Oberman, Heiko A. *Luther: Man Between God and the Devil*. Translated by Eileen Walliser-Schwarzbart. New York: Image Books, 1989.

Olson, Roger. *The Story of Christian Theology: Twenty Centuries of Tradition and Reform*. Downers Grove, IL: InterVarsity Press, 1999.

Ormsby-Lennon, Hugh. "From Shibboleth to Apocalypse: Quaker Speechways During the Puritan Revolution." In *Language, Self, and Society: A Social History of Language*. Edited by Peter Burke and Roy Porter, 72-112. Cambridge: Polity Press, 1991.

Owens, W. R. "Reading the Bibliographical Codes: Bunyan's Publication in Folio." In *John Bunyan: Reading Dissenting Writing*. Edited by N. H. Keeble, 59-77. Oxford: Peter Lang, 2002.

Pelikan, Jaroslav. *The Christian Tradition: A History of the Development of Doctrine*. Vol. 3: *The Growth of Medieval Theology (600-1300)*. Chicago: The University of Chicago Press, 1978.

_____. *The Christian Tradition: A History of the Development of Doctrine*. Vol. 4: *Reformation of Church and Dogma (1300-1700)*. Chicago: The University of Chicago Press, 1984.

Pestana, Carla Gardina. *Quakers and Baptists in Colonial Massachusetts.* Cambridge: Cambridge University Press, 1991.
Pierce, C. A. *Conscience in the New Testament.* London: SCM Press Limited, 1955.
Piper, John. *The Hidden Smile of God: The Fruit of Affliction in the Lives of John Bunyan, William Cowper, and David Brainerd.* Wheaton: Crossway Books, 2001.
Pooley, Roger. "*Grace Abounding* and the New Sense of Self." In *John Bunyan and His England, 1628-88.* Edited by Anne Laurence, W. R. Owens, and Stuart Sim, 105-114. London: The Hambledon Press, 1990.
_____. "Plain and Simple: Bunyan and Style." In *John Bunyan: Conventicle and Parnassus.* Edited by N. H. Keeble, 91-110. Oxford: Clarendon Press, 1988.
Puckett, David L. *John Calvin's Exegesis of the Old Testament.* Louisville: Westminster John Knox Press, 1995.
Randall, J. G. "Against the Backdrop of Eternity: Narrative and the Negative Casuistry of John Bunyan's *The Life and Death of Mr. Badman*." *The Baptist Quarterly* 35:7 (July 1994): 347-359.
Renaut, Alain. *The Era of the Individual: A Contribution to a History of Subjectivity.* Translated by M. B. DeBevoise and Franklin Philip. Princeton: Princeton University Press, 1997.
Reynolds, Anna Maria. "Julian of Norwich." In *Pre-Reformation English Spirituality.* Edited by James Walsh, 198-209. New York: Fordham University Press, 1965.
Rivers, Isabel. "Grace, Holiness, and the Pursuit of Happiness: Bunyan and Restoration Latitudinarianism." In *John Bunyan: Conventicle and Parnassus.* Edited by N. H. Keeble, 45-70. Oxford: Clarendon Press, 1988.
Rivkin, Julie, and Michael Ryan. "The Class of 1968 – Post-Structuralism *par lui-même*." In *Literary Theory: An Anthology.* Edited by Julie Rivkin and Michael Ryan, 333-357. Malden, MA: Blackwell, 1999.
Ross, Aileen. "'Baffled and Befooled': Misogyny in the Works of John Bunyan." In *Awakening Words: John Bunyan and the Language of Community.* Edited by David Gay, James G. Randall, and Arlette Zinck, 153-168. Newark: University of Delaware Press, 2000.
Rowse, A. L. *Milton the Puritan: Portrait of a Mind.* New York: University Press of America, 1977.
Rust, Eric C. *Towards a Theological Understanding of History.* New York: Oxford University Press, 1963.
Sams, Horace, Jr. "Temptation in Imaginative Literature of Milton and Bunyan: Two Faces of the Puritan Persona." Ph. D. diss., University of South Florida, 1985.
Sandel, Michael J. *Democracy's Discontent: America in Search of a Public Philosophy.* Cambridge, MA: The Belknap Press of Harvard University Press, 1996.
Saurat, Denis. *Milton: Man and Thinker.* New York: The Dial Press, 1925.
Schaff, Philip. *The Principle of Protestantism as Related to the Present State of the Church.* Translated by John W. Nevin. Chambersburg, PA: Publication Office of the German Reformed Church, 1845.

Schmidt, Martin. "Biblizismus und natürliche Theologie in der Gewissenslehre des englischen Puritanismus," Zweiter Teil. *Archiv für Reformationsgeschichte* 43:1 (1952): 70-87.

Schweitzer, Friedrich. "Church, Individual Religion, Public Responsibility: Images of Faith Between Modern and Postmodern Adulthood." *The Princeton Seminary Bulletin* 21:3 (November 2000): 287-300.

Seed, David. "Dialogue and Debate in *The Pilgrim's Progress*." In *The Pilgrim's Progress: Critical and Historical Views*. Edited by Vincent Newey, 69-90. Totowa, NJ: Barnes and Noble Books, 1980.

Shain, Barry Alan. *The Myth of American Individualism: The Protestant Origins of American Political Thought*. Princeton: Princeton University Press, 1994.

Sharrock, Roger. "Bunyan Studies Today: An Evaluation." In *Bunyan in England and Abroad: Papers Delivered at the John Bunyan Tercentenary Symposium, Vrije Universiteit, Amsterdam 1988*. Edited by M. van Os and G. J. Schutte, 45-59. Amsterdam: Vrije Universiteit Press, 1990.

⎯⎯⎯⎯. *John Bunyan*. London: Macmillan, 1968.

⎯⎯⎯⎯. "*The Life and Death of Mr. Badman*: Facts and Problems." *The Modern Language Review* 82:1 (January 1987): 15-29.

Shawcross, John T. "The Higher Wisdom of *The Tenure of Kings and Magistrates*." In *Achievements of the Left Hand: Essays on the Prose of John Milton*. Edited by Michael Lieb and John T. Shawcross, 142-159. Amherst: The University of Massachusetts Press, 1974.

⎯⎯⎯⎯. *John Milton: The Self and the World*. Lexington, KY: The University of Kentucky Press, 1993.

Sim, Stuart, and David Walker. *Bunyan and Authority: The Rhetoric of Dissent and the Legitimation Crisis in Seventeenth-Century England*. Bern: Peter Lang, 2000.

Simpson, J. A., and E. S. C. Weiner, eds. *The Oxford English Dictionary*, 2nd ed. Vol. 14. Oxford: Clarendon Press, 1989.

Simpson, Ken. "'For the Best Improvement of Time:' *Pilgrim's Progress* and the Liturgies of Nonconformity." In *Awakening Words: John Bunyan and the Language of Community*. Edited by David Gay, James G. Randall, and Arlette Zinck, 113-126. Newark: University of Delaware Press, 2000.

Smith, Karen. "The Covenant Life of Some Eighteenth-Century Calvinistic Baptists in Hampshire and Wiltshire." In *Pilgrim Pathways: Essays in Baptist History in Honour of B. R. White*. Edited by William H. Brackney and Paul S. Fiddes with John H. Y. Briggs, 165-183. Macon, GA: Mercer University Press, 1999.

Smith, Nigel. *Perfection Proclaimed: Language and Literature in English Radical Religion 1640-1660*. Oxford: Clarendon Press, 1989.

Southern, R. W. *Western Society and the Church in the Middle Ages*. London: Penguin Books, 1990.

Spargo, Tamsin. *The Writing of John Bunyan*. Aldershot: Ashgate Publishing Limited, 1997.

Stachniewski, John. *The Persecutory Imagination: English Puritanism and the Literature of Religious Despair*. Oxford: Clarendon Press, 1991.

Stauffer, Richard. "'Le Voyage du Pélerin,' de John Bunyan." *Bulletin de la Societé de l'Histoire du Protestantisme Français* 134 (October-December 1988): 709-722.

Stendahl, Krister. *Paul Among Jews and Gentiles, and Other Essays*. Philadelphia: Fortress Press, 1976.

Stout, Jeffrey. *The Flight from Authority: Religion, Morality, and the Quest for Autonomy*. Notre Dame: University of Notre Dame Press, 1981.

Stranahan, Brainerd P. "Bunyan's Satire and Its Biblical Sources." In *Bunyan in Our Time*. Edited by Robert G. Collmer, 35-60. Kent, OH: The Kent State University Press, 1989.

Talon, Henri. *John Bunyan*. Writers and Their Works 73. London: Longmans, Green & Co., 1956.

_____. *John Bunyan: The Man and His Works*. Cambridge, MA: Harvard University Press, 1951.

Taylor, Charles. *Sources of the Self: The Making of the Modern Identity*. Cambridge, MA: Harvard University Press, 1989.

Thickstun, Margaret Olofson. *Fictions of the Feminine: Puritan Doctrine and the Representation of Women*. Ithaca, NY: Cornell University Press, 1988.

Thomas, Keith. "Cases of Conscience in Seventeenth-Century England." In *Public Duty and Private Conscience in Seventeenth-Century England: Essays Presented to G. E. Aylmer*. Edited by John Morrill, Paul Slack, and Daniel Woolf, 29-58. Oxford: Clarendon Press, 1993.

Thompson, Philip E. "Re-envisioning Baptist Identity: Historical, Theological, and Liturgical Analysis." *Perspectives in Religious Studies* 27:3 (Fall 2000): 287-302.

Tillyard, E. M. W. *The Miltonic Setting Past and Present*. Cambridge: Cambridge University Press, 1938.

Tindall, William York. *John Bunyan: Mechanick Preacher*. New York: Russell and Russell, Inc., 1964.

Trim, Mary. "Bunyan's Burial Place." *The Recorder* 6 (Spring 2000): 2-3.

Trueblood, D. Elton. *The People Called Quakers*. New York: Harper and Row, Publishers, 1966.

Underwood, T. L. *Primitivism, Radicalism, and the Lamb's War: The Baptist-Quaker Conflict in Seventeenth-Century England*. New York: Oxford University Press, 1997.

Van Til, L. John. *Liberty of Conscience: The History of a Puritan Idea*. Nutley, NJ: Craig Press, 1972.

_____. "The Appeal to Conscience." *Christianity Today* 13:17 (23 May 1969): 6-8.

Wakefield, Gordon. *Bunyan the Christian*. London: HarperCollins, 1992.

_____. "'To be a Pilgrim': Bunyan and the Christian Life." In *John Bunyan: Conventicle and Parnassus*. Edited by N. H. Keeble, 111-136. Oxford: Clarendon Press, 1988.

Walton, George W. "Bunyan's Proverbial Language." In *Bunyan in Our Time*. Edited by Robert G. Collmer, 7-34. Kent, OH: The Kent State University Press, 1989.

Weber, Max. *The Protestant Ethic and the Spirit of Capitalism*. Translated by Talcott Parsons. New York: Charles Scribner's Sons, 1958.

Weintraub, Karl Joachim. *The Value of the Individual: Self and Circumstance in Autobiography*. Chicago: The University of Chicago Press, 1978.

Wendel, François. *Calvin: Origins and Development of His Religious Thought*. Translated by Philip Mairet. Grand Rapids: Baker Books, 1997.
West, Jessamyn, ed. *The Quaker Reader*. New York: The Viking Press, 1962.
White, B. R. "The Fellowship of Believers: Bunyan and Puritanism." In *John Bunyan: Conventicle and Parnassus*, 1-19. Edited by N. H. Keeble. Oxford: Clarendon Press, 1988.
Williams, D. H. *Retrieving the Tradition and Renewing Evangelicalism: A Primer for Suspicious Protestants*. Grand Rapids: William B. Eerdmans Publishing Company, 1999.
Wolff, Hans Walter. *Anthropology of the Old Testament*. Translated by Margaret Kohl. Philadelphia: Fortress Press, 1974.
Woods, Susanne. "Elective Poetics and Milton's Prose: *A Treatise of Civil Power* and *Considerations Touching the Likeliest Means to Remove Hirelings Out of the Church*." In *Politics, Poetics, and Hermeneutics in Milton's Prose*. Edited by David Loewenstein and James Grantham Turner, 193-211. Cambridge: Cambridge University Press, 1990.
Zachman, Randall C. *The Assurance of Faith: Conscience in the Theology of Martin Luther and John Calvin*. Minneapolis: Fortress Press, 1993.
Zagorin, Perez. *A History of Political Thought in the English Revolution*. Bristol, England: Thoemmes Press, 1997.
_____. *Milton, Aristocrat and Rebel: The Poet and His Politics*. Rochester, NY: D. S. Brewer, 1992.
Zinck, Arlette M. "'Doctrine by ensample': Sanctification through Literature in Milton and Bunyan." *Bunyan Studies* 6 (1995/1996): 44-55.
_____. "From Apocalypse to Prophecy: The Didactic Strategies of *The Holy War*." In *John Bunyan: Reading Dissenting Writing*. Edited by N. H. Keeble, 183-198. Oxford: Peter Lang, 2002.
_____. "Of Arms and the Heroic Reader: The Concept of Psychomachy in Spenser, Milton and Bunyan." Ph.D. diss., University of Alberta, 1993.
Zizioulas, John D. *Being as Communion: Studies in Personhood and the Church*. Crestwood, NY: St. Vladimir's Seminary Press, 1985.

Index

A

Aaron, Melissa D. 151
Ahenakaa, Anjov 176, 206-207
Ahlstrom, Sidney E. 44, 10-101
Althaus, Paul 70
Ambrose 199, 201
Ames, William 6, 90, 92-96, 102, 113, 123, 125
Anselm of Canterbury 22-23
antinomian/ism 26, 31, 82, 118, 176, 204-208, 215-216
Apocrypha 199
Aquinas, Thomas 60
Arminian 93, 114, 204
Athanasius 199
Atkins, Gaius Glenn 142
atonement 22-23, 32, 41, 73, 205
Audley, Robert 179
Augustine 2, 49-51, 60, 199, 201

B

Bainton, Roland H. 58
Baker, J. Wayne 208
baptism (see also Sacraments, Ordinances) 11, 69, 85, 106, 114, 153-157, 159-160, 177, 204, 211
Baptist/s 5, 8-9, 19, 25, 33, 35, 41, 45, 80, 82, 96, 100, 103-104, 106, 110, 118, 120, 128, 147, 153, 155-157, 175-176, 179, 191, 199, 215-216, 218-219, 221-227
Barclay, Robert 10, 18, 25, 31, 34, 38
Basil of Caesarea 22
Baxter, Richard 7, 82, 196, 203-204, 206-209
Baylor, Michael G. 83-85
Bayly, Lewis 171, 198
Baynham, James 199
Beaumont, Agnes 148
Bebbington, D. W. 176
Bell, Mark R. 104
Bellah, Robert N. 1, 3, 38
Bercovitch, Sacvan 5, 45
Berry, Wendell 175
Bible (see also Scripture) 1, 12-13, 16-18, 20, 25, 32, 37, 40-44, 48, 51, 53, 75, 85, 97, 105, 115, 117, 139, 145-146, 148, 195-198, 200-203, 220
Bloom, Harold 84
Book of Common Prayer/Prayer Book 10, 105, 107, 124
Bowman, Glen 109
Brantley, Richard 38
Brown, John 21, 38
Brown, Meg Lota 83, 163
Browne, Sir Thomas 52
Bultmann, Rudolf 43
Bunyan, John
  A Case of Conscience Resolved 148-149, 211
  A Defence of the Doctrine of Justification, By Faith 10, 14, 27, 83, 154, 197, 204, 211
  Differences in Judgment About Water-Baptism, No Bar to Communion 153, 211
  The Doctrine of the Law and Grace Unfolded 10, 13, 20, 22, 61, 63-65, 70, 72, 153, 197, 205, 211
  An Exposition on the Ten First Chapters of Genesis 102, 212
  Grace Abounding to the Chief of Sinners xv, 4-5, 10, 15, 46-87, 112, 169, 182, 211
  The Holy City 108, 117, 122, 195-198, 200, 202, 211
  The Holy War xv, 4, 7, 15, 111, 125, 128, 130, 148, 167-168, 178-193, 195-196, 207, 211, 223, 228
  The House of the Forest of Lebanon 106, 109, 212
  The Life and Death of Mr. Badman xv, 4, 7, 28, 107, 111, 117, 125, 128, 133-134, 138, 148, 159, 163,

167-178, 182-183, 187, 193, 198-199, 203, 207, 211, 217, 219-221, 223, 225-226
A Mapp Shewing the Order & Causes of Salvation & Damnation 212
Of Antichrist, and His Ruine 106-107, 109, 111-112, 116, 122, 212
Of Justification By an Imputed Righteousness 212
The Pilgrim's Progress xv, 3-4, 6, 10-11, 13, 15, 21, 26-29, 41, 50, 61, 64, 74, 76, 86, 103, 125, 127-165, 167, 170, 172, 174, 177, 180, 182, 186-187, 196, 198, 200, 202, 204, 206, 208, 212, 214-218, 220-222, 224, 226
Some Gospel-Truths Opened 10-12, 18, 23-25, 28-29, 33, 35, 37, 45-46, 53, 72, 74, 129, 211
A Vindication of Some Gospel-Truths Opened 10, 13, 15, 20, 22-25, 28-29, 53, 72, 111, 116, 211
Burckhardt, Jacob 89
Burgess, Anthony 205
Burrough, Edward 9-10, 21, 24, 30-31, 33
Burton, Henry 205
Burton, John 35, 45, 107
Bushnell, Horace 19

C

Caldwell, Patricia 141
Calvin, John 50-51, 55, 60, 64, 77, 83, 93, 97, 120, 129-130, 161, 165, 176-177, 197-198, 202, 207
Calvinist/Calvinism 47, 82, 87, 90-91, 94-95, 102, 112, 114, 127, 147, 154, 189, 204, 208, 217, 226
Camden, Vera J. 47, 62, 67, 76
Campbell, Gordon 128, 200
Catholic/ism 17, 25, 27, 36, 49, 83, 90-91, 93, 97, 107-108, 110, 117, 119, 159, 183, 195-196, 203, 207
Charles I 90, 93, 120
Charles II 21, 90, 108, 112, 178-179, 200
Cheever, George B. 151
Christ, Jesus 5, 7, 10-14, 16-20, 22-27, 29-30, 32-37, 39-40, 42-46, 51, 55-57, 59, 61-62, 64-80, 85-86, 94, 101-102, 104, 106, 108, 112-113, 115-116, 118-119, 121-122, 124, 128-129, 132-133, 137, 139, 146-147, 149-151, 153-154, 156-157, 159-162, 164, 170-172, 175-178, 182, 185-186, 192, 198-199, 201-203, 205-210
Christology 10, 22-23, 42-43, 117, 128, 199
Church of England 32, 91, 97, 105-106, 204
Clarke, Samuel 198
Clarkson, Lawrence 206
Cobb, Paul 15, 104-105, 179
Coleridge, Samuel Taylor 4, 47, 127, 162, 188, 200
Conn, Walter E. 160
conscience 2-16, 20, 22-25, 27, 29, 32-34, 37-38, 42, 44, 47-50, 52-75, 77-87, 89-101, 103-106, 108-119, 121-125, 127, 132, 134-139, 141, 148-150, 154, 160, 164, 167-173, 175-177, 179-190, 195-196, 198, 201-202, 204-205, 207-208, 210-211, 214-223, 225, 227-228
Constantine 98, 121
Cooper, Tim 206
Corns, Thomas N. 120
Cotton, John 32, 90, 93, 95-101, 108, 111, 113, 123
Cranmer, Thomas 117, 199
creed/s 8, 19-20, 22, 30, 37, 40, 44, 118, 159, 196-198, 214
Crisp, Tobias 206
Cromwell, Oliver 89, 107, 122
Crutwell, Patrick 124

D

Damrosch, Leo 31
Danby, John F. 124
Dante 147
Davies, Horton 18
Davies, Michael 50, 52, 130

Index 231

Dell, William 206
Dent, Arthur 170, 198
Descartes, René 2, 36-37, 51-52, 84, 195
Dever, Mark E. 86-87
Dickens, A. G. 51
Dillistone, F. W. 138
Dixon, Sandra Lee 50
Docherty, Thomas 161
Donne, John 152, 162
Douglas, Constance A. 68-69
Dunan, Anne 177
Dunn, James D. G. 49

E

Eagleton, Terry 120
Eckhart, Meister 50
Edward VI 107
Edwards, Jonathan 109
Elizabeth 92, 105, 107, 121
Emerson, Ralph Waldo 5, 38
Enlightenment 5, 36-37, 40, 52, 89, 100, 115
Erasmus, Desiderius 209
Esau 74, 80, 169, 192, 216
Eusden, John Dykstra 92

F

Feuerbach, Ludwig 41, 43
Fiddes, Paul S. 154
Fish, Stanley 31, 139
Fisher, Samuel 41
Flannagan, Roy 119
Forrest, James F. 158, 161, 168, 184, 189, 191, 203
Fosdick, Harry Emerson 4, 14
Fowler, Edward 25-27, 106, 154, 187, 204, 207
Fowler, Stanley K. 156
Fox, George 9-10, 17-18, 20-21, 30-31, 33, 35-36, 39, 45
Foxe, John 56, 131, 199
Franck, Sebastian 199
Franklin, Benjamin 208
Frei, Hans 164

Freud, Sigmund 2
Frost, Kate Gartner 163
Froude, James Anthony 127
Furlong, Monica 3, 141, 148, 179

G

Geisst, Charles R. 115
Gerrish, B. A. 207, 210
Goldman, Peter 161
Grantham, Thomas 19
Greaves, Richard L. 47, 66, 82, 85, 102-103, 109, 111, 154, 179, 200, 205-206
Green, I. M. 127
Gregory "The Great", Pope 199
Gregory of Nazianzus 22
Gregory of Nyssa 22
Guibbory, Achsah 152

H

Habermas, Jürgen 29
Haller, William 96
Hambrick-Stowe, C. E. 103
Hancock, Maxine 202
Hanford, James Holly 123
Hardin, Richard 26
Harding, M. Esther 3
Harnack, Adolf von 41, 42
Harrison, Frank Mott 167, 178
Harrison, G. B. 47, 147, 167, 180
Haskin, Dayton 26, 47, 85
Hauerwas, Stanley 1
Hawkes, David 174, 178
Hawthorne, Nathaniel 26
Henry VIII 107, 122
Herbert, George 70, 152, 159
Herreshoff, David 142
Hicks, Elias 39
Hicks, Thomas 20
Hill, Christopher 3, 31, 51, 85, 89, 102, 110, 120, 142, 161, 175, 189, 200
Hobbes, Thomas 124-125
Holifield, E. B. 100
Honeygosky, Stephen R. 120

Hubbard, Geoffrey 34, 43
Hus, John 202-203
Hussey, Maurice 103, 167

I

Ignatius 198
imputation/imputed righteousness 70-72, 114, 132, 205
individualism 1-5, 8-10, 19, 28, 34-35, 37-38, 41, 44-45, 48, 51, 65, 76, 82-83, 86, 89, 95, 100-101, 103-104, 119-120, 124, 127, 132, 140-142, 145, 151, 153, 161, 180, 208, 210, 215, 221, 226

J

Jagodzinski, Cecile M. 2, 86, 200
James I 90
James II 109
James, William 67
Jeffrey, David Lyle 7, 46, 195-198, 200-201, 209
Jerome 199, 201
Jerome of Prague 199
Jewett, Robert 48-50
Johnson, Jeffrey 164
Johnson, Thomas H. 96
Judas 75, 169, 201
Julian of Norwich 50, 190
Jüngel, Eberhard 86

K

Kant, Immanuel 2, 40
Kaufmann, U. Milo 76
Keach, Benjamin 179
Keeble, N. H. 80, 127, 132, 135, 149, 162, 179, 208
Kelyng, John 105
Kenyon, J. P. 36, 51, 145
Kierkegaard, Søren 143, 192
Kiffin, William 153
Knott, John R. 137, 162
Knox, Edmund Arbuthnott 179, 190

Knox, Ronald 127
Kretzschmar 176

L

Lamont, Daniel 178, 186, 196, 209
Lamont, William 208
Langland, William 181
Latimer, Hugh 117
Latitudinarian/ism 25-27, 106, 187-188, 204, 225
Leavis, F. R. 21, 127, 138
Leveller/s 46, 89, 104, 191
Lewis, C. S. 164, 200
Lindbeck, George 208
Lindsay, Jack 180, 189
Lloyd-Jones, Martyn 103
Locke, John 2, 36-38, 51-52, 84, 89, 95, 105, 117-118
Lohse, Bernhard 57, 84
Lord's Supper/Communion/ Eucharist (see also Sacraments, Ordinances) 11, 17, 51, 69, 153-154, 156-157, 159-160, 164, 187, 193, 204, 228
Low, Anthony 151
Luther, Martin 5-6, 14-16, 23, 47-51, 53, 55-61, 63-64, 66-67, 69-71, 73, 75, 79, 82, 84-85, 87, 115, 120, 128, 132-135, 138, 151, 156, 160, 171, 176, 182, 188, 196-199, 201-204, 206-209
Lutheran/ism 5, 47-49, 52, 57, 65, 77, 83, 87, 93, 114, 128, 135-136, 168, 176, 186, 188, 203, 207-208, 210, 219
Luxon, Thomas H. 51, 149, 192
Lynch, Beth 168, 189, 196
Lyotard, Jean-François 191

M

Marius, Richard 138
Marvell, Andrew 112
Marxist/ism 52, 142, 180, 220
Mascuch, Michael 2
McAdoo, H. R. 101

Index 233

McGrath, Alister E. 83
Mill, John Stuart 125
Miller, Perry 92, 96, 100-101
Milton, John 4, 6, 49, 75, 112-113, 115-125, 151-152, 161, 179, 185, 190, 195, 198-199, 209
Moody, Dwight A. 100
Morgan, Edmund S. 95
Morris, John N. 52, 85
Muggletonians 46
Muller, Richard A. 52, 102
Mullett, Michael A. 24, 38, 47, 54, 101-102, 130-131, 133, 142, 148, 178-179

N

Nayler, James 18, 20, 34, 45, 107
Nellist, Brian 28
Newey, Vincent 3, 142, 161
Newton, John 131, 206, 209
Nicene Creed 22, 30, 159
Nuttall, Geoffrey F. 17, 128, 147

O

Oberman, Heiko 67
Offor, George 108
ordinance/s (see also Sacraments, Baptism, Lord's Supper) 11, 108, 134, 153-154, 160-161
Origen 199
Ormis, Cicely 199
Owen, John 200
Owens, W. R. 107

P

Pannenberg, Wolfhart 7
Paul, St 48, 50, 59, 93, 104, 151, 201
Pelikan, Jaroslav 14, 51, 64, 129
Penn, William 10, 16, 18, 20, 23, 25, 30, 36, 42, 100
Pennington, Isaac 18
Perkins, William 6, 90-97, 99, 101-103, 123, 125
Peter, St 201

Piper, John 80, 200
Plato 2
Polycarp 198
Pooley, Roger 80, 85
postmodern/ism 2, 7, 151, 191, 226
Presbyterian/s 107, 113, 116, 120, 147, 177, 191, 216, 223
Protestant/ism 7, 17, 27, 33, 36, 41, 44, 50, 85, 90, 107, 109, 113-115, 117-118, 120-122, 124, 128, 149, 195, 198, 204, 208, 217, 219, 221, 225-228
Puckett, David L. 129
Puritan/s/ism 3, 5-7, 17-18, 27, 35-36, 38, 44-46, 50-52, 57, 71, 82, 85-87, 89-93, 95-96, 98-104, 107, 109-110, 113, 119, 122-123, 125, 141-142, 145, 149, 152, 161-162, 164, 171, 178, 189, 191, 196, 199, 204, 206, 208, 214-221, 223-228

Q

Quaker/s 3-5, 9-21, 23-45, 47, 49, 53, 72, 77, 82-83, 96, 99, 107, 111, 116, 119-120, 130, 154, 161, 169, 186-187, 191, 195, 202, 207, 211, 215, 217, 220-221, 224-225, 227-228

R

Ramus, Petrus 94
Ranter 25, 29, 31, 46, 83, 206
Reformation 1, 14, 19, 25, 44-45, 50, 51, 57, 61, 83, 106, 109, 112-115, 117, 121-122, 125, 129, 130-131, 135, 160, 188, 195, 198, 210-211, 215, 217-219, 223-226
Renaut, Alain 8
Reynolds, Anna Maria 50
Ridley, Nicholas 117
Rivers, Isabel 187
Romanticism 36, 38, 40, 120, 215-216
Ross, Aileen D. 149, 161
Ross, Hugh McGregor 16
Rutherford, Samuel 205

S

sacrament/s (see also Ordinances, Baptism, Lord's Supper) 6, 57, 69, 120, 156-157, 160-161, 187, 201, 209, 214
Saltmarsh, John 206
Sams, Horace Jr. 152, 167
Sandel, Michael J. 44
Sanders, E. P. 49
Schaff, Philip 7, 45
Schleiermacher, Friedrich 40
Schmidt, Martin 6, 125
Schweitzer, Friedrich 2
Scripture (see also Bible) 1, 5, 10-19, 21, 25, 27, 29, 32, 35-37, 39, 41-42, 56, 70, 79-80, 82-84, 91-92, 97, 114-119, 124-125, 135-136, 175, 193, 196-198, 201, 205, 220
Seed, David 142
Shain, Barry Alan 44
Shakespeare, William 39, 124, 171
Sharrock, Roger 3, 21, 32, 36, 51, 85-86, 107, 131, 141-142, 148, 155, 158, 160, 168, 179, 184, 189, 203
Shaw, George Bernard 4, 28, 167
Shawcross, John T. 119
Sibbes, Richard 86-87, 203
Sim, Stuart 4, 7, 22, 137, 140, 149-150, 152, 171, 191-192, 196
Simpson, Ken 146, 154
Smith, Karen 147
Smith, Nigel 20
Socinian/ism 23, 25, 113, 205
Southern, R. W. 50
Spargo, Tamsin 41, 149-150
Spurgeon, Charles 157
Stachniewski, John 31, 50, 76, 85
Stauffer, Richard 26-27, 135
Staupitz, Johannes 51
Stendahl, Krister 48-49
Stout, Jeffrey 195
Stranahan, Brainerd P. 187
subjectivism 4-5, 7-8, 10, 39, 51-52, 76, 82-83, 127, 141, 186, 195-196, 198, 210
Sykes, John 39

T

Talon, Henri 10, 11, 13, 38, 47, 135, 143, 164, 171, 179, 180
Taylor, Charles 2, 37, 39, 51, 142, 161
Teresa of Ávila 183
Thickstun, Margaret Olofson 149-150
Thirty-Nine Articles 25, 106
Thomas, Keith 2
Thompson, Philip E. 8
Tillyard, E. M. W. 95
Tindall, William York 26, 106-107, 110, 179
Tombes, John 20
Traherne, Thomas 52
Trim, Mary 9-10
Trinity 22, 113, 117, 128, 199, 212
Trueblood, D. Elton 18, 39-40
Twain, Mark 27

U

Underwood, T. L. 26, 32, 35, 150, 153

V

Van Gogh, Vincent 4, 139
Van Til, L. John 5, 6, 48, 92, 94, 99
Vaughan Williams, Ralph 4

W

Wakefield, Gordon 147, 179
Walker, David 4, 7, 22, 137, 140, 149-150, 152, 171, 191, 192, 196
Walton, George W. 129, 135
Watkins, Owen C. 110
Weber, Max 204
Weintraub, Joachim 208
Wesley, John 131
West, Alick 52
White, B. R. 145
Whitman, Walt 39
Williams, D. H. 198
Williams, Roger 32, 49, 90, 93, 95-101, 103-106, 111, 113, 118, 122-123, 125

Winthrop, John 92, 96, 99
Wyclif, John 120

Z

Zachman, Randall C. 5, 55
Zinck, Arlette 178, 192

Studies in Christian History and Thought
(All titles uniform with this volume)
Dates in bold are of projected publication

David Bebbington
Holiness in Nineteenth-Century England
David Bebbington stresses the relationship of movements of spirituality to changes in their cultural setting, especially the legacies of the Enlightenment and Romanticism. He shows that these broad shifts in ideological mood had a profound effect on the ways in which piety was conceptualized and practised. Holiness was intimately bound up with the spirit of the age.
2000 / 0-85364-981-2 / viii + 98pp

J. William Black
Reformation Pastors
Richard Baxter and the Ideal of the Reformed Pastor
This work examines Richard Baxter's *Gildas Salvianus, The Reformed Pastor* (1656) and explores each aspect of his pastoral strategy in light of his own concern for 'reformation' and in the broader context of Edwardian, Elizabethan and early Stuart pastoral ideals and practice.
2003 / 1-84227-190-3 / xxii + 308pp

James Bruce
Prophecy, Miracles, Angels, *and* Heavenly Light?
The Eschatology, Pneumatology and Missiology of Adomnán's Life of Columba
This book surveys approaches to the marvellous in hagiography, providing the first critique of Plummer's hypothesis of Irish saga origin. It then analyses the uniquely systematized phenomena in the *Life of Columba* from Adomnán's seventh-century theological perspective, identifying the coming of the eschatological Kingdom as the key to understanding.
2004 / 1-84227-227-6 / xviii + 286pp

Colin J. Bulley
The Priesthood of Some Believers
Developments from the General to the Special Priesthood in the Christian Literature of the First Three Centuries
The first in-depth treatment of early Christian texts on the priesthood of all believers shows that the developing priesthood of the ordained related closely to the division between laity and clergy and had deleterious effects on the practice of the general priesthood.
2000 / 1-84227-034-6 / xii + 336pp

Anthony R. Cross (ed.)
Ecumenism and History
Studies in Honour of John H.Y. Briggs
This collection of essays examines the inter-relationships between the two fields in which Professor Briggs has contributed so much: history—particularly Baptist and Nonconformist—and the ecumenical movement. With contributions from colleagues and former research students from Britain, Europe and North America, *Ecumenism and History* provides wide-ranging studies in important aspects of Christian history, theology and ecumenical studies.
2002 / 1-84227-135-0 / xx + 362pp

Maggi Dawn
Confessions of an Inquiring Spirit
Form as Constitutive of Meaning in S.T. Coleridge's Theological Writing
This study of Coleridge's *Confessions* focuses on its confessional, epistolary and fragmentary form, suggesting that attention to these features significantly affects its interpretation. Bringing a close study of these three literary forms, the author suggests ways in which they nuance the text with particular understandings of the Trinity, and of a kenotic christology. Some parallels are drawn between Romantic and postmodern dilemmas concerning the authority of the biblical text.
2006 / 1-84227-255-1 / approx. 224 pp

Ruth Gouldbourne
The Flesh and the Feminine
Gender and Theology in the Writings of Caspar Schwenckfeld
Caspar Schwenckfeld and his movement exemplify one of the radical communities of the sixteenth century. Challenging theological and liturgical norms, they also found themselves challenging social and particularly gender assumptions. In this book, the issues of the relationship between radical theology and the understanding of gender are considered.
2005 / 1-84227-048-6 / approx. 304pp

Galen K. Johnson
Prisoner of Conscience
John Bunyan on Self, Community and Christian Faith
This is an interdisciplinary study of John Bunyan's understanding of conscience across his autobiographical, theological and fictional writings, investigating whether conscience always deserves fidelity, and how Bunyan's view of conscience affects his relationship both to modern Western individualism and historic Christianity.
2003 / 1-84227- 151-2 / xvi + 236pp

R.T. Kendall
Calvin and English Calvinism to 1649
The author's thesis is that those who formed the Westminster Confession of Faith, which is regarded as Calvinism, in fact departed from John Calvin on two points: (1) the extent of the atonement and (2) the ground of assurance of salvation.

1997 / 0-85364-827-1 / xii + 264pp

Byung-Ho Moon
Lex Dei Regula Vivendi et Vivificandi
Calvin's Christological Understanding of the Law in the Light of his Concept of Christus Mediator Legis
This book explores the coherence between Christology and soteriology in Calvin's theology of the law, examining its intellectual origins and his position on the concept and extent of Christ's mediation of the law. A comparative study between Calvin and contemporary Reformers—Luther, Bucer, Melancthon and Bullinger—and his opponent Michael Servetus is made for the purpose of pointing out the unique feature of Calvin's Christological understanding of the law.

2005 / 1-84227-318-3 / approx. 370pp

John Eifion Morgan-Wynne
Holy Spirit and Religious Experience in Christian Writings, c.AD90–200
This study examines how far Christians in the third to fifth generations (c.AD90–200) attributed their sense of encounter with the divine presence, their sense of illumination in the truth or guidance in decision-making, and their sense of ethical empowerment to the activity of the Holy Spirit in their lives.

2005 / 1-84227-319-1 / approx. 274pp

James I. Packer
The Redemption and Restoration of Man in the Thought of Richard Baxter
James I. Packer provides a full and sympathetic exposition of Richard Baxter's doctrine of humanity, created and fallen; its redemption by Christ Jesus; and its restoration in the image of God through the obedience of faith by the power of the Holy Spirit.

2002 / 1-84227-147-4 / 432pp

Andrew Partington,
Church and State
The Contribution of the Church of England Bishops to the House of Lords during the Thatcher Years

In *Church and State*, Andrew Partington argues that the contribution of the Church of England bishops to the House of Lords during the Thatcher years was overwhelmingly critical of the government; failed to have a significant influence in the public realm; was inefficient, being undertaken by a minority of those eligible to sit on the Bench of Bishops; and was insufficiently moral and spiritual in its content to be distinctive. On the basis of this, and the likely reduction of the number of places available for Church of England bishops in a fully reformed Second Chamber, the author argues for an evolution in the Church of England's approach to the service of its bishops in the House of Lords. He proposes the Church of England works to overcome the genuine obstacles which hinder busy diocesan bishops from contributing to the debates of the House of Lords and to its life more informally.

2005 / 1-84227-334-5 / approx. 324pp

Alan P.F. Sell
Enlightenment, Ecumenism, Evangel
Theological Themes and Thinkers 1550–2000

This book consists of papers in which such interlocking topics as the Enlightenment, the problem of authority, the development of doctrine, spirituality, ecumenism, theological method and the heart of the gospel are discussed. Issues of significance to the church at large are explored with special reference to writers from the Reformed and Dissenting traditions.

2005 / 1-84227330-2 / xviii + 422pp

Alan P.F. Sell
Hinterland Theology
Some Reformed and Dissenting Adjustments

Many books have been written on theology's 'giants' and significant trends, but what of those lesser-known writers who adjusted to them? In this book some hinterland theologians of the British Reformed and Dissenting traditions, who followed in the wake of toleration, the Evangelical Revival, the rise of modern biblical criticism and Karl Barth, are allowed to have their say. They include Thomas Ridgley, Ralph Wardlaw, T.V. Tymms and N.H.G. Robinson.

2006 / 1-84227-331-0

Alan P.F. Sell and Anthony R. Cross (eds)
Protestant Nonconformity in the Twentieth Century
In this collection of essays scholars representative of a number of Nonconformist traditions reflect thematically on Nonconformists' life and witness during the twentieth century. Among the subjects reviewed are biblical studies, theology, worship, evangelism and spirituality, and ecumenism. Over and above its immediate interest, this collection provides a marker to future scholars and others wishing to know how some of their forebears assessed Nonconformity's contribution to a variety of fields during the century leading up to Christianity's third millennium.

2003 / 1-84227-221-7 / x + 398pp

Mark Smith
Religion in Industrial Society
Oldham and Saddleworth 1740–1865

This book analyses the way British churches sought to meet the challenge of industrialization and urbanization during the period 1740–1865. Working from a case-study of Oldham and Saddleworth, Mark Smith challenges the received view that the Anglican Church in the eighteenth century was characterized by complacency and inertia, and reveals Anglicanism's vigorous and creative response to the new conditions. He reassesses the significance of the centrally directed church reforms of the mid-nineteenth century, and emphasizes the importance of local energy and enthusiasm. Charting the growth of denominational pluralism in Oldham and Saddleworth, Dr Smith compares the strengths and weaknesses of the various Anglican and Nonconformist approaches to promoting church growth. He also demonstrates the extent to which all the churches participated in a common culture shaped by the influence of evangelicalism, and shows that active co-operation between the churches rather than denominational conflict dominated. This revised and updated edition of Dr Smith's challenging and original study makes an important contribution both to the social history of religion and to urban studies.

2005 / 1-84227-335-3 / approx. 300pp

Martin Sutherland
Peace, Toleration and Decay
The Ecclesiology of Later Stuart Dissent

This fresh analysis brings to light the complexity and fragility of the later Stuart Nonconformist consensus. Recent findings on wider seventeenth-century thought are incorporated into a new picture of the dynamics of Dissent and the roots of evangelicalism.

2003 / 1-84227-152-0 / xxii + 216pp

G. Michael Thomas
The Extent of the Atonement
A Dilemma for Reformed Theology from Calvin to the Consensus
A study of the way Reformed theology addressed the question, 'Did Christ die for all, or for the elect only?', commencing with John Calvin, and including debates with Lutheranism, the Synod of Dort and the teaching of Moïse Amyraut.
1997 / 0-85364-828-X / x + 278pp

Mark D. Thompson
A Sure Ground on which to Stand
The Relation of Authority and Interpretive Method of Luther's Approach to Scripture
The best interpreter of Luther is Luther himself. Unfortunately many modern studies have superimposed contemporary agendas upon this sixteenth-century Reformer's writings. This fresh study examines Luther's own words to find an explanation for his robust confidence in the Scriptures, a confidence that generated the famous 'stand' at Worms in 1521.
2004 / 1-84227-145-8 / xvi + 322pp

Carl R. Trueman and R.S. Clark (eds)
Protestant Scholasticism
Essays in Reassessment
Traditionally Protestant theology, between Luther's early reforming career and the dawn of the Enlightenment, has been seen in terms of decline and fall into the wastelands of rationalism and scholastic speculation. In this volume a number of scholars question such an interpretation. The editors argue that the development of post-Reformation Protestantism can only be understood when a proper historical model of doctrinal change is adopted. This historical concern underlies the subsequent studies of theologians such as Calvin, Beza, Olevian, Baxter, and the two Turrentini. The result is a significantly different reading of the development of Protestant Orthodoxy, one which both challenges the older scholarly interpretations and clichés about the relationship of Protestantism to, among other things, scholasticism and rationalism, and which demonstrates the fruitfulness of the new, historical approach.
1999 / 0-85364-853-0 / xx + 344pp

Shawn D. Wright
Our Sovereign Refuge
The Pastoral Theology of Theodore Beza

Our Sovereign Refuge is a study of the pastoral theology of the Protestant reformer who inherited the mantle of leadership in the Reformed church from John Calvin. Countering a common view of Beza as supremely a 'scholastic' theologian who deviated from Calvin's biblical focus, Wright uncovers a new portrait. He was not a cold and rigid academic theologian obsessed with probing the eternal decrees of God. Rather, by placing him in his pastoral context and by noting his concerns in his pastoral and biblical treatises, Wright shows that Beza was fundamentally a committed Christian who was troubled by the vicissitudes of life in the second half of the sixteenth century. He believed that the biblical truth of the supreme sovereignty of God alone could support Christians on their earthly pilgrimage to heaven. This pastoral and personal portrait forms the heart of Wright's argument.

2004 / 1-84227-252-7 / xviii + 308pp

Paternoster
9 Holdom Avenue
Bletchley
Milton Keynes MK1 1QR
United Kingdom

Web: www.authenticmedia.co.uk/paternoster

November 2004

www.ingramcontent.com/pod-product-compliance
Lightning Source LLC
Chambersburg PA
CBHW062013220426
43662CB00010B/1307